D1099793

**SAMS**
**Teach Yourself**

# Visual Basic® .NET
# Web Programming
# in 21 Days

# Sams Teach Yourself Visual Basic .NET Web Programming in 21 Days

## Copyright © 2002 by Sams Publishing

International Standard Book Number: 0-672-32236-6

Library of Congress Catalog Card Number: 2001089218

Printed in the United States of America

First Printing: December 2001

## Trademarks

## Warning and Disclaimer

**ASSOCIATE PUBLISHER**
Linda Engelman

**ACQUISITIONS EDITOR**
Sondra Scott

**DEVELOPMENT EDITOR**
Susan Shaw Dunn

**MANAGING EDITOR**
Charlotte Clapp

**PROJECT EDITOR**
Natalie Harris

**COPY EDITOR**
Charles A. Hutchinson

**INDEXER**
Larry Sweazy

**PROOFREADER**
Andrea Dugan

**TECHNICAL EDITOR**
Jawahar Puvvala

**TEAM COORDINATOR**
Lynne Williams

**MEDIA DEVELOPER**
Dan Scherf

**INTERIOR DESIGNER**
Gary Adair

**COVER DESIGNER**
Aren Howell

**PAGE LAYOUT**
Plan-it Publishing

# Contents at a Glance

**Week 3** In Review

# Table of Contents

# About the Authors

**Peter Aitken** has been writing about computers and programming for more than 10 years, with some 30 books and more than 1.5 million copies in print as well as hundreds of magazine and trade publication articles. His book titles include *Sams Teach Yourself Internet Programming With Visual Basic in 21 Days* and *Sams Teach Yourself C in 21 Days*. A regular contributor to *Office Pro* magazine and the DevX Web site, Peter is the proprietor of PGA Consulting, providing custom application and Internet development to business, academia, and government since 1994. You can reach him at peter@pgacon.com.

**Philip Syme** has been writing applications with C++ and Visual Basic since the release of Windows 3.1. He has helped create several enterprise scale projects developed for Fortune 500 companies that use Microsoft technologies. Phil has also coauthored articles published in IEEE symposiums. Phil lives in Baltimore, Maryland, and can be reached at psyme@home.com.

# Dedication

*To my two terrific children, Benjamin and Claire.*
*—Peter Aitken*

*To Ann, for all your support while I wrote this book.*
*—Phil Syme*

# Acknowledgments

First and foremost we acknowledge the editors at Sams for their invaluable and professional contributions to this book. In particular, we thank Sondra Scott for all her help and advice in getting this project started, and Susan Dunn for her many contributions. Our thanks also go to Linda Engelman, Charlotte Clapp, Natalie Harris, and Chuck Hutchinson. Last, but definitely not least, thanks go to the technical editor, Jawahar Puvvala, whose extra efforts associated with the code samples were essential for the publication of this book.

# Tell Us What You Think!

As the reader of this book, *you* are our most important critic and commentator. We value your opinion and want to know what we're doing right, what we could do better, what areas you'd like to see us publish in, and any other words of wisdom you're willing to pass our way.

As an Associate Publisher for Sams Publishing, I welcome your comments. You can fax, e-mail, or write me directly to let me know what you did or didn't like about this book—as well as what we can do to make our books stronger.

*Please note that I cannot help you with technical problems related to the topic of this book, and that due to the high volume of mail I receive, I might not be able to reply to every message.*

When you write, please be sure to include this book's title and authors as well as your name and phone or fax number. I will carefully review your comments and share them with the authors and editors who worked on the book.

Fax:    317-581-4770

Email:  feedback@samspublishing.com

Mail:   Linda Engelman
        Associate Publisher
        Sams Publishing
        201 West 103rd Street
        Indianapolis, IN 46290 USA

# Introduction

It's not news any more—the Internet and World Wide Web are *hot*. This means that there's an ever-increasing demand for programs that run on the Web or use the Web in various ways. Old-fashioned programming tools just can't cut the mustard. This is why Microsoft has developed the .NET (say "dot net") Framework, a rich and sophisticated set of programmer tools for developing and deploying Web-enabled programs. .NET is not only for Web applications, but also seems to be where most of the excitement is— and is what this book is about.

Over the next 21 days, you will learn how to create Internet applications, including dynamic Web sites and Web Services, using the significantly improved Visual Basic language within the .NET Framework. .NET offers an enjoyable way to create Internet applications; much of the tedious work previously associated with Internet programming has been subsumed into the framework. You therefore can concentrate on making your Web applications fit your customers' needs. If you have done any Web programming using older tools, you will probably be surprised and how easy .NET is in comparison.

One of the most exciting technologies that the .NET Framework offers is Web Services, which allow you to create distributed applications using Internet standards that are in use today. This book contains four lessons specifically dedicated to this area, along with lessons detailing configuration, deployment, security, and architectural considerations for Web Services.

This book focuses on how to develop Web applications and Web Services using Visual Basic, the .NET Framework, ASP.NET, and supplementary tools provided by Visual Studio .NET. Each section in each lesson introduces you to a new aspect of Web development in .NET. In addition to providing explanations of the theory behind a technique, this book provides many self-contained examples that you can adapt to your own projects.

## Who Should Read This Book?

This book assumes that you are already familiar with Visual Basic. However, you don't have to be an expert with the language; every code sample contains an analysis section to give you an in-depth explanation of the sample, and any new language technique in a sample contains a special description. This book won't teach you Visual Basic from the ground up, but it will teach you how to use Visual Basic along with the .NET Framework to create Web applications.

**Note** If you've already seen the extensive Microsoft .NET documentation, you're probably wondering why you should buy this book. By its very nature, the .NET documentation must cover every nitty-gritty detail. Most of those details you will never need, particularly when you are just getting started. This book cuts to the chase and teaches you those central aspects of .NET that you must know to get started creating your own applications. The Microsoft documentation is essential as a backup and as a source for the many details that can't be included in a book. Remember that we've spent hundreds of hours working with beta versions of .NET and learning all its ins and outs, with the goal that our experience can save you time and frustration.

# How This Book Is Organized

This book is organized into 21 daily lessons. Each lesson contains information about a specific aspect of Internet programming with .NET. Some of the broader topics are spread out over two or more lessons.

To reinforce what you've learned, read through the Questions and Answers (Q&A) and Workshop sections at the end of each lesson. The answers for the quiz questions and exercises are provided in Appendix A, "Answers to Quizzes and Exercises." (Try to answer each quiz question, and make an attempt to complete each exercise before peeking at Appendix A.) Some exercises are open-ended, so you may come up with a different or better solution.

You will see many code examples in each lesson. To get the most information from your study, run each sample yourself. You may want to modify or enhance the samples not only to help you learn the material, but also to give you a great foundation for writing your own applications.

## Week 1

Week 1 quickly brings you up to speed with all the essential information you will need to start creating Web-based applications with Visual Basic and .NET:

- Day 1, "Introducing Web Programming with .NET," will help acquaint you with .NET and set up your development environment. It will also spell out exactly which parts of .NET you will learn in the following lessons, and give references for more detailed coverage of concepts that this book does not cover in full.

- Day 2, "Introducing ASP.NET," gives you the basics of this important technology. You will use ASP.NET for many of your Internet applications, so a good understanding of it is important. You can use any .NET-compatible language in

ASP.NET programs (including Visual Basic, as we use in this book). ASP.NET and Visual Basic form a powerful combination for Web application development.

- Day 3, "Using Web Forms," introduces Web Forms, which you can use to create even the most complex Web applications. A Web Form provides your Internet applications with controls and other user-interface elements that have previously been available only in non-Web programs. Day 3 will explain how to use Visual Basic to create Web Forms for your Internet applications.

- Day 4, "Working with Web Controls"; Day 5, "Using Advanced ASP.NET Web Controls"; and Day 6, "Working with User Controls," provide instruction for using Web controls in your Internet applications. Web controls provide visual user interface elements, such as text boxes and option buttons, that you can use in your Web pages. Each lesson will also show how to use Visual Basic to make the best use of Web controls.

- Day 7, "Writing Internet Applications for Mobile Devices," shows you how to easily integrate support for mobile devices, such as Web-enabled cell phones and personal digital assistants (PDAs) in you Web application.

## Week 2

Week 2 broadens your knowledge of Visual Basic Internet programming by introducing XML and ADO.NET and explaining how to use them in your own Web applications. Week 2 concludes with an introduction to creating Web services with Visual Basic. Week 2's lessons are as follows:

- Day 8, "Using XML with Your Applications," introduces you to XML and how it's used in .NET with Visual Basic.

- Days 9 through 11 show how to use ADO.NET, a new set of Web-enabled database tools, in your Internet applications. Day 9, "Introducing ADO.NET," and Day 10, "Working with Datasets," get you started with the .NET version of ActiveX Data Objects. Day 11, "Using ADO.NET and XML Together" shows how you can combine the two technologies in exciting new ways.

- Day 12, "Putting It All Together With ASP.NET," shows you how to combine the knowledge you've learned from the past 11 days to create powerful Web applications.

- Day 13, "Introducing Web Services," explains what Web Services are and shows you the basic techniques for creating Web Services in .NET using Visual Basic. You'll learn why Web Services are considered so important for the future of Web-based computing.

- Day 14, "Publishing a Web Service," explains important new standards emerging that allow you to describe your Web Service, and allow client programs to find your Web Service.

## Week 3

During Week 3 you will master advanced Internet programming techniques using Visual Basic and .NET. Week 3 provides more lessons on Web Service development, and concludes with lessons that show you how to configure, secure, and architect your Internet programs. This last week's lessons cover the following areas:

- Days 15 and 16 continue the coverage of Web Services. Day 15, " Data Access and Web Services," gives detailed examples showing you how to pass complex objects between client applications and Web services. Day 16, "Putting It All Together With Web Services," shows advanced techniques that you can apply to your Web Services and client applications.
- Day 17, "Using Legacy Code with .NET," guides you through techniques and migration strategies for using .NET alongside your existing base of applications. This lesson will give specific examples on how to integrate ASP and ASP.NET side by side, and how to write .NET components that your existing applications can use.
- On Day 18, "Configuring Internet Applications," you will learn how to use .NET configuration files to fine-tune your applications. This lesson will show you techniques for using Web applications and Web Services in both development and production environments.
- You can use .NET's security services to ensure that your Visual Basic code is secure. Day 19, "Securing Internet Applications," shows you how. This lesson will give examples that you can use to create your own secure Internet applications.
- Day 20, "Deploying Internet Applications," helps you set up your applications on remote and hosted servers for your end users.
- Finally, Day 21, "Creating Your Application Architecture," gives you the background you need to choose the best architecture for your Internet projects.

## Downloading the Book's Source Code

This book contains plenty of sample code to get you started. Every concept introduced in each lesson contains at least one sample program that should allow you to quickly become proficient with the new concept. One of the best approaches you can take while reading this book is to first download the samples for a lesson from www.samspublishing.com (enter this book's ISBN in the search field), and then follow along with your development computer.

At this site, you will find a link that will help you find extra projects, including supplementary Web site and Web Service projects. The linked site also contains news about late-breaking changes and new features in .NET.

# Conventions

All the books in the *Sams Teach Yourself* series enable you to start working and become successful with the product as quickly as possible. Interspersed in each lesson are graphic elements that help you identify special information:

Tips offer advice or suggest easier or alternative methods of doing something.

Notes indicate additional information that may help you avoid problems or that you should consider when using the described features.

Cautions alert you to possible problems or hazards and advise you on how to avoid or fix them.

**NEW TERM** This special icon indicates a new term that's defined and explained in a paragraph. The term being defined is formatted in *italic*.

**ANALYSIS** This icon identifies text that explains the code preceding it.

You also will find certain typographical conventions used throughout this book:

- Names of all dialogs and dialog options use initial capital letters.

- Messages that appear onscreen, as well as all program code, appear in a special monospace font, as in the following example: `Variable undefined`. Text that you are to type appears in **`monospace boldface`**; syntax variables that you need to replace with an appropriate value appear in *`monospace italic`*.

# WEEK 1

# At a Glance

During this week, you will learn about the fundamentals of the .NET Framework and ASP.NET, and how to use them effectively in your Visual Basic projects. At the end of this week, you will know a great deal about how to create dynamic Web sites using .NET. This week will be challenging and you will learn quite a bit of material. Be patient—mastering all the concepts in each lesson takes time.

The best way to learn about .NET is to use it. You will see many examples in the next few days that will give you a starting point to use .NET. You should download the samples from www.samspublishing.com and run them as you read the text. Also, each lesson ends with a workshop containing a quiz and some exercises. At the end of each lesson, you should be able to answer all the quiz questions and complete the exercises. Answers are provided in Appendix A, "Answers to Quizzes and Exercises."

This first week is mainly concerned with Visual Basic and ASP.NET:

- On Day 1, "Introducing Web Programming with .NET," you will learn about important new concepts in the .NET Framework so that you can start building applications productively. You will also learn how to set up your development environment so that you can follow along with the sample programs in the remaining lessons.

- On Day 2, "Introducing ASP.NET," you will learn the fundamentals of ASP.NET.

- Day 3, "Using Web Forms," explains how to use ASP.NET Web forms in your Web applications.

1

2

3

4

5

6

7

- Day 4, "Working with Web Controls," shows you how to use the numerous stock ASP.NET controls in your applications.

- Day 5, "Using Advanced ASP.NET Web Controls," introduces the DataGrid, DataList, and DataAdapter controls, which give you powerful ways to display and manipulate data in your programs.

- Day 6, "Working with User Controls," shows you how to create your own Web controls.

- Day 7, "Writing Internet Applications for Mobile Devices," shows how you can easily support Web-enabled personal digital assistants (PDAs) and cellular phones by using the concepts from the last six lessons.

# DAY 1

# Introducing Web Programming with .NET

For the past few months, you've been hearing all the hoopla and marketing buzz surrounding .NET. You've heard claims that .NET will totally change the way all programming is done, that .NET will revolutionize the Internet. Like many major new technologies, .NET is a significant improvement from the current state of the art and makes Web programming a much easier task than many current technologies that you can choose from.

Today's lesson will focus on the basics, including an explanation of the fundamental concepts that you will use throughout the rest of this book. By reading today's lesson, you will see how to create simple .NET Web programs using Visual Basic, and you will have a good foundation that you can use to understand the concepts of future lessons.

Today you will learn the following:

- What is the .NET Framework?
- Fundamental concepts in .NET programming, such as the Common Language Runtime, assemblies, and namespaces

- How to configure your development environment so that you can develop .NET Web applications
- How to write a basic Web service and dynamic Web page

# What is the .NET Framework?

Over the past few years, the importance of the Internet has grown enormously for almost all areas of computing and information processing. A direct result of this growth is that programmers are asked to create applications that take advantage of the Internet's capabilities, whether for order processing, broadband content delivery, online collaboration, or any of a host of uses. Unfortunately, the development tools previously available to developers, such as Visual C++ 6 and Visual Basic 6, had their origins in the pre-Internet world. Any Internet capabilities they had were afterthoughts, tacked on to meet developer demands. Some earlier Internet programming technologies were actually quite impressive, and many terrific applications have been created with them. Even so, that Internet capabilities weren't built into these programming tools from the ground up led to unavoidable problems with development efficiency, bugs, and program maintenance.

Microsoft's answer to this dilemma was to start essentially from scratch, creating a new framework of developer tools that was designed from day 1 with fully integrated Internet support. The .NET Framework is not only about Internet programming; it also provides for more traditional desktop application development. However, there's no doubt that the excitement about .NET is mostly about its Internet capabilities—and we can tell you from experience, they are really great!

.NET has two main parts:

- The .NET Framework Software Development Kit, an extensive set of classes and interfaces, along with various supporting elements, are designed to work together to meet just about any imaginable development need. The .NET Framework must be installed on any system that will be used to run .NET applications or to develop them. The .NET SDK includes compilers for three languages: the venerable C++, a new language called C# (C sharp), and—most relevant to this book—a vastly improved Visual Basic.
- The Visual Studio development environment. This sophisticated tool provides a comprehensive set of programmer tools, such as code editors, interface designers, and debuggers that greatly simplifies the task of creating .NET applications. Strictly speaking, you don't need Visual Studio to develop .NET programs, but few programmers will want to do without its time- and effort-saving capabilities.

# Fundamental Concepts

This book teaches you how to create Internet applications using the .NET Framework and the Visual Basic language. At least 90% of the material you need to learn is related to the .NET Framework, not to Visual Basic. We therefore don't try to teach Visual Basic, but assume you have at least a fundamental knowledge of the language. When needed, however, we do explain advanced Visual Basic language concepts when they are used in the examples.

To completely understand the code listings in the following chapters, you need to understand a few key terms, including the common language runtime (CLR), assemblies, namespaces, and event handlers. Today's lesson will give you enough information about each topic so that you have a good foundation to build your .NET knowledge.

## The Common Language Runtime

**New Term** The *common language runtime* (CLR) is the infrastructure that .NET uses to execute all your applications. The CLR includes a huge set of class libraries that you can use in your applications. Some interesting non-Internet–related classes include utilities that allow you to manipulate the Windows NT event log, Active Directory, cryptographic services, performance counters, COM+ services, object serialization, and Windows native services. If you aren't familiar with these terms, don't worry! This book will focus on the large amount of Internet programming-related classes, such as Web-based controls, Web Service classes, and Web security classes.

The CLR also takes care of compiling "intermediate language," or IL, code into native machine code. The basic process works as follows:

1. The Visual Basic compiler converts your code into IL. In terms of functionality and language complexity, IL is somewhere between assembly language and C. IL is optimized for quick compilation into machine code. Normally, you won't deal with IL in any of your development efforts. You can think of IL as an intermediate product of the compilation process.

2. Your Internet application is called by a user, or more precisely, by the Web server in response to a user's request.

3. The CLR takes over and compiles the IL into machine code. This happens function by function. If a function is used, it's compiled into machine code. If not, it remains as IL. The odds of an error occurring during this process are extremely small, equivalent to a compiler crash.

If this process seems roundabout and destined to make your application too slow, please suspend judgment until you've worked with .NET for a little while. You should be pleasantly surprised. At the minimum, this process makes development much faster, as the first step is much faster than other methods. You can also compile your .NET code directly into machine code by using standard tools installed with the .NET Framework.

**NEW TERM** The CLR contains other services, including support for running multiple .NET applications inside one process with a guarantee that they won't interfere with each other. This is a result of a concept called *type safety*. Any .NET language must guarantee type-safe code, which ensures that arrays and collections will never be accessed incorrectly, among other things. The Visual Basic compiler always enforces type safety when it compiles your code into IL.

## Assemblies

**NEW TERM** All .NET code is compiled into *assemblies*. From the outside, an assembly looks exactly like a dynamic link library (.dll) or an executable program (.exe). The first few bytes inside each assembly contain machine code that invokes the common language runtime when the assembly is accessed by another program or by a user.

Inside the assembly is a mix of IL and machine code, depending on how much of the assembly has been compiled by the CLR. Assemblies also contain *metadata*. The metadata for a .NET program includes:

- Information about every public class or type, including the name, what classes the class is derived from, and every interface that the class implements
- Information about every public method in each class, including the name and return value
- Information about every public parameter for every method, including each parameter's name and type
- Information about every public enumeration, including the names and values for each enumeration member
- Information about an assembly's specific version

Why have metadata? It solves a number of problems and enables some nice features. One problem DLL files have is that there is no way to examine what kinds of functions they support; you can find the names, but that's about it. COM, or component, files are usually built on top of DLL files and have the same problem. You can associate COM-type libraries with a COM object, depending on myriad Windows Registry entries that can easily become inconsistent.

By having such rich data in each assembly, the .NET Framework doesn't need to use the Registry to run assemblies. If a .NET program needs to use another .NET assembly, they only have to be located in the same directory. This means that if you want to deploy a .NET program on another computer, you can get away with simply copying the required files. Deployment is a complicated issue, however, and Day 20 will give you the necessary details.

You can write .NET code to examine another assembly's metadata to find out whether it supports the functions you need. This is an advanced topic, and this book won't explore the issue in much depth. This process is called *Reflection*, and Microsoft's online documentation contains plenty of details.

## Namespaces

**NEW TERM** If you've used C++, you are familiar with the term *namespace*. A namespace is used in .NET languages to provide a container for a set of classes. This container allows you to create classes with the same names that other developers or the CLR uses. For example, you might use a set of utility Visual Basic classes that you downloaded from a Web site. These utility classes might contain a class named `ErrorLogger`, which writes out error messages to a text file. Unfortunately, you've already developed a class that also happens to be named `ErrorLogger`. Having the same name isn't a problem because the utility class uses a different namespace from your own.

To go into a little more detail, let's look at some Visual Basic code. The following example is typical of what you will see in the remaining lessons in the book because it contains a numbered code listing (*don't include the line numbers in any code you develop*) along with an Analysis section.

**LISTING 1.1** HelloWorld.vb: The Common "Hello, world" Program That Every Book Requires

```
 1: Imports System
 2:
 3: Module Module1
 4:
 5: Sub Main()
 6:
 7:    Console.Writeline("Hello, world")
 8:
 9: End Sub
10:
11: End Module
```

**ANALYSIS** Line 1 uses the `Imports` keyword, which tells the compiler to include the `System` namespace into this program. Line 7, which writes out `Hello World.`, could be written differently. If the listing didn't use the `Imports` keyword on Line 1, Line 9 would turn into the following:

```
System.Console.WriteLine("Hello World.")
```

As you can see, namespaces group similar classes into one logical group to prevent naming conflicts.

Line 3 declares a module for the program's code, one way in which VB .NET organizes its code. Lines 5–9 define the subprocedure named Main(), where execution starts.

# Configuring Your Environment

This lesson and all future lessons in this book focus on teaching you by example. To learn from the examples, you must be able to execute them on your own computer. To execute the sample programs, you need three things installed on your development computer:

- One of the following operating systems: Windows NT 4.0 Workstation or Server, Windows 2000 Professional or Server, or Windows XP or higher, such as Advanced Server or Datacenter Server. Windows NT isn't recommended, however as many people have reported problems getting .NET to work properly on that operating system.

**Caution**   As of this book's writing, there's no way to perform .NET Internet development on the Windows 95/98/ME platforms.

- A Web server that supports ASP.NET. Essentially, this means Microsoft Internet Information Services (IIS) 4.0 or higher, or Microsoft Personal Web Server (PWS) on NT 4.0 Workstation. We assume IIS for the remainder of this book, but you can adapt the instructions to PWS easily.
- The .NET Framework, which includes the CLR, the Visual Basic compiler, and ASP.NET.

Although it's optional, we strongly recommend that you install Visual Studio .NET as well (which includes the .NET Framework). You can create .NET applications without Visual Studio by using any text editor and the command-line compilers, but Visual Studio makes the whole process—debugging in particular—a lot easier.

## Installing IIS

This section will give instructions for installing IIS on Windows 2000 Professional. IIS comes with Windows 2000 Professional but isn't installed by default. To install IIS, you must take the following steps, and you must have your Windows 2000 CD handy.

> **Note**
>
> If you are currently running Windows NT 4.0, you should install Personal Web Server. The installation process for PWS on Windows NT 4.0 Workstation is similar, but you must download the latest Option Pack from http://www.microsoft.com/downloads. Select the keyword search option on this Web page, Windows NT 4.0, from the Operating System drop-down list and then click the Find It button.

Follow these steps:

1. In the Windows Control Panel, select Add/Remove Programs.
2. Select Add/Remove Windows Component on the bottom left of the Add/Remove Programs window.
3. Look at the check box next to the Internet Information Services item.
4. Insert your Windows 2000 CD into your computer.
5. Click Next and wait for the installation to complete.

## Installing Visual Studio .NET

Before you install Visual Studio .NET, take a quick glance at the Microsoft Developer Network home page at msdn.microsoft.com. This site contains any late-breaking news about the product.

Follow the specific instructions that the setup program offers. Depending on the options you select for installation, the process can take some time. Don't expect to get much programming done immediately.

# Internet Applications and Request Processing

Before running any of the code listings in this book, you need a good understanding of how the Web server executes your Web page or Web Service. Internet applications such as dynamic Web sites or custom Web Services are concerned with one task—processing user requests. These requests come as HTTP requests from a client Web browser or as SOAP requests from a Web Service client program. Web Services can also be called from a Web browser, in addition to being called by custom client programs. In most cases, a custom client is needed to do anything useful with the data that a Web Service returns.

**NEW TERM**  HTTP stands for Hypertext Transfer Protocol. A *protocol* is simply an agreed-on method for transmitting data—in this case, for transmitting data between Web servers and browsers. HTTP requests are streams of text characters sent over the Internet, each containing a request to download a Web page's contents. A typical HTTP request looks like this:

```
GET http://www.mycompany.com/index.htm HTTP 1.1
```

This request asks the Web server residing on the machine named www.mycompany.com to send back the page called index.htm.

SOAP stands for Simple Object Access Protocol. Just like HTTP, it's another standard for sending and receiving data from a server computer. In fact, SOAP relies on HTTP and adds additional levels of sophistication to permit more complex interactions. In most cases, SOAP requests are sent to a Web server to handle the request. SOAP requests and responses are customized for calling functions instead of returning Web pages. Day 13 will explore SOAP requests and responses in detail.

## Dynamic Pages Process Overview

So what happens when a user points a Web browser to one of your pages? The Web browser generates an HTTP request for the specific page the user wants to view. The Web server, which is listening at all times for HTTP requests, takes the request and looks up the file for that specific page. If the page ends in an .htm or .html extension, the Web browser simply returns the contents for the file exactly.

Of course, Web servers can do more than just display files ending in an .htm extension. Currently, you can find Web sites that do all sorts of complicated tasks, such as a bank's online check writing service, which will let you pay all your bills using just a Web browser. How do such "dynamic" Web sites work?

The trick to the process is that dynamic pages that contain complex program logic use a different file extension. For instance, the next few chapters will detail ASP.NET pages, which end in an .aspx extension. When the Web server sees a request for such a page, it doesn't read the file. Instead, it knows to hand off the HTTP request to .NET (specifically, to the ASP.NET process), and let ASP.NET take over the task of processing the page and sending the response. The result is that ASP.NET executes your code, which performs whatever tasks it was designed for. Figure 1.1 illustrates how the process works.

## Web Services Processing Overview

Web Services perform a similar task to dynamic Web sites because Web Services simply respond to client requests from the Internet and return data. As we mentioned in the preceding section, rather than receive HTTP requests, Web Services receive SOAP requests. Each SOAP request contains the name of a particular function, such as GetMyAppointments, and a parameter for the function, such as today's date. Each SOAP response contains data that the function returns. For example, the GetMyAppointment method might return a data structure that lists all of a user's scheduled appointments for a certain day.

**FIGURE 1.1**

*Dynamic page proces-sing and Web servers.*

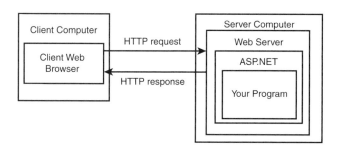

SOAP allows client programs to pass in almost any kind of data structure to the Web Service; that's why Web Services use SOAP. Similarly, Web Services can return almost any kind of data structure to a client program using SOAP.

Most Web Services still use a Web server to communicate with the outside world. After all, Web servers are good at listening for requests and spitting back data. .NET Web Services use ASP.NET to handle the SOAP requests and translate them into a data struc-ture that they can use. This process works the same way as dynamic Web pages. All .NET Web Services end in the file extension .asmx. Internet Information Services knows that it should hand off all requests ending in .asmx to ASP.NET, which then takes over and processes the SOAP request and hands it to your custom Web Service code. Figure 1.2 shows a diagram of how the process works.

**FIGURE 1.2**

*Web Services and Web servers.*

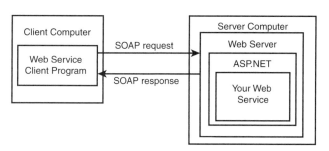

If this whole process sounds a little complicated, you can take comfort in the fact that all the ugly details around SOAP requests and responses are taken care of by the .NET Framework and ASP.NET. You don't have to worry about how to send data structures to Web Services or how to decipher a SOAP request in your Web Service code. You there-fore can concentrate on getting your own project done quickly.

# Creating a Web Service

Assuming that you've installed both Internet Information Services and Visual Studio .NET on your development computer, this section will show you how to create a Web Service. This description is just an "appetizer," to give you a feel for what .NET can do and how to use it. This Web Service will be quite limited in terms of its functionality but will offer a taste of how easy development can be using .NET. Web Services will be covered in detail in future lessons. As is traditional for first programs, this Web Service will deliver a "Hello World" message. This section uses Visual Studio. If you want to create a Web Service "by hand" using the Visual Basic compiler and without using Visual Studio, glance at Day 13's lesson.

To create a Web Service, follow these steps:

1. Start Visual Studio. Click the Get Started option on the left to view the Start Page (see Figure 1.3).

**FIGURE 1.3**

*The Visual Studio Start Page.*

2. Click the New Project button to open the New Project dialog. This dialog contains two main panes. On the left, you can select from different project types. On the right, you can select project templates for each kind of project that you might create.

3. Select Visual Basic Projects from the Project Types pane. Select ASP.NET Web Service from the Templates pane. Name the service **FirstService** (see Figure 1.4) and click OK to create a new virtual directory and several stock files commonly used in a Web Service project.

**FIGURE 1.4**

*Naming a new Web
Service project.*

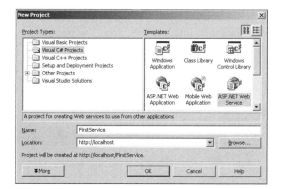

**NEW TERM**   A *virtual directory* is a directory name that corresponds to a directory on your
hard disk. For instance, a virtual directory named Documents might be linked to
the directory C:\DocumentArchive\Current. When a Web browser requests a page
in the virtual directory, such as `http://localhost/Documents/SomePage.htm`, the
Web server looks for the file `C:\DocumentArchive\Current\SomePage.htm`.

---

**Tip**   Internet Information Services uses the directory C:\Inetpub\wwwroot as the
base path for new virtual directories. In step 3, Visual Studio created a new
directory called C:\Inetpub\wwwroot\FirstService and a virtual directory
called FirstService.

---

4. Look at the new project. The Solution Explorer window is located at the upper
   right. You can use the Solution Explorer to browse for any files in your project.

   Right-click the Service1.asmx file in the Solution Explorer and select View Code.

5. Uncomment the `HelloWorld` method and remove the rest of the template code so
   that your Service1.asmx file looks like Listing 1.2.

**LISTING 1.2**   Service1.asmx with `HelloWorld` Uncommented

```
Imports System.Web.Services

Public Class Service1
    Inherits System.Web.Services.WebService

  <WebMethod()> Public Function HelloWorld() As String
      HelloWorld = "Hello World"
  End Function

End Class
```

6. Press F5 to test the Web Service. Pressing this key will compile the project and launch a new instance of Internet Explorer. You should see something similar to Figure 1.5.

**FIGURE 1.5**

*Testing your first Web Service.*

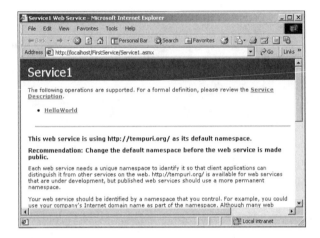

You've now created a working Web Service, albeit a simple one. To use the Web Service, click the HelloWorld link and then click the Invoke button to call the `HelloWorld` method. By clicking Invoke, you are using Internet Explorer as a Web Service client. We'll defer a full explanation for how Web Services like this work until Day 13.

# Running the Code Listings

You will, of course, want to run and experiment with the samples that we provide in this book. The following sections explain how to do so.

**Note**

The code listings in this book have been triple-checked to be error free. However, if a bug happens to creep into a code listing, let us know about it, and it will be fixed and ready for downloading on the book's Web site, at `www.samspublishing.com`.

## Running the Code Listings with a Web Browser

You can run almost all the samples in this book by simply using your favorite Web browser. You don't need to use the Visual Basic compiler or Visual Studio unless the section gives explicit instructions to do so. Most of the samples rely on ASP.NET, which will compile each listing automatically when it's first requested by a browser.

> **Note**
>
> Of course, future lessons will explain how to use the Visual Basic compiler directly if you choose to do so, and today's section titled "Running the Samples Using Visual Studio" will show you how to use Visual Studio for this book's listings.

Let's take a dry run using an extremely simple ASP.NET page to see how you can use a Web browser to run the code listing.

## Using Internet Services Manager

Being an effective Internet developer means being familiar with the Internet Services Manager (ISM), among other things. ISM is an administrative program that allows you to configure the IIS Web server program. By using ISM, you can add and remove virtual directories and change security settings. ISM is essential for developing any kind of Web application using IIS, and you will use it frequently in subsequent lessons. When IIS is installed onto a computer, ISM is installed along with it automatically. Here's how to run ISM:

1. In the Windows Control Panel, double-click the Administrative Tools icon.
2. In the Administrative Tools dialog, double-click the Internet Services Manager icon. If the icon doesn't appear in the window, IIS hasn't been installed properly on your computer.

## Finding the Root Virtual Directory

Now that you've started the Internet Services Manager application, you need to find the root virtual directory for IIS:

1. Expand the tree view on the left. You should see three nodes: Default FTP Site, Default Web Site, and Default SMTP Virtual Server.
2. Right-click the Default Web Site node and select Properties.
3. In the Default Web Site Properties dialog, select the Home Directory tab. The directory in the Local Path text box corresponds to the IIS root virtual directory. Normally, this path is C:\inetpub\wwwroot, but yours may vary. Make note of this folder's name.

## Creating and Running an ASP.NET Page at the Root

Create a file named HelloWorld.aspx with a text editor such as Notepad, type the contents of Listing 1.3, and save the file into the directory that corresponds to the IIS root virtual directory. (You can also download this listing from the book's Web site.)

**LISTING 1.3**   HelloWorld.aspx: A Trivial ASP.NET Page

```
<%@ Page Language="VB" %>
<html>
<body>
<% Response.Write("Hello World from asp.net") %>
</body>
```

Now you can view the file by using your favorite Web browser. To do so, use the name "localhost" for your computer. The URL to access Listing 1.3 is `http://localhost/HelloWorld.aspx`. Instead of using the name localhost, you can use the numerical address 127.0.0.1. You can run Listing 1.3 by using the URL `http://127.0.0.1/HelloWorld.aspx`.

Tomorrow's lesson will explain how to create new virtual directories. By creating new virtual directories, you can make a new project for each new day's code examples.

## Running the Samples Using Visual Studio

When working with samples in Visual Studio, you will need to make some small changes to the single-file sample programs, and you will spend a good amount of time deleting template code that Visual Studio generates while trying to be helpful. We suggest that you take the following approach for each book sample if you want to convert it into a Visual Studio project:

1. Open Visual Studio and start a new Empty Web Application project, assigning it a descriptive name.

2. Add a new Web Configuration file to the project. To do so, choose Add New Item from the Project menu. In the resulting dialog box, select Web Configuration File and click Open.

3. Add a new Web form to the project, assigning it a descriptive name. To do so, choose Add New Web Form from the Project menu, type the descriptive name, and click Open.

4. Replace the entire contents of the Web form with the contents of the sample.

5. The Web form you created will appear in the Solution Explorer window on the right. Right-click the Web form in the Solution Explorer and select the Set as Start Page option.

6. Run the listing by pressing F5.

This six-step process can become tedious. As a result, we have created installation programs that will create Visual Studio projects containing all the code listings for each lesson. These installation programs are available on the book's Web site at `www.samspublishing.com`.

# Summary

Today's lesson introduced basic concepts of Visual Basic, .NET, and Internet Information Services. The remaining lessons will build on this foundation, showing you how to develop sophisticated Web applications and Web Services. Although today's lesson took basic steps, including two "Hello World"–style applications, future lessons will use much more sophisticated examples.

If you aren't comfortable with the Internet Services Manager, take time out to experiment with the program before moving on to tomorrow's lesson. Try to locate all the directories on your hard disk that are associated with each predefined virtual directory on your computer. You may even experiment by creating some new virtual directories, or starting and stopping the Internet Information Services Web server.

# Q&A

**Q  If I use .NET for my Internet project, does this mean that Microsoft will have control over my application and possibly charge usage fees?**

**A**  Absolutely not. Microsoft will have some indirect control because its developers wrote the compilers and code libraries that .NET uses. It's in Microsoft's best interest to provide top-notch development tools for you. Microsoft has done so in the past and will likely continue to do so in the future.

**Q  I have been reading about Web Services and the "Hailstorm" initiative. Will Microsoft control access to my Web Service?**

**A**  Again, no. Web Services and the Hailstorm initiative are only loosely related. Hailstorm includes, among other things, services for your Web Services. By using Hailstorm services, you can let Microsoft take care of user authentication (usernames and passwords). You don't have to use Hailstorm, and it's not appropriate for many Web Services. .NET includes alternate classes that you can use for user authentication. The best part is that these alternative methods are easy to use and give you complete control over usernames and passwords and all security aspects of your application. Day 19's lesson will give details and sample programs that you can use.

**Q  .NET sounds interesting. Do I have to throw away all my existing code?**

**A**  No. You can continue to use your existing code, such as Active Server Pages, for the foreseeable future. You can also convert all or part of your code to .NET, or create new .NET components from your existing programs, and you can use existing code in your .NET Internet applications without much extra work. Day 17's lesson gives details and sample programs.

**Q**  **I don't know if I should use Visual Basic, C#, or another language available with .NET. Which is better?**

**A**  Your choice of language should be based completely on your own preference. There is no real performance difference between any of the languages you can use with .NET. Any performance differences between programs written in any of the languages are so small that they make no practical difference. As of this book's writing, the performance differences between Visual Basic and C# are essentially zero. This book, of course, focuses on Visual Basic.

**Q**  **I have heard that the Visual Basic and C# languages are compiled into *intermediate language*, similar to Java bytecodes. Will my .NET programs run slowly compared to code from previous versions of Visual Basic and C++?**

**A**  All .NET code is compiled into native assembly language instructions, either before the code is deployed or as the code is executing. You can control which compilation method is used. .NET code is, in general, slower than a quality C++ program. By the same token, C programs are faster than C++ programs, and assembly language programs are faster than C programs. With today's fast computer hardware, considerations like this are a thing of the past. If you need to write a program with extremely tight performance constraints, such as a device driver or operating system, .NET isn't for you. If you need to create an Internet site or a service available over the Internet, .NET is a perfect choice.

**Q**  **What does .NET buy me in real terms?**

**A**  First, faster Internet application development. .NET contains a huge amount of plumbing that most Internet applications require, which you can use "out of the box." Today's lesson showed how you can create a Web Service with about five minutes work. Second, better performing Internet sites. Web pages that use .NET are faster than the old ASP and other interpreted solutions by a large margin because they use compiled code. There are many more reasons, including rich XML support, better debugging and tracing, database access classes designed for scalability (ADO.NET), and many more. Read the rest of this book to find out the complete answer!

# Workshop

The Workshop provides quiz questions to help you solidify your understanding of the material covered today as well as exercises to give you experience using what you have learned. Try to understand the quiz and exercises before continuing to tomorrow's lesson. Answers are provided in Appendix A, "Answers to Quizzes and Exercises."

## Quiz

1. What is the common language runtime?

2. What is an assembly?

3. What is a namespace?

4. What is Internet Information Services, and what's it used for?

5. What makes a Web page dynamic?

6. What is a Web Service?

7. What's the difference between a Web Service and a Web server? How are they related?

## Exercises

1. Does your Internet Information Services Web server have help files installed? Locate the virtual directories that contain these help files and take some time to browse through them.

2. Create a project directory for tomorrow's lesson on your computer's hard drive. Next, create a virtual directory that "points" to the project directory just created.

3. Try adding some HTML files to a virtual directory on your computer. If you aren't familiar with HTML, look for HTML documentation on the Internet, using a search site such as www.yahoo.com or www.google.com.

# DAY 2

# Introducing ASP.NET

This lesson will explain the basics of using ASP.NET. If you are already familiar with the old ASP model, this lesson will introduce some new concepts, such as code behind and assemblies in ASP.NET applications.

Today you will learn about the following:

- Making an interactive login page using ASP.NET
- Using Web forms
- Using ASP.NET's code behind feature
- Using simple Web controls in your applications
- Working with the Request and Response objects

## What Is ASP.NET?

ASP.NET, or Active Server Pages for the .NET Framework, is a technology for providing dynamic Web page content to your users. Its name is very descriptive, and we can analyze it in reverse order:

- **Page.** An ASP page is a Web page that the user navigates to and is displayed in his or her browser.

- **Server.** An ASP page contains script code that the Web server executes.
- **Active.** An ASP page provides dynamic content that's updated every time the page is accessed.

Here's how it works: An ASP.NET page resides on the Web server and contains code written in one of the .NET languages. When a user requests the ASP.NET page, the Web server loads the page and executes the program associated with the page. The code associated with the page can carry out numerous actions, such as accessing a database on the server, calling Web services, or performing calculations. Finally, the code displays HTML output to the user in the browser.

Much of ASP.NET's power comes from its capability to accept user information. When an ASP.NET page is requested, the request can include user-defined information. For example, an online book seller could permit users to search for books by topic. The desired topic—let's say, "Japanese history"—would be sent to the ASP.NET code, which would search a database for relevant books and send the results list to the user.

# Your First ASP.NET Page

Let's begin the discussion of ASP.NET by creating a simple login page. For this discussion, we will use IIS 5.0 (Internet Information Server), the standard Web server on the Windows NT/2000 platform. For this initial example, we will also use a text editor instead of Visual Studio 7.0 so that we can see how things work "under the hood." Pick the text editor of your choice—you can even use Notepad.

## Setting Up the Source Code Directory

Create a source code directory to contain the ASP.NET project. For example, you could create a directory called c:\src\beginasp. Each new ASP.NET project should reside in its own directory.

## Setting Up the Web Server

NEW TERM  Now that you have created the directory for the project, you need to create a virtual directory on the Web server pointing to the project directory. A *virtual directory* is a path accessed from a URL pointing to a directory on the machine running a Web server. More than one virtual directory can point to a single physical directory on disk, and the virtual directory can be named anything you like. For instance, in the URL www.mydomain.com/companyindex, companyindex is a virtual directory. It may actually point to a directory on the Web server named c:\private\indexproject, which would contain HTML files for the Web site.

Follow these steps to create a virtual directory with IIS:

1. Open the Control Panel from the Start menu's Settings option. Select the Administrative Tools icon. In the new window that appears, select the Internet Services Manager.

2. Expand the tree view so that the Default Web Site node appears, as Figure 2.1 shows.

**FIGURE 2.1**

*The Internet Information Services controller application.*

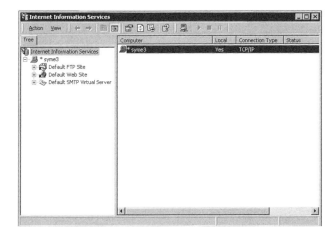

3. Right-click the Default Web Site node, choose New, and then choose Virtual Directory.

4. Follow the wizard steps. For the second step, type the alias **ASPNET**. For the third step, browse to the project directory that you created before, such as c:\src\begi-nasp (see Figure 2.2). In the remaining steps, just use the default selections.

**FIGURE 2.2**

*Step 3 of the New Virtual Directory Wizard.*

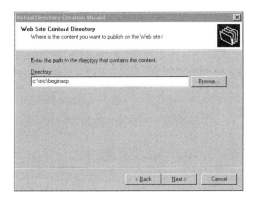

Now that the virtual directory is created, you can browse to it using a URL such as
http://localhost/aspnet/mypage.htm. Of course, for this example to work, you would
have to add an HTML page named mypage.htm into the project directory.

## Creating the Login.aspx Page

Create a new file called Login.aspx using your favorite text editor. As you might have
guessed, ASP.NET pages end in an .aspx extension. ASP.NET files can use other extensions, such as .ascx for user controls and .asmx files for Web Services. We will cover
user controls on Day 6 and Web Services starting on Day 13.

Your first ASP.NET page will be a simple login screen. Listing 2.1 shows the code for
the page.

**LISTING 2.1**   Login.aspx: A Simple Login Page Using Visual Basic and ASP.NET

```
 1: <%@ Page language="VB" %>
 2: <script runat="server">
 3: sub Page_Load(Sender as Object, e as EventArgs)
 4:
 5:    ' If the page has posted back results, then check them
 6:    if IsPostBack then
 7:       ' Grab the username and password fields
 8:       dim strUserName as string = Request("username")
 9:       dim strPassword as string = Request("password")
10:
11:       ' Write out a success/failure message
12:       if (strUserName = "Joe Smith") and (strPassword = "secret") then
13:          Response.Write("<h2>Log on successful as " & strUserName & "</h2>")
14:       else
15:          Response.Write("<h2>Your username/password were not found.</h2>")
16:       end if
17:    end if
18: end sub
19: </script>
20:
21: <html>
22: <body>
23: <h2>Welcome to the Sample Login Page</h2>
24: <form runat="server">
25: <table>
26:   <tr>
27:     <td>UserName:</td>
28:     <td><input type="text" name="username"></td>
29:   </tr>
30:   <tr>
31:     <td>Password</td>
32:     <td><input type="password" name="password"></td>
```

**LISTING 2.1**   continued

```
33:    </tr>
34:    <tr>
35:      <td></td>
36:      <td>
37:        <input type="submit" value="Login">
38:      </td>
39:    </tr>
40:  </table>
41:  </form>
42:  </body>
43:  </html>
```

2

 Line 1 of Listing 2.1 tells ASP.NET that you are using Visual Basic for the code in the page. This line is referred to as the *page directive*. You can specify other things with the page directive, as will be explained soon.

> **Note**
>
> Although ASP.NET allows you to use any of the .NET languages, you can use only one language type for each single page of server-side code. If your page contains client-side code, you can write this with a different language, such as JavaScript.

Line 2 denotes the start of scripting code. Notice the directive `runat="server"`, which ensures that the code in the script tags is executed on the Web server. This code is never sent to a client browser.

The first (and only) method inside the script tag is called `Page_Load` (Line 3). This method is an ASP.NET event handler, which I describe later in this lesson. For the moment, the important point to remember is that ASP.NET calls this method every time the page is rendered. This method also is called before any HTML output is created.

The `Page_Load` method uses code to check the entered username and password. The code uses the `Request` (Lines 8 and 9) and `Response` (Lines 13 and 15) objects to get and send code to the client browser, as covered in more detail later in this lesson.

You may have noticed the test in the first `if` statement that uses the `IsPostBack` flag (Line 6). ASP.NET automatically sets this flag when the page is called after the user clicks the submit button. On the first hit to the page, this flag is false, so most of the code is skipped. This is what we want—we want to check the username and password only if the user has actually submitted some data.

The HTML code in the remaining lines of Listing 2.1 is standard except for the `<form>` tag containing the `runat="server"` attribute (Line 24). This tag is the first example you will see of an ASP.NET Web control. For the moment, remember that this tag functions just like a regular form tag, except that it ensures that ASP.NET will call the `Page_Load` event. Figure 2.3 shows the login page.

**FIGURE 2.3**

*The login page created using ASP.NET.*

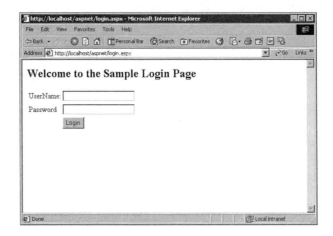

The remaining HTML in Listing 2.1 consists of two input boxes (Lines 28 and 32) and a submit button (Line 37). After the user clicks the submit button, the form's contents are posted back to the login page. After this post back, the code in the `Load` event will be re-executed. However, this time the `IsPostBack` flag will be true, and the input to the form will be checked.

## Using Web Controls

Over the next four days, we will explain ASP.NET Web controls in greater detail. Web controls offer many advantages over HTML controls in applications, including properties, events, and state management. You can convert Listing 2.1 to use Web controls for input boxes and the submit button to get a glimpse of some of these advantages. Listing 2.2 shows such converted code.

**LISTING 2.2**   LoginControl.aspx: Using Web Controls Instead of HTML Controls

```
1: <%@ Page language="VB" %>
2: <script runat="server">
3: sub LoginClicked(Sender as Object, e as EventArgs)
4:
5:    ' If the page has posted back results, then check them
6:    if IsPostBack then
```

**LISTING 2.2**   continued

```
 7:      ' Grab the username and password fields
 8:      dim strUserName as string = Request("username")
 9:      dim strPassword as string = Request("password")
10:
11:      ' Write out a success/failure message
12:      if (strUserName = "Joe Smith") and (strPassword = "secret") then
13:          Response.Write("<h2>Log on successful as " & strUserName & "</h2>")
14:      else
15:          Response.Write("<h2>Your username/password were not found.</h2>")
16:      end if
17:    end if
18: end sub
19: </script>
20:
21: <html>
22: <body>
23: <h2>Welcome to the Sample Login Page</h2>
24: <form runat="server">
25: <table>
26:   <tr>
27:    <td>UserName:</td>
28:    <td><asp:textbox id="username" runat="server"/></td>
29:    </tr>
30:   <tr>
31:    <td>Password</td>
32:    <td><asp:textbox id="password" textmode="password" runat="server"/></td>
33:    </tr>
34:   <tr>
35:    <td></td>
36:    <td>
37:       <asp:button text="Login" onClick="LoginClicked" runat="server"/>
38:    </td>
39:    </tr>
40: </table>
41: </form>
42: </body>
43: </html>
```

**2**

**ANALYSIS**    Notice that the username text box, password text box, and Login button are all Web controls. Web controls are denoted by `<asp:controlname` and end with `/>` (Lines 28, 32, and 37). Each Web control definition contains directives to set a control's attributes, such as `textmode="Password"` for a password field.

Listing 2.2 doesn't use the Page_Load event. Instead, it uses a custom event handler, LoginClicked (Line 3), called by the button control on Line 37. Notice the program text onclick="LoginClicked" instead of the Login button definition. All ASP.NET Web controls use events that you can handle with your own code on the page.

Each ASP control in Listing 2.2 contains the attribute `runat="server"`. This attribute is essential for any Web control definition; without it, the control won't work properly.

If you run the code in Listing 2.2, you might notice that the username field keeps its value even after the Login button is clicked. The password field doesn't keep its state by default. ASP.NET Web controls preserve their state without any programming effort on your part.

## Available Web Controls

Tomorrow's lesson covers most of the ASP.NET Web controls and how you can use them in your own applications. So that you can have a taste of what's to come, the following built-in ASP.NET Web controls are available:

| | |
|---|---|
| Button | Table, TableCell, TableHeaderCell, TableRow |
| Checkbox, RadioButton | TextBox |
| HyperLink | AdRotator |
| Image, ImageButton | Calendar |
| Label | ListControl (Checkbox, Dropdown, RadioButton) |
| LinkButton | DataGrid, DataList |
| Panel | Validator controls |

# Defining Web Forms

NEW TERM    The login page sample in the preceding section is an example of an ASP.NET Web form. If you've programmed with Visual Basic version 6 or earlier, you will be familiar with the term *form* as it's used here. In Visual Basic, a *form* is a window that the user interacts with; for ASP.NET, a *Web form* is a Web page that interacts with users. Web forms have programming state, events, and properties, just like a window on the desktop.

# Coding Behind Forms in ASP.NET

If you've ever written large applications using ASP or a similar technology, you may have had pages that became extremely large, with HTML and script code sprinkled together. Maintaining these pages is troublesome; the code is hard to understand because of the combination of HTML and script. You can easily make syntax errors in the script that cause the entire page to error out, and often the ASP engine doesn't give good error information about coding errors.

Wouldn't it be nice to put all the code and logic in one file, and have all the HTML and user interface elements in another? You can do just that by using ASP.NET's "code behind" feature.

## Using Code Behind with the Login Page

Let's change the login page example to use code behind, shown in Listings 2.3 and 2.4.

**LISTING 2.3**    LoginCodeBehind.aspx: Just HTML and UI Elements

```
 1: <%@ Page language="VB" inherits="MyLoginPage" src="Login.vb" %>
 2: <html>
 3: <body>
 4: <h2>Welcome to the Sample Login Page</h2>
 5: <form method="post" runat="server">
 6: <table>
 7:   <tr>
 8:    <td>UserName:</td>
 9:    <td><asp:textbox id="UserName" runat="server" /></td>
10:    </tr>
11:    <tr>
12:    <td>Password</td>
13:    <td><asp:textbox id="Password" textmode="Password"
14:                    runat="server" /></td>
15:   </tr>
16:    <tr>
17:      <td></td>
18:      <td>
19:        <asp:button id="LoginButton" text="Login"
20:                   onclick="LoginClicked" runat="server" />
21:      </td>
22:    </tr>
23: </table>
24: </form>
25: </body>
26: </html>
```

**ANALYSIS**    Line 1 of Listing 2.3 uses the `inherits` and `src` attributes inside the page directive. The `inherits` attribute specifies the code behind class that this Web form (ASP.NET page) will use. Each Web form uses only one class.

The `src` directive tells ASP.NET where to locate the source code-behind file for this Web form.

The remaining lines in Listing 2.3 are identical to the previous version of the login page, except that all the code is removed. This means that all the user interface code is in one place.

Listing 2.4 contains the source code for the login page.

**LISTING 2.4**   Login.vb: A Visual Basic File Containing All the Code for the Login Page

```
 1: imports System
 2: imports System.Web
 3: imports System.Web.UI
 4: imports System.Web.UI.WebControls
 5:
 6: public class MyLoginPage
 7:    inherits Page
 8:    'Declarations for the web controls
 9:    protected UserName as TextBox
10:    protected Password as TextBox
11:    protected LoginButton as Button
12:
13:    'Code for the LoginClicked Event from the LoginButton control
14:    public sub LoginClicked(Sender as Object, e as EventArgs)
15:
16:       ' Grab the username and password fields
17:       dim strUserName as string = UserName.Text
18:       dim strPassword as string = Password.Text
19:
20:       'Write out a success/failure message
21:       if (strUserName = "Joe Smith") and (strPassword = "secret") then
22:          Response.Write("<h2>Log on successful as " & strUserName & "</h2>")
23:       else
24:          Response.Write("<h2>Your username/password were not found.</h2>")
25:       end if
26:    end sub
27: end class
```

**ANALYSIS**   This code declares a class derived from the Page class, MyLoginPage, on Lines 6 and 7. MyLoginPage is the class name used in the inherits attribute in Listing 2.3. All code behind classes for Web forms must be derived from the Page class.

Notice that the MyLoginPage class declares each Web control used in the .aspx file as protected members of the class (Lines 9–11). We made these declarations because we use the controls in the LoginClicked event-handling method.

We also added imports directives for each namespace that the MyLoginPage class uses (Lines 1–4).

Although the combined code from Listings 2.3 and 2.4 is longer than the original version that didn't use code behind, this new implementation is more organized. Such organization becomes more important when Web forms grow larger, as they do in practical applications.

## Using Assemblies and Code Behind

As you will see in the next section, Visual Studio .NET uses code behind for all Web forms by default. However, it doesn't use the `src` attribute to point to the code-behind files. Instead, Visual Studio .NET compiles code-behind files into assemblies. After source files are compiled, ASP.NET automatically loads the corresponding assemblies for a page. ASP.NET looks for compiled assemblies in a special subdirectory called bin, which must be present in your application if you plan to use compiled assemblies this way. Of course, Visual Studio .NET will create this directory for you when you start a new project.

To illustrate how this process works, let's compile the login.vb file from Listing 2.4 into an assembly. Follow these steps to use an assembly for the login sample:

1. Start the Visual Studio .NET command prompt (from the Windows Start menu choose Programs, Microsoft Visual Studio .NET 7.0, Visual Studio .NET Tools, and then Visual Studio .NET Command Prompt).

2. Change to the project directory by entering the following command into the command prompt window:

   ```
   cd \src\beginasp
   ```

3. Create a subdirectory named bin in the project directory:

   ```
   mkdir bin
   ```

4. Use the Visual Basic compiler to compile the code in Listing 2.4. You can do this by typing the following line into the command prompt:

   ```
   vbc /out:bin\login.dll /t:library /r:system.dll /r:system.web.dll login.vb
   ```

5. Remove the `src` directive from the first line of LoginCodeBehind.aspx so that it looks like this:

   ```
   <% language="VB" inherits="MyLoginPage" %>
   ```

In step 4, the Visual Basic compiler automatically creates an assembly named login.dll for the class in the bin directory. ASP.NET looks for all assemblies in the bin directory immediately under the project directory.

You should be able to rerun the sample LoginCodeBehind.aspx file at this point. It no longer depends on the login.vb file because it's using the compiled code placed in login.dll. Visual Studio .NET uses a very similar technique for ASP.NET Web applications, by compiling all source code into assemblies in the bin directory.

# Creating a Web Application with Visual Studio .NET

Now that you've seen how to create an ASP.NET page by using a text editor and the command-line tools, you should have a sense of how easy it develops applications with ASP.NET. ASP.NET allows you to create full-featured Web pages with nothing more than a text editor. However, creating larger applications requires a more powerful development tool, and Visual Studio .NET is an excellent tool for such a task. Visual Studio .NET provides many features to help you in your development efforts, including the ability to keep track of multiple source files and a drag-and-drop environment for designing the user interface portion of Web page. Let's use Visual Studio .NET to create and extend the Login sample.

To begin, open Visual Studio .NET, where you should see the Start Page, as in Figure 2.4.

**FIGURE 2.4**

*The Visual Studio Start Page, your home base for development.*

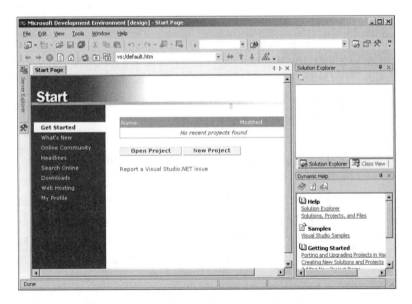

Next, click the New Project button on the Start page. In the New Project dialog box, select Visual Basic Projects as the Project Type and ASP.NET Web Application as the Template.

Enter a name for this new project, such as ASPNetDemo. Then, click OK. You will be greeted with a screen that looks like Figure 2.5.

**FIGURE 2.5**

*The default view for a new Web application.*

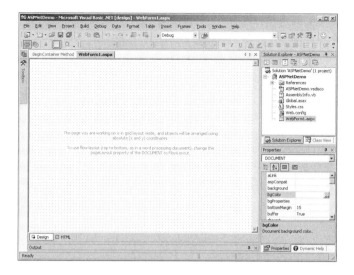

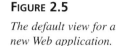

**Note**

Visual Studio .NET will create a new virtual directory with the same name as the project—in this case, ASPNetDemo. It will also create two project directories. The first directory will be under Visual Studio Projects in the My Documents folder. The second directory will be in the root directory for public Web pages (C:\Inetpub\wwwroot for a default IIS installation). Any new Web pages and associated code-behind files will be placed in this second directory.

All ASP.NET pages generated by Visual Studio contain a .aspx file and a code-behind file. You can see a typical .aspx page by locating the WebForm1.aspx page in the Solution Explorer pane on the upper right side of the screen. To view the code-behind file, right-click WebForm1.aspx and select View Code. You will then see the default code for this page that Visual Studio .NET has generated automatically.

To switch between an HTML view and the Drag-and-Drop or Design mode for a page, select one of the two buttons on the lower left part of the window.

Now, you can add items to the WebForm1.aspx page by dragging and dropping controls from the toolbox on the left. You can manipulate each control's properties in the Properties pane on the lower right of the screen. Double-clicking any control will switch the current view to an event-handler in the code-behind file.

When you are satisfied with the layout and code for a page, you can run the project by choosing Start from the Debug menu. Visual Studio .NET will compile the entire project and launch a new browser to view the program.

For the most part, the code examples in this book will be in the form of single files that you can run directly from a browser. However, each can be easily adapted to fit into a Visual Studio .NET project.

# The Response Object

Let's dig a little deeper into some of ASP.NET's essential classes. So far you've used the Response object's Write method in the login page samples. The Response object also contains other useful methods that you should be aware of.

## Cache Property

Use the Response object's Cache property to cache variables, objects, and data. This is one of the most important features of ASP.NET for making high-performance sites.

## Redirect Method

The Redirect method allows you to send the client browser to another page. You can't use this method if you've already written any HTML out to the client browser. For instance, the following code will cause an error:

```
Response.Write("You will be redirected...");
Response.Redirect("newpage.aspx");  //error!
```

## BufferOutput Property

The BufferOutput property controls whether Response.Write commands are buffered in the Response object. By default, BufferOutput is set to true. This feature should be turned off in only a few situations, such as a page that performs a time-consuming process and updates its status on the page at regular intervals. Listing 2.5 simulates this kind of page.

LISTING 2.5   NoBuffer.aspx: Turning Off Buffering and Then Writing Out HTML Periodically

```
1: <%@ Language="VB" %>
2: <%@ Import Namespace="System.Threading" %>
3: <html>
4: <body>
5: <h3>This shows an unbuffered Response object</h3>
```

**LISTING 2.5**   continued

```
 6: <%
 7:    Response.BufferOutput = false
 8:    Response.Write("One...")
 9:    Thread.Sleep(2000)
10:    Response.Write("Two...")
11:    Thread.Sleep(2000)
12:    Response.Write("Three...")
13: %>
14: </body>
15: </html>
```

**ANALYSIS**   Listing 2.5 contains a new language feature on Line 2—the Import directive. This directive allows you to reference namespaces from the .NET Framework (or other .NET components) inside script on the page. Of course, you don't need this directive if you are using code behind; you would just use the Visual Basic Imports keyword.

Listing 2.5 places code directly inside HTML by using the <% and %> tags (Lines 6–13). ASP programmers will be familiar with these tags. ASP.NET includes them for backward compatibility with ASP. Day 5, "Using Advanced ASP.NET Web Controls," explains a better alternative to these tags.

Line 11 uses the Thread.Sleep command. This command makes the current execution thread yield to other threads in the current application, or other threads in different processes. You must specify the amount of time to yield in milliseconds. For this demonstration, we chose a time of 2 seconds. See the Visual Studio documentation for more information on the Thread class.

# The Request Object

You can use the Request object to read parameters from HTML form submissions or to detect the client's browser. You also can use the Request object to read cookies, as explained tomorrow.

## Browser Detection

The Request object's Browser property gives detailed information about the client's Web browser. Listing 2.6 shows a program that will write out all this information.

**LISTING 2.6**   ShowBrowser.aspx: Showing Client Web Browser Information

```
1: <%@ Page Language = "VB" %>
2: <script runat="server">
```

**LISTING 2.6**   continued

```
 3: sub PrintTableLine(Name as string, Value as string)
 4:
 5:    Response.Write("<tr><td><b>" & Name & "</b></td><td>" & Value & _
 6:          "</td></tr>")
 7: end sub
 8: sub PrintTableLine(Name as string, Value as boolean)
 9:
10:    dim strYesNo as string = "No"
11:    if Value = true then strYesNo = "Yes"
12:
13:    Response.Write("<tr><td><b>" & Name & "</b></td><td>" & strYesNo & _
14:            "</td></tr>")
15: end sub
16: </script>
17: <html><body>
18: <h2> Here is some information about your browser </h2>
19: <table>
20:   <%
21: dim bc as HttpBrowserCapabilities  = Request.Browser
22: PrintTableLine( "Browser Type", bc.Type)
23: PrintTableLine( "Browser Name", bc.Browser)
24: PrintTableLine( "Version", bc.Version & " " & bc.MajorVersion & " " & _
25:          bc.MinorVersion)
25: PrintTableLine( "Operating System", bc.Platform)
26: PrintTableLine( "Is it a Beta Version?", bc.Beta)
27: PrintTableLine( "Is it a Web Crawler?", bc.Crawler)
28: PrintTableLine( "You're not one of those AOL users?", bc.AOL)
29: PrintTableLine( "Frames Compatible", bc.Frames)
30: PrintTableLine( "Tables Compatible", bc.Tables)
31: PrintTableLine( "Cookies Compatible", bc.Cookies)
32: PrintTableLine( "VB Script Compatible", bc.VBScript)
33: PrintTableLine( "Java Script Compatible", bc.JavaScript)
34: PrintTableLine( "Java Applets Compatible", bc.JavaApplets)
35: PrintTableLine( "ActiveX Compatible", bc.ActiveXControls)
36: %>
37: </table>
38: </body>
39: </html>
```

**ANALYSIS**   In this example, we use a custom method, `PrintTableLine`, that outputs a line in an HTML table. This method is overloaded so that it can be called with two string arguments (Line 3) or with one string and one Boolean argument (Line 8). By using the `Browser` property of the `Request` object (Line 21), we find out all the details of the client browser for this particular page request. The two most important properties, `Type` and `Browser` (Lines 22 and 23), allow us to distinguish what kind of browser has hit our page.

## Form Collection

You can use the `Form` collection to gather all input from an HTML form. The login page example used the `Form` collection to get the username and password. The `Form` object is indexed by each object's HTML or ASP ID. For example, the following text box,

```
<input type="text" id="Phone">
```

can be accessed in the `Form` object by using a line such as the following:

```
Dim strPhoneNumber As Strong=Request.Form("Phone")
```

The `Form` object is of .NET type `NameValueCollection`. The Form object is populated from HTTP `POST` requests.

## QueryString Collection

Similar to the `Form` object, the `QueryString` object contains a collection of all parameters submitted in an HTTP `GET` request. For instance, you may have a link in a page like the following:

```
<a href="SalesByStateLister.aspx?StateName=Ohio&Department=Marketing>
  Show Ohio's sales figures</a>
```

The SalesByStateLister.aspx file can access these parameters by using code like this:

```
dim strState as string = Request.QueryString("StateName")
dim strDept as string = Request.QueryString("Department")
```

The `QueryString` object is also of .NET type `NameValueCollection`.

## Parameters Collection

The `Parameters` collection combines the contents of the `Form` and `QueryString` collections. You can use the `Parameters` collection as a more general way of accessing any kind of data that the user has entered or chosen. It contains the contents of user input from HTTP `POST` and HTTP `GET` requests.

## Advanced Methods of the Request Object

The `HttpRequest` class contains various more advanced methods. Table 2.1 gives a summary.

**TABLE 2.1**  Advanced Methods in the *Request* Object

| Method | Description |
| --- | --- |
| ServerVariables | All the Web server variables, some of which are more easily accessed using the other methods listed here |
| Headers | The HTTP headers for this request |

**TABLE 2.1** continued

| Method | Description |
|---|---|
| HttpMethod | Specifies if GET or POST was used for this request |
| IsAuthenticated | Flag telling whether the current user is authenticated |
| IsSecureConnection | Flag telling whether the HTTPS protocol is in use |
| RawUrl | The raw URL for this request |
| TotalBytes | A byte count of the current request |
| Url | A property of type Uri that gives information about the current request's URL, such as the protocol |
| UrlReferrer | A property of type Uri that tells what page referred this request (can be null) |
| Path | The URL's virtual path |
| PhysicalPath | The path on the Web server for this URL; this is how the MapPath method (discussed in the following section) works |

The code in Listing 2.7 prints the ServerVariables collection.

**LISTING 2.7** ServerVars.aspx: Printing the Entire Contents of the *ServerVariables* Collection

```
<%@ Page Language="VB" %>
<html>
<body>
<h2>All of the Server Variables, in gory detail</h2>
<table border="1">
<%
dim Vars as NameValueCollection
dim nKeyIndex as integer
Vars = Request.ServerVariables
for nKeyIdx = 0; to Vars.Count - 1
  Response.Write( "<tr><td>" & Vars.Keys[nKeyIdx] & "</td>")
  Response.Write( "<td>" & Vars[nKeyIdx] & "</td></tr>" )
next
%>
</table>
</body>
</html>
```

# Handy Methods in the Page Class

Now that you have a good understanding of the Request and Response objects, let's conclude our overview of ASP.NET with a short discussion of the Page class. Tomorrow's lesson contains a more complete discussion of this class. For today, you learn about a few of the utility methods that you might use in your own applications.

## MapPath Method

The MapPath method converts filenames from a virtual directory, as the Web server sees them, into physical paths on disk. For instance, Listing 2.8 uses the Response.WriteFile and MapPath methods to write the contents of a text file to a Web browser. For this example to work, myfile.txt must reside in the physical directory corresponding to the virtual directory named beginasp.

**LISTING 2.8**   WriteFile.aspx: Writing the myfile.txt File into the Web Browser

```
<%@ Page Language="VB" %>
<html>
<body>
<h2>Here is a text file</h2>
  <pre>
<% Response.WriteFile(MapPath("/beginasp/myfile.txt")) %>
  </pre>
</body>
</html>
```

## ResolveUrl Method

You can use the ResolveUrl method to map the current virtual directory name onto an HTML page. For instance, ResolveUrl("login.aspx") will return "\beginasp\login.aspx" for the project, as Listing 2.9 shows.

**LISTING 2.9**   Resolve.aspx: Resolving the User Path to the Login Page

```
<%@ Page Language="VB" %>
<script runat="server">
sub ResolveClicked(sender as Object, e as EventArgs)
  Response.Write(ResolveUrl("login.aspx"))
end sub
</script>
<html>
<body>
<form runat="server">
<asp:button text="ResolveLoginPage" onclick="ResolveClicked"
            runat="server" />
</form>
</body>
</html>
```

### User Property

You can use the Page object's User property to determine the remote user's security identity. Day 19, "Securing Internet Applications," explains .NET security in more detail and
how to use this property.

# How ASP.NET Works

After reading through this lesson, you've seen some of the ways that ASP.NET varies
from the old ASP model. It's true that ASP.NET retains many features of ASP to help
with porting efforts. However, ASP.NET uses a much different mechanism to serve pages
than ASP or many of the other existing Web programming technologies.

As mentioned in yesterday's lesson, ASP.NET pages are compiled. Pages are either compiled on first use or precompiled if code behind is used. This makes ASP.NET a viable
solution for high-traffic Web sites.

A simplified explanation of how ASP.NET processes pages is as follows:

1. When a page is hit, ASP.NET checks to see whether it has a precompiled version
   of the page in its compiled page cache directory.
2. If the page has been updated since the last compilation, the page is recompiled on-
   the-fly. The compiled page is placed into the compiled page cache directory.
3. The ASP.NET engine renders the compiled version of the page.

This model is simplified for a couple of reasons:

- ASP.NET has a powerful caching mechanism. Entire pages can be cached for a
  certain time window, and pieces of a page can be cached by using Web controls
  and user controls.
- You can configure and customize the way pages are rendered in the ASP.NET
  engine.

Although a full treatment of these advanced techniques is beyond the scope of this book,
I will explain how to use the caching engine on Day 6.

# Summary

Today's lesson introduced ASP.NET Web page programming. You saw a number of different approaches for constructing ASP.NET pages, including code-behind techniques for
pages. You constructed an ASP.NET application by using a text editor, and you also saw
how to use Visual Studio .NET for your Web projects. During the last half of today's les-

son, you saw an overview of some objects you will frequently use in your own ASP.NET Web applications. You learned about some of the most useful properties and methods in the Request and Response objects. This lesson also showed some of the methods from the Page class that you frequently use in your own applications. Last, this lesson gave a high-level view of how ASP.NET handles page requests.

We've just scratched the surface of ASP.NET Web programming. Tomorrow's lesson elaborates on Web Forms, including the processing model and event sequence that occurs when users browse to one of your pages. You will also learn about some of the fundamental programming techniques used with ASP.NET, including state management.

Before moving on to the next chapter, read through the following Q&A section. You can also use the Quiz and Exercises to enhance your knowledge.

# Q&A

**Q Do pages written using ASP.NET require Internet Explorer to function properly, because .NET is supported on only Microsoft platforms?**

**A** No. Because all .NET code in ASP.NET pages run on the Web server, the Web server running ASP.NET pages must support .NET. However, client browsers see only HTML and any JavaScript that is included in the page.

**Q Does using code-behind techniques with ASP.NET result in faster code?**

**A** No. All ASP.NET code is compiled, whether or not it uses code-behind. Using code-behind may or may not result in faster performance, and the difference will be trivial. Instead, code-behind is used to make pages more maintainable.

# Workshop

The Workshop provides quiz questions to help you solidify your understanding of the material covered and exercises to provide you with experience in using what you've learned. The answers to the quiz questions are provided in Appendix A, "Answers to Quizzes and Exercises."

## Quiz

1. Does every ASP.NET page require you to implement the Page_Load event?
2. How can an ASP.NET page be made to use code-behind?
3. What's the simplest way to write an HTML string to the output of an ASP.NET page?

4. What ASP.NET class reads the contents of a form after the user clicks the Submit button?

5. What's the difference between the Form collection and the QueryString collection in the HttpRequest class?

6. What is the MapPath method used for?

7. What class determines the type of browser being used?

8. How can you redirect users to a different page?

9. Why would you use the Parameters collection from the HttpRequest class instead of the Form or QueryString collection?

10. List three different Web controls that you might use in a form used for surveying user preferences.

## Exercise

1. Rewrite Listing 2.2 so that users are redirected to a new page when they log in successfully.

2. Write an ASP.NET page that will redirect users to two different pages depending on the kind of browser they are using.

DAY **3**

# Using Web Forms

Yesterday's lesson introduced ASP.NET programming. You saw how to implement a basic ASP.NET page using a simple Web form and how to use code behind with Web forms. Today's lesson will introduce more techniques that you can use with Web forms, including basic state management and some details about the life cycle of Web forms. Today you will learn about the following:

- The way Web forms are processed
- An introduction to Web form state management
- The Session and Application objects
- The way global objects are stored

## Understanding How Web Forms Are Processed

As we discussed yesterday, a Web form is another name for an ASP.NET page. You learned yesterday that a Web form can be made up of a single file with an .aspx extension. You also saw how an .aspx file and a code behind file can be combined to make a Web form. As we'll show in the following few days, Web forms can also contain your own custom controls, defined similarly to .aspx pages, called *user controls*.

Because a Web form can include HTML, ASP.NET Web controls, custom (user) controls, and code behind, creating them can get complicated pretty quickly. However, you need to remember only a few key ideas about ASP.NET page processing so that you can develop and debug effectively.

The first key idea is that much of the ASP.NET infrastructure is set up so that a single ASP.NET page can post form data back to itself repeatedly. You saw this "postback" technique in yesterday's examples with the Login page. This technique is most useful when you divide your Web site's functionality into a few main pages. We'll explore this kind of design in the first bonus programming project in this book, after Day 12.

The second key idea to remember is that all ASP.NET pages are eventually compiled into executable files by the ASP.NET infrastructure. This means that every time a page is processed and rendered, a small program corresponding to each Web form is executed by the ASP.NET infrastructure.

Let's explore in more detail how Web forms are processed. Listing 3.1 shows a sample Web form that performs an English unit to metric unit conversion, and Figure 3.1 shows the resulting page.

**LISTING 3.1**    EnglishToMetric.aspx: Converting Feet and Inches to Meters

```
 1: <%@ Page Language="VB" %>
 2: <html>
 3: <body>
 4:   <form runat="server">
 5:    <h2>English to Metric conversion</h2>
 6:    <h3>Please enter your height, and then click the Convert button</h3>
 7:    <asp:Textbox id="Feet" runat="server"/>Feet
 8:    <br>
 9:    <asp:Textbox id="Inches" runat="server"/>Inches
10:    <br>
11:    <asp:Button OnClick="OnConvert" Text="Convert" runat="server"/>
12:    <br>
13:    <br>
14:    <asp:Label id="lblMeters" runat="server"/>
15:   </form>
16: </body>
17: </html>
18:
19: <script runat="server">
20: Sub Page_Load(Sender As object, e As EventArgs)
```

**LISTING 3.1** continued

```
21:
22:    If IsPostBack Then
23:       If Feet.Text = "" Then Feet.Text = "0"
24:       If Inches.Text = "" Then Inches.Text = "0",
25:    End If
26: End Sub
27:
28: Sub OnConvert(Sender as Object, e As EventArgs)
29:
30:    Dim fFeet As Single = Single.Parse(Feet.Text)
31:    Dim fInches as Single = Single.Parse(Inches.Text)
32:    Dim fMeters As Double = 0.305*fFeet + 0.0254*fInches
33:    lblMeters.Text = "<b>You are " & fMeters.ToString() & " meters tall</b>"
34:
35: End Sub
36: </script>
```

**FIGURE 3.1,**

*The English unit to metric unit conversion page.*

**ANALYSIS** Let's examine how Web forms work using Listing 3.1 as our reference. Web forms like Listing 3.1 are processed in two different ways:

- A Web form is rendered when the user initially browses to the .aspx file. In this case, the Web form doesn't process any events because there has been no user interaction.

- A Web form may be processed after the user interacts with one of the page controls. For instance, the user might click a button on the page or select an item from a drop-down list. When the user does so, the same Web form gets hit by the user's browser, this time with information about what the user has done.

Through both cases, a Web form goes through five distinct stages when it's rendered, as shown in Figure 3.2.

FIGURE 3.2

*Web forms processing
stages.*

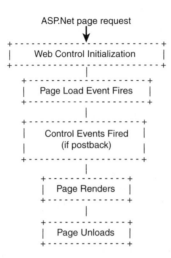

In Figure 3.2, the first stage deals with Web control initialization. We'll learn more details about how controls save and then remember their state in tomorrow's lesson. You don't need to be too concerned about this stage in your own programming tasks.

Your code is frequently involved in the second stage of Web forms processing, when the ASP.NET infrastructure fires the Load event in the Page class. As Listing 3.1 shows, you can use the Page_Load event (Lines 20-26) to change the contents of controls or to perform any other kinds of processing before a page is rendered. If the page posts back to itself (that is, if the user clicks the Convert button), the Page_Load event will fill in zeros if the user leaves any field blank (Lines 22–25).

The third stage of Web forms processing is for control event handling, which happens only if the user manipulates one of the Web controls on the page. This stage won't happen if this is the first time the user is browsing to this particular page. In Listing 3.1, the OnConvert method is called during this stage (Lines 28–35). Note that event handling happens after the Page_Load event. You will learn about more complex Web controls that contain many events on Day 5, "Using Advanced ASP.NET Web Controls."

In the fourth stage, the HTML for the page is rendered. This process involves calling the Render method for the page, which will call the Render method for every control, among other things.

**Note**

Listing 3.1 doesn't contain an explicit Render method, because the page class and Web control classes have default implementations for it already. You will need to override the Render method only if you want to customize the exact HTML that each class produces.

In the last stage, , the `Page_Unload` event gets called. You can use the `Unload` event to clean up database connections and other objects that have to be closed explicitly, for example. (Listing 3.1 also doesn't define the `Page_Unload` event, because it doesn't need to clean up any objects.)

# Performing Basic State Management in Web Applications

**NEW TERM** Most Web applications are customized for each individual site user. Even if the site behaves the same way for every user, a user will often perform an operation on the site that spans two or more pages. For instance, if your Web application has a search feature, you might use one page to gather a search string. You might use a second page to display the results and a third page to hold a history of search queries. Designing your ASP.NET code to keep track of search queries, search results, and search history entries involves state management. In the broadest terms, *state management* refers to the ways an ASP.Net page "remembers" what a user has done previously.

If the searching feature was part of a standalone program, such as a Visual Basic Windows application, storing the user's state, including search queries and results, isn't an issue—just store the search strings and results on the client computer. With Web applications, you can't store much of anything on the client computer because the client is just a Web browser.

Web programmers have invented a number of methods for storing state in Web applications. The most basic methods include cookies, query strings, and hidden fields. These methods allow you to store a small bit of information, such as a key to a database table.

By using ASP.NET, you have these and several other more powerful state options at your disposal. These methods include the `Session` and `Application` objects and the `ViewState` property. ASP.NET also adds a new class for page caching, `Response.Cache`. You can use this feature to achieve significant performance improvements in your Web applications, usually after the bulk of coding is complete. Page caching will be explained in more detail on Day 7.

# Using Cookies

Cookies allow you to store small bits of data on the user's computer. They take up a small amount of space on the user's hard drive and are often useful for storing nonessential information, such as user preferences.

**Tip** | Store information that you are willing to lose in cookies. Users can delete cookies at any time, and some users disable them altogether.

ASP.NET lets you manipulate cookies quite easily with the `Cookies` collection on the `Request` and `Response` objects. Listings 3.2 and 3.3 are two companion pages that will read and write cookies that you enter. Figures 3.3 and 3.4 show the two pages.

**LISTING 3.2** WriteCookies.aspx: Writing Arbitrary Cookies

```
 1: <%@ language="VB" %>
 2: <script runat="server">
 3: Sub WriteClicked(Sender As Object, e As EventArgs)
 4:
 5:    'Create a new cookie, passing the name into the constructor
 6:     Dim cookie as HttpCookie = new HttpCookie(NameField.Text)
 7:
 8:    'Set the cookies value
 9:     cookie.Value = ValueField.Text
10:
11:    'Set the cookie to expire in 1 minute
12:     Dim dtNow as DateTime  = DateTime.Now
13:     Dim tsMinute as New TimeSpan(0, 0, 1, 0)
14:     cookie.Expires = dtNow.Add(tsMinute)
15:
16:     'Add the cookie
17:     Response.Cookies.Add(cookie)
18:     Response.Write("Cookie written. <br><hr>")
19:
20: End Sub
21: </script>
22: <html>
23: <body>
24: <h3>Use the button below to write cookies to your browser </h3>
25: The cookies will expire in one minute.
26: <form runat="server">
27: Cookie Name <asp:textbox id="NameField" runat="server"/><br>
28: Cookie Value <asp:textbox id="ValueField" runat="server"/><br>
29: <asp:button text="WriteCookie" onclick="WriteClicked" runat="server" /><br>
30: </form>
31: <a href="readcookies.aspx">Read the cookies</a>
32: </body>
33: </html>
```

**LISTING 3.3**  ReadCookies.aspx: Reading Cookies Written from the WriteCookies Example

```
 1: <%@ language="VB" %>
 2: <script runat="server">
 3: Sub ReadClicked(Sender As Object, e As EventArgs)
 4:
 5:   'Get the cookie name the user entered
 6:   Dim strCookieName as string = NameField.Text
 7:
 8:   'Grab the cookie
 9:   Dim cookie as HttpCookie = Request.Cookies(strCookieName)
10:
11:   'Check to make sure the cookie exists
12:   if cookie Is Nothing then
13:     Response.Write("Cookie not found. <br><hr>")
14:   else
15:     'Write the cookie value
16:     Dim strCookieValue as string = cookie.Value.ToString()
17:     Response.Write("The " & strCookieName & " cookie contains: <b>" _
18:                          & strCookieValue & "</b><br><hr>")
19:   end if
20:
21: End Sub
22: </script>
23: <html>
24: <body>
25: Use the button below to read a cookie<br>
26: <form runat="server">
27: Cookie Name <asp:textbox id="NameField" runat="server" />
28: <asp:button text="ReadCookie" onclick="ReadClicked" runat="server" />
29: </form>
30: <a href="writecookies.aspx">Write Cookies</a>
31: </body>
32: </html>
```

3

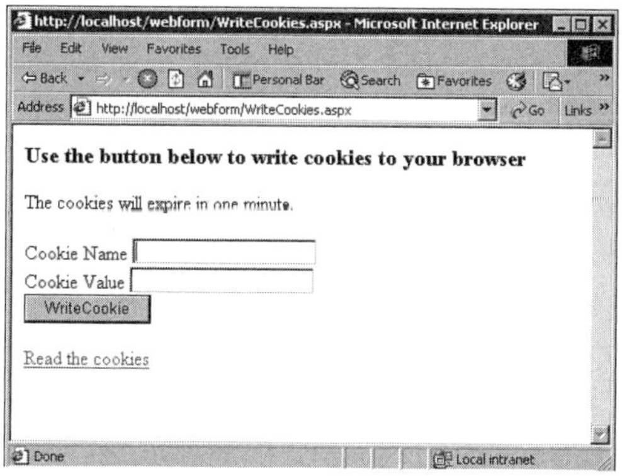

**FIGURE 3.3**

*The WriteCookies.aspx page writes cookies to the user's browser.*

**FIGURE 3.4**

*The ReadCookies.aspx page reads cookies stored on a user's browser.*

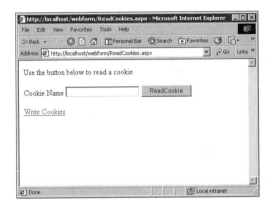

ANALYSIS To write a cookie, create a new HttpCookie object (Line 6 of Listing 3.2), assign a string to its Value property (Line 9), and then call the Add() method on the Response.Cookies object (Line 17). You can also set the time of expiration for a cookie by setting the Expires property to a DateTime value (Line 14).

ReadCookies.aspx in Listing 3.3 shows that it's equally easy to read cookies back, using the Request.Cookies collection (Line 9), which is indexed by cookie name.

Cookies can store only strings, so if you need to store a more complex data type, it must be converted into a string. One possibility for storing complicated data structures is to write the structure out as an XML string and convert it back when reading the cookie.

You can store multiple strings in a cookie by treating each cookie as a collection object. For example, the following would work fine:

```
Dim cookie As HttpCookie = new HttpCookie("UserFavorites")
cookie("FavoriteColor") = "blue"
cookie("FavoriteFlavor") = "chocolate";
cookie("FavoriteDrink") = "coffee";
```

The HttpCookie class contains some advanced properties, listed in Table 3.1.

**TABLE 3.1** Advanced Properties of the HttpCookie Class

| Property | Description |
|---|---|
| Domain | Gets/sets the domain name that this cookie belongs to. If set, it restricts access to this cookie from Web servers in the specified domain, such as mycompany.com. |
| Path | Gets/sets the path that this cookie belongs to. If set, it restricts access to this cookie from Web pages in the specified path. |
| Secure | Gets/sets a flag that tells whether the cookie should be transmitted securely to the client browser using the HTTPS protocol. You must have HTTPS set up on your Web server for this option to work. |
| HasKeys | Tells whether the cookie is made up of a collection of strings. |

# Using Hidden Fields and Query Strings

You also can store small amounts of information on the client by using hidden fields. Hidden fields are HTML elements, similar to text boxes, where you can store strings. Web browsers don't display hidden fields in page output. However, when you use a hidden field within an HTML form, the contents are submitted back to your program.

To use hidden fields, use a code line that looks similar to the following within a `<form>` area:

```
<input type="hidden" value="Value That You Need to Store" id="KeyName">
```

You can extract the hidden field's value by using the `Params` collection in the `Request` object, using a code line like this:

```
Dim strValue As HttpCookie = Request.Params("KeyName")
```

As you will see in the following lessons, hidden fields play a much smaller role in ASP.NET Web programming than in other technologies, such as the older ASP. This is true because ASP.NET Web controls keep track of their own state and because the `Page` class contains a `ViewState` collection in which you can store string data easily.

You can also use query strings to pass parameters from page to page. Query strings are bits of information appended to an URL, as in the following line:

```
<a href="ShowSales?Dept=Mfg&Year=2001>Maufacturing Sales</a>
```

Listings 3.4 and 3.5 show examples of one page that passes a parameter to another page using a query string.

**LISTING 3.4**  ShowSales.htm: Passing a Query String to SalesFigures.aspx

```
<html>
<body>
<h2>Please select one of the links below
for Widgets Inc quarterly sales figures</h2>
<a href="salesfigures.aspx?Department=Manufacturing">Manufacturing</a>
<br>
<a href="salesfigures.aspx?Department=RD">Research & Development</a>
```

**LISTING 3.5**  SalesFigures.aspx: Showing Different Sales Depending on a Query String

```
<%@ Page Language="VB" %>
<html>
<body>
<h2>Sales figures for Widgets Inc</h2>
```

**LISTING 3.5**  continued

```
<% WriteSales() %>
</body>
</html>
<script runat="server">
Sub WriteSales()

  if Request.Params("Department") = "Manufacturing" Then
    Response.Write("<b>Manufacturing Quarterly Sales</b><br>")
    Response.Write("Quarter 1 Sales: $24M<br>")
    Response.Write("Quarter 2 Sales: $34M<br>")
    Response.Write("Quarter 3 Sales: $12M<br>")
  End If
  if Request.Params("Department") = "RD" Then

    Response.Write("<b>Research and Development Quarterly Sales</b><br>")
    Response.Write("Quarter 1 Sales: $2M<br>")
    Response.Write("Quarter 2 Sales: $3M<br>")
    Response.Write("Quarter 3 Sales: $1M<br>")
  End If
End Sub
</script>
```

# Working with the `Session` Object

Programming with query strings and hidden fields is cumbersome if you need to manipulate more than a trivial amount of state data. Luckily, ASP.NET gives you a better way to store state for each user on the server with the `Session` object. Every time a new browser hits your ASP.NET application, a new `Session` object is created for that Web browser. You can store data in the `Session` object, and it will be available from hit to hit for the same Web browser. Sessions expire after 20 minutes of inactivity by default, although you can change this behavior, as we'll show shortly.

Sessions aren't magic. By default, ASP.NET uses a cookie containing a unique and random ID that it uses to look up the `Session` object in the ASP.NET server process.

Tip

> If needed, you can turn off the cookies to instantiate *cookieless sessions*. You can also offload the storage of session state onto a different server or into a SQL Server database, for "Web farm" scenarios. We'll explain these different session configurations on Day 18, "Configuring Internet Applications."

# Adding Data to the `Session` Object

You can easily add data to the `Session` object. The line

```
Session("ValidUser") = true
```

automatically creates a new variable called `ValidUser` (if it doesn't exist already) and sets it to `true`. By default, every variable added to the `Session` object is of the .NET `Object` type.

Because variables in the `Session` object are of type `Object`, proper programming practice argues that you should cast them to the appropriate type when accessing them:

```
Dim strUserName As String = CStr(Session("UserName"))
```

Because Visual basic is very good at automatic data conversions, however, you can usually leave out the explicit cast as shown here:

```
Dim strUserName As String = Session("UserName")
```

You might be wondering whether it's appropriate to store large custom objects in `Session`. The answer is that you should avoid storing large amounts of data in session if possible. You can easily overburden your Web server by storing large amounts of data in `Session`, especially if your Web site has many users. Databases are a better choice for storing large amounts of state data.

The `Session` object is of type `HTTPSessionState`. Its default property is the `Item` collection, which allows you to access the stored items by using the `()` notation.

# Lifetime of the `Session` Object

A new session is created once for each new browser that hits your ASP.NET Web site. If a user stops hitting your Web site, his `Session` will time out after 20 minutes of inactivity, by default.

You can find out how long the `Session` timeout setting is by using the `Timeout` method. The following code line prints `"20"` by default:

```
<% Response.Write(Session.Timeout.ToString()) %>
```

You can change the timeout for the `Session` object by assigning the `Timeout` property to a certain value, in minutes, such as

```
Session.Timeout = 5
```

# Removing Objects from the `Session` Object

Because sessions time out, you don't really need to remove objects from them. However, you can remove objects by using the `Session.Remove()` method. You also can remove everything in the Session object by using the RemoveAll() method. You might want to use these two methods to conserve Web server resources, especially if you store large objects in Session.

Listing 3.6 shows a page that lets you add and remove strings to the current Session.

**LISTING 3.6**  SessionPopulate.aspx: Adding and Removing Strings from Session State

```
<%@ language="VB" %>
<script runat="server">
Sub AddClicked(Sender As Object, e As EventArgs)

   Session(Key.Text) = Value.Text

End Sub

Sub RemoveClicked(Sender As Object, e As EventArgs)

   Session.Remove(Key.Text)

End Sub
</script>
<html>
<body>
<h3>Current items in Session</h3>
<form method="post" runat="server">
<table border="1">
  <tr>
    <td><b>Item Name</b></td>
    <td><b>Value</b></td>
  </tr>
<%
  Dim strSesKeyName As String
  Dim strSesItem As String
  Dim i As Integer
  for  i=0 to Session.Count - 1
    strSesKeyName = Session.Keys(i)
    strSesItem = Session(i)
    Response.Write("<tr><td>" & strSesKeyName & "</td><td>" & _
                   strSesItem & "</td></tr>")
  Next
%>
</table>
<br>
Key <asp:textbox id="Key" runat="server"/>
Value <asp:textbox id="Value" runat="server" /><br>
<asp:button text="Add/Modify Key/Value pair"
            onclick="AddClicked" runat="server" />
<asp:button text="Remove Key" onclick="RemoveClicked" runat="server" />
```

**LISTING 3.6**   continued

```
</form>
</body>
</html>
```

> **Tip**
>
> You also can kill off a session immediately by using the Abandon() method.
> As soon as Abandon is called, a new session is created automatically.

# Working with the `Application` Object

Not all data in your Web applications is specific to individual users of your Web site. For instance, if your application tracks stock prices, this data should be available to all users. Data like this is called *global data*, and using global data in session doesn't make sense. Fortunately, ASP.NET provides the `Application` object just for this purpose.

The `Application` object is stored in memory and unlike `Session`, objects can't be offloaded to another server or a SQL database. This limits the usefulness of the `Application` object for Web farm scenarios. However, if your Web application contains a large amount of read-only data that takes awhile to load, the `Application` object is a good place to store it.

## Adding Objects to the Application

You can add objects to the `Application` object in the same way that you can in `Session` objects. For instance,

```
Application("WebStoreName") = "Stanley Sprockets Online"
```

stores a string into the `Application` object. Conversely,

```
Dim strStoreName As String = Application("WebStoreName")
```

fetches the value.

## Synchronizing Code in the `Application` Object

If more than one Web page tries to store or update a value in the `Application` object at the same time, the data can become corrupt unless the updates are synchronized. This situation could easily happen with a site that experiences even a moderate amount of traffic, so using the `Lock()` and `Unlock()` methods of the `Application` object is important when you're storing data. Listing 3.7 shows how to synchronize code properly.

**LISTING 3.7**   HitCounter.aspx: Updating a Hit Counter for the Web Site

```
<%@ language="VB" %>
<%
    'We need to check if the "Hits" object
    'has never been assigned and is null.
    'If it is null, then we set it equal to 0
    if Application("Hits") Is Nothing Then
      Application.Lock()
      Application("Hits") = 0
      Application.UnLock()
    End If
    Dim nHits As Integer = Application("Hits")
    nHits = nHits + 1
    Application.Lock()
    Application("Hits") = nHits
    Application.UnLock()
%>
<html>
<body>
<h2>This site has been hit
    <% Response.Write(Application("Hits").ToString()) %>
    times </h2>
</body>
</html>
```

> **Caution**
>
> Locking the Application object blocks other pages that use the object from running until it is unlocked. For best performance, don't make many updates to the Application object. The best use for the object is for infrequently updated read-only data. An example might be an application that tracks sporting events and stores the latest scores from current games every five minutes.

## Removing Objects from the Application

You can remove objects from the Application object by using the Remove() and RemoveAll() methods, just like with the Session object.

## Lifetime of an Application

The Application object is created on the first hit from the first user to your ASP.NET application. The Application object remains in memory until the Web server is shut down, or the web.config site configuration file has changed. (We introduce the web.config file shortly.) Unlike the Session object, the Application object doesn't have an Abandon() method.

# Setting Up Global Objects with the global.asax File

ASP.NET uses a special file, called global.asax, to establish any global objects that your Web application uses. The .asax extension denotes an application file rather than .aspx for a page file.

Each ASP.NET application can contain at most one global.asax file. The file is compiled on the first page hit to your Web application. ASP.NET is also configured so that any attempts to browse to the global.asax page directly are rejected.

Listing 3.8 shows a global.asax file that you can use to make a more complete hit counter.

**LISTING 3.8**   global.asax: Event Handlers for the Application and Session Objects

```
 1: <%@ language="VB" %>
 2: <script runat="server">
 3: Sub Application_Start(Sender As Object, e As EventArgs)
 4:
 5:   Application("Hits") = 0
 6:   Application("Sessions") = 0
 7:   Application("TerminatedSessions") = 0
 8:
 9: End Sub
10:
11: 'The BeginRequest event is fired for every hit
12: 'to every page in the site.
13: Sub Application_BeginRequest(Sender As Object, e As EventArgs)
14:
15:   Application.Lock()
16:   Application("Hits") = Application("Hits") + 1
17:   Application.UnLock()
18:
19: End Sub
20:
21: Sub Session_Start(Sender As Object, e As EventArgs)
22:
23:   Application.Lock()
24:   Application("Sessions") = Application("Sessions") + 1
25:   Application.UnLock()
26:
27: End Sub
28:
29: Sub Session_End(Sender As Object, e As EventArgs)
30:
31:   Application.Lock()
32:   Application("TerminatedSessions") = _
```

3

**LISTING 3.8** continued

```
33:        Application("TerminatedSessions") + 1
34:     Application.UnLock()
35:
36: End Sub
37:
38: Sub Application_End(Sender As Object, e As EventArgs)
39:
40:     'Write out our statistics to a log file
41:     '...code omitted...
42:
43: End Sub
44: </script>
```

**ANALYSIS** The global.asax file in Listing 3.8 contains event handlers for the Session and Application objects. Each event handler has the same signature as the Page_Load event handler.

The code in Listing 3.8 handles three Application object-related events: Start (Lines 3–9), End (Lines 38–43), and BeginRequest (Lines 13–19). Start and End are called when the Web application starts and ends, respectively. BeginRequest is called for every page hit that the site receives. Listing 3.8 updates the total number of hits in this event.

The Session Start (Lines 21–27)and End (Lines 29–36)events are handled in the middle of the listing. These two events count how many different Web users have accessed the site.

You can write a simple page to utilize the statistics that Listing 3.8 tracks. Listing 3.9 shows a page that writes out the results of the hit-counting code in the global.asax file. Figure 3.5 shows the statistics page after a few hits.

**LISTING 3.9** Statistics.aspx: The Results of the Tracking in the global.asax File

```
<%@ page language="VB" %>
<html>
<body>
<h2> Statistics for the Test Web Application </h2>
Total hits: <% Response.Write(Application("Hits").ToString()) %> <br>

Total sessions: <% Response.Write(Application("Sessions")) %> <br>

Expired sessions:
  <% Response.Write(Application("TerminatedSessions")) %> <br>
</body>
</html>
```

**FIGURE 3.5**

*The Statistics page after some traffic.*

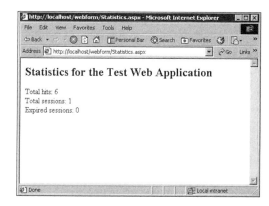

**Statistics for the Test Web Application**

Total hits: 6
Total sessions: 1
Expired sessions: 0

**Tip**

If the global.asax file is modified, the Web application is restarted on the next page hit and the global.asax file is recompiled.

3

## Adding Objects to the global.asax File

To use global objects in your ASP.NET application, add the <object> tag in the global.asax file for each one. The <object> tag has an optional attribute called scope, which determines if the added object will be created on-the-fly, associated with the Application object, or associated with the Session object.

**NEW TERM** To explore the <object> tag, let's create a simple class that stores and retrieves strings. The sample is going to associate an object of this class with the Application object in the global.asax file, so the class must be thread-safe. The term *thread-safe* means that many client threads can access the class at the same time without any data corruption. Because ASP.NET uses one thread per page, ensuring that the class is thread-safe is critical if multiple users browse the site at the same time.

### Understanding Threads

What's a thread? To answer, let's review *processes* first. All Windows applications are processes that run on your computer. Processes contain their own code and memory space, and can interact with computer peripherals, such as the screen or the network card. ASP.NET runs as a process, and it executes your code, of course.

Each process contains one or more threads. A *thread* is like a process or an individual program, because it also executes a certain set of code. However, a thread is a "lightweight" version of a process. Threads live inside processes, and use a process's memory. The Windows operating system gives each thread a small amount of time to execute and quickly switches between threads so that it seems like more than one thread is executing at the same time. For all practical intents, the threads are running at the same time.

Because threads use their parent process's memory, they can potentially change the same object (in memory) at the same time. For two threads, A and B, thread A might add 10 to the counter object. Thread B might subtract 10 from the counter. If the two threads are switched on and off by the operating system in an "unlucky" way, the counter object could contain a scrambled result.

When each ASP.NET page is being processed, it gets its own thread. If more than one user accesses the Web site at the same time, many threads will appear even if both users are accessing the same ASP.NET page.

To prevent threads (and ASP.NET pages) from interfering with each other when accessing the same object, use the technique in the example that follows.

To make the class thread-safe, use the Synchronized method of the base collection class, Hashtable. This class is shown in Listing 3.10.

**LISTING 3.10**  MyClass.vb: Implementing a Class to Store and Retrieve Strings in a Thread-Safe Way

```
Imports System
Imports System.Collections

Namespace TestApplication

  public class MyClass1
    private m_col As Hashtable
    'm_colSync will be a thread-safe container for m_col
    private m_colSync As Hashtable

    Public Sub New()
        m_col = new Hashtable()
        m_colSync = Hashtable.Synchronized(m_col)
    End Sub

    Public Sub AddItem(Name As String, Value As String)
        m_colSync(Name) = Value
    End Sub

    Public Function GetItem(Name As String) As String
        return m_colSync(Name)
    End Function

End Class
```

**LISTING 3.10**  continued

```
End Namespace

'note: use "vbc /out:bin\myclass.dll /t:library myclass.cs /r:system.dll"
'        to compile with the command line utility
```

Note that the DLL file is placed in the bin directory off the project directory. The next step is to add this object to the global.asax file with the <object> tag. A short global.asax file that does this follows:

```
<object id="MyStringCollection" runat="server"
        class="TestApplication.MyClass1" scope="Application" />
```

The id attribute tells ASP.NET what to call our object when it's used later. The class attribute can be used to specify COM objects in addition to .NET components, but by using their ProgID.

If the listing omitted the scope attribute, a new object is created on-the-fly for every page that uses the StringCollection object.

Let's write a sample page that uses StringCollection. Listing 3.11 shows just such a page.

**LISTING 3.11**  UseObject.aspx: Using the Global Object

```
<%@ language="VB" %>
<script runat="server">
Sub Page_Load(Sender As Object, e As EventArgs)

  MyStringCollection.AddItem("FirstUser", "Joe Smith")

End Sub
</script>
<html>
<body>
The name of the first user is
   <% Response.Write(MyStringCollection.GetItem("FirstUser")) %>
</body>
</html>
```

# Putting Code Behind the global.asax File

If you use Visual Studio. NET to create your Web project, it will use the code behind feature of ASP.NET for global.asax. The code behind file that is generated is named global.asax.vb, when using the Visual Basic compiler. To use code behind in global.asax manually, use the `Application` directive instead of the `Page` directive, like this:

```
<@ Application Inherits="MyApplication.GlobalClass" %>
```

Listing 3.12 shows a code behind example for the global.asax file.

**LISTING 3.12**   GlobalClass.vb: Implementing the Code for the global.asax File

```
Namespace MyApplication

    Imports System
    Imports System.Web
    Imports System.Web.SessionState

    Public class GlobalClass
        Inherits System.Web.HttpApplication

      protected Sub Session_Start(Sender As Object, e As EventArgs)

        Response.Write("Session started <br>")

      End Sub
    End Class
'note: use "vbc /out:bin\globalclass.dll /t:library globalclass.cs
/r:system.dll"
'       to compile with the command line utility

End Namespace
```

**Tip**   You can mix code behind and the `<object>` tag in the global.asax file.

# Configuring the Application

Configuring Web sites is much easier using ASP.NET than it is with many other solutions. ASP.NET allows you to configure almost every aspect of your site using an XML file called web.config.

The web.config file is a boon for developers who have their Web applications hosted by another company. Rather than have to deal with surly support technicians from your hosting company, you can simply upload new versions of a web.config file at will.

The web.config file is similar to the global.asax file, in that it can be stored at the root of an ASP.NET application. Also, whenever you modify the file, the ASP.NET application is automatically restarted.

Look at a sample web.config file in Listing 3.13.

**LISTING 3.13** Sample web.config File to Specify a Session Timeout of Five Minutes

```
<?xml version="1.0" ?>
<configuration>
  <system.web>
    <sessionState
            timeout="5"
    />
  </system.web>
</configuration>
```

Visual Studio.NET creates a more detailed web.config file by default when you create a new Web application. On Day 18, we'll describe how to construct web.config files in detail.

As a prelude to Day 18's lesson, here is a list of some changes you can make with a web.config file:

- Set default language for ASP.NET pages
- Turn debugging and tracing on and off
- Specify error-handling pages
- Specify where session state is stored
- Set the authentication mode
- Set globalization parameters
- Prevent pages ending in a specific extension from being downloaded
- Set the browser capabilities of your site
- Add assemblies to your Web site
- Configure Web service

Although this book won't go into the details of each feature until Day 18, this list should give you a starting point for figuring out the default web.config file that Visual Studio generates.

3

# Summary

Today's lesson covered the state management features of ASP.NET, including cookies, the `Application` and `Session` objects, `ViewState`, hidden fields, and query strings. You saw how to use cookies to store items such as user preferences on the client computer. You also saw how to use strings and objects in `Session` and `Application` state on the Web server.

Today's lesson didn't give you enough information for you to decide when to use session state, ViewState, and application state. Day 12 will contain instructions for making an intelligent choice in your own state management approach.

You learned about the global.asax file and how to use it to specify which objects are stored in `Session` and `Application` state.

Today's lesson explained the order of events in a typical ASP.NET Web form as it's rendered to the client computer. You saw an example that read and modified the values of some simple Web controls on a Web form.

Last, today's lesson introduced the web.config file and explained how it's used to configure your ASP.NET Web site. You saw a simple example of a web.config file that set the timeout value for `Session` objects.

Tomorrow you will learn about Web controls in detail and how to use them in your Web forms to produce powerful Web applications.

# Q&A

**Q I want to make my ASP.NET Web site extremely fast. What strategies should I take?**

**A** For ultimate performance, don't use ASP.NET sessions, and don't use Web Control ViewState (which will be explained in full tomorrow). As you absorb tomorrow's lesson, this strategy will become more clear.

**Q I have heard that ASP.NET contains special features for so called *Web Farms*, where multiple Web servers are used to host one site. How does this work?**

**A** ASP.NET has features that allow you to store sessions on another computer (the session server) or in a Microsoft SQL Server database. These techniques are explained on Day 18. You can't use the `Application` object this way.

# Workshop

The workshop provides quiz questions to help you solidify your understanding of the material covered today as well as exercises to give you experience using what you have learned. Try to understand the quiz and exercise before continuing to tomorrow's lesson. Answers are provided in Appendix A, "Answers to Quizzes and Exercises."

## Quiz

1. What is a postback, and when is it used in ASP.NET Web forms?

2. What are the five different ways of handling state in ASP.Net Web forms?

3. Where are cookies stored, and what kinds of data can they contain?

4. Why would you store an object in `Application` state instead of `Session` state?

5. How do you change the timeout for a `Session` object?

6. What events does the `HttpSession` class support?

7. What file do you use to handle `Session` and `Application` events?

8. What tag do you use to declare an object in the global.asax file?

9. What file do you use to configure a Web application?

10. What method do the .NET collection classes use to return thread-safe versions of themselves?

## Exercises

1. Create a new Web service using Visual Studio. What files did Visual Studio create that we didn't in today's examples?

2. Add a method called `Clear` to the MyClass.vb application. How can you ensure that the method is thread-safe?

3. Create a two-page Web application that allows a user to log on and then select her favorite football team. Save the user's response in a cookie so that subsequent uses of the application will remember the user's preference.

# DAY 4

# Working with Web Controls

Using ASP.NET Web controls is a powerful way to generate and use HTML controls in your applications. Web controls make the process of creating interactive Web pages much less tedious than with other Web programming technologies.

You've seen a number of simple control examples in the past two lessons, such as the TextBox and Button. Today you will learn about many of the other Web controls, and how to start using them productively in your development efforts. This chapter covers the following topics:

- Events, properties, and methods that all Web controls share
- Commonly used features of each basic Web control
- List controls, such as drop-down and check box lists
- Validation controls, to validate user input from other Web or HTML controls

- Basic data binding, including storing the contents of an ADO.NET DataSet in a list control
- Integrating Cascading Style Sheets and Web controls

# Understanding the Benefits of Web Controls

Web controls offer several advantages over raw HTML for items such as text input boxes, drop-down lists, and buttons:

- Web controls send events back to your .NET code, allowing you to handle user interaction in an organized way. You saw a small example of this in the login page on Day 2, "Introducing ASP.NET."
- They manage their own state. If your Web page posts back to itself from a submit button or link, you don't have to write a lot of tedious code to repopulate the controls with their original values. Instead, the Web controls remember their previous values through POST and GET requests.
- They contain various properties that allow you to customize their behavior and display appearance. You can write server-side code to change a Web control's appearance or point the Web controls to a style from a Cascading Style Sheet (CSS).
- Web controls can render their HTML in a browser-specific way. You therefore can concentrate on making your program logic correct rather than deal with the intricacies of all the different browsers that your users may be using.

# Understanding the Common Features of Web Controls

Before diving into the details of Web controls, you should survey the entire collection of Web controls offered in ASP.NET, as shown in Figure 4.1.

Notice that Web controls fall into three main groups:

NEW TERM Controls such as Button, TextBox, Label, and DropDownList are thin wrappers around the standard HTML controls. A *wrapper* for an object is some code in a library that allows you to program with that object more easily. For example, the TextBox, Label, and DropDownList controls help you produce the corresponding HTML controls more easily.

- Validation controls have no HTML equivalent. They allow you to include validation rules and error messages that trigger based on the contents of other controls on the page.

FIGURE **4.1**

*ASP.NET Web Controls ready for use in your own applications.*

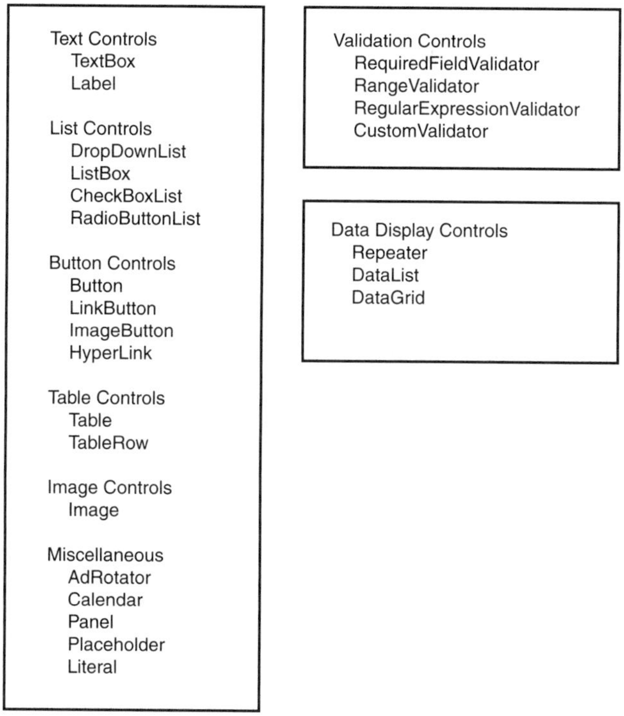

Text Controls
  TextBox
  Label

List Controls
  DropDownList
  ListBox
  CheckBoxList
  RadioButtonList

Button Controls
  Button
  LinkButton
  ImageButton
  HyperLink

Table Controls
  Table
  TableRow

Image Controls
  Image

Miscellaneous
  AdRotator
  Calendar
  Panel
  Placeholder
  Literal

Validation Controls
  RequiredFieldValidator
  RangeValidator
  RegularExpressionValidator
  CustomValidator

Data Display Controls
  Repeater
  DataList
  DataGrid

4

- Data display controls allow you to create more complex interaction in your Web pages. They create complex HTML output and save you time for many data display tasks.

You can pick from several Web controls, and each has numerous methods, properties, and events. To tackle learning all of them, let's explore what all the controls have in common.

## Common Events

All ASP.NET controls expose events that you can handle with server-side code. Events work by having the ASP.NET page post form variables to itself after a user action. Undercover, ASP.NET generates a small amount of client-side JavaScript that will generate a form submit request when a control is activated. As a result, you must use the <form runat="server"> tag in any ASP.NET page that uses events.

Table 4.1 shows the most common events a typical ASP.NET page can handle.

**Table 4.1** Commonly Handled Events from Web Controls

| Event | Description |
|-------|-------------|
| Click | The Button, HyperLink, ImageButton, and LinkButton controls send this event when users click them. |
| SelectedItemChanged | The ListBox, DropDownList, CheckBoxList, and RadioButtonList controls send this event when the selected item is changed. |
| CheckChanged | The CheckBox control sends this event when the control becomes checked or unchecked. |

Handling a Web control event involves two steps:

1. Specify the name of the event you want to handle. Of course, the event name must be an event that the control can send. To specify an event, set On to the event name and add the name of the event handling method in code. To specify the Click event for a Button control, you might use code like the following:

```
<asp:Button id="MyButton" OnClick="ClickEventHandlingMethod"
            runat="server" />
```

2. Write the event handler. From the preceding line, you would need to write code like the following:

```
sub ClickEventHandlingMethod(sender as Object, e as Eventargs)

   'code that takes some action
end sub
```

The Calendar, DataList, and DataGrid controls have special events that we cover tomorrow.

## Other Events

All controls can fire several other events (see Table 4.2). You probably won't handle these events as frequently in your code, but they are worth a quick look.

**TABLE 4.2** Other Events in ASP.NET Web Controls

| Event | Description |
|-------|-------------|
| Init | Called when the control is initialized. This is the first event called for every control. |
| Load | Called when the Page object loads the control. |
| PreRender | Called right before the control is rendered into the HTML result stream. |
| DataBinding | Called when the control is bound to a data source. |
| Disposed | Called when the control is released from memory. This call can happen at any time after the page is fully rendered, when the .NET garbage collector runs. |

Every Web control inherits these events from the `Control` class. Notice that some events are similar to the events in the `Page` class. This is no coincidence—the `Page` class is derived from the `Control` class.

## The `AutoPostBack` Property

By default, list box controls and selection controls, such as a check box list, won't repost form data every time the user changes a selection. However, you can force these controls to repost data whenever their selection changes by setting the `AutoPostBack` property to `true`.

**Note**

> If the client's browser supports DHTML, ASP.NET can render the Web controls so that events won't cause another hit to the server unless absolutely necessary. You don't have to worry about the DHTML details when writing code. However, for earlier browsers that don't support DHTML, each control event requires a round-trip to the Web server.

The sample in Listing 4.1 handles the events listed in Table 4.1.

**4**

**LISTING 4.1**  HandleEvents.aspx: Handling Common Events in Some Web Controls

```
1: <html>
2: <body>
3: <script runat="server" language="VB">
4: sub ButtonPress(Sender as Object, e as EventArgs)
5:     lblOutput.Text = "You pressed the button<br>"
6: end sub
7: sub MyDropSelected(Sender as Object, e as EventArgs)
8:     lblOutput.Text = ExDrop.SelectedItem.ToString() & _
9:         " is selected in the drop down box<br>"
10: end sub
11: sub MyCheckSelChange(Sender as Object, e as EventArgs)
12:     dim i as Integer
13:     lblOutput.Text = ""
14:     for i=0 to ExCheck.Items.Count - 1
15:         if ExCheck.Items(i).Selected then
16:             lblOutput.Text += "Check box " + i.ToString() & " is checked<br>"
17:         else
18:             lblOutput.Text += "Check box " & i.ToString() & _
19:                 " is not checked<br>"
20:         end if
21:     next
22: end sub
23: </script>
24: <form runat="server">
```

**Listing 4.1**   continued

```
25:  <asp:Button id="ExButton" text="Press Me" OnClick="ButtonPress"
26:               runat="server"/>
27:  <br>
28:  <asp:DropDownList id="ExDrop" runat="server"
29:                   OnSelectedIndexChanged="MyDropSelected"
30:                   AutoPostBack="True">
31:    <asp:ListItem>Item 1</asp:ListItem>
32:    <asp:ListItem>Item 2</asp:ListItem>
33:    <asp:ListItem>Item 3</asp:ListItem>
34:  </asp:DropDownList>
35:  <br>
36:  <asp:CheckBoxList id="ExCheck" runat="server"
37:                   OnSelectedIndexChanged="MyCheckSelChange"
38:                   AutoPostBack="True">
39:    <asp:ListItem>Check 1</asp:ListItem>
40:    <asp:ListItem>Check 2</asp:ListItem>
41:    <asp:ListItem>Check 3</asp:ListItem>
42:  </asp:CheckBoxList>
43:  <hr>
44:  <asp:Label id="lblOutput" runat="server" />
45:
46:  </form>
47:  </body>
48:  </html>
```

**ANALYSIS**   In Listing 4.1, the DropDownList and CheckBoxList controls both use the ListItem subcontrol (Lines 31–33 and 39–41). Use ListItem to add entries to each control. ListItem is an example of a Web control contained within another Web control. You'll see other examples of contained Web controls in the next few lessons.

Each control in Listing 4.1 has its AutoPostback property set to "True" (Lines 30 and 38). This forces the control to repost the form data whenever the user selects a different item in the controls.

If you've written .NET code that handles events, the event handlers for each Web control in Listing 4.1 should look familiar. If you haven't, know that each event handler takes two parameters: the Sender and EventArgs objects. We don't use either object in Listing 4.1 because we can query each Web control for the currently selected item.

## Control Properties

All ASP.NET Web controls share a set of common properties. Because there are several, we will explore the most common ones. Table 4.3 lists some of the more interesting common properties.

**TABLE 4.3**  Common Properties of Web Controls

| Property | Description |
| --- | --- |
| ID | The control's ID, which you can use to refer to the control in code. |
| Parent | The control's parent, which is usually the Page object. |
| Visible | If set to false, the control won't be displayed. Defaults to true. |
| ToolTip | Sets the ToolTip that's displayed when the user hovers the mouse pointer over the control. Not all browsers support this feature. |
| Page | The Page object, for convenience. |
| Height, Width, ForeColor, BackColor, BorderColor, Font, Style, CssStyle | We will cover these properties later in the "Beautifying Your Controls" section. |

Table 4.3 shows that each Web control can be manipulated as though it were a regular GUI control. For example, you can write code in the Page_Load event to set a control's Visible property to true or false depending on the application's needs.

## Specific Properties of Web Controls

Several properties are specific to a few controls that you will use commonly in your ASP.NET applications (see Table 4.4).

**TABLE 4.4**  Properties Used with Web Controls

| Property | Description |
| --- | --- |
| Text (set) | Sets the text associated with the Label, ListItem, Button, ImageButton, LinkButton, and HyperLink controls |
| Text (get) | Receives the text associated with the ListItem control when calling the SelectedItem method of its parent |
| Checked | Truc if a CheckBox or RadioButton control is checked or selected |
| Selected | True if a ListItem control is selected in a ListBox, DropDownList, RadioButtonList, or CheckBoxList control |

Of course, the properties in Table 4.4 aren't the only ones you will use in your code. I will show examples of many others, and the Visual Studio documentation contains the full explanation of each property for each Web control.

## Control Methods

All Web controls share two interesting methods: DataBind and ApplyStyle. ApplyStyle lets you apply a Style object to the control to set the control's look and feel. I will cover this method later in the section "Beautifying Your Controls."

DataBind is handy for automatically displaying data in a control. The data can come either from properties in a class that you create or from an ADO.NET DataSet. On Day 12, "Putting it All Together with ASP.NET," we will explain how to use Web controls and ADO.NET together to make interesting applications. Tomorrow, you will learn how to create complex data grid controls using the DataBind method.

# Working on the Web Controls Example

More than 25 Web controls are available in ASP.NET. Let's write a sample program that includes many of the basic ASP.NET controls. This example will include the controls that you haven't seen previously, including CheckBox, HyperLink, Image, Label, and LinkButton. Listing 4.2, an online survey form, shows these controls, along with many of the ListBox style controls.

**LISTING 4.2**   SimpleControls.aspx: An Example with Most of the Simple ASP.NET Web Controls

```
 1: <html>
 2: <body>
 3: <script runat="server" language="VB" Debug="true">
 4: sub DoneClicked(Sender as Object, e as EventArgs)
 5:   dim i as integer
 6:   Response.Write("Here are the results of the survey<br>")
 7:   if ToLong.Checked then
 8:     Response.Write("1) You thought this example was much too long.<br>")
 9:   else
10:     Response.Write("1) You were comfortable with the length " & _
11:       "of the example.<br>")
12:   end if
13:   Response.Write("2) Your level of ASP.NET knowledge is : " _
14:    & NetKnow.SelectedItem.Text + "<br>")
15: Response.Write("3) Your favorite programming language is " _
16:    & Lang.SelectedItem.Text + " which is number " _
17:    & Lang.SelectedIndex.ToString + " on the list<br>")
18: Response.Write("4) You prefer the following drinks: ")
19: for i=0 to Drinks.Items.Count - 1
20:   if Drinks.Items(i).Selected then
21:     Response.Write(Drinks.Items(i).Text + " ")
22:   end if
23: next
```

**LISTING 4.2**   continued

```
24:   Response.Write("<br>5) You indicated that: <br>")
25:   for i=0 to Misc.Items.Count-1
26:     if Misc.Items(i).Selected then
27:       Response.Write(Misc.Items(i).Text + "<br>")
28:     end if
29:   next
30:   Response.Write("Thanks for taking the survey.<br><hr>")
31: end sub
32: </script>
33: <form runat="server">
34:
35: Click here to go to MSDN online:
36: <asp:HyperLink Text="MSDN"
37:       NavigateUrl = "http://msdn.microsoft.com"
38:       runat="server"/><br>
39: <br>
40:
41: <asp:Label
42:       Text="Check this box if you think the example is too long."
43:       runat="server"/>
44: <asp:Checkbox id="ToLong" runat="server"/>
45:
46: <br>
47:
48: Please select your level of ASP.NET knowledge from the list below<br>
49: <asp:RadioButtonList id="NetKnow" runat="server">
50:   <asp:ListItem Selected="True">Beginning</asp:ListItem>
51:   <asp:ListItem>Intermediate</asp:ListItem>
52:   <asp:ListItem>Advanced</asp:ListItem>
53: </asp:RadioButtonList>
54:
55: <br>
56:
57: Please select your favorite programming language<br>
58: <asp:DropDownList id="Lang" runat="server">
59:   <asp:ListItem>C#</asp:ListItem>
60:   <asp:ListItem>C++</asp:ListItem>
61:   <asp:ListItem>Visual Basic</asp:ListItem>
62:   <asp:ListItem>Java</asp:ListItem>
63:   <asp:ListItem>Assembly Language</asp:ListItem>
64:   <asp:ListItem>Other</asp:ListItem>
65: </asp:DropDownList>
66:
67: <br>
68:
69: Please select your favorite drinks<br>
70: <asp:CheckBoxList id="Drinks" runat="server">
71:   <asp:ListItem>Soda</asp:ListItem>
72:   <asp:ListItem>Coffee</asp:ListItem>
```

4

LISTING 4.2   continued

```
73:    <asp:ListItem>Beer</asp:ListItem>
74:    <asp:ListItem>Wine</asp:ListItem>
75: </asp:CheckBoxList>
76:
77: <br>
78:
79: Please select all that apply<br>
80: <asp:ListBox id="Misc" SelectionMode="Multiple" runat="server">
81:    <asp:ListItem>I'm going to use .NET immediately</asp:ListItem>
82:    <asp:ListItem>I prefer coding in ANSI C</asp:ListItem>
83:    <asp:ListItem>I use Java all the time</asp:ListItem>
84: </asp:ListBox>
85:
86: <br>
87:
88: <asp:Button id="Done" text="Done With Survey"
89:             OnClick="DoneClicked" runat="server"/><br>
90: <asp:LinkButton Text="I'm Really Done"
91:                 OnClick="DoneClicked" runat="server"/><br>
92:
93: </form>
94: </body>
95: </html>
```

**ANALYSIS**   All the List controls (ListBox, DropDownList, and so on) use the ListItem Web control to specify each contained element. In code, you can get the value of each list item by accessing a control's Items collection. Each object returned from the Items collection is specific to the type of the parent list control. For instance, an object from the Items collection of a CheckBoxList is of type CheckBox.

Listing 4.2 also shows how to use the Label control (Lines 41–43), which shows static text. You can set the Label control's contents programmatically by using code on the Page_Load event or another event handler and by setting the Text property.

The LinkButton control is used at the end of the listing (Lines 90–91) as an alternative to the regular Button control. This control behaves like an HTML hyperlink but sends a Click event rather than automatically navigating to the target.

The HyperLink control (Lines 36–38), which also wraps the HTML hyperlink, lets you specify the destination of the link by using the NavigateURL method.

Figure 4.2 shows the results of running the code in Listing 4.2.

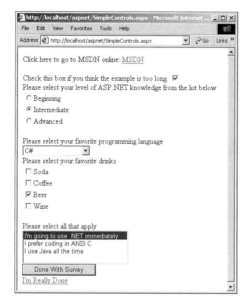

**FIGURE 4.2**

*The*
*SimpleControls.aspx*
*page.*

## Control Properties

You can set any of the other common properties in each control in this sample, such as
`ToolTip`, `Height`, `Width`, and style properties, by specifying each parameter. Just add
code such as `Height="100"` inside the control definition to specify any of the parameters.

## Control State

Web controls maintain their state between multiple page hits by using *view state*.
For instance, the view state of a TextBox contains the text that the user has typed
in. The view state for a checkbox group would include which checkboxes have been
selected. Every time the user clicks a submit button and the form's contents are sent back
to the Web server, each control will remember its state; the TextBox will redisplay what
the user previously typed, and the checkbox group will remember which checkboxes
have been selected.

ASP.NET implements view state through hidden text boxes. ASP.NET puts a string
inside the text box that contains data about the state of all the Web controls on the current Web form.

You can control whether a Web control persists its state this way by using its
`EnableViewState` property. By default, `EnableViewState` is set to `true` so that the contents of the control will be preserved. For controls that don't need to preserve their state,
this property should be set to `false`, as a performance optimization. Because ASP.NET

sends the data for the hidden text box in the GET or POST method, turning off view state saves on the amount of information that must be transmitted.

If your Web page uses some of the more complicated Web controls, such as a DataGrid (explained in tomorrow's lesson), you will almost certainly want to turn off view state. Similarly, if your Web page uses more than two or three simple Web controls, consider turning off their view state to enhance performance.

# Working with Validation Controls

Almost every Web application contains many code lines that validate user input. For example, many online storefront applications contain a page that asks the user for his or her shipping address. Fields such as the Street, City, and ZIP code are often required. Validation code checks to see that each required field isn't blank. In addition to required fields, validation code can check a field's format, such as making sure that every character in a ZIP code field is numeric.

Writing code to validate user input is tedious, but important. ASP.NET relieves much of the burden in validation input on Web pages with a group of Web controls designed specifically for this task. These controls simplify your code, make your ASP.NET pages simpler to maintain, and cut down on the bugs that can creep in from complicated validation algorithms.

## RequiredFieldValidator

The RequiredFieldValidator control is the simplest of the validation controls. It checks to make sure that the user has entered text or made at least one selection in a control group. Listing 4.3 shows how to use this control with a text box.

**LISTING 4.3**   RequiredText.aspx: Checking to Make Sure That Users Enter Their Home Phone Numbers

```
 1: <html>
 2: <body>
 3:  <form runat="server">
 4:   <h2>Please update your telephone numbers</h2>
 5:
 6:   Home Phone: <asp:textbox id="HomePhone" runat="server" />
 7:
 8:   <asp:RequiredFieldValidator id="RequiredPhoneV"
 9:       ControlToValidate="HomePhone" runat="server">
10:   Your Home Phone Number is Required
11:   </asp:RequiredFieldValidator>
12:
13:   <p>
```

**LISTING 4.3**   continued

```
14:    Work Phone: <asp:textbox id="WorkPhone" runat="server" />
15:    <p>
16:    <asp:button text="Update" runat="server"/>
17:  </form>
18: </body>
19: </html>
```

**ANALYSIS**   Notice that the RequiredFieldValidator control (Lines 8–11) contains two tags. Enter the error message that should be displayed by the control inside these two tags, such as Your Home Phone Number is Required (Line 10).

The second parameter in the RequiredFieldValidator control example, ControlToValidate, (Line 9) should be set to the ID of the control that needs to be validated.

The custom error text will be displayed in red by default. You can specify the font type, size, and color within the beginning tag, using the parameters Font-Face, Font-Size, and Font-Color, as you will see in the next code listing.

You can also use the RequiredFieldValidator control if you need to make sure that the user has made a selection from a group of radio buttons. Listing 4.4 shows how.

**4**

**LISTING 4.4**   RequiredRadio.aspx: Requiring a Selection and Specifying a Custom Font

```
 1: <html>
 2: <body>
 3:  <form runat="server">
 4:   <h2>Select your age group</h2>
 5:   <asp:RadioButtonList id="AgeGroup" runat="server">
 6:     <asp:ListItem>1-24</asp:ListItem>
 7:     <asp:ListItem>25-34</asp:ListItem>
 8:     <asp:ListItem>35-44</asp:ListItem>
 9:     <asp:ListItem>45-54</asp:ListItem>
10:     <asp:ListItem>55-64</asp:ListItem>
11:     <asp:ListItem>65 and up</asp:ListItem>
12:   </asp:RadioButtonList>
13:   <asp:RequiredFieldValidator id-"AgeV"
14:       ControlToValidate="AgeGroup" runat="server"
15:      Font-Name="Helvetica" Font-Size="20">
16:      <font color="purple">You must select one of the age groups</font>
17:   </asp:RequiredFieldValidator>
18:   <p>
19:   <asp:button text="Update" runat="server"/>
20:  </form>
21: </body>
22: </html>
```

**ANALYSIS** In Listing 4.4, the Font-Name and Font-Size (Line 15) parameters are specified for the RequiredFieldValidator, and custom HTML has been inserted into the error message to make the error message font purple. You can insert any amount of custom HTML inside the RequiredFieldValidator control for complete control over error messages. As you will see in the SummaryValidator section later today, ASP.NET also offers a validation control that allows you to summarize all validation errors together.

The RequiredFieldValidator control uses the "validation property" of target Web controls. Not every Web control contains a validation property; only TextBox, ListBox, DropDownList, and RadioButtonList have validation properties.

## CompareValidator

You can use the CompareValidator control to compare the contents of a Web control to a value, such as a minimum amount. The CompareValidator control can also compare the contents of two Web controls. You might use the following code snippet to make sure a user enters a non-negative age:

```
Your Age: <asp:Textbox id="Age" runat="server " /><br>
<asp:CompareValidator id="MinAgeV" ControlToValidate="Age"
                      ValueToCompare="0" Operator="GreaterThan"
                      Type="Integer" runat="server">
You must enter an age greater than 0
</asp:CompareValidator>
```

You must specify an Operator parameter to tell which kind of comparison is needed and a Type parameter to cast the target control's contents into a particular data type. The possible operators are as follows:

- Equal
- NotEqual
- LessThan
- LessThanEqual
- GreaterThan
- GreaterThanEqual

The following data types are possible:

- String
- Integer
- Date
- Currency
- Double

The CompareValidator control will do its best to convert whatever the user has entered into the type that you specify. However, for finer grained control over checking what the user entered, you can use the RegularExpressionValidator and CustomValidator controls, as explained next.

> **Note**
>
> To compare the contents of two controls, use the `ControlToCompare` parameter instead of `ValueToCompare` in the CompareValidator control. When using `ControlToCompare`, you still need to specify the `Operator` and `Type` parameters.

## RangeValidator

Similar to CompareValidator, the RangeValidator control checks to make sure that user input falls within a valid range that you specify. Rather than use the `ValueToCompare` parameter, use the `MinimumValue` and `MaximumValue` parameters. The following code snippet shows how you might check that the age a user has entered is between 0 and 120:

```
Your Age: <asp:Textbox id="Age" runat="server" /><br>
<asp:RangeValidator
  id="AgeV"
  ControlToValidate="Age"
  MinimumValue="0"
  MaximumValue="120 "
  Type="Integer"
  runat="server">
You must enter an age between 0 and 120
</asp:RangeValidator>
```

## RegularExpressionValidator

Using regular expressions is a compact and powerful way of specifying the exact values for input. Regular expressions work by pattern matching: You specify a pattern that user input must match exactly. The RegularExpressionValidator control checks your regular expression against what the user types.

Regular expressions are a complex subject, so we will talk only about the basics. Let's look at an example of a regular expression that matches only one digit:

```
\d
```

This example would match 3 but not 34 or 122 because the latter two have more than one digit. To match any number of digits, use the following regular expression:

```
\d+
```

To match five digits (not four or six), use

\d{5}

In another example, you might want to match a ZIP or ZIP+4 code. The regular expression to do so would be the following:

\d{5}[-\s-]?(\d{4})?

The [-\s] part means "match either a '-' character or a space," and the question mark means "match either zero or one occurrence of this pattern." Likewise, (\d{4})? means "match zero or one occurrence of a group of four digits." Table 4.5 shows the more common keywords in regular expressions.

**TABLE 4.5**   Common Keywords for Regular Expressions

| Keyword | Description |
| --- | --- |
| \d | Match a digit |
| \s | Match a whitespace character |
| \w | Match a "word" character (a to z, A to Z, 1–9, and _) |
| [abc] | Match any one of a, b, or c |
| [^abc] | Match any character except a, b, or c |
| \W\S\D | Match nonword, nonwhitespace, nondigit character |
| (abc) | Match abc exactly one time |
| (abc)? | Match abc zero or one time |
| (abc)+ | Match abc any number of times (abc, abcabc, abcabcabc) |

Consult the Visual Studio help system for complete documentation on regular expressions.

The following code snippet shows how to validate a ZIP code field for five digits or ZIP+4 formatted input:

```
Zip Code: <asp:Textbox id="Zip" runat="server" /><br>
<asp:RegularExpressionValidator
  id="ZipChecker"
  ControlToValidate="Zip"
  ValidationExpression = "\d{5}[-\s-]?(\d{4})?"
  runat="server">
Please enter your five digit zip code
</asp:RegularExpressionValidator>
```

The RegularExpressionValidator control needs a ValidateExpression parameter that contains the regular expressions to check against. Listing 4.5 shows a sample page where you can enter your own regular expressions and test input against them. It also shows how to use validation Web controls programmatically.

**LISTING 4.5**  RegExpValidator.aspx: Specifying a Regular Expression to Check

```
 1: <%@ Page language="VB" clienttarget="downlevel" %>
 2: <html>
 3: <body>
 4: <script runat="server">
 5: sub CheckClicked(Sender as Object, e as EventArgs)
 6:
 7:   RegValidator.ValidationExpression = RegExp.Text
 8:   RegValidator.Validate()
 9:   if RegValidator.IsValid then
10:     Response.Write("The input matches!")
11:   else
12:     Response.Write("The input is not valid according to " & _
13:       "the regular expression.")
14:   end if
15: end sub
16: </script>
17: <form method="post" runat="server">
18:  <h3>Regular Expression Tester</h3>
19:  Regular Expression <asp:TextBox id="RegExp" runat="server"/><br>
20:  Input <asp:TextBox id="Input" runat="server"/><br>
21:  <asp:RegularExpressionValidator
22:    id="RegValidator"
23:    runat="server"
24:    ControlToValidate="Input" />
25:  <asp:button text="Check Input" onclick="CheckClicked" runat="server"/>
26: </form>
27: </body>
28: </html>
```

4

**ANALYSIS**  The RegularExpressionValidator control (Line 21) is set to validate the TextBox control with an ID of "Input". Notice that the regular expression isn't specified in the control declaration. Instead, the CheckClicked method sets the ValidationExpression property in code, on Line 7.

# CustomValidator

You can write your own validation code and integrate it with the CustomValidator control. The CustomValidator control takes a parameter called OnServerValidate, which specifies the name of an event handler in your code. A typical event handler framework might look like the following:

```
sub MyValidator(Sender as Object, e as ServerValidateEventArgs)
  dim nVal as Integer = e.Value
```

```
   'do some checking
   e.IsValid = true 'the value is ok
end sub
```

## SummaryValidator

You can summarize the results of multiple validation controls by using the
SummaryValidator control. This control takes the results of all other Validator controls
and allows you to format them however you prefer. For instance, you can group all the
errors on a page at the top the screen, as shown in Listing 4.6.

LISTING 4.6 GroupErrors.aspx: Using SummaryValidator to Group Multiple Errors from
Validation Controls

```
 1: <%@ Page clienttarget=downlevel %>
 2: <html>
 3: <body>
 4: <h2>Grouping Errors Together</h2>
 5: <form runat="server">
 6: <!— Note that we are enclosing the Validation Summary control inside of a
 7:     table. The control generates a table itself with a default width of
 8:     100%, which we don't want in this case —>
 9: <table>
10:   <tr>
11:     <td>
12: <asp:ValidationSummary ID="AllErrs" runat="server"
13:     HeaderText="Please resolve the errors listed below. "
14:     DisplayMode="List"
15:     Font-Name="Arial"
16:     Border="1"
17:     CellPadding="2"/>
18: </asp:ValidationSummary>
19:     </td>
20:   </tr>
21: </table>
22: <table>
23:   <tr>
24:     <td>Name</td>
25:     <td><asp:TextBox id="Name" runat="server"/></td>
26:     <td>
27:
28:     <!— Note that we have added the ErrorMessage tag to each Validator
29:         control, so that they will display an error message in the
30:         summary control —>
31:     <asp:RequiredFieldValidator
32:       id="VName"
33:       runat="server"
34:       ErrorMessage="<b>Name</b> - You must enter your name"
35:       ControlToValidate="Name">
36:       *
37:     </asp:RequiredFieldValidator>
```

**LISTING 4.6**    continued

```
38:
39:        </td>
40:      </tr>
41:      <tr>
42:        <td>Email Address</td>
43:        <td><asp:TextBox id="EMail" runat="server"/></td>
44:        <td>
45:
46:        <asp:RequiredFieldValidator
47:         id="VEmail"
48:         runat="server"
49:         ErrorMessage="<b>Email</b> - You must enter your email address"
50:         ControlToValidate="Email">
51:         *
52:        </asp:RequiredFieldValidator>
53:
54:        <asp:RegularExpressionValidator
55:         id="VRegEmail"
56:         runat="server"
57:         ControlToValidate="Email"
58:         ErrorMessage="<b>Email</b> - Please re-enter your email address"
59:         ValidationExpression="\w+@\w+.\w+">
60:         *
61:        </asp:RegularExpressionValidator>
62:
63:        </td>
64:      </tr>
65:    </table>
66:    <asp:button text="Submit" runat="server"/>
67:  </form>
68:  </body>
69:  </html>
```

**4**

**ANALYSIS**    Listing 4.6 adds the ErrorMessage parameter to each validation control (Lines 34, 49, and 58). The set ErrorMessage will be displayed in the contents of the ValidationSummary control (Line 12). To indicate which controls have a problem, we included an asterisk inside the two control definition tags (Lines 36, 51, and 60).

We added the ValidationSummary control itself (Line 12), which contains two key parameters: HeaderText and DisplayMode. DisplayMode can be set to "List", "BulletList", or "Paragraph".

**Tip**

To remove the error message that each validation control displays individually (an asterisk in Listing 4.6), set each control's DisplayMode property to "None".

# Data Binding: Integrating Results with Code

 *Data binding* allows you to take the results of properties, collections, method calls, and database queries and integrate them with your ASP.NET code. You can combine data binding with Web control rendering to relieve much of the programming burden surrounding Web control creation. You can also use data binding with ADO.NET and Web controls to populate control contents from SQL select statements or stored procedures. We will tackle this last feature on Day 12.

## Syntax and Semantics of Data Binding

Data binding uses a special syntax:

```
My custom property contains the following value: <%# myProp %>
```

Notice the opening three-character tag, <%#, which instructs ASP.NET to evaluate the expression. The difference between a data-binding tag and regular code insertion tags (<% and %>) becomes apparent when the expressions are evaluated. Expressions within the data-binding tags are evaluated only when the DataBind method in the Page object or Web control is called.

Let's look at an example to see the differences between the two tags. Listing 4.7 shows how a property's data-bound value stays the same, even if the value is changed later in the page.

**LISTING 4.7**   SimpleBind.aspx: Simple Data Binding to a Property and Data-Binding Evaluation

```
<html>
<body>
<script runat="server" language="VB">
sub Page_Load(Sender as Object, e as EventArgs)
  m_strMyProp = "First Value"
  Page.DataBind()
end sub

dim m_strMyProp as String

'A custom property added to the Page object, called myProp
property myProp() as string
  get
    return m_strMyProp
  end get
  set(byval value as string)
    m_strMyProp = value
  end set
```

**LISTING 4.7** continued

```
end property
</script>

<h2>Demo of the DataBinding evaluation</h2>

The DataBound value of myProp is : <%# myProp %><br><br>

Setting myProp to "Second Value"...<br><br>
<% myProp = "Second Value" %>

The value of myProp is: <%= myProp %><br><br>

The DataBound value of myProp is still: <%# myProp %>
</body>
</html>
```

Running Listing 4.7 results in output similar to that shown in Figure 4.3.

**FIGURE 4.3**

*The output of Listing 4.7 in Internet Explorer.*

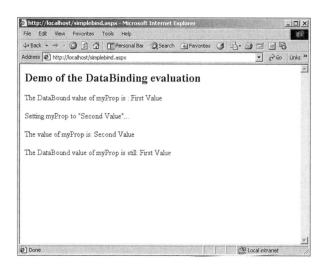

Notice that the last line in this output shows that the property's data-bound value is the original value (First Value), even after we update the property. The value appears the same because anything in the data-binding tags <%# and %> is evaluated only on the Page.DataBind method.

## Practical Data Binding

Let's talk about more practical uses of data binding. You can use data binding to populate list and data controls with values from an array by setting their DataSource properties, as Listing 4.8 shows.

**Listing 4.8**   DataRadioList.aspx: Populating a Radio Button List with an Array's Contents

```
 1: <script runat="server" language="VB">
 2: sub Page_Load(Sender as Object, e as EventArgs)
 3:
 4:     dim arDropList as ArrayList = new ArrayList()
 5:     arDropList.Add("Red")
 6:     arDropList.Add("Blue")
 7:     arDropList.Add("Green")
 8:     arDropList.Add("Other")
 9:
10:     'Set the data source of the radio button list to our array
11:     ColorRadioList.DataSource = arDropList
12:
13:     'Call databind on the radio button list itself
14:     ColorRadioList.DataBind()
15: end sub
16: </script>
17: <html>
18: <body>
19: <form runat="server">
20:
21: <h2>Databound radio button list</h2>
22: Please select your favorite color.<br>
23:
24: <asp:RadioButtonList id="ColorRadioList" runat="server"/>
25:
26: </form>
27: </body>
28: </html>
```

**Analysis**   Each Web control that supports data binding has a DataBind method. After you set the DataSource property on Line 11, call the control's DataBind method on Line 14 to make it read the DataSource's contents.

The ListBox, DropDownList, CheckBoxList, and RadioButtonList controls all have a DataSource property for binding them to collections.

## ADO.NET Tables and Data Binding

As a prelude to Day 12, when we look at ADO.NET and ASP.NET together, let's talk about data binding with ADO.NET tables. You don't need to have a database to make an ADO.NET table. Instead, you can create a data table programmatically, using the DataView and DataTable classes.

To make an ADO.NET data table, just create a new DataTable object, add column definitions, and then add data rows. When the data table is created and populated, create a DataView object and associate it with the DataTable. We will explore all the details of these classes on Day 10, "Working with Datasets," but Listing 4.9 shows a simple data table and view created on-the-fly in the Page_Load event.

**LISTING 4.9**  ADODataRadioList.aspx: Populating a RadioButtonList Control with an ADO.NET Table

```
 1: <%@ Import Namespace="System.Data" %>
 2: <script runat="server" language="VB" debug="True">
 3: sub Page_Load(Sender as Object, e as EventArgs)
 4:
 5:    'Make a new data table object
 6:    dim dt as DataTable = new DataTable()
 7:
 8:    'Add two columns
 9:    dt.Columns.Add(new DataColumn("Index"))
10:    dt.Columns.Add(new DataColumn("Color"))
11:
12:    'Add three rows
13:    dim dr as DataRow
14:    dr = dt.NewRow()
15:    dr("Index") = 1
16:    dr("Color") = "Red"
17:    dt.Rows.Add(dr)
18:
19:    dr = dt.NewRow()
20:    dr("Index") = 2
21:    dr("Color") = "Blue"
22:    dt.Rows.Add(dr)
23:
24:    dr = dt.NewRow()
25:    dr("Index") = 3
26:    dr("Color") = "Green"
27:    dt.Rows.Add(dr)
28:
29:    'Create a data view object to encapsulate the data table
30:    dim dv as DataView = new DataView(dt)
31:
32:    'Set the data source of the radio button list to our ADO.NET table view
33:    ColorRadioList.DataSource = dv
34:
35:    'Set the Color column as the text source for each
36:    'item in the radio button list
37:    ColorRadioList.DataTextField = "Color"
38:
39:    'Set the Index column as the value source for each
40:    'item in the radio button list
41:    ColorRadioList.DataValueField = "Index"
42:
43:    'Call databind
44:    ColorRadioList.DataBind()
```

4

**LISTING 4.9** continued

```
45: end sub
46: </script>
47: <html>
48: <body>
49: <form runat="server">
50:
51: <h2>ADO.NET Databound radio button list</h2>
52: Please select your favorite color.<br>
53:
54: <asp:RadioButtonList id="ColorRadioList" runat="server"/>
55:
56: </form>
57: </body>
58: </html>
```

**ANALYSIS** Listing 4.9 also uses the RadioButtonList control's `DataTextField` (Line 37) and `DataValueField` (Line 41) properties. They tell the list control which column to use for the text and value of each radio button, respectively.

Populating the ADO.NET table from a SQL statement or stored procedure involves setting up the data source of the table, as you will see on Day 12.

# Beautifying Your Controls

All the sample code listings so far have been functional, but the output they produced is quite plain, to put things mildly. Fortunately, ASP.NET Web controls give you complete and easy control over their appearance, using Cascading Style Sheets (CSS).

CSS allows you to specify the look and feel of almost every aspect of an HTML page. Both Internet Explorer and Netscape support CSS to varying degrees; creating some CSS that will fool earlier versions of each browser isn't difficult, so careful testing or a good style sheet expert is needed when using CSS.

A complete description of CSS is beyond the scope of this book. However, you can find a good reference online at `http://msdn.microsoft.com/workshop/author/css/reference/attributes.asp`.

## Native UI Support

Before seeing how to use CSS with Web controls, note that all ASP.NET Web controls have built-in properties for the most common UI settings. Visual Studio .NET has complete documentation for all the properties, but Listing 4.10 shows a sample program with two controls that exercise most of the built-in style properties. Figure 4.3 shows the resulting two controls.

**LISTING 4.10**   NativeStyle.aspx: A Sample Program with Colorful Label and TextBox Web Controls

```
<html>
<body bgcolor="lightblue">
<form runat="server">
  <asp:label id="lbl1" runat="server"
    Height="30"
    Width="75"
    BackColor="LightGreen"
    BorderColor="Green"
    BorderStyle="Solid"
    BorderWidth="1"
    ForeColor="Blue"
    Font-Name="Arial"
    Font-Size="20pt"
    Font-Underline="false"
    Text=" Name "
    ToolTip="Please enter your full name"/>
  <asp:textbox id="Name" runat="server"
    Height="30"
    Width="300"
    BackColor="LightGreen"
    BorderColor="Green"
    BorderStyle="Dashed"
    BorderWidth="1"
    ForeColor="Blue"
    Font-Name="Arial"
    Font-Size="18pt"/>
</form>
</body>
</html>
```

**FIGURE 4.4**

*NativeStyle.aspx shows Web controls with style changes applied as properties.*

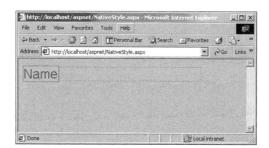

Underneath the covers, ASP.NET renders the HTML controls by using CSS references. ASP.NET doesn't create a new style sheet on-the-fly, but uses the inline style sheet directives within each HTML control.

It's quite tedious to program Web control style in the manner of Listing 4.10, which has nearly 30 lines of code for just two controls. Instead, you can use CSS explicitly with Web controls inline, from a reference on your HTML page, or programmatically.

## Inline Specification and References

As you can do with any HTML page, you can include style sheet classes inline, as Listing 4.11 shows:

**LISTING 4.11**   An ASP.NET Page That Uses a Cascading Style Sheet

```
 1: <style>
 2:   H1
 3:   {
 4:     font-weight: bold;
 5:     font-size; 20pt;
 6:     color: green;
 7:     font-family: Arial, Sans-Serif;
 8:   }
 9:   .textstyle
10:   {
11:     font-weight: normal;
12:     font-size; 14pt;
13:     color: blue;
14:     font-family: Arial, Sans-Serif;
15:   }
16: </style>
17: <body>
18:   <H1>Here is my 20pt Green Arial Header</H1>
19:   <asp:textbox id="Text" runat="server" CssClass="textstyle"/>
20: </body>
```

**ANALYSIS**   Notice the `CssClass` parameter on Line 19 to make the textbox Web control use the custom style.

If you plan to use style sheets for most of your pages, a better alternative is to create one master sheet for your Web site and have each page reference it. If you need to create special styles for a page, you can override them inline or make another style sheet file especially for that page. This way, the client browser can cache the style sheet.

Visual Studio .NET contains a style sheet editor that makes creating and manipulating style sheets easy. Follow these steps to access the editor:

1. Create a new Web Project in Visual Studio, if you haven't done so already.

2. In the Project Explorer window, right-click the main project, choose Add, and then choose Add New Item. You can also select this option from the Project menu on the top menu bar.

3. Select Style Sheet in the dialog box that appears.

After you create your style sheet, you can add new style sheet classes or override the default look of existing ones, such as the H1 class in Listing 4.11.

To reference a style sheet that you've created, use the HTML LINK directive:

```
<html>
 <head>
  <LINK REL=StyleSheet HREF="globalstyle.css" TYPE="text/css">
...
```

As with inline style sheets, you can use the CssClass attribute for each Web control that needs to conform to a certain style.

## Using Style Sheets in Code

An interesting feature of ASP.NET is that the style of both Web controls and HTML elements can be controlled in code.

To programmatically control the style of a Web control, you can use the ApplyStyle method after creating a Style object and setting its properties. The Style object contains most of the properties available through CSS classes. Complete documentation of the Style class is available in Visual Studio, but it contains properties similar to those used in the Web controls in Listing 4.11.

You can also modify the styles of individual HTML elements. As long as the HTML element contains the directive runat="server", you can access the HTML tag's Style property. This second Style property varies from the Style class in the preceding paragraph. The Style property is a collection indexed by CSS attribute name. You can assign string values to each member of the collection similarly to CSS properties. Listing 4.12 shows an example of both Style objects.

**LISTING 4.12**   ProgramStyle.aspx: Manipulating a Web Control and the HTML *<body>* Tag Programmatically

```
<%@ page language="VB"%>
<%@ import namespace="System.Drawing" %>
<html>
<script runat="server">
sub Page_Load(Sender as Object, e as EventArgs)
```

**LISTING 4.12**   continued

```
'Web controls can have styles applied to them using a
' Style object and the ApplyStyle method
dim myStyle as Style = new Style()

select case  TextColorList.SelectedIndex
  case 0
      myStyle.BackColor = Color.Red
  case 1
      myStyle.BackColor = Color.Blue
  case 2
      myStyle.BackColor = Color.Green
  end select
  txtName.ApplyStyle(myStyle)

  'HTML elements can have their Cascading Style Sheet attributes
  'set programmatically.
  'Note that the SelectedItem.Text field is a string,
  'such as "Pink" or "Orange"
  body.Style("background-color") = BodyColorList.SelectedItem.Text
end sub
</script>
<body id="body" runat="server">
<form runat="server" method="get">
 <h2>Programmatic Styles in Web Controls</h2>
 Name: <asp:textbox id="txtName" runat="server"/><br>

 Change Textbox Background Color to:
 <asp:DropdownList id="TextColorList" runat="server"
                   OnSelect="ColorSelected" AutoPostBack="true">
   <asp:ListItem>Red</asp:ListItem>
   <asp:ListItem>Blue</asp:ListItem>
   <asp:ListItem>Green</asp:ListItem>
 </asp:DropDownList>
 <br>

 Change Body Background Color to:
 <asp:DropdownList id="BodyColorList" runat="server"
                   OnSelect="ColorSelected" AutoPostBack="true">
   <asp:ListItem>Pink</asp:ListItem>
   <asp:ListItem>LightGreen</asp:ListItem>
   <asp:ListItem>Orange</asp:ListItem>
 </asp:DropDownList>
</form>
</body>
</html>
```

**Note**  You must set control styles in the Page_Load event only; if you write a custom event handler, the ApplyStyle method will have no effect.

# Summary

Today you had a crash course on the basic Web controls that ASP.NET offers for use in Web development. You should have a good understanding of how to use the basic Web controls in your own development projects.

We're not done yet with our discussion of ASP.NET Web controls. Tomorrow we will discuss the most powerful Web controls, including the DataGrid, Calendar, Repeater, and XML controls. In the following days, we will also learn about making custom Web controls to extend the built-in controls ASP.NET offers.

# Q&A

**Q Is the `Page_Load` event the best place to validate the contents of an ASP.NET page?**

**A** No. The ASP.NET validation controls are the best way to validate a Web page's contents. They allow you to encapsulate any rules surrounding an input control.

**Q I like to set the properties of each control using the Visual Studio .NET editor. Why should I bother to learn about Cascading Style Sheets?**

**A** Although learning about CSS does take some time, it will save you effort if your site involves more than a few pages. By using CSS, you can alter the look and feel of your site by changing a few definitions in one file, rather than reworking many ASP.NET pages.

**Q How do I decide when to turn off a control's view state?**

**A** You can look at the source for a page in your browser. In Internet Explorer, right-click the page and select View Source. Within the source for your page, you can see the hidden field that contains the view state for a page, called __VIEWSTATE. If the view state hidden field is quite large, you might want to disable view state for the control.

# Workshop

The Workshop provides quiz questions to help you solidify your understanding of the material covered and exercises to provide you with experience in using what you've learned. The answers to the quiz questions are provided in Appendix A, "Answers to Quizzes and Exercises."

## Quiz

1. What tag is required for each ASP.NET page to process events from Web controls?
2. Which commonly handled event does the LinkButton control generate?
3. What property should you set to force a CheckBoxList to generate form requests every time a user changes a selection?
4. How can you programmatically suppress the generation of a control?
5. Which control will compare the contents of two controls and generate an error message if their contents don't meet a specific condition?
6. How can you suppress the error message from a validation control?
7. What are Cascading Style Sheets used for?
8. What control property is used to bind a Web control to a Cascading Style Sheet element definition?
9. What control method must you call after using a `Style` object?
10. How can you set the display width of a TextControl?

## Exercise

1. Change Listing 4.1 so that it contains an Update button. Make the listing display only the status of its contained controls when the Update button is clicked.
2. Create a page with a `HashTable` object that contains the days of the week. Create a control on the page that's bound to the `HashTable`.
3. Create your own style sheet that contains three custom fonts for heading, regular text, and hyperlinks. Apply the style sheet to Listing 4.2.

# DAY 5

# Using Advanced ASP.NET Web Controls

Yesterday you learned about the basic Web controls offered by ASP.NET. You can use the basic Web controls to create rich user interfaces for Internet applications. However, ASP.NET offers additional controls that allow you to display and manipulate more complex data. Today you will harness the full power of the remaining ASP.NET Web controls by learning about the Repeater, DataList, and DataGrid controls.

Today you will learn how to do the following:

- Bind data to controls by using the `DataSource` property
- Use the `DataBinder` class to extract and format data in Web controls
- Create interactive grids, lists, and tables
- Use the special properties of the DataGrid, DataList, and Repeater controls

# Building Controls with Code

You can drag and drop any Web control onto a Web form by using the Visual Studio design view. However, your project may need to customize the look and feel of each control using custom logic. One way of accomplishing this is by using the Panel control. For example, Listing 5.1 is a two-line Web form that will generate a Label and ListBox control. Figure 5.1 shows the output of the listing.

**FIGURE 5.1**

*Using the ASP.NET Panel Control*

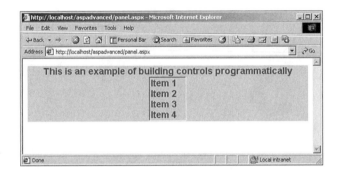

**LISTING 5.1**    Panel.aspx: An HTML File with a Label and a List Box

```
<%@ Page Src="Panel.vb" Inherits="MyPanelClass" %>
<html><body><asp:Panel id="MyPanel" runat="server"/></body></html>
```

Of course, Panel.aspx won't work by itself; it needs Listing 5.2 to create controls inside the panel.

**LISTING 5.2**    Panel.vb: The Code to Generate HTML and ASP.NET Controls

```
 1: Imports System
 2: Imports System.Web
 3: Imports System.Web.UI
 4: Imports System.Web.UI.WebControls
 5: Imports System.Drawing
 6:
 7: public class MyPanelClass
 8:    Inherits Page
 9:    'Declarations for the web controls
10:    Protected MyPanel As Panel
11:
12:    'This procedure is executed when the page loads.
13:    Public Sub Page_Load(Sender As Object, e As EventArgs)
14:
15:    Dim itemIdx As Integer
16:
```

**LISTING 5.2**  continued

```
17:     'Add an HTML tag to the Panel
18:     MyPanel.Controls.Add(new LiteralControl("<center>"))
19:
20:     'Add a label to the panel
21:     Dim lbl As New Label()
22:     lbl.Text = "This is an example of building controls programmatically"
23:     lbl.ID = "Label1"
24:
25:     'Set the style and font for the label
26:     Dim sty As new Style()
27:     sty.BackColor = Color.LightBlue
28:     sty.Font.Name = "Arial"
29:     sty.Font.Bold = true
30:     sty.Font.Size = New FontUnit(14)
31:     sty.ForeColor = Color.Blue
32:
33:     lbl.ApplyStyle(sty)
34:
35:     'Add the label to the panel, using its controls collection
36:     MyPanel.Controls.Add(lbl)
37:
38:     'Add an HTML tag to the Panel
39:     MyPanel.Controls.Add(new LiteralControl("<br>"))
40:
41:     'Add a ListBox to the Panel, with five arbitrary items
42:     Dim lst As New ListBox()
43:     lst.ID = "List1"
44:     for itemIdx = 1 To 4
45:       lst.Items.Add(new ListItem("Item " & itemIdx.ToString()))
46:     Next
47:
48:     'Use the same style for the ListBox as we did with the label
49:     lst.ApplyStyle(sty)
50:     MyPanel.Controls.Add(lst)
51:
52:     MyPanel.Controls.Add(new LiteralControl("</center>"))
53:     MyPanel.BackColor = Color.LightGray
54:   End Sub
55: End Class
```

**ANALYSIS**  Listing 5.2 adds Label and ListBox controls to the panel. First, it creates the Label and ListBox control objects (Lines 21 and 42) and then assigns properties to each (Lines 22–33 and 43–49). Finally, the listing adds the two controls to the panel by calling the Add method on the Panel control's Controls collection (Lines 36 and 50).

5

> **Note**
>
> Many Web controls have a `Controls` collection that stores child Web controls. For instance, the ListBox `Controls` collection stores all of the items that the list box contains.

You may have noticed the `LiteralControl` objects added on Lines 18, 39, and 52 of Listing 5.2. To add generic HTML tags or any string of HTML code programmatically to the Panel control, just add a new `LiteralControl` to the Panel's `Controls` collection.

> **Tip**
>
> Creating a `LiteralControl` is easy. Just pass the HTML that it should contain into the constructor. For instance, to add a table and heading, you might write
>
> ```
> MyPanel.Controls.Add(new LiteralControl("<div>Heading</div>")
> ```

## Practical Uses of the Panel Control

Although Listings 5.1 and 5.2 aren't the most practical examples of using the Panel control, in some situations the Panel control can save on programming effort. During development, more than a few pages may be quite similar but vary slightly in the number of controls or in small sections of HTML. Rather than create these multiple pages individually, you can make one page with a Panel control or two containing the differences. Then, on the `Page_Load` event, you can change the Panel's contents or disable it altogether by setting its `Visible` property to `false`.

---

**The `DataSource` Property**

Almost all the code examples in today's lesson use data binding and the relevant control's `DataSource` property. *Data binding*, if you'll recall from yesterday's lesson, means that some kind of data, such as the result of a method or rows in a table, is combined with a Web control to populate its output.

On Day 12, "Putting it All Together with ASP.NET" we will harness the full power of data binding. Even without using ADO.NET, you can write properties and methods to feed sample data into controls. Today's examples will use methods with data binding. After we cover programming with ADO.NET, converting these data-binding samples to use ADO.NET will be a straightforward task.

---

# Repeating Templates with the Repeater Control

**NEW TERM** The Repeater control's job is to repeat a set of templates once for every field of data in its DataSource collection. An ASP.NET *template* is a set of HTML and Web controls that are repeated inside a containing Web control. All controls covered today contain templates. For example, a template might consist of HTML and ASP.NET code that displays a row of data. The Repeater control repeats this row, supplying new data items each time the template is rendered.

Templates are best explained with a code example, as in Listing 5.3.

**LISTING 5.3** CountToFive.aspx: A Repeater Control That Counts from 1 to 5

```
 1: <html><body>
 2:
 3: <asp:Repeater id="MyRepeater" runat="server">
 4:   <ItemTemplate>
 5:     <%# Container.DataItem %>, 
 6:   </ItemTemplate>
 7: </asp:Repeater>
 8:
 9: </body></html>
10:
11: <script language="VB" runat="server">
12: Sub Page_Load(Sender As Object, e As EventArgs)
13:
14:   Dim arNumbers() As Integer = {1, 2, 3, 4, 5}
15:   MyRepeater.DataSource = arNumbers
16:
17:   'Don't forget to bind the data to the repeater
18:   MyRepeater.DataBind()
19: End Sub
20: </script>
```

**ANALYSIS** Lines 3–7 of Listing 5.3 define a Repeater control. The `<ItemTemplate>` tag on Line 4 defines a template that specifies the ASP.NET code used to render each repeated item.

Line 5 uses the `<%#` and `%>` data-binding tags to specify that the containing control's DataItem property should be displayed inside the template.

Between the `<script>` tags (lines 11–20), we define what each data item will be by setting the Repeater control's DataSource property to an array containing a list of numbers. We must call the DataBind method (line 18) after setting the DataSource property. Any time the contents of the DataSource change, DataBind must be called again.

The Repeater control contains five templates, as listed in Table 5.1.

**TABLE 5.1**  Repeater Control Templates

| Template | Description |
| --- | --- |
| ItemTemplate | Specify what each repeated item should look like inside this element. The data binding usually happens in this element, which is the only required part of the Repeater control. |
| SeparatorTemplate | Define HTML to display after each item in this optional element. |
| HeaderTemplate | Put the header HTML in this optional element. |
| FooterTemplate | Put the footer HTML in this optional element. |
| AlternatingItemTemplate | Specify a second set of HTML and data-binding commands in this template so that alternating (even numbered) items are displayed differently. |

## Using `DataBinder.Eval`

Before constructing an example with these different templates, let's study the `DataBinder.Eval` method. You use `DataBinder.Eval` to extract data from any collection and format the data with a format string. The following code would format the key and value elements from a `HashTable` collection:

```
1: <ItemTemplate>
2:    Employee Name:
3:    <%# DataBinder.Eval(Container.DataItem, "Key") %> <br>
4:    Employee Salary
5:    <%# DataBinder.Eval(Container.DataItem, "Value", "{0:C}") %> <br>
6: </ItemTemplate>
```

**Tip**   .NET includes many different kinds of built-in collections, all in the `System.Collections` namespace. The `HashTable` collection stores elements made up of key and value pairs. For instance, you might store employee records in a hash table, using the employee's identification number as a key and a custom employee class as a value.

**ANALYSIS**   The preceding code snippet uses two versions of the `Eval` method. The `Eval` method on Line 3 uses two parameters:

- The `Eval` method always specifies the collection element to extract, usually `Container.DataItem`.

- The second parameter is the name of the property in the collection to extract. Notice that the second parameter passed into Eval is a string, such as "Key", and must include quotation marks.

The Eval method on Line 5 takes an optional third parameter that specifies a format string. Like most format strings, it's quite cryptic. Table 5.2 shows some of the more commonly used format strings, but you should consult the Visual Studio documentation for complete details.

**TABLE 5.2** Common Format Strings

| Format String | Description |
| --- | --- |
| {0:C} | Currency: $xx,xxxx.xx |
| {0:N} | Number: xx,xxxx.xx |
| {0:D} (with number objects) | Decimal: xxxxxx |
| {0:d} (with datetime objects) | Short Date: m/d/yyyy |
| {0:D} (with datetime objects) | Long Date: Wednesday, February 12, 2001 |

With DataBinder.Eval as a part of our programming toolbox, let's return to the Repeater control. Listing 5.4 uses the AlternatingItemTemplate, HeaderTemplate, FooterTemplate, and DataBinder.Eval method to construct the table showing fictitious employee names and salaries. Figure 5.2 shows the result of running Listing 5.4.

**FIGURE 5.2**

*Using the Repeater Control.*

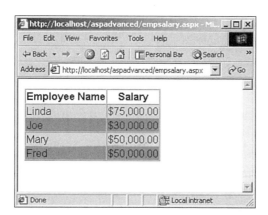

**LISTING 5.4** EmpSalary.aspx: Creating a Table of Employee Names and Salaries with the Repeater Control

```
1: <%@ Import NameSpace="System.Collections" %>
2: <script language="VB" runat="server">
```

**LISTING 5.4**  continued

```
 3: Sub Page_Load(Sender As Object, e As EventArgs)
 4:
 5:   Dim ht as new Hashtable()
 6:   ht.Add("Joe", 30000)
 7:   ht.Add("Mary", 50000)
 8:   ht.Add("Linda", 75000)
 9:   ht.Add("Fred", 50000)
10:
11:   MyRepeater.DataSource = ht
12:   MyRepeater.DataBind()
13:
14: End Sub
15: </script>
16: <html>
17: <body>
18: <font face="Arial" size="10pt">
19:
20: <asp:Repeater id="MyRepeater" runat="server">
21:
22:   <HeaderTemplate>
23:     <table border="1" cellspacing="0">
24:       <tr><th>Employee Name</th><th>Salary</th></tr>
25:   </HeaderTemplate>
26:
27:   <ItemTemplate>
28:     <tr>
29:     <asp:TableCell BackColor="LightGray" runat="server">
30:       <%# DataBinder.Eval(Container.DataItem, "Key") %>
31:     </asp:TableCell>
32:     <asp:TableCell BackColor="LightGray" runat="server">
33:       <%# DataBinder.Eval(Container.DataItem, "Value", "{0:C}") %>
34:     </asp:TableCell>
35:     </tr>
36:   </ItemTemplate>
37:
38:   <AlternatingItemTemplate>
39:     <tr>
40:     <asp:TableCell BackColor="Gray" runat="server">
41:       <%# DataBinder.Eval(Container.DataItem, "Key") %>
42:     </asp:TableCell>
43:     <asp:TableCell BackColor="Gray" runat="server">
44:       <%# DataBinder.Eval(Container.DataItem, "Value", "{0:C}") %>
45:     </asp:TableCell>
46:     </tr>
47:   </AlternatingItemTemplate>
48:
49:   <FooterTemplate>
50:     </table>
51:   </FooterTemplate>
```

**LISTING 5.4**   continued

```
52:
53: </asp:Repeater>
54:
55: </font>
56: </body>
57: </html>
```

**ANALYSIS**   In Lines 3–14, the `Page_Load` event handler creates a `HashTable` collection, adds some sample entries, and binds the `HashTable` to the Repeater control defined in the second half of the listing.

Most of the code in Listing 5.4 specifies HTML and Web controls for each of the Repeater's built-in templates. Notice the use of the TableCell Web control (Lines 29–45), which wraps the HTML `<td>` tag.

The Repeater control saves you from writing code to iterate through a dataset or collection and lets you roll your own code for rendering the data. If you plan to display data on your Web page, the Repeater control gives you great flexibility for rendering HTML to the browser.

# Displaying Tables with the DataGrid Control

One of the most common tasks Web pages perform is displaying tabular data, such as search results or sale items in an inventory. You could use the Repeater control to display these elements, but ASP.NET offers two controls to make the job of displaying data easier: DataGrid and DataList. Both controls offer a flexible and powerful way to display data in tabular form. Let's look at the DataGrid first.

As you might expect, the DataGrid control gets attached to the data it should display by setting the `DataSource` property. You can bind this control to various data sources, including a `DataSet` or a `DataView`. If the data source contains multiple tables, you must specify the table to bind to with the `DataMember` property.

**Tip**   You don't need to attach ADO.NET dataset collections to a database. Instead, you can create a table in memory and set the contents with your own algorithms. The samples in today's lesson show exactly how to create these datasets.

Listing 5.5 shows a simple example of a DataGrid control in action.

5

**LISTING 5.5** DGEmpSalary.aspx: A Table of Employees and Salaries Using a DataGrid Control

```
 1: <%@ Import NameSpace="System.Data" %>
 2: <script language="VB" runat="server" >
 3: Sub Page_Load(Sender As Object, e As EventArgs)
 4:
 5:    Dim dt as new DataTable()
 6:    Dim iRowIdx As Integer
 7:
 8:    dt.Columns.Add(new DataColumn("Name"))
 9:    dt.Columns.Add(new DataColumn("Salary"))
10:
11:    'Create a random number generator for salary figures
12:    Dim randGen as new Random()
13:
14:    'Populate the data set with things like "Employee 3", "24567.23"
15:    for iRowIdx = 0 to 4
16:      Dim dr as DataRow
17:      dr = dt.NewRow()
18:      dr("Name") = "Employee " & iRowIdx.ToString()
19:      dr("Salary") = Math.Round(randGen.NextDouble() * 100000, 2)
20:      dt.Rows.Add(dr)
21:    Next
22:
23:    Dim dv as new DataView(dt)
24:
25:    MyDataGrid.DataSource = dv
26:    MyDataGrid.DataBind()
27:
28: End Sub
29: </script>
30: <html>
31: <body>
32:   <ASP:DataGrid id="MyDataGrid" runat="server"
33:     BorderColor="black"
34:     BorderWidth="1"
35:     GridLines="Both"
36:     CellPadding="2"
37:     Font-Name="Arial"
38:     Font-Size="14"
39:     ItemStyle-BackColor="LightGray"
40:     AlternatingItemStyle-BackColor="Gray"
41:     />
42: </body>
43: </html>
```

**ANALYSIS**  The DataGrid control has all the standard user interface properties we have come to expect with every ASP.NET Web control. You can see how Listing 5.5 uses these properties in the declaration of the DataGrid control starting at Line 32.

The DataGrid also has the alternating item template you saw in the Repeater control. To set style properties for the alternating items, just precede each property name with `AlternatingItemStyle` and a hyphen, as shown on Line 40.

Often, when we display data from a search query or large set of records, the entire set won't fit on one screen page. The DataGrid control has a built-in capability to display multipage datasets, using the `AllowPaging`, `PagerSize`, and `PagerStyle` properties (coming up in Listing 5.6). The `PagerStyle` property is a regular .NET style object, allowing you to set the standard UI properties such as `Font` and `ForeColor`, as well as letting you set the number of page buttons to display. We will see a complete example including these properties shortly.

You can put Web controls inside each DataGrid column. For instance, you can place a read-only check box indicating whether an item is in stock at your online store. The DataGrid control lets you specify any number of controls for each column in the grid. This will be shown in Listing 5.6.

The DataGrid also has built-in sorting and a `Visible` property if you want to hide a column.

Lastly, the DataGrid allows data editing in each column. You can turn editing on and off depending on events generated from another column, which might have Edit, Save, and Cancel buttons. This will be shown shortly in Listing 5.6.

Listing 5.6 shows a sample that uses all these features. It's another employee list with randomly generated values like our last sample. However, this sample is much more powerful because it allows you to edit all the information about an employee, delete the employee record, sort, and page through the data. Figure 5.3 shows how the grid looks onscreen.

**FIGURE 5.3**

*Using the ASP.NET DataGrid Control.*

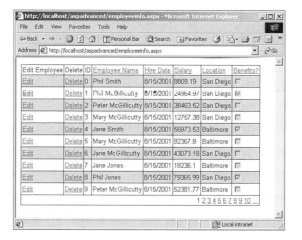

**Tip**

Don't even think about typing in the code for the following sample.
Download the source code for all the listings in this book from this book's
Web page at www.samspublishing.com.

**LISTING 5.6**   EmployeeInfo.aspx: Displaying Employee Information in a Grid for
Viewing and Editing

```
 1: <%@ page debug="true" %>
 2: <%@ Import NameSpace="System" %>
 3: <%@ Import NameSpace="System.Data" %>
 4:  <script language="vb" runat="server">
 5:
 6:   dim randGen as Random
 7:
 8:   'Declare our data table and view objects at Page scope
 9:   dim dt as DataTable
10:   dim dv as DataView
11:   dim strSortField as String
12:
13:   'Get a random number between 0 and max
14:   'used for generating random
15:   Function GetRandom(max as Integer) as Integer
16:     return CType(Math.Round(randGen.NextDouble() * (max-1), 0), Integer)
17:   End Function
18:
19:   'This method will populate the DataTable with 500 employees. If we
20:   'were using a database to populate the grid, then this routine would
21:   'be much shorter
22:   Sub CreateDataSet
23:     'Create the columns for the data table
24:     dt.Columns.Add(new DataColumn("Index", GetType(Integer)))
25:     dt.Columns.Add(new DataColumn("Name", GetType(string)))
26:     dt.Columns.Add(new DataColumn("Salary", GetTYpe(double)))
27:     dt.Columns.Add(new DataColumn("Location", GetTYpe(string)))
28:     dt.Columns.Add(new DataColumn("Has Benefits", _
29:         GetType(System.Boolean)))
30:     dt.Columns.Add(new DataColumn("Hire Date", GetType(System.DateTime)))
31:
32:     'Set the primary key for the data table
33:     dim primaryKeys(1) as DataColumn
34:     primaryKeys(0) = dt.Columns(0)
35:     dt.PrimaryKey = primaryKeys
36:
37:     'Create some lists for Location - we will randomly pick from the
38:     'list to generate our data set
39:     dim locations as ArrayList
40:     locations = new ArrayList()
```

**LISTING 5.6**   continued

```
41:     locations.Add("Denver")
42:     locations.Add("Baltimore")
43:     locations.Add("San Diego")
44:
45:     'Create some lists for random names
46:     dim firstnames as ArrayList
47:     firstnames = new ArrayList()
48:     firstnames.Add("Peter")
49:     firstnames.Add("Phil")
50:     firstnames.Add("Mary")
51:     firstnames.Add("Jane")
52:
53:     dim lastnames as ArrayList
54:     lastnames = new ArrayList()
55:     lastnames.Add("Smith")
56:     lastnames.Add("Jones")
57:     lastnames.Add("McGillicutty")
58:     lastnames.Add("Finkelstein")
59:
60:     'Populate the data table
61:     dim iRowIdx as Integer
62:     for iRowIdx = 1 to 500
63:       dim dr as DataRow
64:       dr = dt.NewRow()
65:       dr("Index") = iRowIdx
66:       dr("Name") = firstnames(GetRandom(4)) + " " _
67:         + lastnames(GetRandom(4))
68:       dr("Salary") = Math.Round(randGen.NextDouble() * 100000, 2)
69:       dr("Location") = locations(GetRandom(3))
70:       dr("Has Benefits") = (randGen.NextDouble() > 0.5)
71:       dr("Hire Date") = System.DateTime.Now.Subtract( _
72:         new System.TimeSpan(GetRandom(365), 0, 0, 0))
73:       dt.Rows.Add(dr)
74:     next
75:   End Sub
76:
77:   Sub Page_Load(Sender as Object , e as EventArgs)
78:     'If our data set is not in session, then create a new one and add
79:     'it in session. Notice that we are creating a new DataView object
80:     'every time we hit the page. The data view object is a lightweight
81:     'wrapper around a data set.
82:     if(Session("DataSet") is nothing)
83:       'create our random number generator
84:       randGen = new Random(System.DateTime.Now.Millisecond)
85:
86:       'Create the data table object and populate it with random values
87:       dt = new DataTable()
88:       CreateDataSet()
89:
```

5

**LISTING 5.6** continued

```
90:      'Make a view for the data
91:      dv = new DataView(dt)
92:
93:      'Store the entire data set in Session
94:      Session("DataSet") = dt
95:      Session("EditIdx") = -1
96:      Session("Sort") = "Index"
97:
98:      'otherwise retrieive the dataset from session store
99:    else
100:      dt = Ctype(Session("DataSet"), DataTable )
101:      dv = new DataView(dt)
102:      dv.Sort = Ctype(Session("sort"), string)
103:      MyDataGrid.EditItemIndex = Ctype(Session("EditIdx"), integer)
104:    end if
105:
106:    'Always bind the DataGrid to the DataSet
107:    'The data for the grid is stored in Session
108:    'The grid does not have view state enabled,
109:    'so re-attach the grid to the DataSet
110:    BindGrid()
111:  end sub
112:
113:  'This is a standard method you define when working with a DataGrid.
114:  'Many of the event handlers have to update the grid after doing their
115:  'work (editing/deleting) so it's useful to have a method that will
116:  'call DataBind on the current data view object
117:  sub BindGrid()
118:    MyDataGrid.DataSource = dv
119:    MyDataGrid.DataBind()
120:  end sub
121:
122:  'This event is triggered when any one of our sortable columns is
123:  'clicked. We need to update the sort field name in session and on
124:  'the data view
125:  protected sub SortGrid(sender as Object , _
126:        e as DataGridSortCommandEventArgs )
127:    strSortField = CType(e.SortExpression, String)
128:    Session("sort") = strSortField
129:    dv.Sort = strSortField
130:    BindGrid()
131:  end sub
132:
133:  'This event is triggered when the Delete linkitem is clicked
134:  protected sub Command(Sender as Object , e as DataGridCommandEventArgs)
135:    if( e.CommandName = "Delete")
136:      'Get the employee id, which will be the third element of the
137:      'Cells collection (the third column in the DataGrid)
138:      dim strempid as string
```

**LISTING 5.6**   continued

```
139:        strEmpID = e.Item.Cells(2).Text
140:
141:        'Convert ID to an Integereger
142:        dim nempid as integer
143:        nEmpID = Int32.Parse(strEmpID)
144:
145:        'Find the data row with this id
146:        dim dr as datarow
147:        dr = dt.Rows.Find(nEmpID)
148:
149:        'Delete the row
150:        dt.Rows.Remove(dr)
151:
152:        'Replace the current data table in session with the
153:        'new data table
154:        Session("DataSet") = dt
155:
156:        'Create a new view
157:        dv = new DataView(dt)
158:        dv.Sort = CType( Session("sort"), String)
159:
160:        BindGrid()
161:      end if
162:    end sub
163:
164:    'This event is triggered when the user decides to update a row they
165:    'have been editing. If we were using a database, we might call an
166:    'update stored procedure. Since we are holding the whole data set
167:    'in memory, we will delete the old row and re-add the new one of a
168:    'of a row in the field.
169:    protected sub Update(sender as Object , e as DataGridCommandEventArgs)
170:
171:        'To delete the old record, we will filter our data view so that
172:        'the old record is the only one that is visible.
173:        'We get the ID again using the Cells collection
174:        dv.RowFilter = "Index=" + e.Item.Cells(2).Text
175:        if(dv.Count > 0)
176:          dv.Delctc(0)
177:        end if
178:
179:        'Now that the old record is gone, we can turn off our row filter
180:        dv.RowFilter = ""
181:
182:        'Create the new row
183:        'Notice that the new data the user has entered is the first
184:        'element of the controls collection of each cell
185:        dim dr as datarow
186:        dr = dt.NewRow()
187:        dr("Index")         = e.Item.Cells(2).Text
```

5

**LISTING 5.6**  continued

```
188:    dr("Name")          = CType(e.Item.Cells(3).Controls(0), TextBox).Text
189:    dr("Hire Date")     = CType(e.Item.Cells(4).Controls(0), TextBox).Text
190:    dr("Salary")        = CType(e.Item.Cells(5).Controls(0), TextBox).Text
191:    dr("Location")      = CType(e.Item.Cells(6).Controls(0), TextBox).Text
192:    dr("Has Benefits") = true
193:    dt.Rows.Add(dr)
194:
195:    'Replace the current data table in session with the
196:    'new data table
197:    Session("DataSet") = dt
198:
199:    'Create a new view
200:    dv = new DataView(dt)
201:    dv.Sort = CType( Session("sort"), String)
202:
203:    MyDataGrid.EditItemIndex = -1
204:    BindGrid()
205:
206:    'Store the EditItemIndex, since viewstate is false
207:    Session("EditIdx") = MyDataGrid.EditItemIndex
208: end sub
209:
210: 'Boilerplate code...
211: 'This event is triggered when the user decides to cancel the editing
212: 'of a row in the field. All we need to do is set the edit item to -1
213: protected sub Cancel(sender as Object , e as DataGridCommandEventArgs )
214:    MyDataGrid.EditItemIndex = -1
215:    BindGrid()
216:
217:    'Store the EditItemIndex, since viewstate is false
218:    Session("EditIdx") = MyDataGrid.EditItemIndex
219: end sub
220:
221: 'Boilerplate code...
222: 'This event is triggered when the user decides to edit a row
223: 'of a row in the field. All we need to do is set the edit item index
224: protected sub Edit(sender as Object , e as DataGridCommandEventArgs)
225:    MyDataGrid.EditItemIndex = CType(e.Item.ItemIndex, Integer)
226:    BindGrid()
227:
228:    'Store the EditItemIndex, since viewstate is false
229:    Session("EditIdx") = MyDataGrid.EditItemIndex
230: end sub
231:
232: 'Boilerplaite code...
233: 'This event is triggered when the user pages to a new set of data
234: protected sub NewPage(sender as Object , _
235:         e as DataGridPageChangedEventArgs)
236:    MyDataGrid.CurrentPageIndex = e.NewPageIndex
```

**LISTING 5.6**   continued

```
237:      BindGrid()
238:   end sub
239: </script>
240:   <html>
241:   <body>
242:     <form runat="server">
243:     <asp:DataGrid id="MyDataGrid" runat="server"
244:       enableviewstate="false"
245:       BorderColor="black"
246:       BorderWidth="1"
247:       GridLines="Both"
248:       CellPadding="2"
249:       Font-Name="Arial"
250:       Font-Size="10pt"
251:       ItemStyle-BackColor="LightGray"
252:       AlternatingItemStyle-BackColor="White"
253:       AutoGenerateColumns = "false"
254:       AllowSorting="true"
255:       OnItemCommand="Command"
256:       OnSortCommand="SortGrid"
257:       OnEditCommand="Edit"
258:       OnCancelCommand="Cancel"
259:       OnUpdateCommand="Update"
260:       AllowPaging="True"
261:       PageSize="10"
262:       PagerStyle-Mode="NumericPages"
263:       PagerStyle-HorizontalAlign="Right"
264:       PagerStyle-NextPageText="Next"
265:       PagerStyle-PrevPageText="Prev"
266:       OnPageIndexChanged="NewPage"
267:       >
268:
269:       <Columns>
270:
271:         <asp:EditCommandColumn
272:            EditText="Edit"
273:            CancelText="Cancel"
274:           UpdatcText="Update"
275:            ItemStyle-Wrap="false"
276:            HeaderText="Edit Employee"
277:            HeaderStyle-Wrap="false"
278:            />
279:
280:         <asp:TemplateColumn HeaderText="Delete">
281:           <ItemTemplate>
282:             <asp:LinkButton id="Delete" text="Delete"
283:                         CommandName="Delete" runat="server"/>
284:           </ItemTemplate>
285:         </asp:TemplateColumn>
```

5

**LISTING 5.6**    continued

```
286:
287:            <asp:BoundColumn HeaderText="ID" DataField="Index"
288:                          ReadOnly="True" />
289:            <asp:BoundColumn HeaderText="Employee Name" DataField="Name"
290:                          SortExpression="Name"/>
291:            <asp:BoundColumn HeaderText="Hire Date" DataField="Hire Date"
292:                          DataFormatString="{0:d}"
293:                          SortExpression="Hire Date"/>
294:            <asp:BoundColumn HeaderText="Salary" DataField="Salary"
295:                          SortExpression="Salary" />
296:            <asp:BoundColumn HeaderText="Location" DataField="Location"
297:                          SortExpression="Location"/>
298:
299:            <asp:TemplateColumn HeaderText="Benefits?"
300:                            SortExpression="Has Benefits">
301:              <ItemTemplate>
302:                <asp:Checkbox id="HasBenefits" runat="server"
303:                  Checked=<%# DataBinder.Eval(Container.DataItem,
304:                          "Has Benefits")%>
305:                  Enabled="false" />
306:              </ItemTemplate>
307:            </asp:TemplateColumn>
308:          </Columns>
309:        </asp:DataGrid>
310:
311:      </form>
312:   </body>
313: </html>
```

Whew! This is a long listing, so let's analyze it in pieces.

## Ordering the Bound Columns

**ANALYSIS**    You may have noticed the <asp:BoundColumn> declarations in the <Columns> section of the data grid, starting at Line 287 of Listing 5.6. You can use these declarations to set the order in which columns are displayed in the grid and to specify formatting for a column. One declaration that binds the employee's Hire Date is as follows:

```
291:            <asp:BoundColumn HeaderText="Hire Date" DataField="Hire Date"
292:                          DataFormatString="{0:d}"
293:                          SortExpression="Hire Date"/>
```

Here, the DataFormatString formats the data into the "short date" format, using the same format string used in the Eval method of the DataBinder object. The DataField property tells which column of data to use as a source for the column. SortExpression is set here to the same column of data used for the DataField property.

**Tip**

To control the ordering of columns in a DataGrid, put all column declarations in the exact order they should appear in the DataGrid's <Columns> declaration. Also, set the property AutoGenerateColumns to false.

## Controlling Column Rendering with Template Columns

**ANALYSIS** For complete control over column rendering, use the list control's
<asp:TemplateColumn> definition, starting at Line 299. Here is the second template column definition of Listing 5.6 relisted for analysis:

```
299:        <asp:TemplateColumn HeaderText="Benefits?"
300:                        SortExpression="Has Benefits">
301:          <ItemTemplate>
302:            <asp:Checkbox id="HasBenefits" runat="server"
303:              Checked=<%# DataBinder.Eval(Container.DataItem,
304:                    "Has Benefits")%>
305:                Enabled="false" />
306:          </ItemTemplate>
307:        </asp:TemplateColumn>
```

Think of the template column as a souped-up Repeater control. Like a Repeater, it allows you to add an ItemTemplate, AlternatingItemTemplate, HeaderTemplate, and FooterTemplate. TemplateColumn also shares many of the same properties that the BoundColumn control has, such as SortExpression.

## Sorting the Columns

**ANALYSIS** To make DataGrid columns sortable, you need to follow a few simple steps. Here are the steps we took to get sorting to work in Listing 5.6:

1. Set the AllowSorting property in the DataGrid definition to true.

2. Set the SortExpression property in each column definition to the name of the data field that should be used for sorting. Normally, it is just the same data field that the column is bound to from the DataField property.

3. Set the OnSortCommand property of the DataGrid to the name of the custom sorting event handler.

4. Add a custom event handler for the SortCommand event. On Lines 125–126 of Listing 5.6, this handler is called "SortGrid".

**5**

**Tip**

Store the current sort column in the Session object so that when the user returns to the page, the grid will still be sorted.

Figure 5.4 shows the list sorted by employee salary.

**FIGURE 5.4**

*Automatic Sorting and the DataGrid*

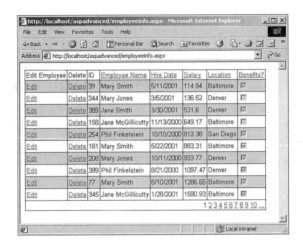

## Deleting Records

 **ANALYSIS** If you look at the column definitions starting at line 277, notice the first `TemplateColumn`:

```
280:          <asp:TemplateColumn HeaderText="Delete">
281:            <ItemTemplate>
282:             <asp:LinkButton id="Delete" text="Delete"
283:                        CommandName="Delete" runat="server"/>
284:            </ItemTemplate>
285:          </asp:TemplateColumn>
```

This column displays a LinkButton control so that the user can delete records by clicking the Delete link next to the appropriate record.

> **Tip**
>
> You could use a regular Button control in the delete column or a custom control of your own design. Just as you can do with the Repeater control, you can create any kind of custom code inside the `ItemTemplate` collection of the `TemplateColumn`.

Notice the special `CommandName` parameter in the definition of the link button (Line 283). Because the link button control is defined inside the DataGrid, it will trigger an `ItemEvent` when the user clicks it. The event will "bubble up" in the DataGrid control to the custom item event handler. We declared the item event handler in the `OnItemCommand` property of the DataGrid.

We named the item event handler Command and wrote an event handling method named Command. This excerpt from Listing 5.6 shows the event handler:

```
133:    'This event is triggered when the Delete linkitem is clicked
134:    protected sub Command(Sender as Object , e as DataGridCommandEventArgs)
135:       if( e.CommandName = "Delete")
```

The handler checks to make sure that the Delete button control called it. If the Delete button was the source of the event, the appropriate record in the data table is deleted.

The record is deleted by using various ADO.NET commands. We won't go into the details of ADO.NET until Day 9, "Introducing ADO.NET." However, if you inspect the sample code closely, you can see that the Find and Delete methods are used to remove the record.

## Editing Data

**ANALYSIS** The first column we defined for the DataGrid was of type EditCommandColumn (Lines 271–278). This column will automatically display Edit, Update, and Cancel buttons. When the user clicks Edit, each cell will be transformed to a text box or check box for editing, without any extra code on our part. The only thing we have to add is an event handler for the Edit, Update, and Cancel events, most of which is just boilerplate code.

> **Tip**
>
> Rather than use the built-in data editing capabilities that EditCommandColumn provides, you might want to make your own controls to edit data. One possible solution is to create a special column that contains your own editing controls. Normally, this column would be hidden. When the edit event is fired, you could write code to make the editable column visible by setting the column's Visible property.

5

## Paging Records

**NEW TERM** *Paging* permits a long list of records to be displayed a page at a time rather than all at once. Because the code in Listing 5.6 works with a table of 500 employees,

**ANALYSIS** paging is needed so that we can look at a few employees at a time. To turn on paging, set the AllowPaging, PageSize, and PagerStyle properties (Lines 257–259), and add an event handler with some boilerplate code.

Tip

> The DataGrid control is the most complicated standard control in the .NET arsenal. Even with this lengthy example, we cover only the high points. You can dig deeper into the more complicated aspects of paging, data editing, and column rendering in the Visual Studio .NET documentation.

# Displaying Data with the DataList Control

After all this discussion about the DataGrid and Repeater controls, you might be wondering whether there's a control with more features than the Repeater, but not quite as complex as the DataGrid. As it turns out, the DataList control is just that, lying between the Repeater and DataGrid in terms of complexity and functionality.

The DataList, as you might infer from the name, can display data in a list format. Consider using the DataList control when your data isn't neatly packaged into a table. It's possible to display DataList items in a grid format, but you aren't required to do so.

The DataList control works like the Repeater control in that you must define an `ItemTemplate` for each item of data that needs to be rendered onscreen. The control also allows you to define a `HeaderTemplate`, `FooterTemplate`, `AlternatingItemTemplate`, and `SeparatorTemplate`.

The DataList control contains two unique template properties: `SelectedItemTemplate` and `EditItemTemplate`. These two templates allow you to specify different visual layouts and controls when the user selects or edits a list item. You make an item selectable or editable by defining a Web control inside the `ItemTemplate` with a special `CommandName` parameter. This might look like the following:

```
<ItemTemplate>
  Employee Record: Name <%# Container.DataItem("EmpName")%> <br>
  <asp:LinkButton id="btnEdit" runat="server"
                  CommandName="RecordSelected"
                  Text="View Employee Details" />
</ItemTemplate>
<SelectedItemTemplate>
  <!-show all of the details of the employee —>
</SelectedItemTemplate>
```

Just as you do with the DataGrid, you would have to add an event handler for the `CommandName` parameter and tell the DataGrid what to do when an item command occurs:

```
<asp:DataList  (parameters omitted) OnItemCommand="MyCommandHander"
    (Template declarations...)
</asp:DataList>
```

```
<script>
Sub MyCommandHandler(Sender As Object, e As DataListCommandItem)
  if e.CommandName = "RecordSelected" then
    MyDataList.SelectedItem = e.Item.SelectedItem
  End If
End Sub
</script>
```

You add event handlers for an Edit command similarly. Let's take all these code snippets and put them together in a working example—Listing 5.7.

**LISTING 5.7**   EmpDataList.aspx: An Employee List in a DataList

```
 1: <%@ Import Namespace="System.Data" %>
 2: <script language="VB" runat="server">
 3:
 4: ' Utility method to create fake data. Normally we would use
 5: ' the database to populate our list
 6: ' This returns a data view object with all of our data
 7: Function CreateData() As ICollection
 8:    Dim dt as new DataTable()
 9:    Dim dr as DataRow
10:
11:    dt.Columns.Add(new DataColumn("EmpName", GetType(string)))
12:    dt.Columns.Add(new DataColumn("Years", GetType(Int32)))
13:    dt.Columns.Add(new DataColumn("BirthDate", GetType(DateTime)))
14:    Dim i As Integer
15:    for i = 0 to 8
16:       dr = dt.NewRow()
17:       dr(0) = "Employee " & i.ToString()
18:       dr(1) = i
19:       dr(2) = DateTime.Now
20:       dt.Rows.Add(dr)
21:    Next
22:
23:    Dim dv as new DataView(dt)
24:    return dv
25:
26: End Function
27:
28: ' Bind the Data List to the Data View if this is the first page hit
29: Sub Page_Load(Sender As Object, e As EventArgs)
30:     if Not IsPostBack then BindList()
31: End Sub
32:
33: ' Standard binding utility method
34: Sub BindList()
35:     MyDataList.DataSource = CreateData()
36:     MyDataList.DataBind()
37: End Sub
```

5

**LISTING 5.7** continued

```
38:
39: ' This method gets called when any of the buttons in our data list
40: ' are pressed. Each button has a CommandName property, which gets
41: ' passed in the method. Depending on the particular command, we
42: ' set the selected index or edit item index of the data list control.
43: Sub MyCommandHandler(Sender as object, e as DataListCommandEventArgs)
44:
45:     Dim strCmd as string = e.CommandName
46:     if strCmd = "RecordSelected" then
47:         MyDataList.SelectedIndex = e.Item.ItemIndex
48:     end if
49:
50:     if strCmd = "RecordDeSelected" then
51:         MyDataList.SelectedIndex = -1
52:     end if
53:
54:     if strCmd = "RecordEdit" then
55:         MyDataList.EditItemIndex = e.Item.ItemIndex
56:     end if
57:
58:     if strCmd = "Update" then
59:         ' Perform the update operation
60:         ' ...Code omitted..
61:         MyDataList.EditItemIndex = -1
62:     end if
63:
64:     if strCmd = "Cancel"
65:         MyDataList.EditItemIndex = -1
66:     end if
67:
68:     BindList()
69: End Sub
70: </script>
71:
72: <html>
73: <body>
74:   <form runat=server>
75:   <asp:DataList id="MyDataList" runat="server"
76:       Font-Name="Arial"
77:       Font-Size="10pt"
78:       BorderColor="black"
79:       BorderWidth="1"
80:       GridLines="both"
81:       CellPadding="3"
82:       OnItemCommand="MyCommandHandler">
83:
84:     <HeaderTemplate>
85:       Employee Records
86:     </HeaderTemplate>
```

**LISTING 5.7** continued

```
87:
88:      <ItemTemplate>
89:        <%# DataBinder.Eval(Container.DataItem, "EmpName") %> <br>
90:        <asp:LinkButton id="btnSelect" runat="server"
91:                        CommandName="RecordSelected"
92:                        Text="Show Employee Details" /> <br>
93:        <asp:LinkButton id="btnEdit" runat="server"
94:                        CommandName="RecordEdit"
95:                        Text="Update Employee Record" /> <br>
96:      </ItemTemplate>
97:
98:      <SelectedItemTemplate>
99:        Employee Name:
100:       <%# DataBinder.Eval(Container.DataItem, "EmpName") %> <br>
101:       Years of Service:
102:       <%# DataBinder.Eval(Container.DataItem, "Years")%> <br>
103:       BirthDate:
104:     <%# DataBinder.Eval(Container.DataItem, "BirthDate", "{0:D}") %> <br>
105:        <asp:LinkButton id="btnDeselect" runat="server"
106:                        CommandName="RecordDeSelected"
107:                        Text="Hide Employee Details" /> <br>
108:      </SelectedItemTemplate>
109:
110:      <EditItemTemplate>
111:        Employee Name:
112:        <asp:TextBox runat="server" Text=
113:          '<%# DataBinder.Eval(Container.DataItem, "EmpName") %>'/> <br>
114:        Years of Service:
115:        <asp:TextBox runat="server" Text=
116:          '<%# DataBinder.Eval(Container.DataItem, "Years")%>' /> <br>
117:        BirthDate:
118:        <asp:TextBox runat="server" Text=
119:           '<%# DataBinder.Eval(Container.DataItem, "BirthDate",
120:               "{0:D}")%>' /> <br>
121:        <asp:LinkButton id="btnUpdate" runat="server"
122:                        CommandName="Update"
123:                        Text="Update Record" /> <br>
124:        <asp:LinkButton id="btnCancel" runat="server"
125:                        CommandName="Cancel"
126:                        Text="Cancel Editing" /> <br>
127:      </EditItemTemplate>
128:
129:    </asp:DataList>
130:    </form>
131: </body>
132: </html>
```

5

Figure 5.5 shows the results of running Listing 5.7. Let's analyze the sample piece by piece.

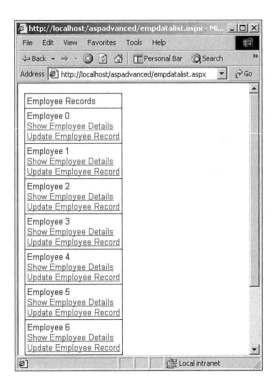

## Displaying Items

**ANALYSIS**  The `ItemTemplate` definition in Listing 5.7 follows:

```
88:        <ItemTemplate>
89:            <%# DataBinder.Eval(Container.DataItem, "EmpName") %> <br>
90:            <asp:LinkButton id="btnSelect" runat="server"
91:                            CommandName="RecordSelected"
92:                            Text="Show Employee Details" /> <br>
93:            <asp:LinkButton id="btnEdit" runat="server"
94:                            CommandName="RecordEdit"
95:                            Text="Update Employee Record" /> <br>
96:        </ItemTemplate>
```

For each data item, we display the employee name (using `DataBinder.Eval`) and two LinkButtons to show record details and edit the record. We set the `CommandName` parameters for each so that we can distinguish which one sent an `Item` command to our command handler. The command handler looks like the following:

```
43: Sub MyCommandHandler(Sender as object, e as DataListCommandEventArgs)
44:
45:     Dim strCmd as string = e.CommandName
46:     if strCmd = "RecordSelected" then
47:         MyDataList.SelectedIndex = e.Item.ItemIndex
...
69: End Sub
```

The ListControl calls the command-handling routine automatically because we defined the OnItemCommand parameter in the MyDataList definition.

## Editing and Viewing Details

**ANALYSIS** If you look at the definitions for SelectedItemTemplate (lines 98–108) and EditItemTemplate (lines 110–132) in Listing 5.7, notice that they look similar to the regular ItemList definition. They both contain appropriate control definitions and more LinkButtons for hiding, updating, and canceling editing. The item event command handler gets called each time one of these LinkButtons gets clicked.

> **Tip**
>
> You can display a DataList in table format by setting the RepeatLayout property to "Table" instead of "Flow", the default. You also can control the order in which the items are displayed by setting the RepeatDirection property to "Horizontal" or "Vertical", the default.

# Summary

5

In yesterday's and today's lessons, we covered almost every standard Web control that ASP.NET has to offer. ASP.NET also offers the Calendar control, an AdRotator control to display rotating online advertisements, and the XML control, which applies an XSL style sheet to XML data for display. We will investigate the XML control on Day 8, "Using XML with Your Applications," when we discuss XML handling in .NET.

After the past few days of work, you have a great deal of knowledge at your disposal for constructing Web applications with .NET. From today's discussion, you learned the fundamentals of the DataGrid, DataList, and Repeater controls. We took a cursory look at the Calendar control. You also found out how to construct dynamic pages with Visual Basic by using the Panel control. With these tools, you should be able to make great-looking, highly functional Web pages.

Stay tuned for tomorrow's lesson, where we will learn about making our own controls.

# Q&A

**Q** **How do I pick between the Repeater, DataGrid, and DataList controls?**

**A** Use the DataGrid for data from a table or XML file. Next week's lessons will show examples using the Northwind database, ADO.NET, and XML files. Use the DataList if the data you need to display contains only one or two items. Use the Repeater control for complete control over data display.

**Q** **What performance advantages, if any, are there when I create Web controls using code-behind only, such as the Panel example in today's lesson?**

**A** There are no performance advantages from using only code-behind created controls. The code in Web forms (.aspx files) is compiled, just as the code-behind files are, so there's no practical difference between the two methods.

# Workshop

The Workshop provides quiz questions to help you solidify your understanding of the material covered and exercises to provide you with experience in using what you've learned. The answers to the quiz questions are provided in Appendix A, "Answers to Quizzes and Exercises."

## Quiz

1. What class adds arbitrary HTML tags to the Panel control?
2. What is a template in the context of ASP.NET controls?
3. What method is used to bind data items to an ASP.NET Web control?
4. What two templates are used to change the style of even and odd numbered rows?
5. Can ASP.NET Web controls be put inside DataGrid columns?
6. How can you enable in-place row editing for the DataGrid control?
7. Why does Listing 5.6 turn off ViewState for the DataGrid?

## Exercises

1. Try experimenting with the Calendar control. What specialized properties does this control contain that the controls in today's lesson didn't use?
2. Try combining a DataGrid and Panel control, so that the grid is created entirely using code-behind logic. What are the benefits of an approach like this?

# DAY 6

# Working with User Controls

Today and tomorrow, you will learn about creating and using your own ASP.NET controls. The two kinds of user-created controls are user controls and custom controls. Today's lesson will explain user controls.

Today you will learn about the following:

- What makes up a user control
- When to use a user control
- How to create custom properties in a user control
- How to use custom events in a user control
- How to use code behind and user controls
- How to use caching with Web Forms and user controls

## Understanding User Controls

User controls are ASP.NET code and HTML snippets that you can include in a page and use just like any other Web control. You can add properties and events to user controls so that they can be used generically throughout pages in a Web site. Creating user controls is a snap because you can build them using regular ASP.NET code and HTML, just like regular pages. They become user controls when the code is saved in a file with the special .ascx extension.

> **Note**  You can write custom controls in any .NET language, but can use only one language in a given control. For instance, you could write a Web form using VB.NET and write a user control in C#. If your team is building an Internet application, you can use user controls to break the project into pieces to be assigned to individual developers. This way, each developer can choose in which .NET language to create his or her user controls.

## A Text-Only User Control

Let's see how this works. The first user control that we will create consists of HTML only (see Listing 6.1).

**LISTING 6.1**  Simple.ascx: A Simple User Control Containing Just Text

```
<h2>Acme Widgets Inc</h2>
<p>At acme Widgets, we can satisfy all of your shopping needs.<p><br>
```

If you are following along with the code samples, be sure to save this file with an .ascx extension. All user controls use the .ascx extension.

The next step is to include this simple user control inside a Web form, as on the sample page in Listing 6.2.

**LISTING 6.2**  ShowSimple.aspx: A Page Including a User Control

```
1: <%@ Register TagPrefix="WebBook" TagName="TextOnlyControl"
2:     src="Simple.ascx" %>
3: <html>
4: <body>
5: <p>Advertisement:<p><hr>
6: <WebBook:TextOnlyControl runat="server"/>
7: <hr>Copyright 2001, Acme Widgets
8: </body>
9: </html>
```

**ANALYSIS** Listing 6.2 uses the `Register` page directive (Line 1) to include the user control. With the `Register` directive, you specify a namespace for the user control, a custom name for the control itself, and the source file containing the code for the control. A typical `Register` tag looks like the following:

```
<%@ Register TagPrefix="NameSpace" TagName="UserControlName"
    src="SourceFile" %>
```

You can create any name you want for your user control by using the `TagName` parameter in the `Register` directive. `TagPrefix`, which corresponds to a namespace for the control, allows you to distinguish between the built-in ASP.NET controls and your own user controls. You can add any number of user controls to a Web form by using the `Register` directive.

To add the user control to a page, you use a declaration similar to a regular Web control. For the line in the preceding paragraph, a user control declaration would look like the following:

```
<Namespace:UserControlName id="MyControlID"
    CustomProperty1="value" runat="server" />
```

This code line will use the user control you registered at the top of the Web form with the `Register` directive.

---

**ASP.NET and Code Reuse**

Reusing ASP code has always been a cumbersome process. One way that Web programmers reused code in ASP.OLD was to use the `#include` directive, which looked similar to the following:

```
<!— #include "mycode.asp" —>
```

This directive would insert the contents of the MyCode.asp file directly into the ASP file where the `#include` directive is located. Although this method works, following the ASP code is difficult, especially for someone else reading the code. Also, knowing every place a file may be included in other pages is difficult. This can cause an unwary programmer to break pages inadvertently when changing an included file. Using the `#include` directive with a large ASP application was a maintenance nightmare, but often it could not be avoided.

To reuse code in ASP.NET, you should use user controls instead of `#include`. Even if the shared code is made up of HTML only, creating a user control still makes sense. If the code targeted for reuse contains programming logic, user controls are an ideal solution because they allow you to specify parameters in the containing Web form.

---

## The `Register` Directive

Let's look more closely at the `Register` directive. Table 6.1 lists its parameters.

6

**TABLE 6.1** The Register Directive Parameters

| Parameter | Description |
|---|---|
| TagPrefix | Specifies an alias for the namespace to which the user control belongs. All references to the user control must have TagPrefix before the control name. |
| TagName | Specifies an alias for the user control. |
| Src | Specifies the source file's location for the user control. |
| NameSpace | Specifies a NameSpace instead of TagName alias for code behind user controls and custom controls. |
| Assembly | Specifies an Assembly instead of source file for code behind and custom controls. |

Notice the NameSpace and Assembly parameters used for code behind user controls and custom controls. We will cover code behind user controls shortly.

# Using Properties

You can use properties in user controls by adding code for the properties inside the <script> tag. Just like Web forms, user controls support the script tag and code behind.

Let's explore properties and user controls by creating a user control that contains a ZIP code field. This user control might be used on a Web form that gathers user information. Of course, we could use a regular text box for the ZIP code field, but with a user control, we can add custom validation code along with the field.

Let's add an IsZipCodeValid property to the control to make sure that the user has entered a valid ZIP code. If the IsZipCodeValid property is false, we should also add an ErrorText property that the containing form can use to display an error message to the user. Also, let's add a Width property so that the containing form can set the width of the ZIP code control.

In Listing 6.3, the ZIP code control contains these properties and a RequiredFieldValidator and RegularExpressionValidator to check the status of the ZIP code text box.

**LISTING 6.3** Zips.ascx: A User Control with Customized Error Checking Using Properties

```
1: <script language="vb" runat="server">
2:
3: 'Get/Set property for the width of the zip code
4:   public property Width() as unit
5:     get
```

**LISTING 6.3** continued

```
 6:         return ZipCode.Width
 7:      end get
 8:      set (byval newvalue as unit)
 9:         ZipCode.Width = newvalue
10:      end set
11:   End Property
12:
13:  'Get property that returns true if both the zipcode is
14:  ' non-blank and 5 digits
15:   public readonly property IsZipValid() as boolean
16:      get
17:         return (ZipValidator.IsValid And ZipValidator2.IsValid)
18:      end get
19:   end property
20:
21:  'Returns the error message associated with the custom zip code control
22:   public readonly property ErrorMessage() as string
23:      get
24:        if not ZipValidator2.IsValid then
25:           return ZipValidator2.ErrorMessage
26:        end if
27:        if not ZipValidator.IsValid then
28:           return ZipValidator.ErrorMessage
29:        end if
30:        return "Zip code ok."
31:      end get
32:   end property
33: </script>
34: <asp:TextBox id="ZipCode" runat="server" />
35: <asp:RegularExpressionValidator
36:       ASPClass="RegularExpressionValidator"
37:       EnableClientScript="false"
38:       id="ZipValidator" runat="server"
39:       ControlToValidate="ZipCode"
40:       ValidationExpression="\d{5}"
41:       ErrorMessage="You must enter a five digit zip code"
42:       Display="None">
43:       </asp:RegularExpressionValidator>
44: <asp:RequiredFieldValidator id="ZipValidator2" runat="server"
45:       ControlToValidate="ZipCode"
46:       EnableClientScript="false"
47:       ErrorMessage="The zip code field cannot be blank"
48:       Display="None">
49:       </asp:RequiredFieldValidator>
```

 **ANALYSIS**  In Listing 6.3, three custom properties for the user control are defined inside the <script> tag:

- Width (Lines 4–11) allows the containing page to specify the width of the user control.

- IsZipValid (Lines 15–19) will be true if the user's input passes the validation rules defined later in the listing.

- ErrorMessage (Lines 22–32) contains an error message if the entered ZIP code isn't valid.

One tricky part of Listing 6.3 is in the declaration of the ZIP code field validators. Lines 37 and 46 set the EnableClientScript property to false so that if the validators fail, they will post back to the page rather than execute their own JavaScript on the client.

For this sample user control, the parent Web page should display the custom error messages itself. To make this behavior work, the listing doesn't include any error message text between the FieldValidator tags (Lines 42–43 and 48–49). However, Listing 6.3 does specify the ErrorMessage property in each FieldValidator (Lines 41 and 47), which the custom ErrorMessage property reads from each validation control (Line 17).

Let's write a page using this control. Listing 6.4 shows how to use the Width property in the declaration of the user control and how to use the IsZipValid and ErrorMessage properties when the Submit button gets clicked.

**LISTING 6.4**    EntryForm.aspx: Using the Custom ZIP Code Control in a Form

```
 1: <%@ Register TagPrefix="WebBook" TagName="ValidatingZip" src="Zips.ascx" %>
 2: <script runat="server" language="vb">
 3:
 4: public sub Submit_Click(Sender as Object, e as EventArgs)
 5:   if MyZip.IsZipValid then
 6:     Response.Write("You entered a valid zip code!<hr>")
 7:   else
 8:     Response.Write(MyZip.ErrorMessage + "<hr>")
 9:   end if
10: end sub
11:
12: </script>
13:
14: <html>
15: <body>
16: <form runat="server">
17:   Please enter your zip code below:<br>
18:
19:   <WebBook:ValidatingZip id="MyZip" Width=200 runat="server"/><br>
20:
21:   <asp:Button Text="Submit" OnClick="Submit_Click" runat="server"/>
22: </form>
23: </body>
24: </html>
```

Figure 6.1 shows the ZIP code user control in an ASP.NET Web form.

**FIGURE 6.1**

*A User Control to Validate Input.*

Of course, this ZIP code control could be reused in other projects that require a ZIP code field on a form.

# Handling Events

User controls can also handle their own events. You can handle an event inside a user control the same way you would for a Web form—by putting the event handler method inside the <script> tags.

Consider a user control that encapsulates an ASP.NET calendar control. This user control might have some extra buttons and drop-down lists to allow the user to change the calendar's colors. Alternatively, a Web form could include the ASP.NET calendar control and extra buttons. However, the Web form would be simpler if you put the extended calendar control inside a user control. This way, you can hide all the details of the extended calendar control, making the containing Web form simpler.

In Listing 6.5, a user control contains an ASP.NET calendar control and extends its functionality to show the number of days left until Christmas.

**LISTING 6.5**   ChristmasCalc.ascx: A Calendar Control That Uses Events

```
1: <script runat="server" language="vb">
2: sub SelectYear(Sender as Object, e as EventArgs)
3:
```

6

**LISTING 6.5**  continued

```
 4:    Dim strYear as String = Year.SelectedItem.Text
 5:    Dim nYear as Integer = Int32.Parse(strYear)
 6:    Cal.VisibleDate = _
 7:      new DateTime(nYear, Cal.VisibleDate.Month, Cal.VisibleDate.Day)
 8:
 9: End Sub
10:
11: sub CalcDaysLeft(Sender as Object, e as EventArgs)
12:
13:    Dim dtSelected as DateTime = Cal.SelectedDate
14:    Dim dtChristmas as new DateTime(dtSelected.Year, 12, 25)
15:    if dtChristmas < dtSelected then
16:      DaysLeft.Text = "You missed Christmas this year."
17:    else
18:      Dim tsDaysLeft as TimeSpan = dtChristmas.Subtract(dtSelected)
19:      DaysLeft.Text = tsDaysLeft.Days.ToString() & _
20:          " days left until Christmas."
21:    end if
22: End Sub
23: </script>
24:
25: <asp:Calendar id="Cal" runat="server"
26:                OnSelectionChanged="CalcDaysLeft" />
27: <br>
28: <asp:DropdownList id="Year" runat="server">
29:    <asp:ListItem>1996</asp:ListItem>
30:    <asp:ListItem>1997</asp:ListItem>
31:    <asp:ListItem>1998</asp:ListItem>
32:    <asp:ListItem>1999</asp:ListItem>
33:    <asp:ListItem>2000</asp:ListItem>
34:    <asp:ListItem>2001</asp:ListItem>
35:    <asp:ListItem>2002</asp:ListItem>
36:    <asp:ListItem>2003</asp:ListItem>
37:    <asp:ListItem>2004</asp:ListItem>
38:    <asp:ListItem>2005</asp:ListItem>
39: </asp:DropdownList>
40: <asp:Button id="YearSel" OnClick="SelectYear"
41:                Text="Change Year" runat="server" />
42: <hr>
43: <asp:Label id="DaysLeft" font-size="18pt" runat="server" />
44: <hr>
```

**ANALYSIS**  Listing 6.5 contains four Web controls: the Calendar control (Lines 25–26), a year selection DropDown control (Lines 28–39), a Button (Lines 40–41), and a Label that displays the number of days left until Christmas (Line 43). The Calendar control contains a definition for the OnSelectionChanged event (Line 26), which will be called whenever a user clicks a particular day on the calendar. Inside the `<script>` tags, the `CalcDaysLeft` event handler (Lines 11–22) calculates the number of days until Christmas, using the `DateTime` and `TimeSpan` classes. After the event handler finds the number of days, it sets the `"DaysLeft"` Label control's text to an appropriate message (Lines 19–20).

This user control also lets a Web user set the calendar control's current year. The Change Year button (Line 40) fires the `SelectYear` event handler (Lines 2–9) that sets the current year on the calendar control.

> **Caution**
>
> Notice that this control doesn't have a `<form>` tag. Never add a `<form>` tag to a user control. If both a user control and containing Web form page have `<form>` tags, the resulting HTML output will contain both tags. Having both tags can lead to unpredictable results.

Let's combine this calendar Web control and the simple control in Listing 6.1 on a Web form. Listing 6.6 shows both controls in action, and Figure 6.2 shows the resulting Web page.

**LISTING 6.6**   TwoControls.aspx: Combining a Simple User Control and a User Control with Events

```
 1: <%@ Register TagPrefix="WebBook" TagName="Calendar"
 2:               src="ChristmasCalc.ascx" %>
 3: <%@ Register TagPrefix="WebBook" TagName="AcmeText" src="Simple.ascx" %>
 4: <html>
 5: <body>
 6:
 7: <form runat="server">
 8:
 9: <table>
10: <tr>
11:   <td valign-"top">
12:   <WebBook:AcmeText runat="server"/>
13: <p>Use the calendar to find out how many days
14:    are left in this shopping season<p>
15:   </td>
16:   <td>
17:    <WebBook:Calendar id="CustomCal" runat="server" />
18:   </td>
19: </tr>
20:</table>
21: </form>
22:
```

6

**LISTING 6.6**   continued

```
23: </body>
24: </html>
```

**FIGURE 6.2**

*Combining two user controls.*

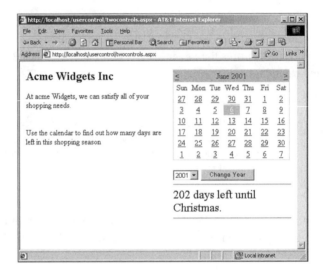

**ANALYSIS**   Listing 6.6 includes the text-only and custom calendar controls from Listings 6.1 and 6.5 through the Register directive (Lines 1–3). Each Register directive includes a user control for use in the page. In addition to the <form> definition (Line 7), the remaining lines in the page just contain HTML code to position the two user controls defined in previous listings. Line 12 includes the simple text-only user control, and Line 17 includes the customized calendar control.

User controls offer great flexibility, especially when combined with more complex built-in Web controls, such as DataGrid, DataList, Repeater, or Calendar.

# Creating Code Behind User Controls

Because you are familiar with using code behind and Web forms from Day 3, "Using Web Forms," learning how to write code behind user controls won't be difficult. Code behind user controls are similar to code behind Web forms.

**Note**

Visual Studio.NET uses code behind by default when you use it to create user controls. The techniques in this section should make clear the process that Visual Studio uses.

Let's convert the extended calendar user control from Listing 6.5 into a code behind version. Listing 6.7 shows part of the new version. Because we are using code behind, the new control will use two files: an .ascx file containing the ASP.NET code and a .vb file containing the code behind.

**LISTING 6.7** ChristmasCalc.vb: The Code Behind for the User Control That Calculates Days Left Until Christmas

```
 1: Imports System
 2: Imports System.Web.UI
 3: Imports System.Web.UI.WebControls
 4:
 5: public class ChristmasCalc
 6:    Inherits UserControl
 7:
 8:    public Cal as Calendar
 9:    public Year as DropDownList
10:    public DaysLeft as Label
11:
12:    public sub SelectYear(Sender as Object, e as EventArgs)
13:
14:      dim strYear as String = Year.SelectedItem.Text
15:      dim nYear as integer = Int32.Parse(strYear)
16:      Cal.VisibleDate = _
17:          new DateTime(nYear, Cal.VisibleDate.Month, Cal.VisibleDate.Day)
18:
19:    end sub
20:
21:    public sub CalcDaysLeft(Sender as Object, e as EventArgs)
22:
23:      Dim dtSelected as DateTime = Cal.SelectedDate
24:      Dim dtChristmas as new DateTime(dtSelected.Year, 12, 25)
25:      if dtChristmas < dtSelected then
26:        DaysLeft.Text = "You missed Christmas this year."
27:      else
28:        TimeSpan tsDaysLeft = dtChristmas.Subtract(dtSelected)
29:        DaysLeft.Text = tsDaysLeft.Days.ToString() & _
30:            " days left until Christmas."
31:      end if
32:    end sub
33: end class
```

**ANALYSIS** We took three steps to create this code behind version of the calendar control:

1. We added the Imports keywords to a new code behind file (Lines 1–3).

2. We put all the code that previously appeared inside the <script> tags inside a custom class derived from the UserControl class (Lines 5–33). All user controls derive from the UserControl class.

3. We added declarations for each Web control that the code references:

```
7:    public Cal as Calendar
8:    public Year as DropDownList
9:    public DaysLeft as Label
```

We also made each event handler a public method, preceding each method declaration with the `public` keyword.

Now we need an .ascx file with the ASP.NET and HTML code, as Listing 6.8 shows.

**LISTING 6.8**  ChristmasCalc.ascx: The Second Half of the Code Behind User Control

```
 1: <%@ Control Inherits="ChristmasCalc" CodeBehind="ChristmasCalc.vb" %>
 2: <asp:Calendar id="Cal" runat="server"
 3:               OnSelectionChanged="CalcDaysLeft" />
 4: <br>
 5: <asp:DropDownList id="Year" runat="server">
 6:    <asp:ListItem>1996</asp:ListItem>
 7:    <asp:ListItem>1997</asp:ListItem>
 8:    <asp:ListItem>1998</asp:ListItem>
 9:    <asp:ListItem>1999</asp:ListItem>
10:    <asp:ListItem>2000</asp:ListItem>
11:    <asp:ListItem>2001</asp:ListItem>
12:    <asp:ListItem>2002</asp:ListItem>
13:    <asp:ListItem>2003</asp:ListItem>
14:    <asp:ListItem>2004</asp:ListItem>
15:    <asp:ListItem>2005</asp:ListItem>
16: </asp:DropdownList>
17: <asp:Button id="YearSel" OnClick="SelectYear"
18:               Text="Change Year" runat="server" />
19: <hr>
20: <asp:Label id="DaysLeft" font-size="18pt" runat="server" />
21: <hr>
```

**ANALYSIS**  Listing 6.8 is similar to the original user control in Listing 6.5, except for two changes. The listing doesn't contain any code within <script> tags because this code has been moved into a code behind file (refer to Listing 6.7).

Listing 6.8 uses the `Control` directive in Line 1. This directive is similar to the `Page` directive used in Web forms because it directs the ASP.NET processor to the code behind file. `Control` directives generally look like the following:

```
<%@ Control Inherits="ClassName" CodeBehind="CodeBehindFileName" %>
```

**Tip**

You also can use the `Assembly` parameter instead of `CodeBehind` in the `Control` directive. Use the `Assembly` parameter when you compile your code behind file into an assembly. Visual Studio.NET uses the `Assembly` parameter instead of the `Src` parameter.

# Caching Web Forms

**NEW TERM**  User controls offer a powerful way to break Web forms into manageable pieces. A second powerful way to manage Web forms involves caching. *Caching* means storing a piece of frequently used data in a place where it can be retrieved quickly.

ASP.NET allows you to cache almost everything that you use in your Web application, including pages, controls, user controls, and objects used on a page. The ASP.NET caching mechanism is flexible enough to allow you to specify a schedule indicating when an item should be removed from the cache. You can set the priority of objects in the cache so that more important objects stay in if memory runs short on the Web server.

## Output Cache Directive

Let's begin the discussion of ASP.NET caching by learning about how ASP.NET caches pages. You might want to cache a page if it doesn't change much but is accessed frequently by users. This might include a page that lists items from a query to the database or a page that uses a complicated algorithm that takes a relatively long time to generate.

**NEW TERM**  ASP.NET has a special name for the cache used to hold pages and controls—the *output cache*. You can control what is put into the output cache by using the `OutputCache` page directive. The following directive puts the current page into the output cache and keeps it there for 10 minutes:

```
<%@ OutputCache Duration="300" VaryByParam="None"%>
```

**Note**

`VaryByParam` tells ASP.NET if different versions of the page should be cached for different HTTP POST or GET parameters. We'll go into more details on caching based on parameters later today.

**6**

You might be wondering where the output cache is located. Most Web browsers cache pages on the client computer, many proxy servers also cache pages, and the Web server itself can cache pages using ASP.NET. You can specify each location by using the

Location parameter. For instance, if you prefer that the current page be cached on the user's browser, you might specify an output cache directive like the following:

```
<@% OutputCache Duration="300" Location="Client" VaryByParam="None" %>
```

The Location parameter can take any of the values listed in Table 6.2.

**TABLE 6.2**  Possible Values for the Location Parameter

| Value | Description |
| --- | --- |
| Server | Cache on the Web server |
| Client | Cache on the Web browser |
| None | Don't cache |
| Downstream | Cache on a proxy server or the client browser |
| Any | Let ASP.NET pick the location |

Let's consider a sample page that gets cached on the server:

```
<@% OutputCache Duration="15" Location="Server" VaryByParam="None" %>
<% Response.Write("Last updated on " + DateTime.Now.ToString()) %>
```

If you try out this page, you will see that the message updates every 15 seconds, even if you click the Refresh button on your browser multiple times.

## Caching Different Versions of Pages

Caching a single ASP page is nice, but many times ASP pages change based on some type of user input. For instance, you might have a page that allows users to pick a certain department in a company and then displays the monthly revenue for each. Caching a different version of the page for each department would be nice. ASP.NET allows you to do just that by using the VaryByParam parameter on the OutputCache directive.

To use VaryByParam, specify a list of the parameters that distinguish each cached version of the page. For instance, the code in Listing 6.9 allows users to pick one of two departments. You can see how each version of the page is cached differently if you run the sample and examine the "last updated" text that's displayed. Notice that we use DeparmentList as the argument for VaryByParam. DepartmentList is the ID of the drop-down list, and when users click the Submit button, one parameter to the page could look like DepartmentList=Manufacturing.

**LISTING 6.9**  ShowDeparmentStats.aspx: Showing Statistics for Each Department of a Company and Caching the Page Based on Department Name

```
<%@ Page Language="vb" %>
<%@ OutputCache Duration="15" VaryByParam="DepartmentList" %>
```

LISTING 6.9   continued

```
<html>
<body>

<script runat="server" >
sub Select_Click(Sender as Object, e as EventArgs)

  Dim strDepName as string = DepartmentList.SelectedItem.Text
  if strDepName = "IS" then
    Response.Write("Information Systems Department<br>")
    Response.Write("Total Revenues: $45m<br>")
    Response.Write("Total Employees: 200<br>")
  else if strDepName = "Manufacturing" then
    Response.Write("Widget Manufacturing Department<br>")
    Response.Write("Total Revenues: $50m<br>")
    Response.Write("Total Employees: 500<br>")
  end if
  Response.Write("Page last generated at " & _
      System.DateTime.Now.ToString())

end sub
</script>

<form runat="server" method="get">
<asp:DropDownList id="DepartmentList" runat="server" >
  <asp:ListItem>IS</asp:ListItem>
  <asp:ListItem>Manufacturing</asp:ListItem>
</asp:DropDownList>
<asp:Button id="Submit" Text="Submit" OnClick="Select_Click" runat="server" />
</form>
</body>
</html>
```

# Page Caching Based on Browser Type

Imagine that you've set up page caching for a frequently accessed page that happens to be rendered differently depending on the client browser type. ASP.NET renders pages differently for browsers that support DHTML automatically, so this client-specific behavior might be happening already on one of your pages. Combined with caching, this behavior can spell trouble because the DHTML version of a page might get cached first. When users with non-DHTML–compliant browsers visit the cached page, they could discover a page that isn't displayed properly.

Luckily, you can cache different versions of a page based on the client browser type by using the VaryByHeader parameter in the OutputPage directive. All you need to do is list the particular HTTP parameters that you care about in the VaryByHeader parameter, and different cached versions of page will be saved for each instance of the parameter. An example is listed in the following code snippet:

6

```
<%@ OutputCache Duration="15" VaryByParam="None" VaryByHeader="User-Agent" %>
```

Every browser sends the User-Agent parameter in with its HTTP requests, and each browser tells its type with this parameter.

Listing 6.10 shows a sample HTTP header string.

**LISTING 6.10** A Sample Header String from a Browser

```
Cache-Control: no-cache
Connection: Keep-Alive
Content-Length: 66
Content-Type: application/x-www-form-urlencoded
Accept: */*
Accept-Encoding: gzip, deflate
Accept-Language: en-us
Host: localhost
Referer: http://localhost/usercontrol/postingpage.aspx
User-Agent: Mozilla/4.0 (compatible; MSIE 6.0; Windows NT 5.0;)
```

Another parameter in the HTTP header that we might use is Accept-Language, which tells us the language of the user's browser.

> **Tip**
>
> To cache by browser and browser language, use the following syntax in the OutputCache command:
>
> VaryByHeader="User-Agent;Accept-Language"
>
> You can append each different parameter with a semicolon.

> **Tip**
>
> You can combine the caching strategies that we have talked about. The VaryByParam and VaryByHeader parameters aren't exclusive.

# Caching User Controls

You saw how Web forms can be cached for better performance on Day 3. Although page caching is flexible, sometimes a page must be regenerated every time the client hits the page. Even in this case, parts of a page might not change frequently. You can put these infrequently changing page parts inside a user control and cache the user control by itself, leaving the rest of the page to regenerate on every page hit.

Consider a page used for searching. The part that displays search results will change for every query the user types. Caching the search results would be counterproductive; soon the cache would grow huge with every different search result. The odds of a cached page being fetched from memory for a second hit would be quite low.

However, suppose that this page also shows a list of topics that could be search targets, along with some text explaining good ways to enter a search string. This part of the page would be a great candidate for caching: It never changes, and it appears every time a user searches the Web site.

**NEW TERM** For this example, one approach might be to encapsulate the static part of the page in a user control, which could then be cached. ASP.NET refers to caching with user controls as *fragment caching*. By caching user controls, you cache fragments of a page. You can cache a user control the same way you cache a page—by using the `OutputCache` directive.

## Implementing a Page with Cached User Controls

Let's look at a page that uses a few cached user controls. We'll revise the sample used in Day 3's lesson that displayed statistics about a company department to use a cached user control. The sample page uses a cached control for the header, a noncached control for the page results, and a containing page to allow the user to select a company department. Listings 6.11, 6.12, and 6.13 show the code, and Figure 6.3 shows the resulting Web page.

**LISTING 6.11** Header.ascx: A User Control That Encapsulates the Header for a Department List Page

```
1: <%@ OutputCache Duration="15" VaryByParam="none" %>
2: <h3>Wonderful Widgets Incorporated - Department Statistics</h3>
3: <p>Select a department from the list below, and press the Submit button<p>
4: <% Response.Write("<i>Header last generated at " & _
5:    DateTime.Now.ToString() & "</i><br>") %>
```

**LISTING 6.12** Results.ascx: A Control That Displays Query Results

```
1: <%@ Control language="vb" %>
2: <script runat="server">
3:
4: 'This is a definition for public property that will change the
5: 'output of this user control
6: public DepartmentName as String
7:
8: </script>
```

6

**LISTING 6.12**   continued

```
 9: <hr>
10: <font size="5">
11: <%
12:   if DepartmentName = "IS" then
13:     Response.Write("Information Systems Department<br>")
14:     Response.Write("Total Revenues: $45m<br>")
15:     Response.Write("Total Employees: 200<br>")
16:   else if DepartmentName = "Manufacturing" then
17:     Response.Write("Widget Manufacturing Department<br>")
18:     Response.Write("Total Revenues: $50m<br>")
19:     Response.Write("Total Employees: 500<br>")
20:   end if
21: %>
22: </font>
```

**LISTING 6.13**   DepartmentStats.aspx: A Department List Using Cached Header User Controls and a Noncached Results Control

```
 1: <%@ Page Language="vb" %>
 2: <%@ Register TagPrefix="WebBook" TagName="Header" src="Header.ascx" %>
 3: <%@ Register TagPrefix="WebBook" TagName="Results" src="Results.ascx" %>
 4:
 5: <script runat="server">
 6: sub Select_Click(Sender as Object, e as CommandEventArgs)
 7:
 8:   'Set the department name property of the Results control
 9:   Results.DepartmentName = DepartmentList.SelectedItem.Text
10:
11: end sub
12: </script>
13:
14: <html>
15: <body>
16: <WebBook:Header runat="server"/>
17:
18: <WebBook:Results id="Results" runat="server"/>
19:
20: <form runat="server">
21: Department: <asp:DropDownList id="DepartmentList" runat="server" >
22:   <asp:ListItem>IS</asp:ListItem>
23:   <asp:ListItem>Manufacturing</asp:ListItem>
24: </asp:DropDownList>
25: <asp:Button id="Submit" Text="Submit" OnCommand="Select_Click"
26:              runat="server" />
27: </form>
28:
29: </body>
30: </html>
```

**FIGURE 6.3**

*Caching the output of user controls.*

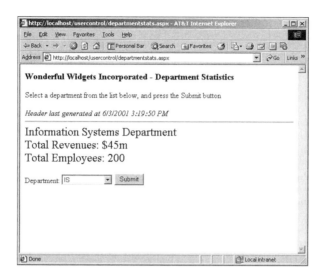

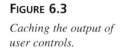 Listing 6.11, containing the file Header.ascx, shows header text for a page. It's cached for a duration of 15 seconds, using the Duration parameter (Line 1). It also contains code that writes out when the page was last generated (Lines 4–5) so that you can see control caching in action if you run the sample.

The user control in Listing 6.12 displays information about two different departments. Depending on how the DepartmentName parameter (Line 6) is set by the containing Web form, the Information Systems department's statistics will be shown (Lines 12–16), or the Manufacturing department's statistics will be shown (Lines 17–21). This control isn't cached. In a practical application, a control like this may query a database to generate statistics about a company department.

The Web form in Listing 6.13 includes both user controls (Lines 16 and 18). This Web form isn't cached but relies on the contained user controls to perform their own caching.

> **Tip**
>
> In many Web forms, you might need to change different parts located at the middle or end when the user makes a selection. The easiest way to do so is to create a user control for the page part that will change and then embed it into a Web form container page.

**6**

## Caching Different Versions of a User Control

Results.ascx in Listing 6.15 contains hard-coded information to display statistics about two departments in a company. A more practical control that displayed department statistics might query a database for the latest information to display.

If the Results control did make several queries to the database, it might be a good candidate for caching. The statistics that you might display for a company department may not change every millisecond. In this case, caching a different version of the Results control for every company department could increase performance by limiting the number of database queries.

You can cache different versions of a user control by using the VaryByParam parameter just like you would with Web forms. For example, you just need to add the following line to the beginning of Listing 6.13 to make caching work for the Results collection:

```
<%@ OutputCache Duration="30" VaryByParam="DepartmentList" %>
```

Next, you would read the value of DepartmentList inside the Results control, with a line like the following:

```
Dim DepartmentName as String = Request("DepartmentList")
```

The modified code would look like Listing 6.14.

**LISTING 6.14**   Results2.ascx: Reading Information from the Request Object

```
<%@ OutputCache Duration="30" VaryByParam="DepartmentList" %>
<%@ Control language="vb" %>
<%
  Dim DepartmentName as string = Request("DepartmentList")
  if DepartmentName = "IS" then
    Response.Write("Information Systems Department<br>")
    Response.Write("Total Revenues: $45m<br>")
    Response.Write("Total Employees: 200<br>")
  else if DepartmentName = "Manufacturing" then
    Response.Write("Widget Manufacturing Department<br>")
    Response.Write("Total Revenues: $50m<br>")
    Response.Write("Total Employees: 500<br>")
  end if
%>
</font>
```

Writing the Results control this way makes the containing page much simpler. Now the containing page doesn't need an event handler for the button because the Results control takes care of the submit action. Listing 6.15 shows a simplified Web form that uses Listing 6.14 to process the results of a submit action.

**LISTING 6.15**   DepartmentStats2.aspx: A Department List Using Two Cached Controls

```
<%@ Page Language="vb" %>
<%@ Register TagPrefix="WebBook" TagName="Header" src="Header.ascx" %>
```

**LISTING 6.15**  continued

```
<%@ Register TagPrefix="WebBook" TagName="Results" src="Results2.ascx" %>
<html>
<body>
<WebBook:Header runat="server"/>

<WebBook:Results id="Results" runat="server"/>

<form runat="server">
Department:
<asp:DropDownList id="DepartmentList" runat="server" >
  <asp:ListItem>IS</asp:ListItem>
  <asp:ListItem>Manufacturing</asp:ListItem>
</asp:DropDownList>

<asp:Button id="Submit" Text="Submit" runat="server" />
</form>

</body>
</html>
```

Listing 6.15 contains a drop-down list and submit button. The user control in Listing 6.14 handles the results of the page when the user clicks the submit button.

# Summary

Today you learned how to create user controls. You saw how user controls are a better alternative to the #include directive and how they can encapsulate groups of related controls in a Web form.

User controls can contain code. ASP.NET Web controls and HTML and are similar to Web forms. These controls contain their own directive, named Control.

You learned how to use the Register directive inside Web forms. This directive includes user controls in your Web forms.

You also saw how to use code behind and user controls together. By using code behind, you can separate code logic from the user interface presentation and make your application easier to maintain.

Last, you learned how to use page caching and fragment caching with your user controls. Caching Web forms and user controls allows you to optimize your Web site's performance.

Tomorrow you will learn a second technique for creating your own controls: custom ASP.NET controls.

6

# Q&A

**Q Will adding user controls slow down my application?**

**A** Adding user controls will introduce a small performance penalty. However, the gains in code encapsulation should more than offset this penalty. You also can apply the caching techniques in today's lesson for faster performance.

**Q I like the idea of adding caching to my Web application. At what point should I do so?**

**A** Add caching at the very last possible moment as an optimization. If caching is applied too early in the development process, it may mask errors in Web form or user control code, and it may also introduce subtle bugs. One approach that you might take is to disable all caching and debug the application completely. Then add caching where needed.

# Workshop

The Workshop provides quiz questions to help you solidify your understanding of the material covered and exercises to provide you with experience in using what you've learned. The answers to the quiz questions are provided in Appendix A, "Answers to Quizzes and Exercises."

## Quiz

1. What is the main mechanism for code reusing in Web forms?
2. What advantages do user controls offer?
3. Do user controls support custom properties? If so, how?
4. Do user controls support events? If so, how?
5. Should the <form> tag be used within a user control?
6. What is fragment caching?
7. What parameter sets the length of time that a Web form or user control should be held in memory when cached?
8. What directive enables caching for a Web form or user control?
9. What parameter is used to store multiple versions of a cached Web form or user control?

## Exercises

1. Add a Height parameter to Listing 6.3 to get and set the height of the text box for the sample.
2. Investigate the Cache property of the Page class. How can it be used for caching?

# DAY 7

# Writing Internet Applications for Mobile Devices

Mobile devices, such as Personal Digital Assistants (PDAs) and cellular phones with Web access, are growing in popularity. The infrastructure that makes up the "wireless web" is becoming larger and more reliable with each passing day, and it's quite likely that the mobile user market will continue to grow. However, many developers discard the idea of supporting PDAs and cell phones for their Web sites because the cost of adding extra pages to support these devices is too high. In particular, cell phones use an entirely different standard for consuming Web pages, called Wireless Markup Language (WML). Creating special WML pages takes extra time and effort.

Fortunately, the "mobile" version of ASP.NET makes writing Web pages for mobile devices a much easier task. By using the ASP.NET Mobile Software Development Kit (*Mobile SDK* in future references), you can create Web pages using the same ASP.NET constructs that you've seen in the last few lessons.

You can use your current server hardware and software configuration to support mobile devices by using the ASP.NET Mobile SDK for your Web pages. The Mobile SDK doesn't eliminate all the headaches surrounding mobile device support, but it makes a daunting task much more manageable.

Today's lesson gives an overview of the ASP.NET Mobile SDK, including explanations of new techniques you can use to create mobile-ready Web applications. Today you will learn how to do the following:

- Write ASP.NET mobile pages that any mobile device can use
- Customize each page for different devices without trouble
- Use each ASP.NET mobile Web control
- Find a suitable mobile device emulation program so that you can be sure your mobile site works

# Introducing Mobile Device Support

Mobile devices come in many flavors, making it difficult to design a Web site that supports all of them. Your users might own a few of these mobile devices:

- Windows CE–compatible PDAs, such as the HP Journada, Casio Cassiopeia, Compaq iPAQ, and @migo. This group of devices are known as Pocket PCs.
- Palm-compatible PDAs, such the Palm III and higher and Handspring Visor.
- Myriad Web-enabled cell phones. For example, the latest models from Nokia, Ericsson, Motorola, Samsung, Sanyo, and other manufacturers can access the Internet.

PDA devices can view most HTML pages. Some support JavaScript, and many don't. Most cell phones can't view HTML pages but use the WML standard for Web access.

## Downloading and Installing the Mobile Internet Toolkit

Before running any of the code samples in today's lesson, you need to download and install the ASP.NET Mobile SDK, contained in the Mobile Internet Toolkit. You can find the toolkit at `www.microsoft.com/ISN/downloads.asp`, under the Software Development Kits link.

After installing the toolkit, you should have a link to the Mobile Internet Toolkit local Web page on your desktop. Open this link to find the SDK documentation.

# HTML and Mobile Devices

PDA devices render HTML and can view many existing Web sites without problems. Many of these devices support JavaScript, cookies, and image files, so designing PDA-accessible Web sites is relatively easy. The main constraint is that PDA devices have smaller screens than desktops.

Currently, only high-end cell phones can render HTML, and even these devices support a limited subset of the HTML standard. As the next section will show, ASP.NET will output pages in a suitable format for the device, so you don't have to be concerned about this problem.

Today's lesson will explain how to interrogate each client device for its screen size, JavaScript capabilities, cookie support, and other attributes so that you can create special logic to render different versions of a page. This way, you can create pages that look as though they were designed especially for each different mobile device.

Input capabilities for mobile devices vary. Every mobile device contains at least some sort of a Back button to display the previous screen. All mobile devices also contain a button to select a link and scroll through the contents of a page; they also have numeric input capabilities. Typically, all mobile devices make it difficult for users to enter alphanumeric text.

You can use this knowledge to create "mobile-friendly" sites. Such sites contain a home page with limited options and many small pages showing a single feature. Most users don't mind tapping the Back button a few times to return to the home page. However, navigating through a lengthy page can involve tapping the Scroll Down button many times, which makes for a bad experience. Avoid creating screens that require detailed input.

Figure 7.1 shows an example of a typical page on a cell phone device. The figure uses a cell phone emulation program. You can download many different mobile device emulation programs for free, as today's lesson will explain shortly.

# Introducing WML

**New Term**  Because all Web-enabled cell phones can view WML pages, it's helpful to know a little bit about the WML standard. WML is based on eXtensible Markup Language (XML). Today's lesson won't explore XML in depth, but tomorrow's lesson will give an extensive review of the standard. XML files use tags similar to HTML but also contain special header lines. XML files can also have *Schema* files associated with them to specify their structure and what kinds of tags the files can support. Listing 7.1 shows a simple WML page.

7

**FIGURE 7.1**

*A web page rendered on a mobile device, using a cell phone emulation program.*

**LISTING 7.1** Code for a Simple WML Page

```
 1: <?xml version="1.0"?>
 2: <!DOCTYPE wml PUBLIC "-//WAPFORUM//DTD WML 1.1//EN"
 3:     "http://www.wapforum.org/DTD/wml_1.1.xml">
 4: <wml>
 5:     <card>
 6:       <p>
 7:         Hello!
 8:       </p>
 9:     </card>
10: </wml>
```

**ANALYSIS** Line 1 is the standard XML header that every XML file, including WML pages, must contain. Lines 2 and 3 specify a Schema file for this WML file. Don't worry about the details of XML Schemas at this time; tomorrow's lesson will give complete details.

**NEW TERM** Every WML page uses the <wml> tag (Lines 4 and 10). WML files are made up of *cards* (Lines 5 and 9), each of which corresponds to a single screen listing on a cell phone. You can use a subset of the standard HTML tags within each card definition. Lines 6–8 contain a hello message within the standard paragraph (<p>) tags.

By using ASP.NET, you don't need to know any more about WML files than what Listing 7.1 illustrates. ASP.NET detects whether the requesting client is a cell phone device and renders WML files automatically. This means that you never have to create WML files explicitly. Not only do you not have to create WML files, you shouldn't use raw WML pages in any of your ASP.NET mobile code because most PDA devices don't know how to render WML files. The best approach is to let ASP.NET deal with how each page should be rendered.

## Finding an Emulator

 You should use a cell phone or PDA emulator program to test your mobile-accessible Web pages. An *emulator program* simulates a cell phone or PDA on your desktop, so you can use it as a virtual mobile device. Although you can browse to each ASP.NET mobile page using a standard desktop Web browser, you won't get a realistic picture of how the page will look on a mobile device unless you use an emulator.

Microsoft has created two emulators: one for cell phones and one for Windows CE–compatible PDAs. You can download the cell phone emulator from `www.microsoft.com/mobile/phones/mme`. The PDA emulator, part of the Microsoft eMbedded Visual Tools package, is available at `www.microsoft.com/mobile/downloads`. Both downloads are free.

> **Note** The Microsoft eMbedded Visual Tools package is a very large file, and you can't download the PDA emulator in its own file.

Openwave makes an excellent cell phone emulator, which can simulate many popular mobile phone devices. It's available at `http://developer.openwave.com/download/index.html`, under the Products link. Figure 7.2 shows the Openwave cell phone emulator and the Microsoft phone and PDA emulation programs, all pointing to Listing 7.1.

You can find Palm emulation programs at `http://www.palmos.com/dev/tech/tools/emulator`. The emulator comes with strict licensing requirements and organizations located outside the United States have limited access.

> **Note** The Palm emulation program requires specialized ROM files to operate correctly. To obtain the ROM files, you must be a member of the Palm development community. To join the community, click the Join link at the emulator download site. Your membership information takes a day or so to check, so you can't use the emulator immediately.

7

FIGURE 7.2

*Mobile device emulation programs.*

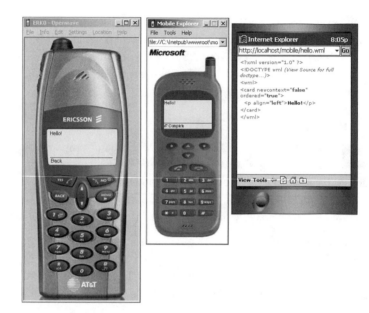

Downloading and installing the mobile device emulation programs will be the most time-consuming and frustrating portion of today's lesson. You have to complete this painful but necessary process only once.

# Creating Mobile Web Forms

Every mobile Web page needs to include the ASP.NET mobile library classes contained in the assembly called System.Web.Mobile.dll. These classes contain definitions of mobile Web controls used extensively in mobile programming. Let's look at simple mobile Web page that uses the Form and TextView controls (see Listing 7.2).

LISTING 7.2    Hello.aspx: A Simple Message for Any Mobile Device

```
 1: <%@ Page Inherits="System.Web.UI.MobileControls.MobilePage"
 2:          Language="vb" %>
 3: <%@ Register TagPrefix="mobile"
 4:              Namespace="System.Web.UI.MobileControls"
 5:              Assembly="System.Web.Mobile" %>
 6:
 7: <mobile:Form runat="server" >
 8:     <mobile:TextView runat="server">
 9: Hello!
10:     </mobile:TextView>
11: </mobile:Form>
```

**ANALYSIS** Lines 1 and 2 include the MobilePage class, which contains definitions for many of the stock mobile classes, including the Form control (Line 7). Lines 3–5 include the Mobile control's namespace, which defines the remaining ASP.NET mobile controls. Every mobile page will use Lines 1–5.

Line 7 declares a mobile form, which corresponds to a single page displayed on a cell phone or PDA. The TextView control (Line 8) includes simple text messages.

The output of Hello.aspx is identical to the output of Listing 7.1, shown in Figure 7.2.

## Using Multiple Forms Per Page

Mobile pages use multiple forms per .aspx file. This way, you can organize your code into a smaller number of files, each containing multiple related screens. The first form defined in an .aspx file is shown first to client programs. You can display other forms by setting the page's ActiveForm property or by appending the second form ID property to the URL using the # character. Listing 7.3 shows an example that uses the Link control to select different forms.

**LISTING 7.3** QandA.aspx: Using Two Mobile Forms on One Page

```
 1: <%@ Page Inherits="System.Web.UI.MobileControls.MobilePage"
 2:         Language="vb" %>
 3: <%@ Register TagPrefix="mobile"
 4:             Namespace="System.Web.UI.MobileControls"
 5:             Assembly="System.Web.Mobile" %>
 6:
 7: <mobile:Form runat="server" id="QuestionForm">
 8:     <mobile:TextView runat="server">
 9:         Is mobile programming difficult?
10:     </mobile:TextView>
11:     <mobile:Link runat="server"
12:         NavigateURL="#AnswerForm">Answer</mobile:Link>
13: </mobile:Form>
14:
15: <mobile:Form runat="server" id="AnswerForm">
16:     <mobile:TextView runat="server">
17:         Not at all!
18:     </mobile:TextView>
19: </mobile:Form>
```

**ANALYSIS** The first form (Lines 7–13) contains a TextView control (Lines 8–10) and a Link control (Lines 11–12). The NavigateURL property uses "#AnswerForm" to invoke the second form, whose full URL is "QandA.aspx#AnswerForm". Lines 15–19 define the second form, which also contains a TextView control.

7

## Pagination

The mobile form control contains automatic pagination features. This form segments a long text message into smaller pages so that users can tap the Select button or tap a link at the bottom of the page to view each screen. ASP.NET paginates the page appropriately for each device, so a PDA sees more information per page than a cell phone. To use automatic pagination, set the `Paginate` property to `true` in the form control. Some other mobile Web controls also contain automatic pagination features, as we'll show shortly. Listing 17.4 shows a mobile form that uses automatic pagination. The `Paginate` property is set in Line 7.

**LISTING 17.4**    LongPage.aspx: Using Automatic Pagination

```
 1: <%@ Page Inherits="System.Web.UI.MobileControls.MobilePage"
 2:          Language="vb" %>
 3: <%@ Register TagPrefix="mobile"
 4:              Namespace="System.Web.UI.MobileControls"
 5:              Assembly="System.Web.Mobile" %>
 6:
 7: <mobile:Form runat="server" Paginate="true">
 8:     <mobile:TextView runat="server">
 9: When in the Course of human events, it becomes necessary
10: for one people to dissolve the political bands which have
11: connected them with another, and to assume among the powers
12: of the earth, the separate and equal station to which the
13: Laws of Nature and of Nature's God entitle them, a decent
14: respect to the opinions of mankind requires that they
15: should declare the causes which impel them to the separation.
16:     </mobile:TextView>
17: </mobile:Form>
```

## Headers and Footers

You can include a header and footer for your mobile forms by using the HeaderTemplate and FooterTemplate subcontrols. The example in Listing 7.5 also uses the Label control.

**LISTING 7.5**    News.aspx: Using Headers and Footers

```
 1: <%@ Page Inherits="System.Web.UI.MobileControls.MobilePage"
 2:          Language="vb" %>
 3: <%@ Register TagPrefix="mobile"
 4:              Namespace="System.Web.UI.MobileControls"
 5:              Assembly="System.Web.Mobile" %>
 6:
 7: <mobile:Form runat="server" Paginate="true" >
```

**LISTING 7.5** continued

```
 8:    <HeaderTemplate>
 9:      <mobile:Label runat="server" Text="Acme News" />
10:    </HeaderTemplate>
11:
12:    <mobile:TextView runat="server">
13: News from around the globe...
14:    </mobile:TextView>
15:
16:    <FooterTemplate>
17:      <mobile:Label runat="server" Text="News all the time" />
18:    </FooterTemplate>
19: </mobile:Form>
```

**ANALYSIS** The HeaderTemplate control is defined in Lines 8–10. You can include any other kinds of mobile controls within the header and footer; in this example, the Label control (Line 9) displays a string. The FooterTemplate control (Lines 16–18) also displays a simple string.

# Working with Mobile Web Controls

ASP.NET mobile includes a few of the standard ASP.NET Web controls that you've seen in previous lessons and also includes some new controls designed specifically for the limited screen sizes of mobile devices.

Table 7.1 shows mobile Web controls used for displaying data. Some of these controls, such as SelectionList and ObjectList, allow users to select the items that they display and send events to event handler methods. Mobile controls also support data binding, either through an explicit DataSource property or by using the DataBinder.Eval method. ASP.NET mobile also contains a limited number of input controls, as listed in Table 7.1.

**TABLE 7.1** Mobile Display and Input Controls

| Control | Description |
| --- | --- |
| **Data Display Controls** | |
| TextView | Displays HTML text in a device-specific way. |
| Label | Displays strings. Text can be set programmatically with the Text property. |
| List | Displays a bulleted list of items, which users can select. Sends the ItemCommand event when users select an item. Can be populated with server code. |
| SelectionList | Displays a list of items. Can be populated with server code. You must use another control to submit user selections. |

7

**TABLE 7.1** continued

| Control | Description |
|---|---|
| **Data Display Controls** | |
| ObjectList | Displays programmer-defined objects. Can be used to create complex list elements that contain graphics. |
| **Input Controls** | |
| TextBox | Allows for alphanumeric input. Can be set to allow only numeric input using the Numeric property. |
| Button | Appears as a link on cell phone devices. |
| Link | Appears as a standard hyperlink control. |

All validation controls are available through ASP.NET mobile. They include the CompareValidator, RangeValidator, RegularExpressionValidator, CustomValidator, and SummaryValidator controls. Review Day 4, "Working with Web Controls," for code examples that use these controls.

The AdRotator, Calendar, and Image controls are also available but might not be supported for every mobile device. The "Customizing Pages by Device Type" section later today describes methods for showing alternate output for these limited mobile devices.

The Call control can be used for cell phones and PDAs that can make telephone calls. Set the Text property to a message that you want to display on the device and the PhoneNumber property to a number that the device should dial when the control is selected.

## Control Example

Listing 7.6 shows a sample mobile application that displays predictions for a user's day and stock market portfolio. It uses multiple pages and a few of the Web controls from today's lesson.

**LISTING 7.6** Predict.aspx: Making Predictions and Using Some Mobile Web Controls

```
1: <%@ Page Inherits="System.Web.UI.MobileControls.MobilePage"
2:          Language="vb" debug="true" %>
3: <%@ Register TagPrefix="mobile"
4:              Namespace="System.Web.UI.MobileControls"
5:              Assembly="System.Web.Mobile" %>
6:
7: <script runat="server" >
8:
9: private class Prediction
```

**LISTING 7.6**    continued

```
10:
11:    private pname as String
12:    private pdayPrediction as String
13:    private pstockPrediction as String
14:
15:    public sub New(name as string, dayPrediction as String, _
16:       stockPrediction as String)
17:
18:      me.pname = name
19:      me.pdayPrediction = dayPrediction
20:      me.pstockPrediction = stockPrediction
21:
22:    End Sub
23:
24:    public ReadOnly Property Name() as string
25:
26:      get
27:        return me.pname
28:      end get
29:
30:    End Property
31:
32:    public ReadOnly Property DayPrediction() as string
33:
34:      get
35:        return me.pdayPrediction
36:      end get
37:
38:    End Property
39:
40:    public Readonly Property StockPrediction() as string
41:
42:      get
43:        return me.pstockPrediction
44:      end get
45:
46:    End Property
47:
48: End Class
49:
50: protected predictionArray as ArrayList
51: protected predictionNumber as integer
52:
53: protected sub Page_Load(sender as Object, e as EventArgs)
54:
55:    predictionArray = new ArrayList()
56:    predictionArray.Add(new Prediction("great", _
57:                         "you will win the lottery!", _
58:                         "the market will gain 500 points!"))
```

**LISTING 7.6**  continued

```
59:    predictionArray.Add(new Prediction("good", _
60:                          "you will lose 1 pound.", _
61:                          "the market will gain 100 points"))
62:    predictionArray.Add(new Prediction("ok", _
63:                          "your car will run smoothly", _
64:                          "the market will close mixed"))
65:    predictionNumber = DateTime.Now.Millisecond Mod 3
66:
67: End Sub
68:
69: protected sub Predict(sender as object, e as ListCommandEventArgs)
70:
71:    Dim p as Prediction
72:    p = CType(predictionArray(predictionNumber), Prediction)
73:
74:    if e.ListItem.Value = "PredictDay" then
75:
76:      DayLabel.Text = p.DayPrediction
77:      ActiveForm = DayForm
78:
79:    End If
80:
81:    if e.ListItem.Value = "PredictStock" then
82:
83:      StockLabel.Text = p.StockPrediction
84:      ActiveForm = StockForm
85:
86:    End If
87: End Sub
88: </script>
89:
90: <mobile:Form runat="server">
91:    <mobile:Label runat="server">Check the Oracle</mobile:Label>
92:    <mobile:List runat="server" OnItemCommand="Predict">
93:      <Item Text="Check your future today"
94:            Value="PredictDay"/>
95:      <Item Text="Check your portfolio's future today"
96:            Value="PredictStock"/>
97:    </mobile:List>
98: </mobile:Form>
99:
100: <mobile:Form id="DayForm" runat="server">
101:    Today, <mobile:Label runat="server" id="DayLabel" />
102: </mobile:Form>
103:
104: <mobile:Form id="StockForm" runat="server">
105:    Today, <mobile:Label runat="server" id="StockLabel" />
106: </mobile:Form>
```

**ANALYSIS** Lines 9–48 define the `Prediction` class, which simply stores three strings: a name, prediction for a day, and prediction for the stock market. Lines 53–67 define the `Page_Load` method, which populates an `ArrayList` object that stores a list of predictions (Line 55). It also calculates a choice from the list based on the current millisecond (Line 65).

The `Predict` event handler (Lines 69–87) moves users to the day prediction form (Lines 76–77) or the portfolio prediction form (Lines 83–84), depending on what menu option users select from the List control. It also sets a label on each prediction form appropriately. The event handler sets the current form using the `ActiveForm` property (Lines 77 and 84).

# Customizing Pages by Device Type

ASP.NET mobile allows you to create device-specific content using two methods:

- You can use the `Request.Browser` class to detect any device's exact capabilities by testing specific properties such as `JavaScript` and `CanSendMail`.
- Another method doesn't rely on any conditional logic and allows you to define specialized versions of each Web control.

The following sections will give examples for both methods.

## Device Capabilities

Although ASP.NET mobile renders customized output for each browser, you may, unfortunately, have to create special logic if your mobile site displays graphics or complex Web controls such as Calendar or AdRotator. Luckily, detecting the exact capabilities of each device is an easy process when you use the `MobileCapabilities` class.

Standard ASP.NET pages can use the `BrowserCapabilities` class to detect the client browser name, version, and scripting support. The `Request.Browser` object is of type `BrowserCapabilities`, and Day 2, "Introducing ASP.NET," gave an example that used it. ASP.NET mobile extends the `BrowserCapabilities` class through the `MobileCapabilities` class. You can access the mobile capabilities of any device by using the same `Request.Browser` class.

Table 7.2 lists a subset of the `MobileCapabilities` public properties. The class contains a huge number of properties that can be used to detect more arcane aspects of each mobile device. Consult the SDK documentation for a complete list of properties.

7

**TABLE 7.2**  MobileCapabilities Properties

| Property | Description |
|----------|-------------|
| ScreenCharactersHeight | The height of the device's screen, in characters |
| ScreenCharactersWidth | The width of the device's screen |
| ScreenPixelsHeight | Height in pixels |
| ScreenPixelsWidth | Width in pixels |
| IsColor | True if the device supports color |
| Cookies | True if the device supports cookies |
| Browser | Name of the client browser |
| JavaScript | True if the device supports JavaScript |
| VBScript | True if the device supports Visual Basic Scripting |
| SupportsCSS | True if the device supports Cascading Style Sheets |
| CanInitiateVoiceCall | True if the device can make telephone calls |
| CanSendMail | True if the device can send e-mail |
| MobileDeviceModel | Device model name |
| MobileDeviceManufacturer | Device manufacturer's name |
| HasBackButton | True if the device has a Back button |

Listing 7.7 shows a program that will display all possible device capability properties in the Request.Browser object.

**LISTING 7.7**  Capabilities.aspx: Showing All Device Capabilities

```
 1: <%@ Page Inherits="System.Web.UI.MobileControls.MobilePage"
 2:         Language="vb" %>
 3: <%@ Register TagPrefix="mobile"
 4:            Namespace="System.Web.UI.MobileControls"
 5:            Assembly="System.Web.Mobile" %>
 6: <%@ Import Namespace="System.ComponentModel" %>
 7:
 8: <script runat="server">
 9: protected sub Page_Load(sender as Object, e as EventArgs)
10:
11:   if  not IsPostBack then
12:     Dim properties as PropertyDescriptorCollection = _
13:       TypeDescriptor.GetProperties(Request.Browser)
14:
15:     CapabilityList.DataSource = properties
16:     CapabilityList.DataBind()
17:   End If
18:
```

**LISTING 7.7**    continued

```
19: End sub
20:
21: protected Sub DisplayProp(sender as object, e as ListCommandEventArgs )
22:
23:     Dim propertyName as string = e.ListItem.Text
24:     Name.Text = propertyName
25:     Value.Text = _
26:       DataBinder.Eval(Request.Browser, propertyName, "{0}")
27:   ActiveForm = ValueForm
28:
29: End Sub
30: </script>
31:
32: <mobile:Form runat="server" Paginate="True">
33:   <mobile:List runat="server" id="CapabilityList"
34:     DataTextField="Name"
35:     OnItemCommand="DisplayProp"  />
36: </mobile:Form>
37:
38: <mobile:Form runat="server" id="ValueForm">
39:   <mobile:Label runat="server" id="Name"
40:         StyleReference="title" />
41:   <mobile:Label runat="server" id="Value" />
42: </mobile:Form>
```

**ANALYSIS**   Listing 7.7 uses the TypeDescriptor object (Line 13). This class can be used to find any collection object's complete list of properties, using the GetProperties method. TypeDescriptor is part of the System.ComponentModel namespace, included on Line 6.

The PropertyDescriptorCollection returned from the GetProperties method (Lines 12–13) contains a Name property used to access the name of each target object's properties. The List control's DataTextField property is set to "Name" (Line 34) so that the control can be bound to the property descriptor collection (Lines 15–16).

The MobileCapabilities class contains the HasCapability method, which you can use as a quick check to see whether the device supports a given capability. For example, you can use the method like this:

```
if Request.Broswer.HasCapability("JavaScript", "true") then

    'render javascript functions
End If
```

**7**

## Device Filters

A second method for creating device-specific code uses device filters. You define these filters using special entries in the web.config file, which you can place in any directory or subdirectory of your site. Day 18, "Configuring Internet Applications," will give a detailed explanation of how to configure Web applications and Web Services using the web.config file. Today's discussion will focus on using the file for mobile devices.

Listing 7.8 shows a sample web.config file that defines a custom filter to detect whether a mobile device supports JavaScript.

**LISTING 7.8**  Creating a Device-Specific Filter

```
1: <configuration>
2:   <system.web>
3:     <deviceFilters>
4:       <filter name="UsesJava"
5:               compare="JavaScript"
6:               argument="true" />
7:     </deviceFilters>
8:   </system.web>
9: </configuration>
```

**ANALYSIS**  Every web.config file must start with the <configuration> and <system.web> tags (Lines 1–2). The <deviceFilters> tag (Line 3) declares the start of one or more custom device filters.

A custom filter contains three attributes: name, compare, and argument. The name attribute (Line 4) can be anything you want. You can use whatever name you come up with later in your ASP.NET pages. The compare attribute must be one of the values from the MobileCapabilities class listed in Table 7.2. The argument attribute defines a value that will be compared against the device property. If the argument matches the device capability property, the filter's value will be true.

Listing 7.9 shows a page that uses the custom filter from the previous listing to display two alternate messages. This listing uses several new Web control elements, including the <DeviceSpecific> and <Choice> tags.

**LISTING 7.9**  Java.aspx: Using Device Filters to Display Different Strings

```
1: <%@ Page Inherits="System.Web.UI.MobileControls.MobilePage"
2:         Language="vb" %>
3: <%@ Register TagPrefix="mobile"
```

**LISTING 7.9**  continued

```
 4:                 Namespace="System.Web.UI.MobileControls"
 5:                 Assembly="System.Web.Mobile" %>
 6:
 7: <mobile:Form runat="server" >
 8:   <mobile:TextView runat="server">
 9:     <DeviceSpecific>
10:       <Choice Filter="UsesJava"
11:             Text="Your device can use JavaScript" />
12:       <Choice Text="Your device does not use JavaScript" />
13:     </DeviceSpecific>
14:   </mobile:TextView>
15: </mobile:Form>
```

**ANALYSIS**   Line 8 defines a standard mobile control—in this case, TextView—which is rendered differently depending on the value of the custom filter from Listing 7.8.

Lines 9–13 contain a special section using the <DeviceSpecific> tag. This tag can contain one or more <Choice> tags, which are used to set a mobile control's properties differently depending on a filter's result.

The first <Choice> tag (Lines 10–11) is used if the custom filter named UsesJava evaluates to true. The <Choice> tag can contain any number of properties from the Web control; in this case, the Text property sets the output of the TextView label control. The second <Choice> tag (Line 12) is used if all the previous <Choice> tags aren't selected. You can use a <Choice> tag with no Filter parameter, like on Line 12, for default behavior.

This declarative style of control customization is elegant because you don't have to write special logic for each kind of device that you need to support. You will probably use a combination of the methods described in this and the previous section for your applications.

# Using Style Sheets

Most mobile devices don't support Cascading Style Sheets (CSS), but ASP.NET mobile provides an easy way to apply custom styles using the Web control attributes and the StyleSheet control. Every mobile Web control supports the style attributes listed in Table 7.3, a limited subset of normal controls.

7

**TABLE 7.3**    Mobile Web Control Style Attributes

| Attribute | Description |
| --- | --- |
| Font-Name | Specifies the font name, such as Arial or Courier |
| Font-Bold | Boldfaces the font when set to `true` |
| Font-Italic | Italicizes the font |
| Font-Size | Sets the font size to Large, Normal, or Small |
| ForeColor | Specifies the foreground text color |
| BackColor | Specifies the background color |
| StyleReference | References one of the styles set in the StyleSheet control. This property will be demonstrated in the next code example. |

Of course, not all mobile devices support different fonts and colors. If the device can't render the color or font, the style information isn't transmitted by ASP.NET mobile.

You can use the StyleSheet control as a scaled-down version of a style sheet. Listing 7.10 shows an example using the control, and Figure 7.3 shows the output from two perspectives.

**FIGURE 7.3**

*Alternate rendering of the same page on two mobile devices.*

**LISTING 7.10**    Colors.aspx: Using the StyleSheet Control

```
1: <%@ Page Inherits="System.Web.UI.MobileControls.MobilePage"
2:           Language="vb" %>
3: <%@ Register TagPrefix="mobile"
```

**LISTING 7.10**   continued

```
 4:                 Namespace="System.Web.UI.MobileControls"
 5:                 Assembly="System.Web.Mobile" %>
 6:
 7: <mobile:StyleSheet runat="server">
 8:    <Style name="RedForm" Font-Name="Arial"
 9:                          BackColor="Red"
10:                          ForeColor="White"/>
11:    <Style name="BigFont" Font-Size="Large" />
12: </mobile:StyleSheet>
13:
14: <mobile:Form runat="server" StyleReference="RedForm">
15:   <mobile:TextView StyleReference="BigFont">
16: If you're using a Windows CE-compatible PDA,
17:    you should see a large message!
18:   </mobile:TextView>
19: </mobile:Form>
```

**ANALYSIS**   Lines 7–12 contain the definition for the StyleSheet control. In the control, two different kinds of styles are defined: one named RedForm (Lines 8–10) and one named BigFont (Line 11). Both style definitions use the attributes from Table 7.3.

The Form control (Line 14) and TextView control (Line 15) use the StyleReference attribute to use the styles defined in the StyleSheet control.

ASP.NET contains two built-in styles called Title and Error. The Title style is defined with a boldfaced font, and the Error style uses a red, non-boldfaced font.

# Understanding State Management Issues

State management, which concerns how you use the ViewState Web control and if you use the ASP.NET session object, is a tricky issue for any kind of Web application. As you might expect, the issue is even more difficult for mobile devices.

As a quick review, the ViewState control is normally stored in each page in the contents of a hidden field. Each ASP.NET page that uses view state has code similar to the following in every HTML page:

```
<input type="hidden" name="__VIEWSTATE"
                     value="dDwyMzgxOTQzODg7dD==" />
```

The content of the value attribute is a compressed encoding of the all data that should be displayed in each Web control.

Sending the information in the view state hidden field could slow down a page significantly because most mobile devices transmit information extremely slowly. As a result, ASP.NET mobile stores view state in session state.

7

To further complicate the issue, ASP.NET sessions use cookies to index a particular session for users. As a result, to use view or session state, the mobile device must support cookies. Many mobile devices, including cell phones, don't support cookies. ASP.NET can use "cookieless" sessions, but doing so involves a rather complex process of browser redirection and URL modification. Day 18 gives a detailed explanation of the process. The important fact to remember for today's discussion is that most mobile devices don't support "cookieless" sessions either.

The concept to take away from this section's discussion is that, in general, you can't use view or session state in your mobile Web applications. This doesn't mean that you have to take any special actions to disable the two state options. Instead, just don't add any variables to the session object.

Day 4 discussed some possible alternatives to session state, including hidden fields and URL parameters. ASP.NET makes using hidden fields easy because the Form class contains a collection called HiddenVariables. You can use this collection (sparingly) to store information that you need to keep around for each user. The following line shows an example:

```
Form.HiddenVariables("UserKey") = "1239343234"
```

You can retrieve the contents of the HiddenVariables collection the same way you might for the session object, such as the following few lines:

```
Dim lookupkey as string = CStr(Form.HiddenVariables("UserKey"))
'make a database query to retrieve the user's preferences
'using "lookupKey" to find the correct record.
'...
Dim favoritecolor as string = CStr(dataRow("color"))
Dim favoritebeverage as string = CStr(dataRow("Beverage"))
```

After you read the lessons in Days 9 and 10, you will know exactly how to implement the code that was conveniently left out of the previous snippet.

## Summary

Today's lesson introduced the fundamentals of mobile Internet programming by using the ASP.NET Mobile SDK. The lesson began by showing you what WML files look like. Any Web-enabled cell phone can use these files to display Web content. You also saw some mobile device emulation programs and information on how to download some of the most popular ones.

The second major section in today's lesson introduced mobile Web forms. You can use multiple Web forms in each .aspx page and group mobile pages that carry out one set of functions together. You saw how to activate each different form, using a qualified URL or the `ActiveForm` property. Mobile forms support automatic pagination, headers, and footers. The second section included sample programs that use each feature.

Today's chapter gave an overview of mobile Web controls, which are similar to ASP.NET Web controls. The mobile controls implement a subset of the standard functions provided by desktop Web controls but can generate events and use customized style properties.

ASP.NET mobile provides rich support for device-specific page rendering and control customization. You can use the `MobileCapabilities` class and device filters to simplify the development burden of supporting PDAs and cell phones with the same code base.

# Q&A

**Q I'm having a lot of trouble with the mobile device emulators. Which ones are the best to use?**

**A** As of this book's writing, the Pocket PC emulator and mobile phone emulator from Microsoft are bit rough around the edges. These tools will undoubtedly improve in the future. The Openwave emulation tools are the most stable emulation at the present time.

**Q Besides being limited to ASP.NET mobile controls, are there any other limitations on my server-side code for mobile devices?**

**A** The last section in today's lesson explained some of the state management issues that you will encounter when supporting mobile devices. However, in addition to these issues, there are no other limitations on server-side code. The following lessons will show how to use ADO.NET, XML, and Web Services in your Web applications. You can create sites for mobile devices that use all these technologies. For instance, you can easily create a mobile page that uses a Web service.

**Q I want to display graphics in my mobile pages, but I don't want to make the pages incompatible with text-only cell phones. What strategy should I use?**

**A** Any graphics that your mobile pages render will simply be skipped by text-only mobile phones. More precisely, ASP.NET mobile won't render the graphics. This means that as long as the graphic images on a page aren't essential for navigation or understanding the page, you don't have to worry about the issue.

# Workshop

The Workshop provides quiz questions to help you solidify your understanding of the material covered today as well as exercises to give you experience using what you've

7

learned. Try to understand the quiz and exercises before continuing to tomorrow's lesson. Answers are provided in Appendix A, "Answers to Quizzes and Exercises."

## Quiz

1. Name two examples of a mobile device emulation program.

2. What widely supported standard do cell phones use to render Web content?

3. What property is used to support automatic pagination in mobile Web forms?

4. Name three mobile Web controls that display list-based data.

5. What are the two methods used to render device-specific content?

6. Can mobile devices use Cascading Style Sheets, in general? What is an alternative?

7. How does ASP.NET mobile store Web control view state?

8. What collection can you use to keep track of per-user data for mobile Web pages?

## Exercises

1. Create a mobile Web form that allows users to enter a numerical password. What differences are there in the form when it's displayed on a PDA versus a cell phone?

2. Create a device filter that can be used to test whether a user has a PDA or cell phone.

# WEEK 1

# In Review

We hope that you've enjoyed your first week of learning how to use Visual Basic and .NET for Web programming. You've covered quite a bit of material including Web forms, user controls, custom controls, and mobile code. You've followed along through many sample applications for each area. With this experience, you should be able to apply .NET to your own Web applications.

At the beginning of the week, you learned how to set up your development environment to use .NET effectively. The remainder of the week was devoted to .NET and dynamic Web sites. You learned how to create code behind files and saw how Web forms work. You also learned about the Web controls that ASP.NET provides for your Web pages. You saw how to create your own user controls, allowing code reuse and caching for better performance. The week ended with a lesson about supporting mobile devices.

Take a break and pat yourself on the back. You've learned a great deal about Web programming with Visual Basic and .NET.

1

2

3

4

5

6

7

# WEEK 2

# At a Glance

After the past seven lessons, you should feel comfortable with Visual Basic and ASP.NET and should be able to apply them in your own Web applications. If you've run and analyzed each sample program, you should be well on your way to becoming an expert .NET Web developer.

This second week of lessons covers three exciting technologies that you will likely employ in your own Internet applications: XML, ADO.NET, and Web Services. You will learn in depth how to use XML and ADO.NET in your Web applications, and you will spend one day becoming familiar with Web Services.

This week builds on last week's lessons. Most of the sample code in this week's lessons will continue to use ASP.NET pages to illustrate new concepts. This will show you how each new technology can be used in your own Web sites.

8

9

10

11

12

13

14

# DAY 8

# Using XML with Your Applications

The eXtensible Markup Language (XML) is quickly becoming a popular standard used throughout the computer industry. Today's lesson will explain XML and how to use the .NET Framework to create and manipulate XML data.

Several complementary technologies are related to XML, such as XSL, XSLT, and XML Schemas. You will learn about XSL, XSLT, and their related .NET classes in today's lesson as well. On Day 11, "Using ADO.NET and XML Together," you will see how to use XML Schemas along with ADO.NET to create powerful data access classes.

Today's topics include how to:

- Represent data as XML
- Read, write, and display XML data in your Web programs
- Understand XSL
- Use XSL to transform your XML data
- Use the `XmlTextReader`, `XmlTextWriter`, and `XmlDocument` classes in your own development efforts

# What Is XML?

XML is a way to represent structured data. Just like HTML, XML uses tags to enclose each piece of data. Unlike HTML, however, with XML you pick the names for each tag so that they are appropriate for your own dataset. One big advantage of XML is that the data contained in XML files is "self-describing," because each data element is enclosed in HTML-like tags that give contextual clues about the data.

Listing 8.1 is a sample XML file that contains data about cars.

**LISTING 8.1**  XML Example

```
 1: <?xml version="1.0"?>
 2: <!— This file contains data for two cars—>
 3: <cars>
 4:   <car>
 5:    <make foreign="true">Honda</make>
 6:    <model>Accord</model>
 7:    <color>Black</color>
 8:    <year>1998</year>
 9:   </car>
10:   <car>
11:    <make foreign="false">Ford</make>
12:    <model>F-150</model>
13:    <color>Blue</color>
14:    <year>2000</year>
15:   </car>
16: </cars>
```

**ANALYSIS**  The first thing you might notice from Listing 8.1 is the code's first line, which is the header line:

```
<?xml version="1.0"?>
```

Every XML file must have this header line as the beginning of the file. As of this book's writing, everyone uses XML version 1.0, and this will probably be true for quite some time.

Line 2 of the XML file contains a comment. You can use comments anywhere inside an XML file, using the same syntax as HTML files.

Now look at lines 3 and 16:

```
<cars>
    . . .
</cars>
```

**NEW TERM**   These two tags form an XML *element*. XML elements can contain other elements. Because this <cars> element isn't contained by any other element, it's called a *root element*. The <cars> element in this example contains two <car> elements, the *children*, and the <cars> element is their *parent*. Each <car> element in turn contains several child elements: <make>, <model>, and so on. XML places no restrictions on your data's complexity. An element can contain as many child elements as you need, and you can nest child elements to any desired level.

Now let's return to the example. Within the first <car> element, notice the <make> element on Line 5:

```
<make foreign="true">Honda</make>
```

**NEW TERM**   Rather than contain another element, this line contains data—in this case, Honda. This kind of element is called a *text element* because it contains text data. Also, this element contains an attribute—foreign, which is marked true in this case. In general, elements can contain any number of attributes and other elements.

The elements in XML files are arranged in a tree structure starting with the root element and extending to the "leaf" elements that contain data but no child elements. Each tree element can have attributes and an unlimited number of child elements. Each leaf element on the tree can contain data in string format. For example, Figure 8.1 shows the simple tree layout of the XML file in Listing 8.1.

**FIGURE 8.1**

*Tree representation of the cars.xml file.*

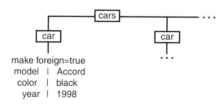

```
make foreign=true
model  |  Accord
color  |  black
 year  |  1998
```

**Tip**

> Internet Explorer 5.0 or higher will display XML files natively You just need to point your browser to a URL containing an XML file, and you will see a formatted version of the file. Figure 8.2 shows an example of the cars.xml flle.

## Advantages of Using XML

XML has become popular for a number of good reasons:

- XML is text-based and very easy to inspect by hand. This makes debugging code that produces or uses XML an easier task.
- It's also very easy to transmit from one computer to another, just like HTML.

- XML is based on industry standards approved by the W3C Group. This means that every computer manufacturer and software producer has an agreed way of using XML.

**FIGURE 8.2**

*Displaying an XML file in Internet Explorer.*

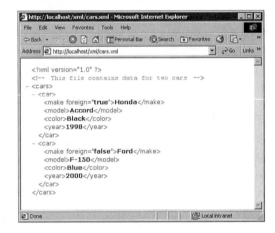

> **Note**
>
> The W3C Group is made up of a large number of experts from academia and industry. They create and maintain many of the standards for the Internet, such as HTML and XML. A W3C standard is called a *recommendation*. You can visit the group's site at http://www.w3c.org.

XML is used almost everywhere in .NET programs. This list describes a few of the places that XML creeps up in .NET:

- Any .NET object can be serialized to an XML representation and deserialized from XML.
- Configuration data for each .NET program, including ASP.NET and Web Services, is stored in XML. We'll see more details on Day 18, "Configuring Internet Applications."
- Web Service method calls are made using SOAP, which uses XML.
- XML is used so that client programs can discover Web Service capabilities.
- ADO.NET uses XML and XML Schemas to persist and validate data. We'll explain ADO.NET in detail in the next few lessons and XML Schemas on Day 11, "Using ADO.NET and XML Together."
- You can use XML Schemas to create classes.

# XML Namespaces

Each tag name that you use in your XML files is part of your own XML vocabulary, which you design to meet the needs at hand. The XML vocabulary in Listing 8.1 consisted of <cars>, <car>, <make>, <model>, <color>, <year>, and <foreign>. Because everyone is free to create his own XML vocabularies, each developer or organization might use the same XML tag to describe a different kind of data. This usage opens the possibility of conflicts with the same XML tag used for different purposes.

**NEW TERM**    To solve the problem of conflicting tag names in shared XML files, you can associate a namespace with each XML file. A namespace is identified by a Uniform Resource Identifier (URI). A *URI* is typically an address on the Internet, such as http://www.w3.org, and can also contain directory information, such as http://www.w3.org/TR/xmlbase. However, a URI is more general than just an Internet address; it can be an e-mail address, FTP address, or Telnet address, such as the following URIs. For a complete definition of URIs, see the W3C standards site at http://www.w3.org.

```
http://www.somecompany.com/xml/inventoryproject
mailto:joe_smith@somecompany.com
news:newsserver.www.servers.somecompany.com
ftp://ftp.somecompany.com
```

To associate a namespace with an XML file, use the xmlns attribute inside the outermost tag where it should apply. Listing 8.2 shows the cars example with a fictitious namespace associated with it.

**LISTING 8.2**   XML File with Namespace Qualification

```
<?xml version="1.0"?>
<cars xmlns="http://www.mysite.com/carproject">
   <car>
    <make foreign="true">Honda</make>
    <model>Accord</model>
    <color>Black</color>
    <year>1998</year>
   </car>
</cars>
```

In Listing 8.2, all elements inside the <cars> element are also associated with the www.mysite.com namespace.

You can also associate a namespace with only selected tags. Listing 8.3 shows how to associate the namespace with just the <make> and <model> tags. Notice that we use the letter z to qualify the tags; we could have used any other letter or string.

**LISTING 8.3** XML File with a Named Namespace Qualification

```xml
<?xml version="1.0"?>
<cars xmlns:z="www.mysite.com/carproject">
  <car>
    <z:make foreign="true">Honda</z:make>
    <z:model>Accord</z:model>
    <color>Black</color>
    <year>1998</year>
  </car>
</cars>
```

## XML Details

**NEW TERM**  You need to know about a few more XML details before diving into the .NET XML classes. All XML documents must be *well-formed*, meaning that they have to abide by the following rules:

- XML tags are case sensitive. This means that the `<Cars>` tag varies from the `<cars>` tag.

- Every opening tag must have a closing tag, and the closing tag an opening tag. For instance, the following lines are invalid because the `<name>` tag doesn't have a closing tag:

```xml
<car>
    <name>Tundra
      </car>
```

  For an empty element, or one that contains only attributes, the tag can contain a closing > character preceded by a / character, as in the following lines:

```xml
<car domestic="true" color="red" />
<car domestic="false" color="blue" />
```

- XML has several reserved characters, including <, >, &, and the word XML itself. Your own tags can't start with the string XML. Every tag is delimited by using the < and > characters, as the previous examples have shown.

  Use the CDATA tag if you need to include reserved characters in your XML data. For instance, the following element contains data with reserved characters:

```xml
<description><![CDATA[
    This tag contains data with reserved characters.  They are: < > &
]]></description>
```

  Notice that the CDATA tag begins with <![CDATA[ and ends with ]]>.

  You can also use escape sequences for reserved characters, as Table 8.1 shows.

**TABLE 8.1**   XML Escape Sequences

| Sequence | Character |
|----------|-----------|
| &lt;     | <         |
| &gt;     | >         |
| &amp;    | &         |

The preceding example could be written as follows:

```
<description>This tag contains reserved characters.
              They are &lt; &gt; &amp;</description>
```

- XML elements must be nested in a tree format, with one root element.

Also, XML ignores whitespace; any formatting in an XML file is there only for readability.

## Writing XML with `XmlTextWriter`

Use the `XmlTextWriter` class to write out XML files. You can use other classes to do the same thing, such as the `XmlDocument` class, which is explained later today. However, `XmlTextWriter` is optimized for fast output.

Table 8.2 shows some of the commonly used methods and properties that you will use with the `XmlTextWriter` class.

**TABLE 8.2**   Commonly Used Methods and Properties in the `XmlTextWriter` Class

| Method/Property | Description |
|-----------------|-------------|
| **Methods** | |
| WriteStartDocument | Writes the `<?xml version="1.0">` string. |
| WriteStartElement | Writes the opening tag for an element. |
| WriteEndElement | Writes the ending tag for an element. |
| WriteAttributeString | Writes an attribute for an element. |
| WriteString | Writes the data for an element as a string. |
| WriteElementString | Writes an element and its string data. |
| WriteComment | Writes a comment. |
| WriteCData | Writes a CDATA section. |
| Flush | Flushes the contents of the writer. |
| Close | Closes the `XmlTextWriter`. (You must close it when you are done with it.) |

**TABLE 8.2**   continued

| Method/Property | Description |
|---|---|
| **Properties** | |
| Formatting | Specifies how the file should be formatted. It can be `Formatting.Indented` or `Formatting.None`. None is the default. |
| Indentation | Specifies by how many characters to indent each subelement. |

Let's put the `XmlTextWriter` class to use by creating an ASP.NET page that creates the cars example shown earlier in Listing 8.1. Listing 8.4 shows the code for the sample page.

**LISTING 8.4**   WriteXML.aspx: Writing an XML File Using `XmlTextWriter`

```
 1: <%@ Page Language="VB" Debug="true"%>
 2: <%@ Import Namespace="System.Xml" %>
 3: <script runat="server">
 4: Sub OnWriteClick(Sender As Object, e As EventArgs)
 5:
 6:    Dim xmlWriter as new XmlTextWriter(Server.MapPath("cars.xml"), Nothing)
 7:
 8:    xmlWriter.Formatting = Formatting.Indented
 9:    xmlWriter.WriteStartDocument()
10:
11:    xmlWriter.WriteStartElement("cars")
12:    xmlWriter.WriteStartElement("car")
13:
14:    xmlWriter.WriteStartElement("make")
15:    xmlWriter.WriteAttributeString("foreign","true")
16:    xmlWriter.WriteString("Honda")
17:    xmlWriter.WriteEndElement()
18:
19:    xmlWriter.WriteElementString("model", "Accord")
20:    xmlWriter.WriteElementString("color", "Black")
21:    xmlWriter.WriteElementString("year", "1998")
22:
23:    xmlWriter.WriteEndElement()
24:    xmlWriter.WriteEndElement()
25:
26:    xmlWriter.Flush()
27:    xmlWriter.Close()
28:
29:    lbl.Text = "XML written successfully!"
30:
31: End Sub
32: </script>
33:
```

**LISTING 8.4**    continued

```
34: <html>
35: <body>
36: <form runat="server">
37: Click the button to generate "cars.xml"
38: <br>
39: <asp:Button runat="server" id="btnGen" Text="Generate XML"
40:                     OnClick="OnWriteClick"/>
41: <br>
42: <asp:Label id="lbl" runat="server" />
43: </form>
44: </body>
45: </html>
```

**ANALYSIS**    The important part of the sample is contained in the `OnWriteClick` event handler (Lines 4–31). First, Listing 8.4 declares a new `XmlTextWriter` (Line 6), passing in the name of the output file. The constructor's second parameter can be used to specify a different encoding scheme for the output file. Listing 8.4 specifies `Nothing` for default encoding.

After writing the XML header with a call to the `WriteStartDocument` method(Line 9), it writes the root <cars> element (Line 11) and then the first <car> element (Line 12).

The next task is to create the <make> element, which has an attribute and some data. We do so with four lines of code (Lines 15–18):

```
14: xmlWriter.WriteStartElement("make")
15  xmlWriter.WriteAttributeString("foreign","true")
16: xmlWriter.WriteString("Honda")
17: xmlWriter.WriteEndElement()
```

Line 17 calls the `WriteEndElement` method. This method is essential because it writes the ending tag for the new element that we created.

Because the remaining elements just have data, the listing calls the `WriteElementString` method to write the begin tag, data, and end tag for each one, as in Line 19:

```
xmlWriter.WriteElementString("model", "Accord")
```

`WriteElementString` will automatically write the ending element.

The last step inside the method is to call the `Flush` and `Close` methods (Lines 26–27). Always call `Close` to ensure that the resulting output file is closed properly.

## Reading XML with `XmlTextReader`

You can read any XML file, including ones you've created, using `XmlTextReader`. `XmlTextReader` allows you only to read the file; if we need to change a part of the file and write it back out, the `XmlDocument` class is more appropriate. (Today's lesson explains the `XmlDocument` class shortly.) However, `XmlTextReader` is optimized for fast, forward-only parsing of an XML file.

**NEW TERM** The most common way to use the `XmlTextReader` class is to create a new object of this type and then call the `Read` method repeatedly. After every call to `Read`, the `XmlTextReader` is populated with the next XML node from the file. Each node is part of an XML element, such as a start tag, end tag, header line, or data string. The term *node* is used by the .NET classes because the XML file is parsed into a tree structure when read. This tree structure contains each tag and data string in a structure that the .NET XML classes can manipulate easily.

After reading a new node, your program can examine the node via the properties of the `XmlTextReader` object itself; each property reflects the properties of the current node in the XML file. Table 8.4 later in this section shows some of the properties that you will likely use in your own code.

Let's create a program that uses the `XmlTextReader` class. Listing 8.5 shows a sample program that will read the cars.xml file and display it on a Web page. Figure 8.3 shows the example in action.

**FIGURE 8.3**

*ShowXML.aspx displaying the cars.xml file*

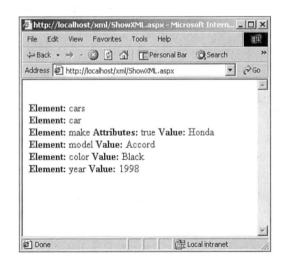

**LISTING 8.5**  ShowXML.aspx: Writing Contents of the XML File to HTML with `XmlTextReader`

```
1: <%@ Page Language="VB" Debug="True" %>
2: <%@ Import Namespace="System.Xml" %>
3: <script runat="server">
4: Sub Page_Load(Sender As Object, e As EventArgs)
5:
```

**Listing 8.5**   continued

```
 6:    Dim xmlReader as new XmlTextReader(Server.MapPath("cars.xml"))
 7:    DisplayXML(xmlReader)
 8:    xmlReader.Close()
 9:
10: End Sub
11:
12: Sub DisplayXML(xmlReader as XmlTextReader)
13:
14:    Dim attIdx As Integer
15:
16:    while (xmlReader.Read())
17:      if xmlReader.NodeType = XmlNodeType.Element then
18:        Response.Write("<br>")
19:        Response.Write("<b>Element: </b>" + xmlReader.Name)
20:        if xmlReader.HasAttributes then
21:          Response.Write(" <b>Attributes: </b>")
22:          for attIdx=0 to xmlReader.AttributeCount - 1
23:            'the Item property retrieves the value for each node's attribute
24:            Response.Write(xmlReader(attIdx))
25:            if attIdx < xmlReader.AttributeCount - 1 then
26:                Response.Write(", ")
27:            End If
28:          Next
29:        End If
30:      else if xmlReader.NodeType = XmlNodeType.Text then
31:        Response.Write(" <b>Value: </b>" + xmlReader.Value)
32:      End If
33:    End While
34:
35: End Sub
36: </script>
```

**ANALYSIS**    The code creates a new XmlTextReader in the Load event handler (Line 6), passing the filename as the only parameter in the constructor. Then this object is passed to the DisplayXML method (Line 7).

Within DisplayXML (Lines 12–35), the code calls the Read method on the XmlTextReader object (Line 16). Each time Read is called, a node of the XML file is read.

In the if statement on Line 17, we check for nodes of type Element or Text. A sample node of type Element would be <color>. We could have tested for other types of elements, such as EndElement. A sample EndElement would be </color>. Table 8.3 lists the common node types that XmlTextReader parses; refer to the Visual Studio documentation for complete details.

**TABLE 8.3**  Common Node Types in the `XmlNodeType` Enumeration

| Node Type | Description |
|-----------|-------------|
| Element | The begin tag in an XML element, such as `<color primary="true" visible="true">` |
| EndElement | The end tag in an XML element, such as `</color>` |
| Text | The text data in an XML node |
| CDATA | A CDATA section of an XML node |
| WhiteSpace | Whitespace in between nodes |
| XmlDeclaration | The XML header `<?xml version="1.0"?>` |

In the middle of the listing, we use the following line for a node of type `Element`:

```
Response.Write(xmlReader[attIdx]);
```

By using the default `Index` property, we can get the value of each attribute in an `Element` tag.

Table 8.4 shows common properties and methods that you might use from the `XmlTextReader` class in your own code.

**TABLE 8.4**  Common Properties and Methods in the `XmlTextReader` Class

| Method/Property | Description |
|-----------------|-------------|
| | **Properties** |
| Name | The name of the current node. It has a value only when the node is of type `Element` or `Attribute`. |
| Value | The value of the current node. It is not empty if the current node is of type `Text`, `Attribute`, or `CDATA`. |
| Depth | Current depth in the XML tree. |
| Item | Value of an attribute. |
| NodeType | Type of the current node, such as `NodeType.Element`. |
| EOF | Returns `true` if at the end of the file. |
| | **Methods** |
| Read | Reads an element of the XML file. It returns `false` if at the end of the file. |
| MoveToAttribute | Moves to the attribute number specified (0 based). |
| MoveToElement | Moves to the element containing the current attribute. |
| Close | The way to close `XmlTextReader`. You should always close `XmlTextReader` when you are done with it. |

> **Tip**
>
> You can read an XML file from another computer on the Internet instead of a local file using XmlTextReader. Just pass in the URL of the XML file in the constructor, such as "http://www.mysite.com/xml/myxmlfile.xml".

# What Is XSL?

The eXtensible Stylesheet Language (XSL) is used to transform XML files into HTML, new and differently formatted XML files, text files, or other formats. As you saw in Listing 8.3, reading through an XML file and transforming the output into HTML through code is a tedious process. By using XSL, you can automate almost all the transformation process.

To see how the process works, look at Figure 8.4.

**FIGURE 8.4**

*How XSL is used to transform XML into new formats.*

How XSL is used to transform XML into new formats

```
xml  -> xsl engine  -> new xml
xsl  ->             -> html
     ->             -> text
     ->             -> other
```

By looking at Figure 8.4, you can see that an XSL transformation engine takes an XML file and an XSL style sheet and combines the two to make a new file.

XSL files are made out of XML. To see how this works, look at the simple XSL file in Listing 8.6.

**LISTING 8.6**  Simple.xsl: A Simple XSL Example

```
 1: <?xml version='1.0'?>
 2: <xsl:stylesheet version="1.0"
 3:         xmlns:xsl="http://www.w3.org/1999/XSL/Transform">
 4:
 5: <xsl:template match="cars">
 6:   <xsl:for-each select="car">
 7:     <xsl:value-of select="make"/>
 8:     <xsl:text>, </xsl:text>
 9:   </xsl:for-each>
10: </xsl:template>
11:
12: </xsl:stylesheet>
```

**ANALYSIS**  XSL uses the XSL Transform (XSLT) language. In Listing 8.4, you can see some of the commands in XSLT, such as template, for-each, and value-of (Lines

5–7). Because XSL uses XML, each XSLT command is embedded in XML elements. This leads to a slightly complicated syntax.

XSL files use the official XSL namespace, from `www.w3.org`, as you can see in Lines 2–3, repeated here:

```
<xsl:stylesheet version="1.0"
    xmlns:xsl="http://www.w3.org/1999/XSL/Transform">
```

With this namespace declaration, any XML element that begins with `xsl:` is parsed as an XSL command.

XSL files use one or more templates. Each template is applied to an XML file to produce output and is matched against XML elements with a certain name. The template in Listing 8.6 is shown in Lines 5–10. This template matches against XML elements named `"cars"` in the source file.

You can create any number of XSL commands within the template. In Listing 8.6, we use the `for-each` command (Line 6) to loop through every `<car>` subelement in the XML file, as repeated here:

```
<xsl:for-each select="car">
  ...
</xsl:for-each>
```

After matching against a car node, the code in Listing 8.3 retrieves the value of the `<model>` tag, using the `value-of` XSLT command. The `value-of` command sends the data within a tag to the output file. Next, we output some text for each car, using the `text` command.

After all this, the final output from applying this XSL style sheet to the cars.xml file is listed as follows:

```
Honda, Ford,
```

## Creating HTML with XSL

The power of XSL comes out when you add your own HTML (or XML) into the XSL style sheet. For instance, Listing 8.7 shows an XSL style sheet that will produce a Web page given the cars.xml file. When this listing is used with Listing 8.8, you can see the results of applying the XSL style sheet in Figure 8.5.

A number of classes in the .NET Framework apply XSLT style sheets to XML files. One of the easiest to use is the XML Web control. Listing 8.8 uses the XML Web control to create a Web page with the XSL in Listing 8.7.

**FIGURE 8.5**

*Applying the cars.xsl style sheet.*

8

**LISTING 8.7**  JerrysCars.xsl: Transforming the Car Data into an HTML Page

```
 1: <?xml version='1.0'?>
 2: <xsl:stylesheet version="1.0"
 3:       xmlns:xsl="http://www.w3.org/1999/XSL/Transform">
 4:
 5: <xsl:template match="/">
 6:   <xsl:apply-templates select="cars"/>
 7: </xsl:template>
 8:
 9: <xsl:template match="cars">
10: <h1>Jerry's Automotive Superstore Inventory</h1>
11: <h2>Cars for sale</h2>
12: <table>
13:   <xsl:for-each select="car">
14:
15:     <tr><td>
16:     <font color="blue"><b>
17:     <xsl:value-of sclcct="make"/>
18:     <xsl:text> </xsl:text>
19:     <xsl:value-of select="model"/>
20:     </b></font>
21:     </td></tr>
22:
23:     <tr><td>
24:     This is a beautiful <xsl:value-of select="color"/> model.
25:     </td></tr>
26:
27:     <xsl:apply-templates select="make"/>
28:
29:   </xsl:for-each>
```

**LISTING 8.7**   continued

```
30: </table>
31: <hr></hr>
32: <b>Call now for our outrageous deals!</b>
33: </xsl:template>
34:
35: <xsl:template match="make">
36:     <xsl:if test="@foreign='false'">
37:     <tr><td>
38:     Made in the USA!
39:     </td></tr>
40:     </xsl:if>
41: </xsl:template>
42:
43: </xsl:stylesheet>
```

**LISTING 8.8**   ShowXSL.aspx: Applying the JerrysCars.xsl Style Sheet to cars.xml

```
1: <html>
2: <body>
3: <asp:XML id="myXML"
4:         DocumentSource="cars.xml"
5:         TransformSource="JerrysCars.xsl"
6:         runat="server" />
7: </body>
8: </html>
```

**ANALYSIS**   Starting with Listing 8.8, the XML and XSL files are specified with the DocumentSource (Line 4) and TransformSource (Line 5) properties inside the XML Web control. Of course, you can set these properties in code, as with any ASP.NET Web control. One possibility is to use the Page_Load event to set these two properties based on your own code logic.

Listing 8.7 uses three XSLT templates. The first template matches the root element in our source XML file, using the match="/" parameter (Line 5). It then uses the apply-templates command (Line 6) to apply all other templates, while selecting the <cars> XML element.

Only one other template matches the <cars> element, the second template in the listing (Lines 9–33). This template outputs most of the HTML in the result. This second template has a similar structure to the Simple.xsl file in Listing 8.6.

The listing contains a second apply-templates command at the end of the second template (Line 27). This command applies the third template in the file (Lines 35–41), which matches the <make> element. This third template uses a new command:

```
<xsl:if test="@foreign='false'">
```

This command is a typical `if` statement. The `test` parameter selects the `foreign` attribute using the @ symbol. To test against data contained in an element, leave off the @. For instance, the following line would test `true` if the current element contained `Ford` inside the tags:

```
<xsl:if test="make='Ford'">
```

## Using XPath

Many XSL commands match against an element of a source XML file. Listing 8.7 uses XML element names, such as `car` and `make`, as well as the `"/"` string to match against the root of the XML file:

```
<xsl:template match="/">
```

You can create match strings like this because every well-formed XML file has a tree structure. For instance, to match against the `<car>` element, you could use a match string like the following:

```
<xsl:template match="/cars/car">
```

Inside the template, after this match has been made, you can create an `if` statement that might match against the `foreign` attribute of the `<model>` tag like this:

```
<xsl:if test="make[@foreign='false']">
```

 All this rather obtuse syntax for navigating through XML files is called *XPath*. As the name implies, XPath strings specify an exact path within an XML document. Although the complete details of XPath are beyond the scope of this book, Table 8.5 shows examples of common XPath strings.

**TABLE 8.5** Common XPath strings

| String | Description |
|---|---|
| / | Indicates the root of an XML document |
| ElementName | Matches a tag named ElementName |
| /ElementName | Matches a tag named ElementName only if it's the root XML element |
| /Element/SubElement | Matches a tag named SubElement only if it has a parent that's the root element and is called Element |
| TagName[@AttributeName] | Matches the attribute AttributeName within an element named TagName |

**TABLE 8.5** continued

| String | Description |
| --- | --- |
| Element/* | Matches all subelements of Element |
| Element[@*] | Matches all attributes of Element |
| ../Parent | Matches any element named Parent of the current element |

In addition to using XPath to match different parts of an XML tree, you can use XPath in if statements. Table 8.6 shows common conditional expressions that you might use in an if statement.

**TABLE 8.6** if Statements Using XPath

| Statement | Description |
| --- | --- |
| <xsl:if test="Year &lt; 2000"> | Select any elements with a year < 2000 |
| <xsl:if test="Year &gt; 1999"> | Select any elements with a year > 1999 |
| <xsl:if test="/cars/car/make[@foreign="true"]> | True if the make child of the car child of the cars element contains a foreign attribute equal to true. |

## Where to Go from Here

Although this introduction to XSL and XPath will give you a good place to start coding, it only scratches the surface of the complete power of XSL style sheets. You can find many good resources on the Web that give more details on XSL, and the Visual Studio documentation also contains good reference material. .NET contains three classes tailored for XSL and XPath, called XPathDocument, XPathNavigator, and XslTransform.

# Understanding the Document Object Model (DOM)

Although XSL is quite powerful, you may need fine-grained control of XML processing within your own code. .NET offers the XmlDocument class to give you a powerful and flexible way to process XML documents.

The XmlDocument class is constructed against another Internet standard called the Document Object Model (DOM). As you may have guessed, this standard was approved by the W3C Group. While an XML file is being parsed, an XmlDocument object treats a source XML file as though it were a tree. In this way, you can navigate from the root element of the XML file down into child and sibling nodes. Because the entire node tree is maintained in memory, you can navigate both forward and backward in the tree structure, unlike the forward-only XmlTextReader. However, this capability results in the XmlDocument class being slower and more resource-intensive.

The XmlDocument class is integrated with the XmlTextReader and XmlTextWriter classes described earlier today. You can pass an XmlTextReader object to the constructor of an XmlDocument object so that it can read the XML file. The XmlDocument class also uses the same XmlNode class to represent each node in the file, just as the XmlTextReader does.

To see the XmlDocument class in action, look at Listing 8.9, which shows an ASP.NET page that will count the number of data elements in an XML file.

**LISTING 8.9**   CountData.aspx: Counting Text Elements in Any XML Document

```
 1: <%@ Page Language="VB" Debug="True" %>
 2: <%@ Import Namespace="System.Xml" %>
 3: <html>
 4: <body>
 5:   <form runat="server">
 6:    <h3>Count data elements in an XML File</h3>
 7:    XML File: <asp:TextBox id="TargetFile" runat="server"/>
 8:    <asp:Button Text="Count" OnClick="OnCountClick" runat="server"/>
 9:    <br>
10:    <asp:Label id="lblCount" runat="server"/>
11:   </form>
12: </body>
13: </html>
14: <script runat="server">
15: Sub OnCountClick(Sender As Object, e As EventArgs)
16:
17:     Dim xmlFile as String = TargetFile.Text
18:
19:     Dim xmlRdr as new XmlTextReader(Server.MapPath(xmlFile))
20:     Dim xmlDoc as new XmlDocument()
21:
22:     xmlDoc.Load(xmlRdr)
23:
24:     Dim dataCount as integer = 0
25:     dataCount = CountData(xmlDoc.DocumentElement)
26:
27:     lblCount.Text = "There are " & dataCount.ToString() & _
28:         " data elements in the file"
29:     xmlRdr.Close()
30: End Sub
31:
32: Function CountData(Node as XmlNode) As Integer
```

**LISTING 8.9** continued

```
33:
34:      Dim Count as integer = 0
35:      Dim ChildNode as XmlNode
36:
37:      if Node.NodeType = XmlNodeType.Text Or _
38:              Node.NodeType = XmlNodeType.CDATA then Count = 1
39:      End If
40:
41:      for each ChildNode in Node.ChildNodes
42:        Count = Count + CountData(ChildNode)
43:      next
44:
45:      return Count
46:
47: End Function
48: </script>
```

**ANALYSIS**  The HTML portion of Listing 8.9 (Lines 3–13) is a simple input form containing TextBox and Button controls. After the user enters the name of the source XML file, the OnCountClick event handler (Lines 15–30)is called.

Within the event handler, the code in Listing 8.9 creates an XmlTextReader and XmlDocument objects (Lines 19 and 20). It passes the text reader into the Load method of the XmlDocument (Line 22) object, which loads the source XML file into memory for manipulation.

The event handler then calls the CountData function (Lines 32–47), passing in the DocumentElement property of the XmlDocument object. This property, of type XmlNode, contains the root node of the source XML document.

The recursive CountData function first checks to see if the type of the node passed in is Text or CDATA (Line 37). If this is the case, the node should be counted, and the Count variable is set to 1 (Line 38). CountData then uses the ChildNodes collection to find any child nodes and calls itself recursively (Line 42).

Table 8.7 shows some of the more commonly used methods of the XmlDocument class. Consult the Visual Studio documentation for a complete list of all methods and properties for these classes.

**TABLE 8.7**  Commonly Used Methods and Properties of the XmlDocument Class

| Method/Property | Description |
| --- | --- |
| **Properties** | |
| HasChildNodes | Returns true if this node has child nodes. |
| ChildNodes | Specifies a collection of child nodes. |

**TABLE 8.7** continued

| Method/Property | Description |
|---|---|
| **Properties** | |
| FirstChild, LastChild | Specifies the first and last child nodes of the current node. |
| NextSibling | Accesses the next child node, after FirstChild. You can iterate through the child nodes with this property. |
| ParentNode | Specifies this node's parent. |
| NodeType | Specifies the type of this node. |
| **Methods** | |
| AppendChild | Adds a child node to this node. |
| InsertAfter, InsertBefore | Inserts a child node after or before the specified node. |
| RemoveChild, RemoveAll | Removes a child node or all children nodes. |
| WriteTo | Writes the current note to an XmlWriter or XmlTextWriter object. |
| Load | Loads XML data from a file, stream, or XmlTextReader. |
| LoadXml | Loads XML data from a string. |
| Save | Saves XML data to a file, stream, or XmlTextWriter. |
| CreateNode, CreateTextNode, CreateElement | Creates an XML element; returns an XmlNode object that can be passed to AppendChild or InsertAfter. |
| CreateAttribute | Returns an XmlAttribute object that can be passed to SetAttributeNode of the XmlElement class. |
| GetElementByName | Returns a list of all child nodes with a specified tag name. |

To see how to use the XmlDocument class to modify and save an XML document, look at Listing 8.10, which shows a page that will allow you to modify the cars.xml file. It also displays the resulting XML file using the XSL style sheet in Listing 8.7. Figure 8.6 shows the page in action.

**LISTING 8.10**   ChangeInventory.aspx: Changing the cars.xml File

```
1: <%@ Page Language="vb" %>
2: <%@ Import Namespace="System.Xml" %>
3: <html>
4: <body>
5:   <form runat="server">
6:     <asp:XML id="myXML"
```

**LISTING 8.10**   continued

```
 7:                  DocumentSource="cars.xml"
 8:                  TransformSource="jerryscars.xsl"
 9:                  runat="server" />
10:      <hr>
11:      <h3>Modify the color of a car</h3>
12:      Car Model: <asp:TextBox id="txtModel" runat="server"/><br>
13:      New Color: <asp:TextBox id="txtColor" runat="server"/><br>
14:      <asp:Button Text="Change Color"
15:                  OnClick="OnChangeColor" runat="server"/>
16:    </form>
17: </body>
18: </html>
19:
20: <script runat="server">
21: Sub OnChangeColor(Sender As Object, e As EventArgs)
22:
23:    Dim Models as XmlNodeList
24:    Dim node as XmlElement
25:    Dim child as XmlNode
26:    Dim TargetModel as String = txtModel.Text
27:    Dim NewColor as String = txtColor.Text
28:
29:    Dim xmlDoc as new XmlDocument()
30:    xmlDoc.Load(Server.MapPath("cars.xml"))
31:    Models = xmlDoc.GetElementsByTagName("model")
32:    for each node in Models
33:       'Retrieve model
34:      if node.InnerXml = TargetModel
35:
36:        Dim parent as XmlNode = node.ParentNode
37:        for each child in parent.ChildNodes
38:           if child.Name = "color" then
39:              'Retrieve color
40:              child.InnerXml = NewColor
41:          End If
42:        Next
43:      end if
44:    Next
45:    xmlDoc.Save(Server.MapPath("cars.xml"))
46: End Sub
47:
48: </script>
```

**ANALYSIS**   The HTML portion of Listing 8.10 (Lines 3–18) displays the car inventory using the XML Web control. It also gets the model and new color for a car to change.

When the user clicks the Change Color button, the OnChangeColor method (Lines 21–46) loads the cars.xml file into an XmlDocument object. Line 31 uses the GetElementsByTagName to get a list of all <model> nodes in the file.

**FIGURE 8.6**

*Changing an XML file using the DOM.*

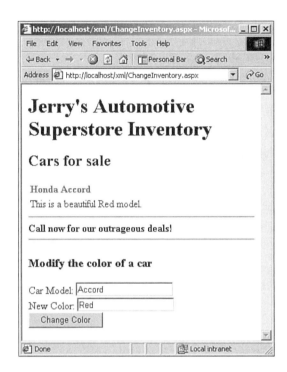

After getting the list of models, the code searches for one that matches the model the user specified. When the correct <model> node is found, the code traverses to the parent <car> node. It then searches for the <color> node and changes its value.

As you can see from the two samples in Listings 8.9 and 8.10, the XmlDocument class gives you a great deal of flexibility for processing XML documents.

# Summary

Today you saw how to use XML to represent data and how you can manipulate it with some of the .NET XML classes. We introduced the major classes used in .NET to help you manipulate XML data, including the XmlTextReader, XmlTextWriter, and XmlDocument classes. You should have a good understanding of how to apply these classes in your own Internet applications to process XML data.

You also learned about XSL and XPath today and saw how they can be used to generate HTML for your Web applications. You saw how XSL style sheets are applied to XML data using the ASP.NET XML control. You now have a foundation for learning more about XSL and XPath if you decide to apply them to your own projects.

# Q&A

**Q** **Why is everyone starting to use XML?**

**A** XML provides a way to store text-based data in a format that is easy for humans to comprehend. Data elements are enclosed by descriptive tags, which leaves less room for error when reading an XML file.

**Q** **I have heard that ADO.NET is integrated with XML. Can I use ADO.NET to manipulate my XML files?**

**A** You certainly can use ADO.NET to manipulate XML files without having to write much extra code. The next few lessons will introduce ADO.NET, and Day 11 will show many examples that use the two together.

**Q** **Because I can manipulate XML files using XSL, XPath, and/or the .NET XML classes, which method should I choose?**

**A** The answer depends on exactly how you need to manipulate the XML data. XSL is great for quickly transforming XML into another format. However, the XPath syntax is obtuse—you may want to use the .NET XML classes for an easier programming model.

**Q** **I have heard about DTD and XSD, but they weren't covered in this lesson. What about these two standards?**

**A** Day 11 will explore both DTD and XSD. As a quick summary, both technologies provide a way to enforce data rules for a target XML file. For instance, you can specify the structure of an XML file and the data types for each element by using DTD and XSD.

# Workshop

The workshop provides quiz questions to help you solidify your understanding of the material covered today as well as exercises to give you experience using what you have learned. Try to understand the quiz and exercises, before continuing to tomorrow's lesson. Answers are provided in Appendix A, "Answers to Quizzes and Exercises."

## Quiz

1. How many top-level nodes can a well-formed XML document have? Why?

2. What is a leaf node in an XML file, and how many child nodes can it contain?

3. List three places that XML is used in the .NET Framework.

4. What are XML namespaces, and why would you want to use them in your own XML files?

5. What are the differences between an element node and a text node in an XML file?

6. Name three data formats that can result from applying an XSL file to an XML file.

7. What are XSL templates, and how are they used in XSL files?

8. How is the XPath standard used in XSL?

9. In what cases would it be better to use the XmlDocument class instead of the XmlTextReader and XMLTextWriter classes?

10. How can you use ASP.NET to transform XML documents?

## Exercises

1. Supplement the cars.xml file with more attributes. How does this change the output of the sample programs in this chapter?

2. Create an ASP.NET page that will count the total number of nodes in any XML file.

3. Create an XSL document that will transform the cars.xml file into a new XML file with new text nodes for each attribute.

# WEEK 2

# DAY 9

# Introducing ADO.NET

Almost any dynamic Web site or service will interact with a database sometime. Databases allow you to store and organize data efficiently and enable your programs to extract and modify data quickly.

ADO.NET, the .NET version of Active Data Objects, provides an easy way to interact with back-end database servers, such as Access, Microsoft SQL Server, and Oracle.

On Day 5, "Using Advanced ASP.NET Web Controls," you learned how to use the more complicated ASP.NET Web controls. That lesson used the ADO.NET `DataSet` object in many examples without explaining the details of ADO.NET. In today's lesson and the following two lessons, you will learn how to use `DataSet` and the complete set of ADO.NET classes in your Internet applications.

Today you will learn the following:

- How ADO.NET is different from ADO and other database technologies
- How to connect to a database
- How to read data from a database
- How to execute SQL commands on a database

- How to interact with a SQL Server database
- How to use ADO.NET and OLE DB to connect to almost any kind of database

# Why ADO.NET?

As a software developer, you may have experience with Data Access Objects (DAO), ActiveX Data Objects (ADO), or one of the many database technologies at your disposal. Each technology has its own API and you may have spent a great deal of effort mastering one or more of them. Now ADO.NET has been added to the mix, and you may be wondering whether learning how to use it is worth your time.

ADO.NET offers several features that make it worth learning:

- ADO.NET is tightly integrated into the .NET framework, so your .NET code will be simpler. You also can write database code for your Internet applications more productively than if you used one of the older models.
- If you are already familiar with ADO, learning ADO.NET will be easy. ADO.NET uses similar kinds of objects, such as Connection and Command. However, you will need to become familiar with several new kinds of objects in ADO.NET. For instance, the ADO Recordset object has been replaced by a set of new objects.
- If you are developing a Web service, ADO.NET provides features that make your life easy. ADO.NET allows you to transmit entire datasets over the Internet and through firewalls as XML strings. It also allows a Web service to reconcile data that a remote client has modified and sent back without writing reams of complicated code. We'll explore these Web service features in the lessons for Days 13 to 16.

## The Disconnected Model

NEW TERM ADO.NET varies from many other database technologies, including ADO, because it is based on a *disconnected* data model. This means that the set of data returned from a SQL query or stored procedure is isolated from the actual connection to the database. You saw an example on Day 5, when you learned how to use the DataGrid Web control with an ADO.NET dataset generated without an underlying database or database connection. Because ADO.NET uses a disconnected model, you can use the DataSet and related classes independently of a database connection. As you might imagine, this kind of functionality is essential for Web services, which may ship entire datasets to a remote client program. ADO.NET makes this kind of operation easy.

The disconnected model is also useful for Web applications. By using a disconnected dataset, a Web application can store the results from a SQL query and close any database connections in between page hits. This way, you can create Web sites that scale well without having to write complicated code.

## ADO.NET Class Categories

Figure 9.1 shows the major classes in ADO.NET.

**FIGURE 9.1**

*Classes used in ADO.NET programming.*

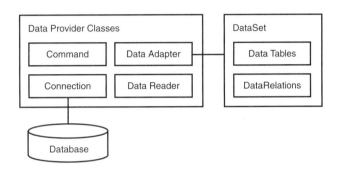

As you can see, ADO.NET consists of classes that fall into two main categories: data provider classes and the DataSet and contained classes. Data provider classes include `SqlConnection`, `OleDbConnection`, `SqlCommand`, and `OleDbCommand`, as well as others. These classes, which are tied directly to a database, allow you to set up connections, execute commands and stored procedures, read data, and populate datasets. Today's lesson shows sample programs that use the data provider classes.

> **Note**
>
> Many of .NET'S database classes come in two versions: Sql*xxxx* and OleDb*xxxx*, where *xxxx* identifies the class. Use the Sql*xxxx* classes when working with a database hosted by Microsoft SQL Server; use the OleDb*xxxx* for other types of databases, such as Microsoft Access and Oracle.

The `DataSet` and related classes make up the disconnected model that ADO.NET uses; they contain several features that make creating and updating data easy. Tomorrow's lesson will explain these data manipulation classes.

 The .NET data provider classes are built to access data using OLE DB or ODBC so that you can connect to almost any commercial database. *OLE DB* and *ODBC* are standards that programs use to connect to databases. Most commercial databases have an ODBC driver, and many have OLE DB drivers. You don't need to worry about the details of these standards, other than that they provide a programming interface for executing database commands.

ADO.NET also contains data provider classes written especially for Microsoft SQL Server. These classes are built for optimal performance when used with a SQL Server back-end database. The SQL Server data provider classes also take advantage of some of the special features in SQL Server, such as native XML support.

Now that you have an overview of ADO.NET, let's look at ways to use ADO.NET in practice.

# Setting Up the Database

Many examples in this lesson require access to either Microsoft Access or Microsoft SQL Server 7.0 or 2000. A section of today's lesson demonstrates how to use SQL Server stored procedures, which requires SQL Server. This chapter will contain notes on how to adapt each example to either database. We'll also show examples of programs that connect to other kinds of databases.

Also, most examples in this lesson use the Northwind database, which is installed by default when you install Access or SQL Server.

As explained earlier, ADO.NET contains two different kinds of data providers: an OLE DB provider and a provider optimized for SQL Server. You can use the OLE DB provider to access Oracle, FoxPro, Access, dBASE, and just about anything else that comes close to being a database, such as Excel.

Each data provider contains four classes: `Connection`, `Command`, `DataReader`, and `DataAdapter`. These four classes are named differently depending on which type of data provider they belong to. For instance, the `Connection` class for the SQL Server data provider is called `SqlConnection`, and the OLE DB data provider connection class is called `OleDbConnection`. The `Command`, `DataReader`, and `DataAdapter` classes are named similarly.

 **Note**

> If you're familiar with ADO, the `Connection` and `Command` classes in ADO.NET might look familiar to you. The ADO and ADO.NET `Connection` and `Command` classes share many methods but are used somewhat differently.

Let's make a simple program that uses the SQL Server data provider. The program will write out the contents of a database table to a Web page. Our program will use the `Connection`, `Command`, and `DataReader` classes. The `DataAdapter` class helps synchronize the database with the `DataSet`, so we won't use it in this first sample.

The first thing we need to do is open a connection to the database. As you might suspect, we will use the Connection object as shown in the following line:

```
Dim con as new SqlConnection("connectionstring")
```

This connection string uses the SQL Server data provider. To use the OLE DB provider for Access or another OLE DB–accessible database, use a line like the following:

```
Dim con as new OleDbConnection("connectionstring")
```

A typical simple connection string used to access the Northwind database on a local SQL Server database would look like the following line:

```
Dim con as _
  new SqlConnection("data source=localhost;uid=sa;pwd=;database=Northwind")
```

A connection string to access the Northwind database using the OLE DB provider is shown here:

```
Dim con as _
   new OleDbConnection("Provider=Microsoft.Jet.OLEDB.4.0;" & _
      "Data Source=C:\Program Files\Microsoft Office\" & _
      "Office\Samples\Northwind.mdb;" & _
      "User ID=;Password=;")
```

**Note**

The connection string contains all the magic to connect to a particular database and can be tricky to get right, especially when you're using the OLE DB provider. We'll explore connection strings later in the lesson.

We also need to open the connection by using the Open method as follows:

```
con.Open()
```

**Note**

Don't call the Open method until the last possible moment, and close the connection as soon as possible. This way, you make sure that the durations of connections to the database are as short as possible, which is good if your program uses many connections or if other programs are also using the database. As we will explain in tomorrow's lesson, you don't need to call Open when using DataAdapter and DataSet together.

After creating our connection, we need to make a SQL SELECT statement to fetch the data. We can use a line like the following for the Customers table in the Northwind database:

```
Dim cmd as new SqlCommand("Select * from Customers", con)
```

Similarly, when we're using the OLE DB provider, we would declare the command object by using the following line of code:

```
Dim cmd as new OleDbCommand("Select * from Customers", con)
```

Notice that we passed in the `Connection` object in addition to the SQL command. Later, we'll see a more sophisticated approach using stored procedures instead of direct SQL text in a string.

Next, we want to execute the command and read the results. In this example, we'll just read the data rather than update or delete records. We'll also read the data from start to finish. The `DataReader` class is optimized for retrieving data in a read-only, forward-only way. We can create a `DataReader` object by calling the `ExecuteReader` method on a `Command` object, as follows:

```
Dim rdr as SqlDataReader = cmd.ExecuteReader()
```

As you might expect, the OLE DB version of the same line looks quite similar, as the following line shows:

```
Dim rdr as OleDbDataReader = cmd.ExecuteReader()
```

Now we can use the `DataReader` object to read through all table rows and then print each line onscreen. The `DataReader` class `Read` method reads one row of data at a time. After `Read` is called, you can access any column in the record that has just been read by calling the `GetString` method, which returns a column as a string. You can use other methods to fetch a column into another data type, such as `GetByte` and `GetBool`. These methods return a column's data as a byte or a bool type, respectively.

A loop to read through all data in a `DataReader` might look like the following:

```
while rdr.Read()
  'fetch column 4, for example
  if not rdr.IsDBNull(3)  then
    Dim strField as OleDbDataReader = rdr.GetString(fldNum)
  end if
    'do something with the field
  end while
```

If you put all this together into a user control, you might get something like Listing 9.1. This listing simply reads through every row and column and prints the value.

**LISTING 9.1**  ShowTable.ascx: A User Control That Displays All the Values in a Table

```
1: <%@ Control Language="vb" %>
2: <%@ Import Namespace="System.Data" %>
3: <%@ Import Namespace="System.Data.OleDb" %>
4: <script runat="server">
```

**LISTING 9.1**    continued

```
 5:
 6: private _TableName as String
 7:
 8: public property TableName() as string
 9:   get
10:     return _TableName
11:   end get
12:   set(byval v as string)
13:     _TableName = v
14:   end set
15: end property
16:
17: </script>
18: <%
19:    'Create a connection to the local NorthWind database
20:      Dim con as new OleDbConnection("Provider=Microsoft.Jet.OLEDB.4.0;" & _
21:            "Data Source=C:\Program Files\Microsoft Office\" & _
22:            "Office\Samples\Northwind.mdb;" & _
23:            "User ID=;Password=;")
24:    con.Open()
25:
26:    'Create a simple command that will select every record from a table
27:    Dim cmd as new OleDbCommand("Select * from " & _TableName, con)
28:
29:    'Create a data reader which will read each record from the select
30:    'command in a forward-only, read-only mode
31:    Dim rdr as OleDbDataReader = cmd.ExecuteReader()
32:
33:    'Loop for every record
34:    while rdr.Read()
35:
36:      'Loop through every column - 0 to FieldCount
37:      dim fldNum as integer
38:      for fldNum = 0 to rdr.FieldCount -1
39:
40:        dim strFieldItem as String = ""
41:
42:        'If the value in the column is not null, retrieve it as
43:        'a String value
44:        if not rdr.IsDBNull(fldNum) then
45:          strFieldItem = rdr.GetString(fldNum)
46:        end if
47:
48:        'Write out the value
49:        Response.Write(strFieldItem)
50:        if (fldNum < rdr.FieldCount - 1)
51:          Response.Write(", ")
52:        else
53:          Response.Write("<br>")
54:        end if
```

9

**LISTING 9.1** continued

```
55:    next
56:    end while
57:    'Close the data reader and the connection - no need to close
58:    'the command object
59:    rdr.Close()
60:    con.Close()
61: %>
```

**ANALYSIS** In Listing 9.1, notice that we need to import the System.Data and System.Data.OleDb namespaces (Lines 2–3). (If we were using the SQL Server provider, we would import System.Data.SqlClient instead on Line 3.)

The first half of the example opens a connection using the OleDbConnection object (Lines 20-24), executes a SQL query using the OleDbCommand object (Line 31), and reads the data through an OleDbDataReader object (Line 31 and the while loop on Lines 34–56.

The OleDbDataReader object contains a FieldCount property, which the innermost loop (Lines 34–56) in the example uses to find the number of columns in the dataset (Line 38). Notice that the dataset used by OleDbDataReader is *not* a true DataSet object; instead, it's just a read-only view of the results of a SQL query.

OleDbDataReader also contains the IsDBNull method, which returns true if the data in a particular column is null (Line 44). If we didn't test for a null value, the GetString method on Line 45 would throw an exception when applied to a null data item.

The sample calls GetString (Line 45) to retrieve and convert the value of every column into a string. You can retrieve the value of a column as Boolean, Byte, Char, DateTime, and many others by using the GetBoolean, GetByte, GetChar, and GetDateTime methods respectively. To find out the specific type of a data field, you can use the GetFieldType method from the SqlDataReader or OleDbDataReader class.

This sample repeatedly calls the OleDbDataReader object's Read method to read each new row (Line 34). The Read method returns false if there are no more rows to read in a set of data from the SqlCommand object.

At the end of the listing, we close both the DataReader and Connection objects using their Close methods (Lines 59–60).

**Note**

It's important to close every database connection that you open. Closing database connections is essential for connection pooling, which ADO.NET uses by default. Also, if you forget to close a connection, your application can quickly exhaust all available database connections.

Let's use this control in a simple page that prints the contents of the Customers table (see Listing 9.2).

**LISTING 9.2**  TableRead.aspx: A Web Page Using ShowTable.ascx

```
1: <%@ Page Language="vb" %>
2: <%@ Register TagPrefix="WebBook" TagName="TableWriter"
3:               Src="showtable.ascx" %>
4: <html>
5: <body>
6: <h3> The Customer table from the Northwind database </h3>
7: <WebBook:TableWriter TableName="Customers" runat="server"/>
8: </body>
9: </html>
```

 Notice that on Line 7 we pass the name of the particular database table to display using the `TableName` property of the ShowTable.ascx user control.

# Using Database Connections

Whenever you need to access the database with ADO.NET, creating an instance of the connections class (`SqlConnection` or `OleDbConnection`) is always the first step. As you saw in Listing 9.1, the connection class constructor takes a connection string that specifies a particular database to access. Correctly using connection strings can be tricky, so the remainder of this section will explore connection strings for both the `SqlConnection` and `OleDbConnection` classes.

## SQL Connection Class

Table 9.1 shows the most common parameters you can use in the `SqlConnection` string.

**TABLE 9.1**  Common Parameters for the `SqlConnection` Provider String

| Parameter | Description |
| --- | --- |
| data source | Tells the machine name of the computer that hosts the SQL Server. Use `"localhost"` for the local computer. You can also use your server's IP address for this parameter. |
| Integrated Security | Enables you to use Windows NT authentication to connect to the database rather than specify a SQL user with a username (`uid`) and password (`pwd`) parameter explicitly. |
| uid | Specifies the user ID used to connect to the database. Use `"sa"` for the administrative account. You don't need to use this parameter if you specified Integrated Security. |

**TABLE 9.1** continued

| Parameter | Description |
|-----------|-------------|
| pwd | Specifies the password to use for the user specified in the uid parameter. |
| database | Specifies the name of the database in the SQL server to connect with. |

Many parameters listed in Table 9.1 also have aliases. For instance, you can use Server, Address, Addr, or Network Address instead of the Data Source parameter, but all the parameters mean the same thing. Consult the Visual Studio documentation if you prefer to use an alias for these parameters.

From looking at Table 9.1, you might wonder whether to use integrated security or to specify a user ID and password explicitly in the connection. Your choice depends on the security policy that you or your database administrator has set up. SQL Server can use Windows NT accounts to authenticate a database user. This means that your client program can identify itself to the SQL Server as a particular Windows user. If your SQL Server has been set up to operate this way, use integrated security.

You can also create user accounts that are different from Windows user accounts on SQL Server. If the SQL Server database is set up this way, you can specify the uid and pwd parameters explicitly. The "sa" user is the account of the database administrator. Although we use this account in our samples, we highly recommend that you use a different, more restricted account in your own applications.

The remaining parameters you can use for the SQL provider connection string are listed in Table 9.2.

**TABLE 9.2** Other Parameters Used in the SQL Provider Connection Class String

| Parameter | Description |
|-----------|-------------|
| Current Language | The SQL Server language record name. |
| Network Library | The networking protocol that should be used to connect to the database. This parameter defaults to TCP/IP, but you can use other values for different protocols. Use dbmssocn for TCP/IP, dbnmpntw for Named Pipes, and dbmsrpcn for Multiprotocol. Consult the Visual Studio documentation for others. |
| Persist Security Info | If the parameter is set to false, the connection doesn't return sensitive information such as passwords. |
| Workstation ID | The name of the client computer. |
| Extended Properties | The name of an attachable database. |

A full explanation of these parameters is beyond the scope of this book. Consult the Visual Studio documentation or your local SQL Server expert for a full explanation of these parameters.

You can easily apply the parameters listed in Tables 9.1 and 9.2. For each parameter, specify the parameter name and value and separate each with a semicolon. The following code shows an example:

```
Dim con as
    new SqlConnection("data source=DBSrv03;integrated security=true;" & _
                      "database=WidgetsInc")
```

## OLE DB Connection Class

The connection string for the OleDbProvider Connection object depends on the particular OLE DB provider that you need to use. The only required parameter in the connection string is "Provider", which specifies the name of the underlying OLE DB provider. However, each OLE DB provider has other required parameters.

We won't list every parameter for every OLE DB provider in this lesson because doing so would involve quite a bit of reference material. You should consult your particular OLE DB provider's documentation for the exact parameters to use. However, instead of a complete OLE DB reference, Table 9.3 lists some connection strings for common providers.

**TABLE 9.3**  Connection Strings for OLE DB Providers

| Provider | Sample Connection String |
| --- | --- |
| Oracle | Provider=OraOLEDB.Oracle;Data Source=MyOracleDatabase;User Id=;Password=; |
| Access | Provider=Microsoft.Jet.OLEDB.4.0;Data Source=C:\Data\MyDatabase.mdb;User ID=;Password=; |
| Excel | Provider=Microsoft.Jet.OLEDB.4.0;Data Source=C:\Data\MyWkbk.xls;Extended Properties="Excel 8.0;HDR=No" |
| DB2 | Provider=DB2OLEDB;Network Transport Library=TCPIP;Network Address=Server;Package Collection=MyPkg;Host CCSID=1142;Initial Catalog=MyDatabase;User ID=;Password=; |

As you can see from Table 9.3, OLE DB connection strings are specific to each individual OLE DB provider. The MSDN Web site (http://msdn.microsoft.com) is a good reference for many OLE DB connection strings. Also, the documentation for the database you are using should contain an explanation of the connection string parameters you can use.

## Connection Errors

The examples so far haven't shown any error handling code. Error handling, especially when you're using databases, is an essential element of your application. In this section, we'll show some patterns for handling errors while opening a database connection.

Both the SqlConnection and OleDbConnection classes will throw exceptions if something is wrong with a connection string or if they have a problem contacting the database server. These two classes will throw SqlException and OleDbException, respectively. Each class contains an Errors collection, which contains at least one member of type SqlError or OleDbError if a problem occurred while connecting.

In your error handler, you can loop through the Errors collection of each exception, extract the SqlError or OleDbError object(s), and then query the error properties of each Error object.

The SqlError class contains a number of specialized properties to handle stored procedure errors, which are listed in the Visual Studio documentation. You can use the Number property for the error number, Message for an error message string, and State to find the state of the SQL Server.

The OleDbError class contains similar properties for querying the error type, including NativeError, Message, and SQLState. However, the OleDbError class doesn't contain methods for querying stored procedure errors.

If the connection string that you provide has an invalid syntax or the database connection is already open, both the SqlConnection and OleDbConnection objects will throw an InvalidOperationException. Calling the Open method will throw an exception if one of the parameters in the connection string is invalid or a problem occurs while trying to open the connection. Some typical code to handle these exceptions might look like the following:

```
Dim con as OleDbConnection
try
  OleDbConnection con =
    new OleDbConnection("Provider=Microsoft.Jet.OLEDB.4.0;" & _
      "Data Source=C:\Program Files\Microsoft Office\" & _
      "Office\Samples\Northwind.mdb;" & _
      "User ID=;Password=;")
  con.Open()
catch ex as InvalidOperationException
  'error handling for an already open connection
  'examine ex.HResult, ex.Message
catch  ex as OleDbException e
  dim err as OleDbError
  for each err in ex.Errors
    'examine e.Number, e.Message
  next
```

```
catch ex as Exception
  'general error handling
end try

if not con is nothing then
  'code to work with a valid database connection
end if
```

## Getting the Current State of the Connection

To find the current state of a Connection object, use the ConnectionState property. This property yields an enumeration of type ConnectionState, whose members are listed in Table 9.4.

**TABLE 9.4**   ConnectionState Enumeration Members

| State | Description |
| --- | --- |
| Open | The connection is open. |
| Closed | The connection is closed. |
| Connecting | The connection is in the process of being opened. |
| Executing | A command or stored procedure is in process. |
| Fetching | Data resulting from a command is being retrieved. |
| Broken | An error occurred with an open connection. To fix a broken connection, close and reopen the connection. |

## Abstracting the Data Provider

ADO.NET provides an easy way to write generic data access code to handle situations such as switching data providers or making your code independent of the underlying database. To create provider-independent code, use the ADO.NET provider interfaces: IDbCommand, IDataReader, and IDataAdapter. When using these classes, you still must use a database-specific Command object, but any other code can use these interfaces. Listing 9.3 shows a snippet of how to create objects using these interfaces.

**LISTING 9.3**   Provider-Independent Data Access Code

```
1: dim con as IDbConnection
2:
3: if bUseSql then
4:    Dim sqlcon as SqlConnection  = MyGetSqlConnectionMethod()
5:    con = sqlcon
6: else
7:    dim oledbcon as OleDbConnection = MyGetOleDbConnectionMethod()
8:    con = oledbcon
```

**LISTING 9.3** continued

```
 9: end if
10:
11: dim cmd as IDbCommand = con.CreateCommand()
12: 'set properties on the command
13: '...
14: dim rdr as IDataReader = cmd.ExecuteReader()
15: 'use the data reader
16: '...
```

**ANALYSIS** In Listing 9.3, MyGetSqlConnectionMethod (Line 4, which you must write your-self) contains code to open a connection to a SQL Server database using the tech-niques discussed earlier to return the reference to the connection. Similarly, MyGetOleDbConnectionMethod (Line 7) would do the same thing for a database connec-tion that uses OLE DB.

Unfortunately, using the generic data provider interface in Listing 9.3 limits the number of ADO.NET features you can use in your code because the SQL and OLE DB provider classes contain specialized methods and properties not accessible through the provider interfaces. However, the method in Listing 9.3 can serve as a good starting place for cre-ating provider-independent routines.

# Changing Data by Using Database Commands

Listing 9.1 showed how to use the SqlCommand object to execute a SELECT statement with the ExecuteReader method. You can also perform any other kind of SQL statement using the Command object. Tomorrow we will explain how to use the DataSet and DataAdapter classes to make data editing easy. This section will show how to update data using raw SQL commands. Using the command object this way forms the foundation for updating data with the DataSet and DataAdapter classes.

## Changing Data with the Command Object

SQL SELECT statements return rows of data. However, other SQL commands such as UPDATE or DELETE don't return any data. A SQL UPDATE command changes the value of one or more fields in a table row and does not return any records. A SQL DELETE com-mand deletes rows and doesn't return any records. In these cases, the Command object's ExecuteReader method object isn't appropriate.

Two other methods in the Command class used for SQL commands don't return records:

ExecuteNonQuery and ExecuteScalar. ExecuteNonQuery is used for SQL commands and stored procedures that don't return data rows, such as UPDATE and DELETE. ExecuteScalar is used for SQL commands that return a single value, such as the following SQL statement:

```
Select Count(*) From Customers
```

**NEW TERM** This SQL statement returns an integer value corresponding to the number of records in the Customers table. The term *scalar* means a numerical value, such as an integer.

Let's look at a couple of examples of changing data with the ExecuteNonQuery command. To change a single row in a table, you might use a SQL command like the following:

```
UPDATE Products SET UnitPrice=25.00 WHERE ProductName='Aniseed Syrup'
```

This statement would change the UnitPrice column in every row of the Products table where the ProductName field was "Aniseed Syrup".

To execute this command using the SqlCommand class, you could use code similar to Listing 9.4.

**LISTING 9.4** Using a SQL UPDATE Command with the *SqlCommand* Class

```
'open the connection as 'con'
'...
dim cmd as SqlCommand = con.CreateCommand()
cmd.CommandText = "UPDATE Products SET UnitPrice=25.00 " & _
                  "WHERE ProductName='Aniseed Syrup'"

con.Open()

dim nRowsAffected as integer = 0
nRowsAffected = cmd.ExecuteNonQuery()

con.Close()
```

ExecuteNonQuery returns the number of rows affected by the SQL statement.

For a second example, Listing 9.5 shows sample code that counts the total number of records in a table, using a SELECT COUNT SQL statement.

**LISTING 9.5** Counting the Total Number of Records in a Table

```
'open the connection as 'con'
'...
```

**LISTING 9.5**  continued

```
dim cmd as leDbCommand = con.CreateCommand()
cmd.CommandText = "SELECT COUNT(*) FROM Products WHERE UnitPrice >= 10.00"

con.Open()

Dim nProductsOverTen as integer = 0
nProductsOverTen = CInt(cmd.ExecuteScalar())
con.Close()
```

From Listing 9.5, we needed to cast the result of the ExecuteScalar method into the desired type because ExecuteScalar has a return type of Object.

Let's put Listings 9.1, 9.4, and 9.5 into a working sample program that will show the names and prices of some products in the Northwind Products table and allow the user to change the price of each. First, we need to make some slight modifications to Listing 9.1 so that we can enter an arbitrary SQL string to select rows of data. Listing 9.6 shows the new ShowTable.ascx user control with this modification.

**LISTING 9.6**  ShowTable2.ascx: Version That Uses an Arbitrary SQL String to Select Records to Display

```
 1: <%@ Control Language="vb" debug=true%>
 2: <%@ Import Namespace="System.Data" %>
 3: <%@ Import Namespace="System.Data.OleDb" %>
 4: <script runat="server">
 5:
 6: private _Sql as String
 7:
 8: public writeonly property Sql() as string
 9:   set(byval value as string)
10:     _Sql = value
11:   end set
12: end property
13:
14: </script>
15: <%
16:   'Create a connection to the local NorthWind database
17:   dim con as new OleDbConnection("Provider=Microsoft.Jet.OLEDB.4.0;" & _
18:     "Data Source=C:\Program Files\Microsoft Office\" & _
19:     "Office\Samples\Northwind.mdb;User ID=;Password=;")
20:   con.Open()
21:
22:   'Build command
23:   Dim cmd as new OleDbCommand(_Sql, con)
24:
25:   'Create a data reader which will read each record from the select
```

**LISTING 9.6**   continued

```
26:   'command in a forward-only, read-only mode
27:   Dim rdr as OleDbDataReader = cmd.ExecuteReader()
28:
29:   'Loop for every record
30:   Response.Write("<table>")
31:   while rdr.Read()
32:     Response.Write("<tr>")
33:
34:     'Loop through every column
35:     dim fldNum as integer
36:     for fldNum = 0 to rdr.FieldCount - 1
37:       dim strFieldItem as String = ""
38:
39:       'If the value in the column is not null, retrieve it as a
40:       'String value
41:       if not rdr.IsDBNull(fldNum) then
42:         strFieldItem = rdr.GetValue(fldNum).ToString()
43:       end if
44:
45:       'Write out the value
46:       Response.Write("<td>")
47:       Response.Write(strFieldItem)
48:       if fldNum < rdr.FieldCount - 1 then
49:         Response.Write("</td><td>")
50:       else
51:         Response.Write("</td></tr>")
52:       end if
53:     Next
54:   end while
55:   Response.Write("</table>")
56:
57:   'Close the data reader and the connection - no need to close
58:   'the command object
59:   rdr.Close()
60:   con.Close()
61: %>
```

**ANALYSIS**   Listing 9.6 is almost identical to Listing 9.1, with the addition of a SQL property string (Lines 8–12) and the capability to show its results in an HTML table, using the Response.Write commands throughout the listing.

Now we need to create a page that will allow users to update the price of a product. Listing 9.7 shows such a sample program, using a SqlCommand object and the ExecuteNonQuery method. Figure 9.2 shows the resulting Web page.

**LISTING 9.7**   UpdateProducts.aspx: Allowing Users to Update Records

```
 1: <%@ Page Language="vb" %>
 2: <%@ Register TagPrefix="WebBook" TagName="TableWriter"
 3:        Src="showtable2.ascx" %>
 4: <%@ Import Namespace="System.Data" %>
 5: <%@ Import Namespace="System.Data.OleDb" %>
 6: <html>
 7: <body>
 8: <form runat="server">
 9:   <h2>Northwind Products Names and Prices</h2>
10:   <WebBook:TableWriter
11:   Sql="Select ProductName, UnitPrice from Products where CategoryID = 1"
12:   runat="server"/>
13:   <br>
14:   <b>Name of Item to Change:</b>
15:   <asp:TextBox id="Name" runat="server" /><br>
16:   <b>New Price: </b> <asp:TextBox id="Price" runat="server" /><br>
17:   <asp:Button id="SetPrice" Text="Update Price"
18:               runat="server" OnClick="UpdatePrice"/>
19:   <asp:Label id="Status" runat="server"/>
20: </form>
21: </body>
22: </html>
23:
24: <script runat="server">
25: sub UpdatePrice(Sender as Object, e as EventArgs )
26:
27:   'Create a connection to the local NorthWind database
28:   dim con as new OleDbConnection("Provider=Microsoft.Jet.OLEDB.4.0;" & _
29:        "Data Source=C:\Program Files\Microsoft Office\" & _
30:        "Office\Samples\Northwind.mdb; User ID=;Password=;")
31:   con.Open()
32:
33:   'Build update command
34:   Dim cmd as new OleDbCommand("Update Products Set UnitPrice = " & _
35:                              Price.Text & " where ProductName = '" & _
36:                              Name.Text & "'", con)
37:   dim nRowsAffected as integer
38:   nRowsAffected = cmd.ExecuteNonQuery()
39:   Status.Text = "<hr>Updated " & nRowsAffected.ToString() & _
40:                " row(s)<hr>"
41:   con.Close()
42: end sub
43: </script>
```

**FIGURE 9.2**

*Updating records
using the ADO.NET
command object.*

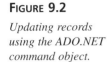

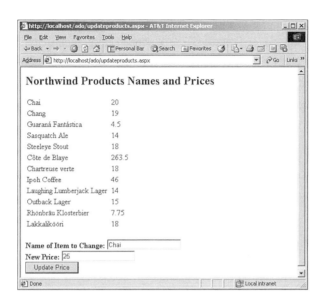

**ANALYSIS** The page contains two TextBox controls (Lines 15–16), with `"Name"` and `"Price"` IDs, which allow the user to choose the name of a product and new price for it. A Button control (Line 17) calls the `UpdatePrice` routine (Lines 25–42), and a Label control (Line 19) shows the operation's status.

Within the `UpdatePrice` method, Listing 9.7 creates a new `OleDbConnection` object (Line 28) in the same way that other listings in this lesson have done. Next, the listing creates a new `OleDbCommand` object (Line 34), building the `UPDATE` SQL statement dynamically using the contents of the Name and Price TextBox controls.

Last, Listing 9.7 calls the `ExecuteNonQuery` method (Line 38) and displays the number of rows updated in the Status Label control (Line 39).

## Using Parameters with the `Command` Object

Listing 9.7 builds an `UPDATE` SQL command dynamically, as the following excerpt shows:

```
34:    Dim cmd as new OleDbCommand("Update Products Set UnitPrice = " & _
35:                        Price.Text & " where ProductName = '" & _
36:                        Name.Text & "'", con)
```

Creating SQL commands this way presents several problems. First, debugging the code is difficult, especially if the SQL statement is complex. Second, creating SQL statements this way can allow a malicious user to enter his or her own SQL code in the program. In this example, text from the Price and Name text boxes is added directly into the SQL statement.

The Command object gives you a better way to handle this situation: using the Parameters collection. Both the SqlCommand and OleDbCommand objects contain a Parameters collection that contains SqlParameter and OleDbParameter objects, respectively. Each Parameter object corresponds to a variable from your program. In the preceding example, Price and ProductName are parameters. By convention, SQL statement parameters are preceded by the @ character, as the following listing shows.

Listing 9.8 shows how to use the Parameters collection and a static SQL string.

LISTING 9.8   Using a Parameterized SQL Statement and the Command Object

```
 1:  'open the connection as 'con'
 2:  '...
 3:  Dim cmd as OleDbCommand = con.CreateCommand()
 4:  cmd.CommandText = "SELECT COUNT(*) FROM Products "& _
 5:                       "WHERE UnitPrice >= @UnitPriceCutoff"
 6:
 7:  OleDbParameter parCutoff = _
 8:      cmd.Parameters.Add("@UnitPriceCutoff", SqlDbType.Int)
 9:  parCutoff.Direction = ParameterDirection.Input
10:  parCutoff.Value = 10
11:
12:  con.Open()
13:
14:  Dim nProductsOverTen as Integer = 0
15:  nProductsOverTen = Cint(cmd.ExecuteScalar())
16:  con.Close()
```

**ANALYSIS**   Listing 9.8 creates a new OleDbParameter object (Lines 7–8) by calling the Add method of the OleDbCommand Parameters collection. The Add method returns a new OleDbParameter object, which you can manipulate later in your code. You must specify the name of the parameter and data type. In this case, we called the parameter "@UnitPriceCutoff" (Lines 5 and 8). Notice that the parameter name must match the parameter in the static SQL statement exactly.

Let's fix Listing 9.7 so that it also uses a static SQL string and the Parameters collection. Listing 9.9 shows one way to fix it.

LISTING 9.9   UpdateProducts2.aspx: A Second Version of That Uses a Static SQL String

```
1: <%@ Page Language="vb" Debug="true" %>
2: <%@ Register TagPrefix="WebBook" TagName="TableWriter"
3:      Src="showtable2.ascx" %>
4: <%@ Import Namespace="System.Data" %>
5: <%@ Import Namespace="System.Data.OleDb" %>
```

**LISTING 9.9**    continued

```
 6: <html>
 7: <body>
 8: <form runat="server">
 9:   <h2>Northwind Products Names and Prices</h2>
10:   <WebBook:TableWriter
11:   Sql="Select ProductName, UnitPrice from Products where CategoryID = 1"
12:   runat="server"/>
13:   <br>
14:   <b>Name of Item to Change:</b>
15:   <asp:TextBox id="Name" runat="server" /><br>
16:   <b>New Price: </b> <asp:TextBox id="Price" runat="server" /><br>
17:   <asp:Button id="SetPrice" Text="Update Price"
18:                 runat="server" OnClick="UpdatePrice"/>
19:   <asp:Label id="Status" runat="server"/>
20: </form>
21: </body>
22: </html>
23:
24: <script runat="server">
25: sub UpdatePrice(Sender as object, e as EventArgs)
26:
27:   'Create a connection to the local NorthWind database
28:     Dim con as new OleDbConnection("Provider=Microsoft.Jet.OLEDB.4.0;" & _
29:         "Data Source=C:\Program Files\Microsoft Office\" & _
30:         "Office\Samples\Northwind.mdb;" & _
31:         "User ID=;Password=;")
32:   con.Open()
33:
34:   'Build update command
35:   Dim cmd as new OleDbCommand("Update Products Set UnitPrice = " & _
36:         "@UnitPrice where ProductName = @ProductName", con)
37:   'Use parameters
38:   Dim parPrice as OleDbParameter = _
39:     cmd.Parameters.Add("@UnitPrice", SqlDbType.Int)
40:   parPrice.Value = Price.Text
41:   Dim parName as OleDbParameter = _
42:     cmd.Parameters.Add("@ProductName", SqlDbType.VarChar)
43:   parName.Value = Name.Text
44:
45:   Dim nRowsAffected as integer
46:   nRowsAffected = cmd.ExecuteNonQuery()
47:   Status.Text = "<hr>Updated " & _
48:                 nRowsAffected.ToString() + " row(s)<hr>"
49:   con.Close()
50: End Sub
51: </script>
```

9

**ANALYSIS** UpdateProducts2.aspx in Listing 9.9 uses a control from Listing 9.6 to display results. This user control is included into the sample using the `Register` directive (Line 2). Lines 10–12 use this user control to display the current contents of the table within the Web form. The Update Price button on Line 17 invokes the `UpdatePrice` event handler (Lines 25–50) using the new price entered in the Price text box (Line 16).

The `UpdatePrice` event handler creates a new `OleDbConnection` (Lines 28–31) and opens the connection on Line 32. The `Update` command (Lines 35–36) uses parameters instead of a dynamic string. The `Add` method (Lines 41 and 42) is used to bind the parameters from the `Update` string to the user-entered values.

The key difference between Listing 9.9 and Listing 9.7 is the use of the parameterized update string (Line 38) and the code to bind the user-entered values to explicit parameter objects (Lines 40–43).

## Using Stored Procedures

Stored procedures are programs that run inside a database server. Many commercial databases, such as Microsoft SQL Server or Oracle, extend the standard SQL language so that you can use these programs. Stored procedures have many advantages: They execute quickly and allow a database administrator to create tight security around a database.

As you have seen from previous examples, you use the `Connection` (`SqlConnection` or `OleDbConnection`) object to execute SQL commands in a database. You also can use the `Connection` object to execute stored procedures by setting the `CommandType` property. Listing 9.10 shows a SQL Server stored procedure for selecting particular products from the Products table in the Northwind database.

**LISTING 9.10** A Sample SQL Stored Procedure to Fetch Particular Products

```
1: CREATE PROCEDURE GetProductByCategoryID
2:   @CategoryID int
3: AS
4:   SELECT ProductName, UnitPrice
5:   FROM Products P
6:   WHERE P.CategoryID = @CategoryID
7:   ORDER BY UnitPrice DESC
```

**ANALYSIS** This stored procedure takes a Category ID as input (Line 2) and returns rows from a simple `SELECT` statement (Lines 4–7). To call this stored procedure, you use code similar to Listing 9.11.

**LISTING 9.11** Calling the `GetProductsByCategoryID` Stored Procedure

```
 1: 'open the connection as 'con'
 2: '...
 3: Dim cmd as SqlCommand = con.CreateCommand()
 4: cmd.CommandType = CommandType.StoredProcedure
 5: cmd.CommandText = "GetProductByID"
 6:
 7: SqlParameter parCatID = _
 8:     cmd.Parameters.Add("@CategoryID", SqlDbType.int)
 9: parCatID.Value = 4
10:
11: con.Open()
12:
13: Dim rdr as SqlReader = cmd.ExecuteReader()
14: 'read the results and do something with them
15: '...
16: rdr.Close()
17: con.Close()
```

**ANALYSIS** Listing 9.11 sets the `CommandType` and `CommandText` properties (Lines 4–5) for the command object to point to the desired stored procedure. The code adds a parameter to the `Parameters` collection of the command object (Lines 7–8) because the stored procedure needs the Category ID to run properly.

# Summary

Today you saw several examples of ADO.NET programs that executed SQL commands, read data, and modified data. After reading this lesson, you should have a good foundation for understanding the ADO.NET data provider classes.

Today's lesson didn't cover one of the most important data provider classes, `DataAdapter`. Tomorrow's lesson will discuss this class and the `DataSet` class in detail.

# Q&A

**Q I'm used to using the ADO `Recordset` class to perform my data access. Why are the new ADO.NET classes better?**

**A** The ADO.NET classes are specialized for the most common types of data access tasks that your application will perform. Thanks to this specialization, each class is optimized to perform one function well. For instance, the ADO.NET `DataReader` class provides an optimized way to read recordset data in a forward-only way. A high percentage of ADO `Recordset` code can be replaced by this construct. As tomorrow's lesson will show, the `DataSet` class provides a less resource-intensive way to manipulate and store data back, allowing your code to support many more concurrent users. As you've seen today, the Command classes are specialized for individual update and deletion commands that might be performed by a stored procedure or SQL statement.

**Q I might change my database before I am through with my project. Which data provider should I use?**

A The OLE DB provider can access almost any kind of database, so it's probably the best choice to begin with. Use the abstract ADO.NET interfaces where possible (the answer to Exercise 2 shows how to implement this interface for Listing 9.1). If you're certain that your project will use SQL Server, use the SQL data provider because it is optimized for the SQL Server.

# Workshop

The Workshop provides quiz questions to help you solidify your understanding of the material covered and exercises to provide you with experience in using what you've learned. The answers to the quiz questions are provided in Appendix A, "Answers to Quizzes and Exercises."

## Quiz

1. What two types of data providers does ADO.NET supply? What determines which one you should use?

2. What two classes are used to open and connect to a database using ADO.NET?

3. What two classes are used to read data only?

4. What two classes are used to execute arbitrary SQL commands in a database using ADO.NET?

5. What method is used by the Command classes to execute SQL commands that do not return resultsets, such as the SELECT COUNT command?

6. What method is used by the Command classes to execute SQL statements that return single values?

7. What is the preferred method for executing SQL commands that contain parameters?

8. What are the two main types of classes associated with errors that are thrown by ADO.NET classes?

9. Why two interfaces can be used to abstract the SQL and OLE DB data providers?

## Exercise

1. Rewrite Listing 9.1 to use SQL Server and the SQL data provider.

2. Rewrite Listing 9.1 to use the abstract ADO.NET interfaces where possible and an `OleDbConnection` object. Use the `Connection` object's `CreateCommand` method to make a new connection.

9

# DAY 10

# Working with Datasets

Yesterday's lesson provided an introduction to ADO.NET and described how you can execute SQL commands and read data from databases. Although you will never create Web pages or a Web service with ADO.NET directly, many of your Internet applications will probably use ADO.NET to store and retrieve data.

Today we'll focus on the DataSet and DataAdapter objects, which provide a powerful model for database programming. We'll also learn about the classes contained in the DataSet object, such as DataTables and DataRelations.

Today you will learn about the following:

- The DataSet object
- The DataAdapter object and how to use it with DataSet
- How to read, modify, and update data with a DataSet
- How to handle errors when reading and writing data
- How to create relationships and constraints in a DataSet

## What Are DataSets and DataAdapters?

The DataSet class stores a copy of data from one or more database tables so that your program can display and manipulate the data. However, DataSets don't have any methods or properties that deal with data providers; they are independent of any database that you choose. We showed an example of a DataSet that didn't use a database on Day 5, "Using Advanced ASP.NET Web Controls," for the examples of the DataGrid and DataList Web controls.

DataAdapter objects bridge the gap between the data provider classes you saw yesterday and the DataSet class. Figure 10.1 shows the relationship between the DataSet, DataAdapter, and data provider classes.

**FIGURE 10.1**

*How the DataAdapter fits into ADO.NET.*

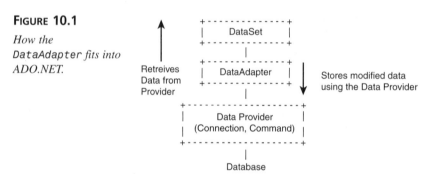

As you may have guessed, ADO.NET comes with OleDbAdapter and SqlDataAdapter classes. Each adapter class references a connection object: OleDbAdapter references OleDbConnection, and SqlDataAdapter references SqlDataConnection. The DataAdapter classes contain methods that fill a DataSet with the contents of a database table using a custom SQL command and write the contents of a modified dataset back to the database.

## Reading Data into a Dataset

Today's first sample program uses the DataAdapter and DataSet classes to display the contents of a database table. The results of this sample are similar to the first sample from yesterday.

Follow these steps to use DataSet and DataAdapter objects in a sample program:

1. Create a connection to the database.
2. Create a new DataSet object.

3. Create a new `DataAdapter` object and pass in a reference to the database connection when creating it.

4. Call the `Fill` method of the `DataAdapter` class to populate the `DataSet` object.

Let's examine each step in more detail:

1. As with the examples from yesterday, our first job is to create a connection to the database. Let's use the Northwind database again, using code like the following:

```
Dim con as _
    new OleDbConnection("Provider=Microsoft.Jet.OLEDB.4.0;" & _
        "Data Source=C:\Program Files\Microsoft Office\" & _
        "Office\Samples\Northwind.mdb;" & _
        "User ID=;Password=;")
```

2. Create a `DataSet` object to store data from the Orders table by adding the following line:

```
Dim ds as new DataSet("Northwind")
```

The parameter passed into the `DataSet` constructor is the new dataset name. We called the dataset Northwind because this is the name of the source database. However, at this moment the Northwind dataset isn't yet related to the Northwind database. We need to bridge the connection from the database to the data set and will do so in the next step.

3. Create a `DataAdapter` object to read all records from the Orders table and put the results in the dataset:

```
Dim adpt as new OleDbDataAdapter("SELECT * FROM ORDERS," con)
```

The `DataAdapter` has a number of constructors. In this example, we're using a simple version which takes an SQL command and a `connection` object as arguments.

You could achieve the same results using a `command` object to execute an SQL command directly against a database. If we were using this technique we would create the command object using the required SQL statement, as shown here:

```
Dim cmdSelOrders as new OleDbCommand("Select * from Orders")
```

Then you would add this command to the `DataAdapter` object, like the following line does:

```
daOrders.SelectCommand = cmdSelOrders
```

The `DataAdapter` class contains four properties that you can set to one of your own command objects, for selecting, updating, deleting, and adding data. `DataAdapter` uses the `SelectCommand` property for the command that will select data.

4. Transfer records from the database into the dataset by using the `Fill` command:

```
da.Fill(dsNorthwind, "Orders")
```

**10**

The `Fill` command performs a number of tasks. First, it creates a new `DataTable` object inside the dataset. As you might expect, a `DataTable` represents the results of a SQL query and stores records in a similar way to a database table. We named the datatable Orders using the second parameter of the constructor.

While using a `DataSet` object, you can access any contained `DataTable` through the `Tables` collection. Within the `Tables` collection, you can access any record by using the `Rows` collection. The `Tables` collection also contains a `Columns` collection, which contains information about each `DataTable` column.

Let's combine these steps into a working sample program. Listing 10.1 shows a sample program that displays the contents of the Northwind Orders table. Figure 10.2 shows the example in action.

**FIGURE 10.2**

*Displaying a table using a data adapter.*

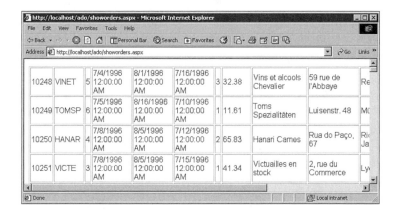

**LISTING 10.1** ShowOrders.aspx: Displaying the Contents of the Orders Table by Using `Command`, `DataSet`, and `DataAdapter` Classes

```
 1: <%@ Page Language="vb" %>
 2: <%@ Import Namespace="System.Data" %>
 3: <%@ Import Namespace="System.Data.OleDb" %>
 4: <html>
 5: <body>
 6: <font face="Arial">
 7: <table border=1>
 8: <%
 9:   Dim con as new OleDbConnection("Provider=Microsoft.Jet.OLEDB.4.0;" & _
10:       "Data Source=C:\Program Files\Microsoft Office\" & _
11:       "Office\Samples\Northwind.mdb;" & _
12:       "User ID=;Password=;")
13:   Dim adpt as new OleDbDataAdapter("SELECT * FROM Orders", con)
14:
15:   Dim ds as new DataSet("Northwind")
```

**LISTING 10.1** continued

```
16:
17:   adpt.Fill(ds, "Orders")
18:   Dim r as DataRow
19:   for each r in ds.Tables("Orders").Rows
20:     Response.Write("<tr>")
21:     Dim i as integer
22:       for i = 0 to r.Table.Columns.Count - 1
23:           Response.Write("<td>" + r(i).ToString() + "</td>")
24:       next
25:     Response.Write("</tr>")
26:   next
27: %>
28: </table>
29: </font>
30: </body>
31: </html>
```

**10**

**ANALYSIS**  Listing 10.1 imports the proper namespaces (Lines 2–3) and creates a connection object (Lines 9–12) as a first step. Next, the code combines some of the steps outlined at the beginning of the section by specifying the SQL SELECT command in the constructor for the data adapter (Line 13).

The end of the code iterates through each row in the Orders table (Lines 19–26). The Rows collection contains objects of type DataRow (Line 18). After each individual row is selected, the code accesses each field in the row by using the default indexing property (Line 23), which allows us to access each DataRow object as though it were an array.

Notice that this code never calls the Open or Close methods of the Connection object. The DataAdapter object takes care of opening and closing the connection to the database for you.

# Changing Data with a Dataset

After you read data into a dataset, you usually modify the data in some way. Keep in mind that any changes you make to a DataSet object aren't automatically reflected in the database. You must use the DataAdapter object to update a database after you modify the DataSet.

To add a row to a DataTable object contained in a dataset, use the NewRow and Add methods:

```
Dim r as DataRow = myDataTable.NewRow()
r("Address") = "11 Elm Street"
r("ModifiedTime") = DateTime.Now()
r(3) = "Another value"  'this will change the fourth column
```

```
myDataTable.Rows.Add(r)
```

If you need to modify a value, you can access the Rows collection on the dataset as though it were a two-dimensional array. This is shown in the following line, which sets the value of the DateTimeCol field in the 35th row to the current date and time:

```
MyDataTable.Rows(35)("DateTimeCol") = DateTime.Now()
```

You can also loop through the Rows collection as follows:

```
Dim r As DataRow
for each r in myDataTable.Rows
  'do something with Row r
next
```

 **Note**      Tomorrow's lesson looks at another way of accessing data tables using properties. This method is called a *typed dataset*.

To delete a row, call the Delete method on the Rows collection:

```
myDataTable.Rows(34).Delete
```

Although DataSet is changed, the database is *not* changed. To persist changes back to the database, use a two-step process:

1. Call the GetChanges method to create a new dataset that contains only changed (or new, or deleted) records.
2. Call the Update method of the DataAdapter to persist the changes back to the database.

You might be wondering how the DataAdapter knows how to update data. As we mentioned earlier, the DataAdapter has four properties, each of which is a command that will access or change data in the database: SelectCommmand, AddCommand, DeleteCommand, and UpdateCommand.

You don't need to create command objects for each property if you've already created the SelectCommand. Instead, use a command builder object, which will create the Add, Delete, and Update commands automatically based on the SelectCommand. Just create a new command builder and assign it to the DataAdapter object:

```
Dim cb as new OleDbCommandBuilder(adptMyAdapter)
```

For the SQL Server–based adapter, use the SqlCommandBuilder class.

> **Note**
>
> Visual Studio.NET automatically generates commands for the DataAdapter object for you. The section "Using Visual Studio.NET" later today contains the details.

After the DataAdapter object is configured with the Select, Add, Delete, and Update commands, you can use it to update the underlying database by using the GetChanges method:

```
Dim dsChanges as DataSet = myDataSet.GetChanges(DataRowState.Modified)
myDataAdapter.Update(dsChanges, "DataTableName")
```

Notice that the GetChanges method returns a new DataSet object containing just the modified rows.

You can pass a number of different parameters to the GetChanges method, including Deleted, New, Modified, and Unchanged. For instance, to update all the rows that have been deleted in a dataset, you use a line like the following:

```
Dim dsDeletedRowsSet as DataSet = myDataSet.GetChanges(DataRowState.Deleted)
```

Table 10.1 explains the parameters that you pass to the GetChanges method.

**TABLE 10.1**  The DataRowState Enumeration

| Parameter | Description |
| --- | --- |
| Modified | Returns records with fields that have changed |
| UnChanged | Returns records that have never been modified |
| Added | Returns any records that have been added |
| Deleted | Returns any records that have been deleted |
| Detached | Represents new DataRows that haven't been added to a DataSet. Won't return any records when used with the GetChanges method. |

Listing 10.2 shows sample code that will change a record in the Northwind Products table. Figure 10.3 shows the example in action.

**FIGURE 10.3**

*Changing records in
the Products table.*

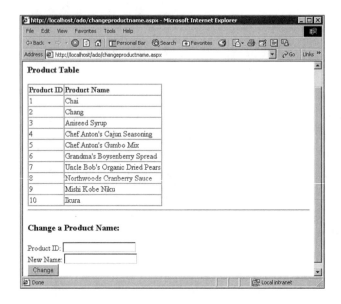

**LISTING 10.2**   ChangeProductName.aspx: Changing the Name of One Record in the
Northwind Products Table

```
 1: <%@ Page Language="vb" debug="true"%>
 2: <%@ Import Namespace="System.Data" %>
 3: <%@ Import Namespace="System.Data.OleDb" %>
 4:
 5: <html>
 6: <body>
 7:   <form runat="server">
 8:
 9:   <hr>
10:   <h3>Product Table</h3>
11:   <% PrintTable() %>
12:   <hr>
13:   <h3>Change a Product Name:</h3>
14:   Product ID: <asp:TextBox id="ProdID" runat="server" />
15:   <br>
16:   New Name:    <asp:TextBox id="NewName" runat="server" />
17:   <br>
18:   <asp:Button Text="Change" OnClick="OnChange" runat="server"/>
19:
20:   </form>
21: </body>
22: </html>
23:
24: <script runat="server">
25:
```

LISTING **10.2** continued

```
26: Dim ds as DataSet
27: Dim adpt as OleDbDataAdapter
28:
29: sub Page_Load(Sender As Object, e As EventArgs)
30:
31:   if not IsPostBack then
32:     ' If this is the first time the page has been hit,
33:     ' create our data set and data adapter
34:     CreateDataSet()
35:
36:     ' Add the data set and data adapter to Session state,
37:     ' so that they can be retrieved after the user clicks
38:     ' the "Change" button
39:     Session.Add("DataSet", ds)
40:     Session.Add("Adapter", adpt)
41:   else
42:      ' Load the data set and data adapter objects
43:      ' from session since this is a page postback
44:     ds = CType(Session("DataSet"), DataSet)
45:     adpt = CType( Session("Adapter"), OleDbDataAdapter)
46:   end if
47: End Sub
48:
49: ' Create a data set and data adapter for the Products table
50: sub CreateDataSet()
51:
52:   Dim con as new OleDbConnection("Provider=Microsoft.Jet.OLEDB.4.0;" & _
53:       "Data Source=C:\Program Files\Microsoft Office\" & _
54:       "Office\Samples\Northwind.mdb;")
55:   adpt = new OleDbDataAdapter("SELECT TOP 10 ProductID, ProductName " & _
56:        "FROM Products ORDER BY ProductID", con)
57:
58:   ' Automatically generate Update, Delete, and Insert commands with a
59:   ' command builder object
60:   Dim cb as new OleDbCommandBuilder(adpt)
61:
62:   ds = new DataSet()
63:
64:   ' Grab all of our data from the database
65:   adpt.Fill(ds, "Products")
66: End Sub
67:
68: '  This is the Change button event handler
69: '  Parse the product id and pass it as a row number to the
70: '  PersistChange method
71: sub OnChange(Sender as Object, e as EventArgs)
72:
73:   Dim nID as integer = CInt(ProdID.Text)
74:   PersistChanges(nID - 1, NewName.Text)
```

**10**

LISTING 10.2 continued

```
75:
76: end sub
77:
78: '  Change a row, and persist the change to the database
79: sub PersistChanges(nId as integer, strName as String)
80:
81:    Dim dt as DataTable = ds.Tables("Products")
82:    dt.Rows(nId)(1) = strName
83:    Dim dsMod as DataSet = ds.GetChanges(DataRowState.Modified)
84:    adpt.Update(dsMod, "Products")
85:    ds.AcceptChanges()
86:
87: end sub
88:
89: ' Print out the contents of a data table
90: sub PrintTable()
91:
92:    Response.Write("<table border='1' cellspacing='0'>")
93:    Response.Write("<tr><td><b>Product ID</b></td>")
94:    Response.Write("<td><b>Product Name</b></td></tr>")
95:
96:    Dim dt as DataTable = ds.Tables("Products")
97:    Dim r as DataRow
98:    Dim i as integer
99:    for each r in dt.Rows
100:      Response.Write("<tr>")
101:      for i = 0 to r.Table.Columns.Count - 1
102:        Response.Write("<td>" & r(i).ToString() & "</td>")
103:      next
104:      Response.Write("</tr>")
105:    next
106:    Response.Write("</table>")
107:
108: end sub
109: </script>
```

**ANALYSIS** Let's start our analysis of Listing 10.2 by examining the HTML portion. Line 11 calls the PrintTable method (Lines 90–108) to display the Products database table and some input boxes that allow users to change a product name.

The Page_Load event (Lines 29–47) performs two tasks:

- On the initial page hit, it calls the CreateDataSet method (Line 34), which is responsible for connecting to the database and creating new DataSet and DataAdapter objects.

- If Page_Load is being called from a postback (the user clicks the Change button), the event retrieves the DataSet and DataAdapter objects from Session (Lines 44–45).

The OnChange method (Lines 71–76)handles the Click event from the Change button (Line 18). It calculates the row number of the Products table that needs to be changed (Line 73) and then calls the PersistChanges method (Line 74). PersistChanges (Lines 79–87) shows the GetChanges (Line 83) and AcceptChanges methods (Line 85) in action.

The CreateDataSet method (Lines 50–66)uses a SQL statement that returns only the first 10 rows from the Products table, repeated here from Lines 55–56:

```
"SELECT TOP 10 ProductID, ProductName " & _
"FROM Products ORDER BY ProductID"
```

You can also limit the records returned by a DataAdapter by using a WHERE clause, such as the following SQL statement does:

```
SELECT ProductID, ProductName from Products WHERE ProductID = 1
```

## Understanding How the Dataset Tracks Changes

You might be wondering how the dataset knows which values have changed and how you can control which rows get returned from the GetChanges method. As you saw in Listings 10.1 and 10.2, each DataTable in each DataSet contains a Rows collection that contains each data row in the table. Each element of the Rows collection is of type DataRow.

Each DataRow contains a RowState property, which can take on the values listed in Table 10.1 (Modified, Added, Deleted, and Unchanged). Whenever your program modifies a value in a row, the RowState changes from Unchanged to Modified. If your program adds a new DataRow, the RowState property is set to Added. Likewise, if your program deletes a row in the DataTable, the RowState property becomes Deleted.

When the GetChanges method is called, you pass in a RowState enumeration value, and the method creates a new DataSet with a DataTable containing rows in the RowState you requested.

If your program needs to add records to the database, you might use the following code lines:

```
Dim dsChanges as DataSet = myDataSet.GetChanges(DataRowState.Added)
myDataAdapter.Update(dsChanges, "DataTableName")
```

Similarly, to delete records in the database, you might use the following two code lines:

```
Dim dsChanges as DataSet = myDataSet.GetChanges(DataRowState.Deleted)
myDataAdapter.Update(dsChanges, "DataTableName")
```

10

## Resetting Properties with the AcceptChanges Method

The DataRow, DataTable, and DataSet classes each contain an AcceptChanges method. This method resets all RowState properties to UnModified. If AcceptChanges is called on a DataSet object, the DataSet object calls AcceptChanges on each DataTable that it contains. In turn, each DataTable object then calls AcceptChanges on each DataRow that it contains. After you call Update in the DataAdapter, you should call AcceptChanges if there are no errors.

| Tip | When AcceptChanges is called for a row with a Deleted RowState, the row is removed from the DataTable that it belongs to. |

Take another look at Table 10.1 listing the RowState enumerations. Each value is relative to the last time AcceptChanges was called on the dataset.

# Handling DataAdapter Errors

The SqlDataAdapter and OleDbAdapter classes fire events if an error occurs when your program calls Fill or Update. Expert developers create special code to handle errors that may occur when reading and writing data to the database. You might ignore the error in your code, log the error, or take a special action. You can do all this by writing error event handling methods in your program.

Two events are associated with the Update command: RowUpdating and RowUpdated. You can add event handlers for them with code similar to the following:

```
AddHandler MyDataAdapter.RowUpdating AddressOf MyUpdatingHandler
AddHandler MyDataAdapter.RowUpdated AddressOf MyUpdatedHandler
```

The preceding code lines add event handlers to an object. In this case, two event handlers are added to the MyDataAdapter object. Each event handler is a method that you must code yourself, so you must code the MyUpdatingHandler and MyUpdatedHandler methods.

Inside your custom event handler, you can find information about the status of the update, update type, and contents of the current row by examining the Update, Status, and Row properties. Listing 10.3 shows some template code.

**LISTING 10.3**    Tracing the Contents of the SqlRowUpdatedEventArgs Object

```
1:  sub MyUpdatedHandler(Sender as Object, e as SqlRowUpdatedEventArgs)
2:
```

**LISTING 10.3** continued

```
 3:     if e.Errors.Count > 0 then
 4:
 5:         'Examine errors
 6:         '...
 7:         'Errors were unrecoverable
 8:         e.Status = SkipAllRemainingRows
 9:
10: End Sub
```

**ANALYSIS**  Line 3 examines the number of errors related to the Update event for the current row. If errors occur, the remaining code lines are skipped.

Line 8 sets the Status property to SkipAllRemainingRows if the error was unrecoverable. This aborts all future updates to the database. You can set the Status property to other values depending on the type of error encountered in the Update event. Table 10.3 shows possible values of the Status property.

**TABLE 10.3**  Status Property Values

| Value | Description |
| --- | --- |
| Continue (default) | No errors occurred; continue processing. |
| ErrorOccurred | There was an error; the Update method should throw an exception. |
| SkipCurrentRow | Don't update this row, and don't throw an exception. |
| SkipAllRemainingRows | Don't update any more rows, and don't throw an exception. |

You can handle errors in the Fill method by adding a SqlFillErrorEventHandler or OleDbFillErrorEventHandler similarly to the way you add to the Update and Updated event handlers. The Fill event handler gets an object of type FillErrorEventArgs, which contains a Continue property. The Continue property is similar to the Status property because it controls whether the Fill process should continue. Set the Continue property to true or false. To stop the Fill method from completing, set Continue to false.

# Working with Multiple Tables

Often you will work with more than one table when using a dataset. You can easily add the contents (or partial contents) of more than one table to a dataset by using two or more DataAdapter objects. For instance, the following snippet shows how you can add both the Customers and Orders tables from the Northwind database to a dataset:

```
'code to establish connection omitted
Dim adptCustomers as _
    new OleDataAdapter("Select * from Customers", con)
Dim adptOrders as new OleDbDataAdapter("Select * from Orders", con)

Dim dsNorthwind as new DataSet("Northwind")
adptCustomers.Fill(dsNorthwind, "Customers")
adptOrders.Fill(dsNorthwind, "Orders")
```

You can integrate data from two different databases by using this method.

In the Northwind database, the Orders table depends on the Customers table. Figure 10.4 shows how the two tables are related.

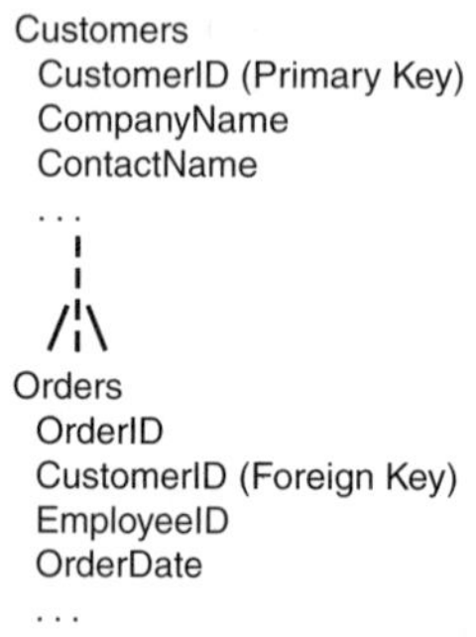

**FIGURE 10.4**

*The relationship between the Customers and Orders tables.*

Customers
CustomerID (Primary Key)
CompanyName
ContactName
. . .

/¦\

Orders
OrderID
CustomerID (Foreign Key)
EmployeeID
OrderDate
. . .

**NEW TERM**  Each Customer record is potentially related to many Orders records because each customer can order many products. The Orders table contains a field called CustomerID, which is a foreign key that identifies the customer who placed the order. A *primary key* is a field (or combination of fields) that uniquely identifies each row in a table. A *foreign key* is a field in a table that has the same value as a primary key in another (parent) table. Primary and foreign keys are often used to make a parent-child relationship between two tables in a database.

Given that a dataset can contain two or more tables with parent-child relationships, it's quite easy to break consistency between the two tables. In the case of the Orders and Customers tables, a Customer with several related Order records might be deleted. The related Order fields would then be stranded because their parent Customer record would be deleted. Making sure that scenarios like this don't happen is called *preserving referential integrity*. With *referential integrity*, every foreign key in every table contains reference to a valid row in a parent table. For example, if a record in the Orders table contains a ProductID field of –50 that doesn't correspond to an existing ProductID in the Products table, referential integrity is violated. Multiple rows in one table can contain the same foreign keys value, meaning that multiple rows can refer to the same parent record.

Every dataset contains a DataRelations collection that allows you to specify foreign key relationships between tables and primary key fields for a single table. Each DataRelation object also contains a set of rules that tell ADO.NET what to do when a record is added or deleted.

Because DataRelations can model parent-child (foreign key) relationships between tables, they allow a dataset to contain nested tables. As an example, consider two tables, Employees and Departments. The Employees table might contain a name, hire date, salary information, and department ID number. The Departments table might contain the ID, name, and location of the department.

We might create a new dataset for our company and add the two tables using code similar to Listing 10.4.

**LISTING 10.4**   Building a Sample Dataset for a Fictitious Company

```
 1: Dim dsCompany as new DataSet("Widgets Inc")
 2: Dim dtEmployees as DataTable = dsCompany.Tables.Add("Employees")
 3: Dim dtDepartments as DataTable = dsCompany.Tables.Add("Departments)
 4:
 5: 'Set up the columns in each table
 6: dtDepartment.Columns.Add("DepId", Type.GetType("System.Int32"))
 7: dtDepartment.Columns.Add("Name", Type.GetType("System.String"))
 8:
 9: dtEmployees.Columns.Add("Name", Type.GetType("System.String"))
10: dtEmployees.Columns.Add("DepId", Type.GetType("System.Int32"))
11:
12: 'Add some sample data
13: Dim r as DataRow = dtDepartment.NewRow()
14: r("DepID") = 1
15: r("Name") = "Denver"
16: dtDepartments.Rows.Add(r)
17:
18: r = dtEmployees.NewRow()
19: r("Name") = "Joe Smith"
20: r("DepId") = 1
21: dtEmployees.Rows.Add(r)
```

**ANALYSIS**   Each employee record contains a DepartmentID field (Line 10), linking the individual employee to a particular department. We can establish the relationship between the Employees and Departments tables in the DataSet object by adding a new DataRelation object into the DataRelations collection, as follows:

```
dsCompany.Relationships.Add("DepartmentEmployee", _
                  dsCompany.Tables("Departments").Columns("DeptID"), _
                  dsCompany.Tables("Employees").Columns("DeptID"))
```

The first parameter is the name of the relationship. As a developer, you specify this name and can choose any reasonable value that you prefer. The second parameter is the primary key column of table, and the third is the foreign key column of the child table. If the primary and foreign keys span multiple columns, you can pass in column arrays for the second and third parameters.

You might want to go to the trouble of establishing this relationship in the dataset for a couple of reasons:

- Creating this relationship makes navigating the dataset easy. When two tables have a relationship, you can use the GetChildRows method of the parent DataTable object to find all related rows in a child table, as shown here:

```
Dim rDept as DataRow = dtd.Rows(0) 'the row for Denver department
'print out the name of every employee for this department
Dim rowEmployee As DataRow
for each rowEmployee in
        rowDept.GetChildRows("DepartmentEmployee"))
   Console.WriteLine(rowEmployee("Name").ToString())
next
```

- You can use the GetParentRow method from the child DataTable to get the related record in the parent table.

When you add a Relationship object to a DataSet, two constraints are created. These constraints set up rules that operate on the two tables.

In ADO.NET, constraints are objects and are attached to the Constraints collection of each DataTable object in the relationship. The first type of constraint that the Relationship object creates is of type UniqueConstraint.

UniqueContraints specify primary keys for a DataTable and enforce the policy that the primary keys in the table must be unique. If your program adds a row with a duplicate primary key, a ConstraintException is thrown when the offending line of code is executed. For instance, if the following code is added to Listing 10.4, it throws an exception because a department with an ID of 1 already exists in the Departments table:

```
r = dtDepartment.NewRow()
r("DepID") = 1
r("Name") = "Atlanta"
dtDepartments.Rows.Add(r)   'this line will throw a ConstraintException
```

The second Constraint object added by creating the Relationship object is of type ForeignKeyConstraint, added to the child table. ForeignKeyConstraint objects, by default, have an action associated with them that cascades deletes and updates and throws an exception if a record is added to the child table with an invalid foreign key. For cascading deletes, the `ForeignKeyConstraint` deletes related objects in a child table when a parent record is deleted. For cascading updates, if a primary key in a parent table is modified, the associated foreign keys in the child table are changed as well. The following code snippet illustrates this behavior:

```
r = dtEmployees.NewRow()
r("Name") = "Pete Smith"
r("DepId") = 5 'this department doesn't exist yet
dtEmployees.Rows.Add(r)  'will throw an InvalidConstraintException

dtDepartment.Rows(0).Delete()  'will delete all records in Employee table
                               'with this record's department id also

dtDepartment.Rows(0)("DepID") = 50  'will change all records in Employee
                                    'table with this record's original
                                    'department id to 50
```

**10**

If you don't like this cascading behavior, you can change it by setting the `Rule` property on the `ForeignKeyConstraint` object in the child table. In our running example, this would look like the following:

```
ForeignKeyConstraint fkc = _
    CType(dtEmployees.Constraints(0, ForeignKeyConstraint)
fkc.DeleteRule = Rule.None
```

If you need complete control over the relationships between tables, you can add `ForeignKeyConstraint` and `UniqueConstraint` objects to each individual `DataTable` object, instead of a `Relationship` object. For the example in this section, we might add the following two constraints:

```
dtDepartment.Columns("DepID").Unique = true
'or
Dim ucId as new UniqueConstraint("DepIdConstraint", _
                                        dtDepartment.Columns("DepId")
dtDepartment.Constraints.Add(udId)

Dim fkcId as new ForeignKeyConstraint("DepartmentEmployees", _
                    dtDepartment.Columns("DepId"), _
                    dtEmployees.Columns("DepId"))
dtDepartment.Constraints.Add(fkcId)
```

## Setting the `PrimaryKey`

Each `DataTable` object has a collection called `PrimaryKey`, which you can set to an array of one or more `DataColumn` objects. Setting the primary key automatically generates a `UniqueConstraint` for the table and also prevents null values in the column or columns.

For the example in this section, you can set the primary key for the Departments table by using the following code:

```
dtDepartments.PrimaryKey = _
    new DataColumn() { dtDepartments.Columns("DepId") }
```

To automate foreign key constraints, the DataAdapter class contains the FillSchema method. When you call FillSchema, the primary key property for the table designated in the SelectCommand is set for you. For the running example in this section, we might have code that looks like the following:

```
'myCon is a connection to the Widgets Inc database
Dim adptDepartments as
    new SqlDatadapter("Select * from Departments", myCon)

'gather primary key information
adptDepartments.FillSchema(dsCompany, SchemaType.Mapped, "Departments")

adptDepartments.Fill(dsCompany, "Departments")

'DataRelations must be added manually
```

Although the FillSchema method sets primary key information, it doesn't add DataRelations—you must add them in code or use Visual Studio's data tools. If the SELECT statement doesn't reference the column or columns containing the table's primary keys, they are added automatically.

 **Note**    If you are using the OLE DB provider, set the MissingSchemaAction property of the OleDbAdapter class to AddWithKey to ensure that each row has its primary key information set correctly.

As you can see from the examples in this section, adding constraints to a dataset is a reliable way to ensure data consistency. Doing so can save you programming effort if you have multiple tables loaded into a dataset and your program makes changes to them. Adding constraints also ensures that only consistent data is persisted back to the database on Update calls.

# Using Visual Studio.NET

Visual Studio.NET automates much of the work shown today with the Server Explorer and drag-and-drop functions. The Server Explorer is a window in the Visual Studio environment that allows you to connect and browse any database on your local machine or local area network. After connecting to a particular database, you can drag and drop

`Connection` and `Adapter` objects onto your Web forms, and Visual Studio automatically generates code to associate with them. After you create the connection-adapter pair, you can also use Visual Studio to generate a corresponding `DataSet` automatically.

Follow these steps to create connection, adapter, and dataset classes for the Northwind database:

1. Create a new Empty Web Project from the Visual Basic Projects group of templates. Name the project **DataExample**.

2. Add a new configuration file to the project (choose Add New Item from the Project menu). In the Add New Item dialog, select Web Configuration File and click OK. Your project should look similar to Figure 10.5.

**FIGURE 10.5**

*A blank Web project containing a Web configuration file.*

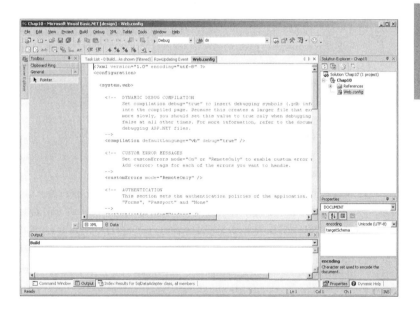

3. Add a new Web form to the project (choose Add Web Form from the Project menu). Call the Web form Example.aspx.

4. Choose Server Explorer from the View menu to open the Server Explorer, which allows you to create `Connection` and `Adapter` objects.

5. In the Server Explorer window, right-click the Data Connections icon and select Add Connection.

6. On the Provider tab of the Data Link Properties dialog, select Microsoft Jet 4.0 OLE DB Provider. On the Connection tab, specify the location of the Northwind.mdb file. Your dialog should look like Figure 10.6.

**FIGURE 10.6**

*Selecting the
Northwind database
using the Data Link
Properties dialog.*

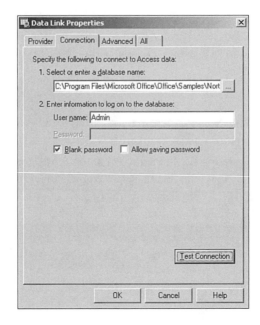

7. Click OK to add the database to the Server Explorer.

8. Expand the Server Explorer tree so that the tables in the Northwind database are shown.

9. Drag and drop the Products table onto the Example.aspx Web form to create a new `OleDbConnection` object called `oleDbConnection1` and a new `OleDbDataAdapter` object called `oleDbDataAdapter1`. Your Visual Studio instance should look like Figure 10.7.

You can modify the properties, including the name of the connection and adapter objects, and examine the code generated by Visual Studio in the code behind file of the Example.aspx Web form.

To generate a `DataSet` for the Products table, select Generate DataSet from the Data menu. Follow the wizard steps, which will allow you to select the data provider generated in the previous steps.

# Using Additional `DataTable` Features

The `DataTable` object has some helper methods and properties that make your life easier as a programmer.

**FIGURE 10.7**

*Automatically generat-ed Connection and Adapter objects.*

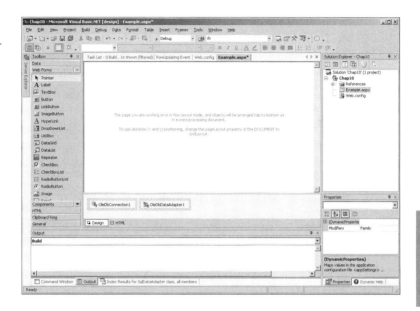

## AutoIncrement

The DataTable class allows you to create columns with values that are automatically incremented any time a new row is inserted. This feature can be useful if you need to make sure that every row in a table is unique, and you are using an integer-based primary key field. Unfortunately, this feature doesn't guarantee uniqueness in all cases. Consider the case of an ASP.NET page that adds rows to a table with an autoincrement column. Because more than one user could hit the page at the same time, each page might add a row with the same (automatically incremented) value.

Each DataTable column has three properties associated with the autoincrement feature, as the following code shows:

```
Dim dcolDepartmentID as DataColumn = dtDepartment.Columns("DepID")
dcolDepartmentID.AutoIncrement = true
dcolDepartmentID.AutoIncrementStep = 1
dcolDepartmentID.AutoIncrementSeed = 500
```

The seed value is the first number that gets generated when Add is called on the Rows collection. You can set the step to a value other than 1 if each incremented value should skip ahead.

## Expression Columns

You can create columns in a DataTable that are based on the values in other columns, instead of being based on data in a database table. These columns calculate their value based on a mathematical expression involving other columns, similar to formula cells in Excel. To create one of these "expression" columns, pass in the desired expression as a string in the third parameter of the Add method in the Columns collection. You can also set a column's Expression property, as the following code shows:

```
dtEmployees.Columns.Add("YearlySalary", Type.GetType("System.Currency"))
'create an expression column based on YearlySalary
dtEmployees.Columns.Add("MonthlySalary", _
                        Type.GetType("System.Currency"), _
                        "YearlySalary / 12")
```

This example only scratches the surface of the kinds of expressions that you can use. Expressions can contain references to parent and child tables as long as you have added the relationship to the dataset's Relations collection. You can also add the string-matching command LIKE to an expression and logic using the IIF statement. For a full explanation of how to use expressions, consult the Visual Studio documentation (look for the Expressions property of the DataSet object).

## Summary

Today's lesson showed how to manipulate data using the DataSet class. You saw how to use the DataAdapter together with DataSet so that your programs read, modify, and persist data to a back-end database.

Today we explained primary and foreign keys in databases and described how you can model these relationships within DataSet objects. These features allow you to maintain consistency in your data even though the data is disconnected from the database.

You learned about three kinds of DataAdapter events that you can handle in your own code to check for errors. Last, you learned how to create DataAdapters and DataSets by dragging and dropping objects in Visual Studio.NET.

## Q&A

**Q  I've heard that ADO.NET provides tight integration with XML. However, none of today's listings used XML. How can I use XML with ADO.NET?**

**A**  Tomorrow's lesson will provide detailed examples for using XML and ADO.NET together. The ADO.NET DataSet object can be attached to an XML file instead of a DataAdapter. You can still use all the functionality that the DataSet provides, including primary and foreign key constraints with XML files.

**Q  It's nice to create all the primary and foreign key constraints mentioned today for a DataSet, but coding this process seems especially tedious. Is there an alternative?**

A Yes. You can use XML Schema files to store metadata information about all the tables in your database. By using these XML schemas, you can use Visual Studio or the .NET framework to generate classes that contain all the built-in constraint rules. Tomorrow's lesson will detail how to generate XML Schemas for any dataset, and how to use them to create datasets with built-in constraints.

Q **Today's lesson provided two methods for handling errors: by using custom event handlers or by catching exceptions in my data access code. Which method should I use?**

A The simplest way to handle data access errors is to surround code with a `try...catch` block and then handle each kind of exception thrown. Adding custom error event handlers is an advanced technique that allows your code to ignore errors and go on, depending on conditions that you set.

**10**

# Workshop

The Workshop provides quiz questions to help you solidify your understanding of the material covered and exercises to provide you with experience in using what you've learned. The answers to the quiz questions are provided in Appendix A, "Answers to Quizzes and Exercises."

## Quiz

1. What method in the `OleDbDataAdapter` class populates a dataset with records?

2. How can you populate one `DataSet` object with data from two different physical databases?

3. If a data table contains records with a currency field containing price information, how can you increase each price field by 10%?

4. Why would you call the `AcceptChanges` method in a `DataSet` object, and when would you do so?

5. How can you handle errors from a `DataAdapter`?

6. What are primary and foreign keys? How are they different?

7. How do you establish a "parent-child" relationship between two tables in a database?

8. What ADO.NET class is used to ensure consistency between primary and foreign keys in a `DataSet`?

9. What are expression columns, and why would you use one?

10. How are `RowStates` used in ADO.NET?

## Exercises

1. Modify Listing 10.1 to use a DataGrid to display the contents of the Orders table.

2. Create an ASP.NET page containing a column that adds 5 cents to the price of every product in the Northwind database without changing the underlying data.

# WEEK 2

# DAY 11

# Using ADO.NET and XML Together

Today's lesson will build on the concepts from Days 8, 9, and 10. Day 8, "Using XML with Your Applications," introduced XML and some of the .NET Framework classes used to read, write, and modify XML files.

On Days 9, "Introducing ADO.NET," and 10, "Working with Datasets," you learned how to create an ASP.NET application that uses data stored in relational databases by using various ADO.NET classes. However, you may be planning to use XML instead of a database to store some or all of your application's data. The good news is that you can still use ADO.NET in your applications. ADO.NET interfaces with XML-based data seamlessly. Today you will learn how to use ASP.NET and ADO.NET to create powerful XML-based Internet applications.

A good portion of today's lesson explains XML Schemas, which describe the structure of XML files. By using XML Schemas, you can access XML files using the same methods that you would use to access data from a relational database.

Today's lesson also explains the fundamentals of *typed datasets*. Typed datasets are a good way to access all ADO.NET datasets because they provide a class structure on top of the generic dataset, data table, and data row objects. By using typed datasets, you can simplify your ADO.NET-based code and eliminate many maintenance problems that might occur.

Today's lesson covers the following topics:

- Reading and modifying XML files using ADO.NET
- Creating XML Schema files and using them in your Internet applications
- Using typed datasets in your applications
- Generating XML Schema files and typed datasets automatically using Visual Studio and the .NET Framework tools

# Manipulating XML Files Using ADO.NET

XML is quickly becoming a popular standard for storing and manipulating all kinds of data. It's not surprising that ADO.NET was designed from the beginning to support XML as well as relational databases.

The DataSet class contains two important methods that you will frequently use when dealing with XML data: ReadXML and WriteXML. To see how to use these methods, let's create a sample XML file to use throughout today's lesson. Listing 11.1 shows a sample XML file containing data about computers.

**LISTING 11.1**  Computers.xml: Sample XML File Used in Today's Lesson

```
 1: <?xml version="1.0" encoding="utf-8" ?>
 2: <computers>
 3:   <computer nic="true" modem="false" server="false">
 4:     <name>Alice 1</name>
 5:     <os>Windows 2000</os>
 6:     <speed>800</speed>
 7:     <memory>256</memory>
 8:   </computer>
 9:   <computer nic="false" modem="true" server="false">
10:     <name>Bob</name>
11:     <os>Windows ME</os>
12:     <speed>500</speed>
13:     <memory>128</memory>
14:   </computer>
15:   <computer nic="true" modem="true" server="true">
16:     <name>Nelson</name>
17:     <os>Windows 2000 Advanced Server</os>
```

**LISTING 11.1**   continued

```
18:      <speed>1000</speed>
19:      <memory>1024</memory>
20:    </computer>
21: </computers>
```

**ANALYSIS**  The XML file in Listing 11.1 contains a root element called <computers> (Line 2), which contains three child <computer>" elements (Lines 3, 9, and 15). Each <computer> element contains three attributes (Line 3) that describe if the computer has a network interface card, a modem, and whether the computer acts as a server. Each <computer> element contains four text elements (Lines 4–7, for example) that describe the name, current operating system, CPU speed, and memory configuration of the computer.

In many of your programs, you will want to display the contents of an XML file in an ASP.NET page. Let's write a sample program that will read the XML file from Listing 11.1 into an ADO.NET DataSet object and display the results in an ASP.NET DataGrid control. Listing 11.2 shows this code.

**LISTING 11.2**   ShowComputers.aspx: Displaying the Contents of Computers.xml Using an ASP.NET DataGrid Control

```
 1: <%@ Page language="vb"%>
 2: <html>
 3:   <body>
 4:     <h3>Research Department Computers</h3>
 5:     <form runat="server">
 6:       <asp:DataGrid HeaderStyle-Font-Bold="True"
 7:                     Font-Name="Arial"
 8:                     Font-Size="10pt"
 9:                     ID="MyDataGrid" Runat="server" />
10:     </form>
11:   </body>
12: </html>
13: <script Runat="server">
14: sub Page_Load(sender as object, e as System.EventArgs)
15:
16:    Dim MyDataSet as new System.Data.DataSet()
17:    MyDataSet.ReadXml(Server.MapPath("Computers.xml"))
18:    MyDataGrid.DataSource = MyDataSet
19:    MyDataGrid.DataBind()
20:
21: End Sub
22: </script>
```

11

**ANALYSIS** Listing 11.2 contains an ASP.NET DataGrid control to display the contents of a dataset (Lines 6–9). The listing sets some Font properties, but otherwise makes no changes to the default DataGrid configuration.

The Page_Load method (Lines 14–21) creates a new DataSet object (Line 16). Page_Load calls the ReadXML method to read the contents of the Computers.xml file into the DataSet (Line 17). After the XML file is read, the DataSet is bound to the grid control (Lines 18–19). Figure 11.1 shows Listing 11.2 in action.

**FIGURE 11.1**

*The results of running the ShowComputers.aspx page. The DataGrid is bound to the contents of a DataSet read from an XML file.*

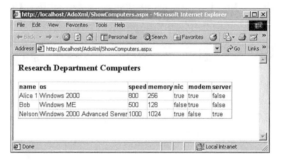

**NEW TERM** You may be wondering about the mechanism that allows a DataSet to automatically read an XML file. The process that a DataSet uses to create the proper tables and rows when reading an XML file is called *inference*. When the ReadXML method is called, ADO.NET follows the inference rules to map the data from the XML file into the DataSet object. Some of these rules follow:

- XML elements that contain child elements are mapped into a new table. For example, the <computers> node in Listing 11.1 contained three child <computer> elements. ADO.NET created a new table called Computers.

- XML elements that contain attributes are mapped into a new table. However, ADO.NET didn't create a new table for each <computer> element—it was intelligent enough to map the attributes in each <computer> element into column names of the Computers table because of the next rule.

- Repeating elements are inferred as a single table. Thus, in Listing 11.1, the <computer> elements were put into the single Computers table.

- Attributes are inferred as columns.

The inference process follows a few more rules for dealing with special cases, such as nested tables, and will even create new DataRelation objects specifying foreign key constraints in a destination DataSet. You can find the complete set of rules for the inference process in the Visual Studio documentation.

As you might imagine, the inference process isn't a sure-fire way to map XML data into a DataSet object. By using inference, you give up control to ADO.NET to make the mapping decisions for you. However, you can have complete control over the way XML data is mapped into DataSet tables by using XML Schemas.

# Understanding XML Schemas

XML Schemas are a relatively new XML-based technology. XML Schemas allow you to specify the structure of elements and data in an XML file. By using the schemas, you can create a "blueprint" for the way other XML files should be constructed. You can create rules for every element in an XML file and the data it contains. XML Schema files end in the extension .xsd.

When combined with the .NET Framework, XSD allows many more powerful options, including the following:

- XML Schemas allow you to validate the contents of an XML document to make sure each element and attribute follows the rules in the schema. The XMLValidatingReader class uses an XSD document to check an XML file.

- By using XML Schemas, you can specify exactly how an XML file should be mapped into an ADO.NET DataSet object.

- Both Visual Studio and a tool called XSD.exe allow you to create an ADO.NET *typed dataset,* which is a wrapper class on top of the generic DataSet object that allows you to program the DataSet using properties. The typed dataset uses the contents of an XSD file to determine what these wrapper classes should look like. (Typed datasets are explained later today.)

- Visual Studio and the XSD.exe tool infer an XML Schema from an XML file, using the same inference techniques that the DataSet.ReadXML method uses. Both tools generate the XML Schema for you.

As you can see from this list, XML Schemas give you a powerful new set of tools that you can use in your own Internet applications.

**11**

# Creating XSD Files

To add a new XML Schema file to your Web project using Visual Studio, follow these steps:

1. Select Add New Item from the Project menu.
2. In the Add New Item dialog box, select the XML Schema icon from the list on the right. The default name for the new file will have an .xsd extension, as all XSD files should.

3. Create a name for the file and click Open.

The default view for an XSD file in Visual Studio is called Schema. You can also select the XML view to see the XSD file's raw contents. Listing 11.3 shows an example of an empty XSD file named Computers.xsd created in Visual Studio. This file was created by using the preceding steps.

**LISTING 11.3** Computers.xsd: A Blank XSD File Created by Visual Studio After Using the Add New Item Feature

```
1: <?xml version="1.0" encoding="utf-8" ?>
2: <xsd:schema id="Computers"
3:             targetNamespace="http://tempuri.org/Computers.xsd"
4:             elementFormDefault="qualified"
5:             xmlns="http://tempuri.org/Computers.xsd"
6:             xmlns:xsd="http://www.w3.org/2001/XMLSchema">
7: </xsd:schema>
```

**ANALYSIS**  XSD files are constructed using XML, similar to other XML-based technologies such as XSL. Listing 11.3 contains the standard XML header line (Line 1).

XSD files use the xsd namespace. In Listing 11.3, the xsd namespace is defined on Line 6, which points to the standard XSD namespace at www.w3.org/2001/XMLSchema. Two other namespace definitions (Lines 3 and 5) define the namespace for this particular XSD file. You can modify these namespaces to suit your project, using your organization's own URL. (Namespaces were explained on Day 8.)

## XSD Step by Step

To start our discussion of creating XSD files, let's write a program that will validate an XML file against an XML Schema. We can use the XmlValidatingReader class to check an XML file against an XSD Schema. Listing 11.4 shows an ASP.NET page that does just such a validation. You can download this listing from www.samspublishing.com because the listing is rather long (to access all source code from this book, enter this book's ISBN in the Search field). We'll postpone analysis of Listing 11.4. For the moment, you can use it as a utility to validate XML files against an XML Schema.

**LISTING 11.4**  ValidateXML.aspx: Validating an XML File Against an XSD Schema

```
1: <%@ Page Language="vb" debug="true"%>
2: <%@ Import Namespace="System.Xml" %>
3: <%@ Import Namespace="System.Xml.Schema" %>
4:
5: <script runat="server">
```

**LISTING 11.4** continued

```
 6: sub CheckXML(Sender as Object, e as EventArgs)
 7:
 8:   Dim sourceXML as String = Server.MapPath(xmlFileName.Text)
 9:   Dim sourceXSD as String = Server.MapPath(xsdFileName.Text)
10:
11:   errorMessage.Text = "Successfully validated " & xmlFileName.Text & _
12:                      " using " & xsdFileName.Text
13:   Dim validatingReader as XmlValidatingReader
14:   Dim xmlReader as XmlTextReader
15:   Dim xsdReader as XmlTextReader
16:   Dim testSchemaCollection as new XmlSchemaCollection()
17:    try
18:     xsdReader = new XmlTextReader(sourceXSD)
19:     testSchemaCollection.Add(xsdFileName.Text, xsdReader)
20:     xmlReader = new XmlTextReader(sourceXML)
21:     validatingReader = new XmlValidatingReader(xmlReader)
22:     validatingReader.Schemas.Add(testSchemaCollection)
23:     validatingReader.ValidationType = ValidationType.Schema
24:     AddHandler validatingReader.ValidationEventHandler, _
25:         AddressOf Me.ValidationCallback
26:
27:     while (validatingReader.Read())
28:     end while
29:    catch ex as Exception
30:     errorMessage.Text = "XXX" & ex.ToString()
31:    finally
32:     if not xmlReader is nothing then xmlReader.Close()
33:     if not xsdReader is nothing then xsdReader.Close()
34:     if not validatingReader is nothing then validatingReader.Close()
35:    end try
36: End Sub
37:
38: sub ValidationCallback(sender as object, args as ValidationEventArgs)
39:
40:    if args.Severity = XmlSeverityType.Warning then
41:       errorMessage.Text = "Warning: "
42:    end if
43:    if args.Severity = XmlSeverityType.Error then
44:       errorMessage.Text = "Error: "
45:    end if
46:    if not args.Exception is nothing then
47:      errorMessage.Text &= args.Message & " at line " & _
48:        args.Exception.LineNumber & _
49:        " position " & args.Exception.LinePosition & ControlChars.CrLf
50:    end if
51: End Sub
52: </script>
53: <html>
54: <body>
```

LISTING **11.4**   continued

```
55:   <font face="arial">
56:   <form runat="server">
57:   <h3>XML validation using XSD</h3>
58:   Source XML File: <asp:TextBox id="xmlFileName" runat="server"/><br>
59:   Source XSD Schema: <asp:TextBox id="xsdFileName" runat="server"/><br>
60:   <asp:Button Text="Validate" OnClick="CheckXML" runat="server"/>
61:   <br>
62:   <asp:Label id="errorMessage" runat="server"/>
63:   </form>
64:   </font>
65: </body>
66: </html>
```

**ANALYSIS**   In Listing 11.4, notice Line 19:

```
testSchemaCollection.Add(xsdFileName.Text, xsdReader)
```

The first argument passed to the Add() method is the namespace, and this code assumes that the XSD file name is being used as the namespace. If this isn't the case, you will have to change this line, because if the namespace passed as the first argument doesn't match the namespace in the XSD file, an exception is thrown.

To warm up, let's create an XML Schema that defines an XML file containing one element with a string value. The XML file might look like Listing 11.5.

LISTING **11.5**   Trivial.XML: A Trivial File Verified with a Simple XML Schema

```
1: <?xml version="1.0" ?>
2: <computer xmlns="trivial.xsd">Bob's computer</computer>
```

**ANALYSIS**   Notice that Listing 11.5 specifies the name of the XSD Schema file to use for this XML file in Line 2, using the xmlns attribute.

The XSD Schema that you might write corresponding to this XML file should use the xsd:element element to specify that the XML file should contain one node named <computer>. XSD contains many different elements that you can use to specify the exact structure of an XML file. Unfortunately, we'll cover only a small portion of them in this book. The Visual Studio documentation contains complete descriptions for every element.

Listing 11.6 shows an XML Schema that will validate Listing 11.5.

**LISTING 11.6**    Trivial.XSD: Validating the Trivial.XML File

```
1: <?xml version="1.0" encoding="utf-8" ?>
2: <xsd:schema xmlns:xsd="http://www.w3.org/2001/XMLSchema">
3:  <xsd:element name="computer" type="xsd:string" />
4: </xsd:schema>
```

**ANALYSIS**  Listing 11.6 declares the XSD namespace at the standard www.w3.org URI (Line 2). Next, it specifies that the target XML file should have one element called computer, which should contain a string. Figure 11.2 shows the XML validation page when run against Listings 11.5 and 11.6.

**FIGURE 11.2**

*Validating XML against XML Schema files.*

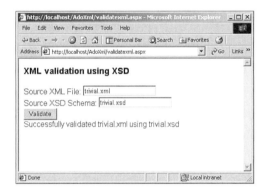

Let's extend the XSD Schema to define the computer element to contain four subelements, called name, os, speed, and memory. Listing 11.7 shows a sample XML file that contains this computer element, and Listing 11.8 shows the matching XSD file. Try checking the two files by using the validation program in Listing 11.4.

**LISTING 11.7**    Simple.XML: A Simple XML Element with Subelements

```
<?xml version="1.0" ?>
<computer xmlns="simple.xsd">
  <name>Bob's Computer</name>
  <os>Windows XP</os>
  <speed>800</speed>
  <memory>256</memory>
</Computer>
```

**LISTING 11.8**    Simple.XSD: Defining a Complex Element

```
1: <?xml version="1.0" ?>
2: <xsd:schema xmlns:xsd="http://www.w3.org/2001/XMLSchema"
```

**LISTING 11.8**   continued

```
 3:                   xmlns="simple.xsd"
 4:                   targetNamespace="simple.xsd"
 5:                   elementFormDefault="qualified">
 6:
 7:    <xsd:element name="computer">
 8:      <xsd:complexType name="computerType">
 9:        <xsd:sequence>
10:          <xsd:element name="name" type="xsd:string" />
11:          <xsd:element name="os" type="xsd:string" />
12:          <xsd:element name="speed" type="xsd:decimal" />
13:          <xsd:element name="memory" type="xsd:decimal" />
14:        </xsd:sequence>
15:      </xsd:complexType>
16:    </xsd:computer>
17: </xsd:schema>
```

**ANALYSIS**   Listing 11.8 contains a schema definition that you can use as boilerplate code in your own files. If you store your XSD file in a publicly available location, such as your own Web server, change the targeNamespace and xmlns keywords to point to the URI of your own XSD file.

Listing 11.8 defines the <computer> element in Lines 7–16. Within the definition for the <computer> element, a complexType element (Lines 8–15) signals that this element will contain subelements in Lines 9–14.

In Line 9 a sequence element signals that the subelements in Lines 10–13 must all be present in the XML file and in the order that they are defined here in the schema file.

Table 11.1 shows some other XSD elements that you can use within a complexType element.

**TABLE 11.1**   XSD Elements That Can Be Contained in a complexType Definition

| Element | Description |
| --- | --- |
| simpleContext | The complexType contains character data or one of the basic XSD types. Use this element in combination with the type attribute to specify the element type. |
| complexContent | The complexType contains only elements. |
| sequence | The complexType contains elements in the order defined in the sequence. Use this element in combination with element nodes to define a sequence of subelements. |
| choice | The complexType contains only one of the elements in the choice group. Use this element in combination with element nodes to define a list of subelements that the target XML file can select from. |

**TABLE 11.1**   continued

| Element | Description |
|---------|-------------|
| all | The complexType contains any of the subelements to appear once. |
| group | The complexType contains elements defined inside the group definition. |

Let's extend Listing 11.8 so that it can parse today's first XML example (from Listing 11.1). To do so, we need to allow for multiple <computer> elements and create definitions for each of the nic, modem, and server attributes. Listing 11.9 shows just such an example. To validate the Computers.xml file from Listing 11.1, add the reference to the Computers.xsd file by changing the main <computers> node to look like the following code line:

```
<computers xmlsn="computers.xsd">
```

You shouldn't have to change any other lines from Listing 11.1.

**LISTING 11.9**   Computers.xsd: Verifying the Computers.xml File from Listing 11.1

```
 1: <?xml version="1.0" ?>
 2: <xsd:schema xmlns:xsd="http://www.w3.org/2001/XMLSchema"
 3:             xmlns="computers.xsd"
 4:             targetNamespace="computers.xsd"
 5:             elementFormDefault="qualified">
 6:   <xsd:element name="computers">
 7:     <xsd:complexType>
 8:       <xsd:choice maxOccurs="unbounded">
 9:           <xsd:element name="computer">
10:               <xsd:complexType>
11:                   <xsd:sequence>
12:                       <xsd:element name="name" type="xsd:string" />
13:                       <xsd:element name="os" type="xsd:string" />
14:                       <xsd:element name="speed" type="xsd:decimal" />
15:                       <xsd:element name="memory" type="xsd:decimal" />
16:                   </xsd:sequence>
17:                   <xsd:attribute name="nic" type="xsd:boolean" />
18:                   <xsd:attribute name="modem" type="xsd:boolean" />
19:                   <xsd:attribute name="server" type="xsd:boolean" />
20:               </xsd:complexType>
21:           </xsd:element>
22:       </xsd:choice>
23:     </xsd:complexType>
24:   </xsd:element>
25: </xsd:schema>
```

**11**

**ANALYSIS**   Line 6 adds a definition for the top-level computers, and the entire definition proceeds through Line 24. In Line 7, the listing defines the computers element to be a `complexType` so that it can contain other elements. Next, Line 8 uses the `choice` element, with the `maxOccurs` attribute set to `unbounded`. Essentially, this means that for the `computers` node, you can choose to use the `computer` element (Lines 9–21) any number of times inside the XML file. Of course, this isn't much of a choice—the XML file is limited to only `computer` elements.

The definition of the `computer` element (again, Lines 9–21) is unchanged from previous examples, except for the addition of the `attribute` elements (Lines 17–19). These elements define each attribute for the `computer` element in the XML file.

Try running the XML verifier page in Listing 11.4 with the modified Computers.xml and new Computers.xsd files. You can also experiment by modifying some values in the Computers.xml file to verify that the Computers.xsd schema is working.

## Generating XML Schemas Automatically

Creating XML Schemas can be quite a daunting task, especially if your XML files have a complicated structure. Luckily, Visual Studio .NET automates the process using simple menu options. To create an XSD file for any XML file, follow these steps:

1. Open the XML file in Visual Studio. You can choose Add Existing Item from the Project menu, or Add New Item if the XML file doesn't exist. In this second case, you must create the XML file.

2. When the XML file is open and selected as the current window, an XML menu will appear in Visual Studio. Select Create Schema from the menu to generate an XSD file.

Visual Studio uses the inference process discussed earlier today to create the XSD file. You can use the XML Schema file generated by Visual Studio as a starting point. However, you will most likely want to change the default XSD file because Visual Studio sets all data types to `string` and may generate a different structure for the file than you prefer.

**Tip**

> You also can generate the XML Schema by using the XSD.exe tool. Just enter the following Visual Studio line at the command prompt:
>
> ```
> Xsd.exe computers.xml
> ```

Let's use Visual Studio to generate an XML Schema file for the Computers.xml file from Listing 11.1. Follow the steps earlier in this section and then browse to the XSD file in the Project Explorer. You should see something similar to Figure 11.3.

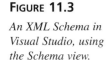

**FIGURE 11.3**

*An XML Schema in Visual Studio, using the Schema view.*

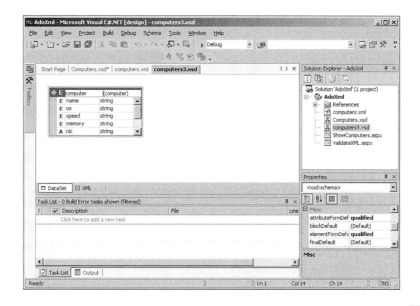

You can also view the XML Schema in XML format by clicking the XML button on the lower left. Listing 11.10 shows the automatically generated XML Schema file. Notice that the schema generator creates a namespace that consists of http://tempuri.org/ followed by the XSD filename, rather than the filename by itself. You must take this into account, for example, if you were using the program in Listing 11.4 to validate with this XSD file.

**LISTING 11.10** The Automatically Generated XML Schema File for Computers.xml

```
 1: <xsd:schema id="computers"
 2:            targetNamespace="http://tempuri.org/computers.xsd"
 3:            xmlns="http://tempuri.org/computers.xsd"
 4:            xmlns:xsd="http://www.w3.org/2001/XMLSchema"
 5:            xmlns:msdata="urn:schemas-microsoft-com:xml-msdata"
 6:            attributeFormDefault="qualified"
 7:            elementFormDefault="qualified">
 8:   <xsd:element name="computers"
 9:               msdata:IsDataSet="true"
10:               msdata:EnforceConstraints="False">
11:     <xsd:complexType>
12:       <xsd:choice maxOccurs="unbounded">
13:         <xsd:element name="computer">
14:           <xsd:complexType>
15:             <xsd:sequence>
16:               <xsd:element name="name" type="xsd:string"
17:                            minOccurs="0" msdata:Ordinal="0" />
```

11

**LISTING 11.10**   continued

```
18:                    <xsd:element name="os" type="xsd:string"
19:                                 minOccurs="0" msdata:Ordinal="1" />
20:                    <xsd:element name="speed" type="xsd:string"
21:                                 minOccurs="0" msdata:Ordinal="2" />
22:                    <xsd:element name="memory" type="xsd:string"
23:                                 minOccurs="0" msdata:Ordinal="3" />
24:                  </xsd:sequence>
25:                  <xsd:attribute name="nic" form="unqualified"
26:                                 type="xsd:string" />
27:                  <xsd:attribute name="modem" form="unqualified"
28:                                 type="xsd:string" />
29:                  <xsd:attribute name="server" form="unqualified"
30:                                 type="xsd:string" />
31:                </xsd:complexType>
32:              </xsd:element>
33:            </xsd:choice>
34:          </xsd:complexType>
35:        </xsd:element>
36: </xsd:schema>
```

**ANALYSIS**   Notice a number of differences between this generated file and the hand-crafted file from Listing 11.9. First, all the data types for each element have defaulted to string. Clearly, this isn't what we want; after all, the main point of the XML Schema is to check the data types in our target XML file. Let's add this to our list of things to change.

Line 5 adds the msdata namespace to the schema. This namespace contains Microsoft-specific extensions to the XSD namespace that allow for easier interaction with ADO.NET. One of these new extensions, IsDataSet (Line 9), signals that the current element should be mapped to a DataSet. In Line 10, the EnforceConstraints flag signals whether any constraints should be applied to the DataSet. This flag is irrelevant for the current schema because the file has no table constraints. However, you will see how to add table constraints later today. The last keyword is Ordinal (Line 17), which specifies a column number for the element if it's mapped to a DataTable object.

## Repairing the Schema

To clean up the automatically generated schema, you must set the data types for each subelement in the computer element. You can do so with Visual Studio by following these steps:

1. Open the Schema view for the automatically generated schema file (Computers1.xsd).

2. Each subelement and attribute is listed as a row in the computer table. Each row contains the element or attribute name and its type. Click the type field, and a drop-down list that lists the possible values for a type appears, as shown in Figure 11.4.

**FIGURE 11.4**

*Selecting a new type for a subelement of the* computer *element by using the XML Schema designer.*

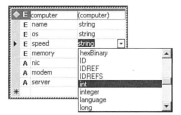

3. Select the appropriate type for each subelement and attribute.

4. Save the corrected schema.

# I Have an XML Schema. Now What?

Now that you have an XML Schema, you might be asking the question, "So what?" The answer is that you can use the schema for a number of things, including creating a typed dataset and automatically generating Visual Basic classes. Let's explore typed datasets.

## Typed Datasets

**NEW TERM** *Typed datasets* are custom wrapper classes built on top of the standard `DataSet`, `DataTable`, `DataColumn`, and `DataRow` classes. Visual Studio can generate a typed dataset automatically by using an XML Schema file. Typed datasets contain properties for each column, so you can access members of a data row by name instead of by column number.

Let's look at an example of untyped and typed datasets and the differences in how to use the two. You saw examples of untyped datasets yesterday and earlier today. A typical example should look like the following code snippet:

```
Dim MyDataSet as new DataSet()
'... Code to fill the DataSet ...
Dim computerTable as DataTable = MyDataSet.Tables("computer")
Dim computerRow as Datarow
For each computerRow in computerTable.Rows
   Dim computerName as string = computerRow(1)
next
```

**ANALYSIS** This code has a few undesirable characteristics. First, to extract the computer table, we index the `Tables` collection using a string value. However, the `DataSet` may not contain a table named computer. At this point, an exception would be raised.

The second and biggest problem with the preceding code is that to extract the name of a particular computer, we use `computerRow(1)`. Code like this is difficult to understand and maintain. What if the name column is moved and can no longer be found at index position 1? Coding values such as 1 for a particular row is bad programming practice.

A new version of the preceding code snippet using typed datasets might look something like this:

```
Dim computersDataSet as new computers()
'... Code to fill the Data Set ...
Dim computerTable as computer = computersDataSet.computer
Dim compRow as computer.computerRow
for each compRow in computer
  Dim computerName as string = compRow.name
next
```

This example corrects all the problems of the first. In particular, both the `computerTable` and `computerName` objects get their values using properties. This allows for much clearer and much more maintainable code. If the underlying database or XML file changes structure, the typed dataset will also change structure to match. This means that if any code tries to access a table or column that doesn't exist, the VB compiler will generate an error. This way, you, as a developer, can catch problems earlier.

## Generating the Typed Dataset

You can generate a typed dataset from an XML Schema easily by using Visual Studio:

1. Open a new, empty Visual Basic Web project.

2. If the XML Schema already exists, add it to the project. If not, add the underlying XML file to the project and generate the schema by using the techniques presented earlier today. Be sure to edit the schema data types as required.

3. Open the schema, and then select Generate DataSet from the Schema menu. A file named *xxxx*.vb, where *xxxx* is the schema name, will be added to your project. You must select View All Files in Solution Explorer to see this file.

For today's examples, use the Computers.xsd file as the XML Schema. The corresponding typed dataset will be named Computers.vb. You can view the file by choosing Show All Files from the Project menu. The typed dataset will appear as a child file from the XML Schema file in the Project Explorer window on the right.

 **Tip**

You can also generate the typed dataset by using the XSD.exe tool. Just add the following options at the command prompt:

```
Xsd.exe /l:vb /d computers.xsd
```

> The /d option signals the XSD tool to generate a typed dataset, and the /l: option specifies to use Visual Basic. The output is a Visual Basic file containing a class representing the typed dataset. Note, however, that at least with the beta version of .NET, command-line compilation doesn't work for typed datasets created in Visual Basic—you must create the typed dataset within a Visual Studio project.

## Using the Typed Dataset

Let's write an ASP.NET page that uses a typed dataset to make changes to the Computers.xml data file. If you are following along in Visual Studio, you would add a Web Form to the project containing the typed dataset, and then enter the code in Listing 11.11. You can't run this example as standalone code; it must be part of a project that includes the typed dataset you created from the computers.xsd schema.

LISTING 11.11  ModifyComputers.aspx: Using a Typed Dataset to Modify the Computers.xml File

```
 1: <%@ Page Language ="vb" debug="true"%>
 2: <html>
 3:   <body>
 4:     <h3>
 5:       Research Department Computers
 6:     </h3>
 7:     <form id="ShowComputers" method="post" runat="server">
 8:       <asp:DataGrid HeaderStyle-Font-Bold="True"
 9:                     Font-Name="Arial" Font-Size="10pt"
10:                     ID="MyDataGrid" Runat="server" />
11:       <br>
12:       <h4>Add a new computer</h4>
13:
14:       <table>
15:       <tr><td>Name: </td>
16:       <td><asp:TextBox ID="Name" Runat="server" /></td></tr>
17:
18:       <tr><td>Operating system: </td>
19:       <td><asp:TextBox ID="OS" Runat="server" /></td></tr>
20:
21:       <tr><td>Speed (MHz): </td>
22:       <td><asp:TextBox ID="Speed" Runat="server" /></td></tr>
23:
24:       <tr><td>Memory (Mb): </td>
25:       <td><asp:TextBox ID="Memory" Runat="server" /></td></tr>
26:
27:       <tr><td>Has NIC? : </td>
```

**11**

LISTING **11.11**   continued

```
28:        <td><asp:CheckBox ID="Nic" Runat="server" /></td></tr>
29:
30:        <tr><td>Has Modem? : </td>
31:        <td><asp:CheckBox ID="Modem" Runat="server" /></td></tr>
32:
33:        <tr><td>Is a Server? : </td>
34:        <td><asp:CheckBox ID="IsServer" Runat="server" /></td></tr>
35:        </table>
36:
37:        <asp:Button Text="Add" OnClick="AddComputer" Runat="server" />
38:      </form>
39:    </body>
40: </html>
41: <script runat="server">
42:    protected computersDataSet as computers
43:
44:    private sub Page_Load(sender as object, e as System.EventArgs)
45:
46:      computersDataSet = new computers()
47:      computersDataSet.ReadXml(Server.MapPath("computers.xml"))
48:      if not IsPostBack then Bind()
49:
50:    End Sub
51:
52:    protected sub AddComputer(sender as object, e as EventArgs)
53:
54:      'Retrieve values and parse as necessary
55:      Dim computerName as String = Name.Text
56:      Dim operatingSys as String = OS.Text
57:      Dim iSpeed as Integer = Int32.Parse(Speed.Text)
58:      Dim iMemory as Integer = Int32.Parse(Memory.Text)
59:      Dim HasNic as Boolean = Nic.Checked
60:      Dim HasModem as Boolean = Modem.Checked
61:      Dim bServer as Boolean = IsServer.Checked
62:
63:      computersDataSet.computer.AddcomputerRow(computerName, operatingSys, _
64:        iSpeed, iMemory, HasNic, HasModem, bServer)
65:
66:      computersDataSet.WriteXml(Server.MapPath("Computers.xml"))
67:
68:      Bind()
69:    End Sub
70:
71:    protected sub Bind()
72:
73:      MyDataGrid.DataSource = computersDataSet
74:      MyDataGrid.DataBind()
75:
76:    End Sub
77: </script>
```

**ANALYSIS** Listing 11.11 adds HTML controls to allow users to enter new computer records (Lines 7–37). These standard Web controls allow users to specify the computer name, operating system, speed, and other attributes.

The Page_Load method (Lines 44–50) initializes the grid that contains computer records. If this is the first time that the page has been accessed, it binds the typed dataset to the grid (Line 48).

The AddComputer method (Lines 52–69) adds a new computer record when the Add button is clicked. First, the method retrieves all the data from the form (Lines 55–61). Next, the AddComputerRow method is called on the computer table (Lines 63–64). This method is created automatically when the typed dataset is generated. AddComputer also writes out the dataset's contents to the Computers.xml file (Line 66) and rebinds the data grid (Line 68).

Figure 11.5 shows the sample in action.

**FIGURE 11.5**

*Adding records to an XML file by using ASP.NET and a typed dataset.*

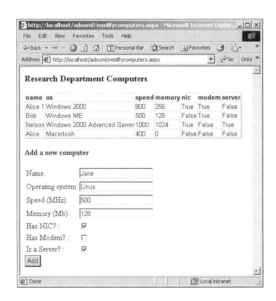

**Note**

Listing 11.11 presupposes that the typed dataset for Computers.xsd is compiled and saved in the project's bin directory. If you're using Visual Studio, this should happen automatically. If not, use the following line at the command prompt within the project directory:

```
vbc /t:library /out:bin\computers.dll computers.vb
```

This line compiles the typed dataset computers.vb into an assembly and puts the assembly in the bin directory.

## Creating Typed Datasets Using a Database

You also can create typed datasets for a database automatically by using Visual Studio. Creating the typed dataset is simply a matter of dragging and dropping the desired tables into your project.

Let's create a Web project that uses a typed dataset. Today's example will use the Northwind database available in Access and SQL Server. Perform the following steps in Visual Studio:

1. Create a new project using the Empty Web Project template. Call the project TypedData.

2. Add a new Web form named ShowProducts.aspx to the project.

3. Open the Server Explorer by choosing Server Explorer from the View menu. The Server Explorer gives you easy access to databases on your computer and local network.

4. Right-click the Data Connections node of the Server Explorer and select Add Connection.

5. In the Data Link Properties dialog, select Microsoft Jet 4.0 OLE DB Provider from the Provider tab.

6. Enter the full path to the Northwind.mdb database in the Connection tab. For my computer, this is C:\Program Files\Microsoft Office\Office\Samples\Northwind.mdb. Figure 11.6 shows an example.

**FIGURE 11.6**

*The Data Link Properties dialog with the Northwind database selected.*

7. Click the Test Connection button to make sure that the database connection works. Then click OK.

8. Expand the Data Connections node in the Project Explorer, expand the ACCESS connection, and then further expand the Tables node. You should see all the tables in the Northwind database.

9. Drag and drop the Products table onto the ShowProducts.aspx Web form you created in step 2 to create new `OleDbConnection` and `OleDbDataAdapter` objects for the Products table. Your environment should look similar to Figure 11.7.

**FIGURE 11.7**

*Dragging and dropping the Northwind Products table onto a Web form using Visual Studio.*

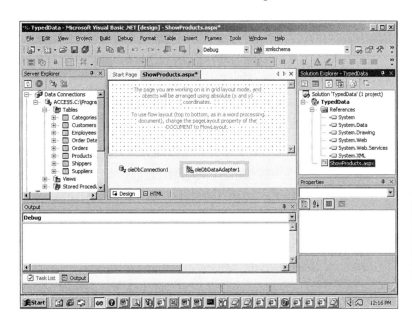

10. Right-click the `oleDbDataAdapter1` object at the bottom of the ShowProducts.aspx Web form and select Generate DataSet. The Generate DataSet dialog will appear.

11. Name the new dataset `Northwind` and click OK to generate a typed dataset for the Products table. This step also creates an XML Schema named Northwind.xsd for the Northwind database containing the Products table.

Now that the you've generated an XML Schema and a typed dataset for the Products table, you can use it in your own code. Try adding the lines from Listing 11.12 to the `Page_Load` event in the ShowProducts.aspx.vb file. Be sure to add an ASP.NET label control named `lblResults` to the HTML portion of the page.

**LISTING 11.12**  Sample Code Using the Northwind Products Typed Dataset

```
private sub Page_Load(sender as object, e as System.EventArgs)

    oleDbDataAdapter1.Fill(northwind1)
    lblResults.Text = ""
```

**LISTING 11.12**  continued

```
    Dim rowProduct as Northwind.ProductsRow
    for each rowProduct in northwind1.Products

      lblResults.Text &= rowProduct.ProductName & " " & _
        rowProduct.QuantityPerUnit & "<br>"  Next
    End Sub
```

You should see a list of all products and their cost when running the project.

# Summary

Today's lesson covered a few different techniques for using ASP.NET, ADO.NET, and XML in combination. At the beginning of the lesson, you learned about the ReadXml and WriteXml methods contained in the DataSet class. You saw a sample illustrating how you can manipulate XML with ADO.NET without writing volumes of code.

Today's lesson also introduced XML Schemas. You learned how to construct XSD files using Visual Studio and the .NET Framework tools. You also learned about the inference process that Visual Studio uses to construct XML Schemas from XML files. You saw examples illustrating how to edit XML Schemas using Visual Studio and how to modify the raw XML source for an XML Schema. Today's lesson also explained some of the XSD elements that you will use in your own schemas.

Last, you saw how to create and use typed datasets and how to modify an XML file using an ASP.NET Web form and typed datasets. You also saw how to easily create your own typed dataset using simple drag-and-drop operations. You can use the techniques in today's lesson as a foundation for your own typed dataset development.

Tomorrow's lesson will build on today's concepts by showing you more advanced techniques for creating dynamic Web applications using ASP.NET and ADO.NET. Before you move on, take some time to answer the quiz questions and exercises.

# Q&A

**Q I want to model my entire database using XML Schema, but I don't want to write the schema by hand. How can I do this?**

**A** You can drag and drop all the tables in a database into an XML Schema using Visual Studio. Use the same techniques that you would use for a single table, but drag the tables node instead of an individual table.

**Q** **I want to generate a new typed dataset every time I modify an XML Schema. How can I do so without calling the XSD.exe tool every time?**

**A** Make sure that you check the Generate DataSet option on the Schema menu in Visual Studio. Every time you save the XML Schema, a new typed dataset will be generated automatically.

**Q** **I want to add a custom method to my typed dataset. How should I do this?**

**A** Don't modify the automatically generated file itself because Visual Studio could rewrite it when you modify the source XML Schema. Instead, create a new class derived from the automatically generated class with your custom methods.

**Q** **How can I find more information about XML Schema?**

**A** The www.w3.org site contains a wealth of information about all XML-based technologies, including XML Schema. On the home page, click the XML Schema link for a tutorial, reference, and links to sample utilities.

# Workshop

The Workshop provides quiz questions to help you solidify your understanding of the material covered and exercises to provide you with experience in using what you've learned. The answers to the quiz questions and exercises are provided in Appendix A, "Answers to Quizzes and Exercises."

11

## Quiz

1. What method is used to populate a dataset using an XML file?
2. What's the process the .NET Framework uses to map XML data into a dataset?
3. Is it possible to enforce referential integrity in an XML file using ADO.NET?
4. What is XML Schema?
5. How do you "point" an XML file to an XML namespace file to verify its contents?
6. What .NET tools are used to automatically generate XML Schemas and typed datasets?

## Exercises

1. Modify Listing 11.2 so that it rearranges the column headings and displays them with capitalized names.
2. Modify Listing 11.1 so that each computer node contains a subelement called `<applications>`. Within the `applications` node, add elements that list sample applications that might be loaded on each computer. Then generate an XML Schema for the new file. What's the structure of the new schema?

# DAY 12

# Putting It All Together with ASP.NET

You've covered quite a bit of ground in the past week and a half. You've learned how to use ASP.NET, ADO.NET, and the .NET Framework XML classes in your own Web applications. Tomorrow's lesson will introduce Web Services, and Days 14, 15, and 16 will explain how to create and use Web Services effectively.

However, before we tackle Web Services, let's spend a day tying together all the concepts from the previous 11 days. Today's lesson will combine XML, ADO.NET, and ASP.NET in new ways.

Today's lesson will begin by revisiting data binding, showing an example of a Web control bound to XML data, and continue by explaining data filtering and sorting methods using the DataView class. Today's lesson will also give advice on how to use session state and view state properly with the DataGrid control. Finally, today's lesson will conclude with an example that combines a user control and an ASP.NET page to display detailed information for individual records in a data grid.

Today you will learn the following:

- How to bind Web controls to XML data
- Which .NET classes support data binding
- How to filter and sort data using the `DataView` class
- How to apply proper state management techniques to your application's data grid controls
- How to use the `HyperLinkColumn` method from the `DataGrid` class to show detailed information about individual records

# Taking a Second Look at Data Binding

On Day 5, "Using Advanced ASP.NET Web Controls," we introduced data binding and gave some examples using the DataList, DataGrid, and Template controls. Now that you are skilled in the use of XML, relational databases, and ADO.NET, you can use this knowledge in combination with data binding to create more complex and useful applications.

To start today's discussion of data binding, let's use an XML file as the source for a ListControl. We'll use the ADO.NET DataSet class as an intermediate object to hold the XML data and then bind the ListControl to the dataset.

To start, look at Listing 12.1, which shows an XML file with some data that we might display in the list.

LISTING 12.1    Music.xml: Listing Music Titles to Display in a ListControl

```
<?xml version="1.0" encoding="utf-8"?>
<music xmlns="http://tempuri.org/Music.xsd">
 <cd>Beethoven Symphony Number 5</cd>
 <cd>Mozart Symphony Number 40</cd>
 <cd>Anthem of the Sun</cd>
 <cd>Electric Ladyland</cd>
 <cd>Rust in Peace</cd>
</music>
```

Before implementing an ASP.NET page with a ListControl, let's generate an XML Schema for the file. This step is important for two reasons:

- You can use the generated XML Schema for insight into how the XML file will be mapped into the ADO.NET dataset that the page will use.
- If you want to customize the mapping of the XML file into the dataset, you can modify the XML Schema appropriately.

You can use techniques described yesterday to generate a schema automatically. Listing 12.2 shows what the schema looks like.

**LISTING 12.2**   Music.xsd: An Automatically Generated Schema for the Music.xml File

```
 1: <xsd:schema id="music"
 2:              targetNamespace="http://tempuri.org/Music.xsd"
 3:              xmlns="http://tempuri.org/Music.xsd"
 4:              xmlns:xsd="http://www.w3.org/2001/XMLSchema"
 5:              xmlns:msdata="urn:schemas-microsoft-com:xml-msdata"
 6:              attributeFormDefault="qualified"
 7:              elementFormDefault="qualified">
 8:   <xsd:element name="music"
 9:              msdata:IsDataSet="true"
10:              msdata:EnforceConstraints="False">
11:     <xsd:complexType>
12:       <xsd:choice maxOccurs="unbounded">
13:         <xsd:element name="cd">
14:           <xsd:complexType>
15:             <xsd:simpleContent msdata:ColumnName="cd_Text"
16:                                msdata:Ordinal="0">
17:               <xsd:extension base="xsd:string">
18:               </xsd:extension>
19:             </xsd:simpleContent>
20:           </xsd:complexType>
21:         </xsd:element>
22:       </xsd:choice>
23:     </xsd:complexType>
24:   </xsd:element>
25: </xsd:schema>
```

**12**

**ANALYSIS**   Listing 12.2 should look familiar to you because it's similar to the example used yesterday (refer to Listing 11.1). Lines 1–7 contain the standard XML Schema header that establishes the file's proper namespaces.

Lines 8–10 define the "music" element, which you can use to map directly into an ADO.NET dataset. Line 9 contains the IsDataSet attribute, which serves as a hint to ensure that this transformation takes place.

Line 12 contains the choice element combined with the maxOccurs attribute to establish that the element definition in Lines 13–21 can occur multiple times.

Lines 15–19 show how the simpleContent XSD element can be used to describe single XML target elements. By default, this simpleContext element is called cd_Text.

Now that we have an XML file and XML Schema to describe it, let's bind a ListControl to them. Listing 12.3 shows a sample application that does just this.

**LISTING 12.3**    ChooseMusic.aspx: Using a ListControl Bound to an XML File

```
 1: <%@ Import Namespace="System.Data" %>
 2: <html>
 3:   <body>
 4:     <form runat="server">
 5:       <h3>Please pick the best album from the list below.</h3>
 6:       <asp:ListBox ID="MusicList" Runat="server" /><br>
 7:       <asp:Button Text="Pick" OnClick="AlbumPicked" Runat="server"/><br>
 8:       <asp:Label ID="Message" Runat="server"/>
 9:     </form>
10:   </body>
11: </html>
12: <script runat="server" language="vb">
13:
14: Private Sub Page_Load(Sender As Object, e As EventArgs)
15:
16:   if Not IsPostBack then BindList()
17:
18: End Sub
19:
20: Private Sub BindList()
21:
22:   Dim MusicSet as new DataSet()
23:   MusicSet.ReadXmlSchema(Server.MapPath("music.xsd"))
24:   MusicSet.ReadXml(Server.MapPath("music.xml"))
25:   MusicList.DataSource = MusicSet
26:   MusicList.DataTextField = "cd_Text"
27:   MusicList.DataBind()
28:   MusicList.SelectedIndex = 0
29:
30: End Sub
31:
32: Sub AlbumPicked(Sender As Object, e As EventArgs)
33:
34:   if MusicList.SelectedIndex mod 2 = 0 Then
35:     Message.Text = "You have truly refined taste in music."
36:   else
37:     Message.Text = "You are a true music aficianado."
38:   End If
39:
40: End Sub
41: </script>
```

**ANALYSIS**    Lines 2–11 contain HTML and ASP.NET Web controls to create the music chooser page. Line 6 contains the MusicList ListControl that is bound to a dataset containing the music data.

The Page_Load method (Lines 14–18) contains logic to call the BindList method (Line 20) when the page is loaded for the first time. The list won't be bound on subsequent page hits or form postbacks because the IsPostBack flag will be true.

The `BindList` method (Lines 20–30) contains all the code needed to bind the XML file to the ListControl. Line 23 introduces a new method, `ReadXmlSchema`, used to read the XML Schema for the source XML file. Calling this method isn't strictly necessary, but you might use it for a couple of good reasons:

- If you use a specific XML Schema, ASP.NET doesn't need to apply the inference process to the source XML file, thus saving processing time.
- Because the XML Schema has already been determined, you don't have to guess what the dataset, datatable, and column names will be in the `DataSet` object declared on Line 22.

Line 26 uses a new property of the ListControl called `DataTextField`. You can use this property to map a column from a dataset into the text of each item in the ListControl. Because the XML Schema has already been generated, we know that the column we need is called `cd_Text`.

You could also use a typed dataset for this example to further simplify Listing 12.3.

## Key Interfaces Needed for Data Binding

You can use ASP.NET data binding in many situations. Specifically, you can bind an ASP.NET control to an object that supports the `IEnumerable`, `ICollection`, or `IListSource` interface. Quite a few .NET Framework objects support these methods. Table 12.1 lists the most common ones that you might use in your own projects.

**TABLE 12.1**   Classes That Support Data Binding by Interface

| Interface | Supported Classes |
|---|---|
| ICollection | Array, ArrayList, BitArray, HashTable, HttpSessionState, ListDictionary, MatchCollection, OleDbErrorCollection, Queue, SortedList, Stack, StateBag, StringCollection, XmlAttributeCollection |
| IEnumerable | All ICollection classes, XmlNode, XmlNodeList |
| IListSource | DataSet, DataTable |

**12**

**Implementing Interfaces**

An *interface* is a specification for certain methods that a class must support. Classes implement interfaces by creating methods that are listed in the interface. For instance, if an interface contains the methods `Walk` and `Run`, a class that implements the interface must contain those two methods. Here is an example of an interface using Visual Basic:

```
Interface IActions
  Sub Walk()
```

```
        Sub Run()
    End Interface
```

Here is an example of a class that implements the interface:

```
    Public Class SomeClass
        Implements IActions
        Sub Sub Walk() Implements IActions:Walk
        ' Code to walk.
        End Sub
        Sub Run() Implements IActions:Run
```

You can find complete information for each class in Table 12.1 in the Visual Studio doc-umentation. Day 4, "Working with Web Controls," presented a sample that uses data binding in combination with the HashTable class, and Day 5, "Using Advanced ASP.NET Web Controls," showed examples using the DataSet and DataTable classes.

# Revisiting the DataView

Previously, when we attached a DataSet to a Web control, most code examples used a code line similar to the following, where *someWebControl* is replaced by one of the Web controls in the sample, and *someDataSet* is replaced by one of the sample's dataset objects:

```
someWebControl.DataSource = someDataSet
```

Surprisingly, Web controls can't bind directly to a DataSet object. So, how have all the previous sample programs worked?

The answer is that Web controls perform some tricks when a dataset is assigned to the DataSource property of a control. First, the Web control examines the object type being assigned. If the object is a DataSet type, the control looks for the first table in the Tables collection. When this table is found, the Web control needs a DataView object. Luckily, every DataTable contains a default data view, accessed using the DefaultView property. Web controls also use this DefaultView object. This means that the previous code line is equivalent to the following line:

```
SomeWebControl.DataSource = someDataSet.Tables(0).DefaultView
```

The default view of a datatable works well in many cases. However, you can create your own table's data views and use them to filter and sort the table's data. Next, let's look at ways to filter and sort data using custom DataView objects.

# Filtering Data

There are two approaches to filtering data in a `DataTable`:

- You can create a custom SQL `Select` statement that contains a command to filter out unwanted rows. Remember that `DataAdapter` contains a `Select` property that you can customize to select particular rows from a table. After the `Select` property is set, you can use the `Fill` command to fill a table in a dataset.

- If you don't want to requery a source database for every kind of filter, or if you will use XML data as the base for your `DataTable` object, using custom `Select` statements isn't an option. Instead, use the `DataView` class. `DataView` contains a property called `Select`, which you can set to a SQL command to filter out unwanted rows. Setting this property saves database queries and allows you to filter XML data easily.

To properly use the `Select` property of the `DataView` object, you must specify the same text that would appear in the `WHERE` clause of a SQL statement. A typical example of a SQL `Select` statement containing a `WHERE` clause might look like the following:

```
SELECT * FROM Products WHERE UnitPrice > 10.00
```

This statement returns all products with a price greater than $10. Of course, you can use more complex statements:

```
SELECT * FROM Products WHERE (UnitPrice * UnitsInStock < 1000) OR
                             (UnitPrice * UnitsOnOrder > 1000)
```

A complete reference on valid SQL expressions is beyond the scope of this book. However, as a quick guide, here are some rules:

- Use the Boolean operators `AND`, `OR`, and `NOT` combined with parentheses, as in the previous example.
- Compare fields using the <, >, <=, >=, <>, and = operators.
- Use `LIKE` and `NOT` to compare strings. Within the `LIKE` or `NOT` comparison, your target string can contain the * and % characters to match any character or one character, respectively.
- Manipulate numerical fields with +, -, ^, /, and % (modulus) operators.
- Use the following statistical functions: `Sum`, `Avg`, `Min`, `Max`, `Count`, `Var`, and `StdDev`.

Let's write a program that allows users to filter the Northwind Products table by price. Listing 12.4 shows the example; Figure 12.1 shows the example in action.

**12**

**FIGURE 12.1**

*Filtering the
Northwind Product
table using the
DataView class.*

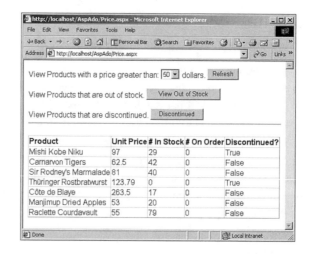

**LISTING 12.4**    FilterProducts.aspx: Filtering Different Views of the Products Table

```
 1: <%@ Import Namespace="System.Data" %>
 2: <%@ Import Namespace="System.Data.OleDb" %>
 3: <html>
 4:   <body>
 5:     <font face="Arial">
 6:     <form runat="server">
 7:
 8: View Products with a price greater than:
 9:       <asp:DropDownList ID="priceList" Runat="server">
10:         <asp:ListItem>0</asp:ListItem>
11:         <asp:ListItem>10</asp:ListItem>
12:         <asp:ListItem>25</asp:ListItem>
13:         <asp:ListItem>50</asp:ListItem>
14:       </asp:DropDownList>
15:       dollars.
16:       <asp:Button Text="Refresh" OnClick="SortByPrice" Runat="server"/>
17:
18:       <br><br>
19:       View Products that are out of stock.
20:       <asp:Button Text="View Out of Stock" OnClick="ShowOutOfStock"
21:                   Runat="server"/>
22:
23:       <br><br>
24:       View Products that are discontinued.
25:       <asp:Button Text="Discontinued" OnClick="ShowDisc" Runat="server"/>
26:
27:       <hr><br>
28: <asp:DataGrid ID="inventoryGrid"
29:                   EnableViewState="False"
30:                   AutoGenerateColumns="False"
```

LISTING **12.4** continued

```
31:                    HeaderStyle-Font-Bold
32:                    Runat="server">
33:   <Columns>
34:    <asp:BoundColumn DataField="ProductName" HeaderText="Product"/>
35:    <asp:BoundColumn DataField="UnitPrice" HeaderText="Unit Price"/>
36:    <asp:BoundColumn DataField="UnitsInStock" HeaderText="# In Stock"/>
37:    <asp:BoundColumn DataField="UnitsOnOrder" HeaderText="# On Order"/>
38:    <asp:BoundColumn DataField="Discontinued" HeaderText="Discontinued?"/>
39:   </Columns>
40: </asp:DataGrid>
41:     </form>
42:    </font>
43:   </body>
44: </html>
45: <script runat="server" language="vb">
46:
47: Protected northwindSet as DataSet
48: Protected filter as String
49:
50: Private Sub Page_Load(Sender As Object, e As EventArgs)
51:
52:   if not IsPostBack then
53:     InitGrid()
54:   else
55:     northwindSet = Session("NorthwindDataSet")
56:     filter = CStr(Session("RowFilter"))
57:   End If
58:   Bind(filter)
59:
60: End Sub
61:
62: private Sub InitGrid()
63:
64:   northwindSet = new DataSet("NorthWind")
65:   Dim nwindCon as new OleDbConnection("Provider=Microsoft. " & _
66:                    " Jet.OLEDB.4.0;Data Source=C:\Program Files\" & _
67:                    "Microsoft Office\Office\Samples\" & _
68:                    "Northwind.mdb;User ID=;Password=;")
69:   Dim nwindAdapt as new OleDbDataAdapter("Select * from Products", _
70:        nwindCon)
71:   nwindAdapt.Fill(northwindSet, "Products")
72:   Session.Add("NorthwindDataSet", northwindSet)
73:   Session.Add("RowFilter", "")
74:
75: End Sub
76: private Sub Bind(strFilter as string)
77:
78:   Session("RowFilter") = strFilter
79:   Dim customView as DataView
80:   customView = northwindSet.Tables("Products").DefaultView
```

**12**

**LISTING 12.4** continued

```
81:     customView.RowFilter = strFilter
82:     inventoryGrid.DataSource = customView
83:     inventoryGrid.DataBind()
84:
85: End Sub
86:
87: Protected Sub SortByPrice(sender as object, e as EventArgs)
88:
89:     Dim price as String = priceList.SelectedItem.Text
90:     Bind("UnitPrice >= " & price)
91:
92: End Sub
93:
94: Protected Sub ShowOutOfStock(sender as object, e as EventArgs)
95:
96:     Bind("UnitsInStock = 0")
97:
98: End Sub
99:
100: Protected Sub ShowDisc(sender as object, e as EventArgs)
101:
102:     Bind("Discontinued = true")
103:
104: End Sub
105:
106: </script>
```

**ANALYSIS** Lines 3–44 contain all the HTML and ASP.NET code to make the sample work. Lines 9–14 define a drop-down list used to filter the Products table by price. Lines 16, 20, and 25 each define button controls that call methods to change the RowFilter property of the default DataView used on Line 80.

The Page_Load event (Lines 50–60) contains code similar to earlier listings. It sets up the grid when the page is first hit by calling InitGrid (Line 53). If this page is being viewed after the initial hit from a postback event, the Page_Load event retrieves the dataset and current row filter from session state (Lines 55–56).

The Bind method (Lines 76–85) contains code to set the RowFilter property of the Products table's DefaultView property (Line 81). The Bind method must be called with a filter string, which can be empty.

Lines 87–104 contain three button-click event handlers, each creating a custom row filter string. Lines 89–90 query the priceList ListControl to find the current value and then use this value to dynamically build a filter string. Lines 96 and 102 of the ShowOutOfStock and ShowDisc methods use a static filter string.

Listing 12.4 shows that you can create powerful dynamic filtering mechanisms in your ASP.NET code without writing huge amounts of code. Much of the code in the listing, such as the `Page_Load` and `Bind` methods, is boilerplate that you can easily reuse.

The `DataView` has other properties that you can use to manipulate table data. Let's look at sorting features next.

## Sorting Data Using the `DataView`

You may want to sort data that has been bound to an ASP.NET Web control. As with data filtering, you can customize `Select` statements in any data adapter objects that you might use to include sorting criteria. However, the `DataView` class is also capable of sorting data in a `DataTable` object easily. You may want to use the `DataView` for sorting for the same reasons explained in the preceding section—namely to reduce queries to a back-end relational database or to sort data from XML files.

You can easily sort data in a `DataTable` by using the `DataView` `Sort` property. This property uses SQL expressions that are part of the `ORDER BY` clause in a SQL `Select` statement. For instance, here's a SQL `Select` statement containing this clause:

```
Select * from Products ORDER BY UnitPrice ASCENDING
```

To use such sort criteria in a `DataView`, you assign the `Sort` property to the string `"UnitPrice ASCENDING"`.

`ORDER BY` clauses frequently use the two keywords `ASCENDING` (also `ASC`) and `DESCENDING` (`DESC`) to specify the order that records should be returned. The default `ASCENDING` keyword sorts records from lowest to highest. You can use these two keywords, in addition to any others mentioned in the previous section, in any strings you assign to the `Sort` property. You can also perform sub-sorting by separating expressions with commas, as in the following example:

```
Select * form Products ORDER BY UnitPrice ASC, UnitsInStock ASC
```

This statement sorts product rows according to their price, and any records with identical prices are sorted again by the number of units in stock.

Because sorting is an expensive operation, you may not want to enable it during the entire lifetime of a `DataView`. To control when a `DataView` should be sorted, you must use the `ApplyDefaultSort` property. Set the property to `true` to enable sorting.

You can add sorting to Listing 12.4 by making the following modifications to the code:

1. Add a declaration for a sort string such as the following just after the `<script>` tag (Line 46):

   ```
   protected sortString As String
   ```

12

2. Add code similar to the following to retrieve the sort string from session in the else clause of the Page_Load event:

```
sortString = CStr(Session.("SortString"))
```

3. Add code to initialize the sortString in session state by adding the following line to the end of the InitGrid method:

```
Session.Add("SortString", "")
```

4. Create a second Bind method that accepts a sort string, such as the following:

```
private void Bind(filterString As String, sortString as String)

    Session("RowFilter") = filterString
    Session("SortString") = sortString
    Dim customView as DataView
    customView = northwindSet.Tables("Products").DefaultView
    customView.RowFilter = strFilter
    customView.Sort = strSort
    customView.ApplyDefaultSort = true
    inventoryGrid.DataSource = customView;  inventoryGrid.DataBind()

End Sub
```

5. Add code, such as event handlers, to apply sorting. They should call the new Bind method.

# Performing Some DataGrid Tricks

The DataGrid is the most powerful ASP.NET Web control, and you'll probably use it quite often in your own Internet applications. You've seen a number of samples in the past few lessons that used the DataGrid to display data in tabular format. Today you've seen how to apply filtering and sorting in a DataGrid. You should be aware of a few important issues when programming with the DataGrid, and there are more features to learn about. The following sections will give important advice on using view state with the DataGrid and when to store the grid in session.

## Fetching Data, the ViewState, and Session State

One decision that you will have to make in your application when programming with the DataGrid is how to keep track of the data that it stores. DataGrids can contain a huge amount of data, and it's important to have solid knowledge about where that data is at any given time. You have three options for storing and maintaining data in the grid:

- Use ViewState to store information in the grid. In this method, you create a DataSet object on the first page hit, populate it, and attach it to the grid using the grid's DataSource property. You do nothing on subsequent page hits and let the grid remember all the data stored inside it. The grid uses ViewState to remember its contents through subsequent page hits. The ViewState is stored in a compressed string in a hidden field on the Web Form.

- Disable ViewState and use session state. In this method, you create a DataSet object, populate it, and then store it in session. Every time the page loads, you retrieve the dataset from session state, attach it to the grid using the grid's DataSource property, and call DataBind. This method was used in Listing 12.4 and many of the listings on Day 5.

- Disable ViewState and don't use session state. In this method, you create a new DataSet object on every page hit, populate it on every page hit, and use the same techniques in the first two methods to bind the dataset to the grid. You never store the grid in Session.

Which method should you use in your own application? The answer depends on your response to the following two questions:

- Will you save data from the grid back to the database or source XML file at any time?

- Will your site be used by a large number of users at the same time? Here, the term *large number* is fuzzy—the exact number depends on your specific Web server and can be determined only by prototyping and testing.

If the answer to the first question is yes, you can't use the first option because it's difficult to save data from a data grid back into a dataset. If you use grid view state, you are limited to a read-only grid. However, in many cases, this method is just fine, and using ViewState is probably the best option.

If you have a read-write grid, you must use the second or third option. In this case, if you have a large number of concurrent users, you should use the third option—don't store the grid in session. You can still store filter and sorting criteria in session and other small strings because sessions eat up memory on your Web server. With a large number of users, you can easily overwhelm your Web server.

However, this decision isn't clear-cut. ASP.NET session state is vastly more powerful than the old ASP session state model. For instance, you can store ASP.NET sessions on a different computer or in a SQL Server database. Depending on the hardware and network that you have at your disposal, you may use one of these options. Day 18, "Configuring Internet Applications," will discuss how to configure session state.

Conventional wisdom says that if you have a huge number of users, you probably will want to disable session state on all your pages. In "fuzzy" cases like this, your best option is to *forget what everyone tells you and run your own tests on your own hardware configuration.*

12

## Using `HyperLinkColumn` to Show Record Details

Many ASP.NET pages that use the `DataGrid` may require displaying supplemental information related to individual records or fields within a row. For instance, you may want to develop a program to show a list of employees in grid format and have a link within each row of the grid to show detailed information about the employee. You can easily add this functionality to your application by using the grid control's `HyperLinkColumn` element.

To demonstrate how to use `HyperLinkColumn`, let's use the Employees table in the Northwind database. This table contains detailed information about each Northwind employee, including address and contact information. The table has 17 columns, and displaying them all at once in a data grid probably isn't the best solution for listing employee information.

Instead, let's create a "master-detail" view of the Northwind employees. This view shows summary information from a master table and then contains a link to display further information in the detailed view. For the following examples, let's use the Northwind Orders table as the detailed view. This table contains all the orders that each Northwind employee is responsible for completing. Listing 12.5 shows a user control that can be placed in any ASP.NET page to show an employee's order details. An example of a containing page for the user control will follow soon.

**LISTING 12.5**  EmployeeDetails.ascx: A User Control Responsible for the Detail View of Orders for an Employee

```
 1: <%@ Control Language="vb" %>
 2: <%@ Import NameSpace="System.Data" %>
 3: <%@ Import NameSpace="System.Data.OleDb" %>
 4: <h3>Employee Sales History</h3>
 5: <asp:DataGrid ID="ordersGrid" Runat="server"
 6:  AutoGenerateColumns="False">
 7:    <Columns>
 8:     <asp:BoundColumn DataField="OrderDate" DataFormatString="{0:d}"
 9:                      HeaderText="Date Ordered"/>
10:     <asp:BoundColumn DataField="ShippedDate" DataFormatString="{0:d}"
11:                      HeaderText="Date Shipped"/>
12:     <asp:BoundColumn DataField="ShipName"
13:                      HeaderText="Shipped To"/>
14:     <asp:BoundColumn DataField="Freight" DataFormatString="{0:C}"
15:                      HeaderText="Freight Cost"/>
16:    </Columns>
17: </asp:DataGrid>
18:
19: <script runat="server" language="vb">
20: protected northwindSet as DataSet
21: protected empRowView as DataRowView
```

**LISTING 12.5** continued

```
22:
23: Private Sub Page_Load(Sender As Object, e As EventArgs)
24:
25:     northwindSet = new DataSet()
26:     Dim empId as String = Request.Params("id")
27:     if empId Is Nothing Or empId = "" then
28:
29:       Me.Visible = false
30:       return
31:
32:     End If
33:
34:     Dim nwindCon as new OleDbConnection("Provider=Microsoft" & _
35:       ".Jet.OLEDB.4.0;Data Source=C:\Program Files\Microsoft Office\" & _
36:       "Office\Samples\Northwind.mdb;User ID=;Password=;")
37:
38:     Dim orderAdapt as new OleDbDataAdapter("Select * from Orders where " & _
39:                            "EmployeeID =" & empId, nwindCon)
40:     orderAdapt.Fill(northwindSet, "Orders")
41:     ordersGrid.DataSource = northwindSet.Tables("Orders")
42:
43:     ordersGrid.DataBind()
44:
45: End Sub
46:
47: </script>
```

**ANALYSIS** Lines 4–17 contain HTML and ASP.NET code that declares a data grid. Each column that needs to be shown is declared by using BoundColumn objects (Lines 8–15). The DataFormatString is used in some of the declarations to format each column properly. Day 5 explained different format string options that you can use in your code.

The Page_Load method (Lines 23–45) contains code that binds the contents of the Orders table to the ordersGrid data grid. Line 26 fetches the employee ID that should be used to filter the Orders table. Lines 27–32 contain special logic to hide this user control if no employee ID is specified. This is important to avoid runtime errors if the containing page doesn't pass an employee ID to the control.

Lines 34–43 should look familiar. We used similar code in many previous samples to open a connection, fill a dataset, and bind the dataset to a data grid.

Now that we have a user control to show the orders that each Northwind employee is responsible for, let's create a containing page to use the control. Listing 12.6 shows just such a page.

**12**

**LISTING 12.6**  ShowEmpDetail.aspx: Using Listing 12.5's User Control to Show a Master-Detail View of an Employee

```
 1: <%@ Register TagPrefix="WebBook" TagName="EmployeeDetails"
 2:     Src="EmployeeDetails.ascx" %>
 3: <%@ Import NameSpace="System.Data" %>
 4: <%@ Import NameSpace="System.Data.OleDb" %>
 5: <html>
 6:   <body >
 7:   <font face="arial">
 8:
 9:     <h3>Employee Sales Information</h3>
10:     Click on the "Details..." link to find out the orders each
11:     employee is responsible for.
12:
13:    <form id="emp" method="post" runat="server">
14:    <asp:DataGrid ID="employeesGrid" Runat="server"
15:     AutoGenerateColumns="False">
16:     <Columns>
17:       <asp:BoundColumn DataField="FirstName" HeaderText="First"/>
18:       <asp:BoundColumn DataField="LastName" HeaderText="Last"/>
19:       <asp:BoundColumn DataField="Title" />
20:       <asp:HyperLinkColumn HeaderText="Details"
21:               DataNavigateUrlField="EmployeeID"
22:               DataNavigateUrlFormatString="ShowEmpDetail.aspx?id={0}"
23:               Text="Details..."/>
24:     </Columns>
25:    </asp:DataGrid>
26:
27:    <br>
28:
29:    <WebBook:EmployeeDetails id=EmpDet1 runat="server"/></FONT>
30:
31:    </form>
32:    </font>
33:   </body>
34: </html>
35: <script runat="server" language="vb">
36:
37: Protected northwindSet as  DataSet
38:
39: private Sub Page_Load(sender as object, e as System.EventArgs)
40:
41:   if Not IsPostBack then
42:     InitGrid()
43:   else
44:     northwindSet = Session("NorthwindDataSet")
45:   end if
46:   Bind()
47:
```

**LISTING 12.6**   continued

```
48: End Sub
49:
50: private Sub InitGrid()
51:
52:   northwindSet = new DataSet("NorthWind")
53:   Dim nwindCon as new OleDbConnection("Provider=Microsoft. " & _
54:   " Jet.OLEDB.4.0;Data Source=C:\Program Files\ " & _
55:   "Microsoft Office\Office\Samples\Northwind.mdb;User ID=;Password=;")
56:   Dim nwindAdapt as new OleDbDataAdapter("Select * from Employees", _
57:       nwindCon)
58:   nwindAdapt.Fill(northwindSet, "Employees")
59:   Session.Add("NorthwindDataSet", northwindSet)
60: End Sub
61:
62: private Sub Bind()
63:
64:   employeesGrid.DataSource = northwindSet
65:   employeesGrid.DataBind()
66:
67: End Sub
68: </script>
```

**ANALYSIS**  Lines 14–25 contain HTML and ASP.NET code to declare a parent data grid listing all Northwind employees. Line 29 contains the same declaration for the user control used in Listing 12.5. This declaration works because the user control was linked into the page using the Register directive in Lines 1–2 of Listing 12.6.

Lines 21–22 use the DataNavigateUrlField and DataNavigateUrlFormatString properties to create a postback request to this same page and set the id parameter. These two properties are essential for enabling the detail view of the data. The DataNavigateUrlField specifies a particular field in the grid's underlying dataset. The DataNavigateUrlFormatString allows you to format a URL request using .NET formatting strings. An alternative way to use these properties is to direct users to a new page to display the detail view. In this case, you could place the user control from Listing 12.5 on this new page.

The Page_Load event on Lines 39–48 uses the standard technique of loading the dataset and binding the data grid, depending on the type of page request. The InitGrid method (Lines 59–60) is responsible for initializing the grid on the first page hit. The Bind method (Lines 62–67) rebinds the grid every time the page is loaded.

Figure 12.2 shows Listings 12.5 and 12.6 in action. Using HyperLinkColumn is an easy way to create master-detail views of any number of datasets.

**12**

**FIGURE 12.2**

*Using the*
*HyperLinkColumn to*
*display master-detail*
*records.*

# Summary

Today's lesson helped you to extend your knowledge of ASP.NET. We began with a sample showing you how to bind XML data to a list box Web control. You can use the same technique to bind XML data to any Web control, such as the data grid or data ListControls. Today's lesson also gave a list of many .NET classes that can be bound to Web controls. These classes support the ICollection, IListCollection, and IEnumerable interfaces, which are key ingredients for allowing data binding to work properly.

**NEW TERM** You also learned about the DataView class and how you can use it to sort and filter data. The DataView is an example of a design technique called *indirection*. This means that the DataView sits between a DataSet and Web control and allows you to manipulate the contents of a DataSet from the Web control's perspective. However, filtering and sorting a DataSet doesn't change the actual data.

The last part of today's lesson explained the key issues surrounding view state and session state for Web controls that can contain significant amounts of data, such as the data grid. You saw three alternative methods for managing the data contained by a grid control and some tips for choosing the best method. Finally, today's lesson demonstrated the use of a user control to implement a master-detail view of the Employees table in the Northwind database. You can use the same techniques for your own application, especially if you have related sets of tables or XML files.

Today's lesson concludes the discussion of ASP.NET. By now, you've learned substantial skills that you can apply to creating your own Web application. Before you get started learning Web services, take some time to read through the Q&A section and try answering the quiz and exercise questions.

# Q&A

**Q I store all my application data using XML. Can I still use the techniques presented in the last part of this chapter?**

**A** Yes, you can fit all the examples that used the Northwind database on top of XML data. Rather than use a data adapter object, read the XML data directly into the dataset by using the `ReadXml` method.

**Q I want to write a custom class that contains data elements and then use data binding to display the contents of the class in a Web control. Can I do this?**

**A** Yes, but this technique is advanced. To start, you must implement the `IEnumerable` interface in your custom class. Start by re-implementing a list class and then build your custom code up from there.

**Q I want to use multiple pages to show detailed data, such as the master-detail section at the end of this lesson. How can I do so?**

**A** You can reuse the sample in this chapter and then change the URL in the `DataNavigateUrlFormatString` property to point to a different page.

# Workshop

The Workshop provides quiz questions to help you solidify your understanding of the material covered and exercises to provide you with experience in using what you've learned. The answers to the quiz questions are provided in Appendix A, "Answers to Quizzes and Exercises."

## Quiz

1. What is an essential interface that a class must provide for data binding to work properly?

2. What property is used by many ASP.NET Web controls to specify a data field to use as the source for data binding?

3. What property is used to retrieve a stock `DataView` for any `DataTable` object?

4. What string would you use to filter all records in a `DataView` that contain the substring `"Inc"`?

12

5. What key property must be set in order for sorting to take place in a `DataView`?

6. Under what circumstances is it a good idea to use the data grid's built-in view state functionality?

7. What performance penalty occurs when using view state?

8. In what circumstances would you disable both view state and session state?

9. Why is it difficult to determine when to disable sessions?

10. What special column in a data grid is used to implement master-detail pages?

## Exercises

1. Extend Listing 12.4 to filter the orders that a Northwind employee has created so that only the most recent year's orders appear in the detail view user control.

2. Modify the XML file from Listing 12.1 to contain a `<locations>` node for each `<cd>` element. Add some locations where each CD can be purchased. Then modify Listing 12.3 to show this XML file in a master-detail style.

# WEEK 2

# DAY 13

# Introducing Web Services

Today's lesson covers the fundamentals of creating and using Web Services, an exciting new way of creating programs that anyone with access to the Internet can use. Although Web Services use sophisticated mechanisms and protocols to communicate with clients, .NET makes the job of creating and using Web Services easy.

**NEW TERM** *Web Services* are programs with methods that can be called over the Internet. Web Services allow you to create *distributed applications*, or applications that live on a number of different computers. The .NET Framework and ASP.NET provide all the underlying mechanisms to make your program Web accessible. .NET provides all the plumbing for Web Services so that you can focus on developing your application.

Today you will learn the following:

- Why Web Services are a viable technology
- How to create a Web Service
- How to create Web Service clients with the .NET Framework utilities
- How to create Web Service clients with Visual Studio .NET
- How Web Services work

# Why Use Web Services?

Already, a number of technologies allow you to create distributed applications, including CORBA, DCOM, RPC, and custom solutions based on TCP sockets. Because these technologies are already in place and are quite mature at this time, why would you or your company make the leap to Web Services?

You might choose Web Services for a number of good reasons if you plan to make a distributed application:

- Web Services are built on industry standard protocols, such as TCP, SSL, XML, SOAP, and WSDL. We'll explain these protocols in detail later today.
- Web Services are easy—even trivial—to implement with .NET. If you've ever tried to implement a CORBA or DCOM solution, you'll be pleasantly surprised by how painless Web Service implementation and configuration are with .NET and ASP.NET.
- You don't need a lot of infrastructure in place to develop a Web Service. The only real requirements are a Web server and a connection to the Internet.

# Implementing Your First Web Service

Rather than dwell on the theoretical aspects of Web Services, let's implement a simple Web Service to demonstrate some of the points from the preceding section. Two pieces are required in any Web Service implementation: the service and the client. We will create the service first.

The easiest way to create Web Services in .NET is to build them using ASP.NET. Web Service files in ASP.NET have the special filename extension .asmx. ASP.NET flags any file with this extension as a Web Service and compiles it as a Web Service.

The first sample service that we will create simply returns the current time on the server as a string. Follow these steps to create the service:

1. As explained for the first ASP.NET page on Day 2, "Introducing ASP.NET," create a directory for the Web Service project on your computer. For this example, use the directory C:\src\timeservice.

2. On your Web server, create a virtual directory named TimeService that points to the project directory in step 1. (Day 2 explained how to create virtual directories.)

3. In the project directory, create a new file called TimeUtilities.asmx using your text editor or download this file from the book's Web site at www.samspublishing.com. Type the contents of Listing 13.1 if you didn't download the file.

Listing 13.1 shows a basic Web Service that will return the time of day as a string on the server.

**LISTING 13.1**   TimeUtilities.asmx: Returning the Current Time on the Server

```
 1: <%@ WebService Language="vb" Class="TimeUtilities" %>
 2: Imports System
 3: Imports System.Web.Services
 4:
 5: <WebService(Namespace:="http://tempuri.org/webservices")> _
 6: public class TimeUtilities
 7:     Inherits WebService
 8:
 9:   <WebMethod> public function GetTime() as String
10:
11:      Dim ret as string = "The current time on the server is: "
12:      ret &= DateTime.Now.ToString()
13:      return ret
14:
15:   End Function
16:
17: End Class
```

**ANALYSIS**   Line 1 uses the WebService page directive. You've seen other ASP.NET page directives such as Page, Import, and Control on previous days. The WebService page directive marks the remaining code in the page as a Web Service. Within the page directive, you must specify the class of the Web Service that you are going to define in the code. Each Web Service must have its own class; the one in this example is called TimeUtilities.

Lines 2 and 3 specify that we are using the System and System.Web.Services namespaces. They are required in any Web Service that we write.

Line 5 shows the definition of the class. Notice that before we define the class, we use an attribute for it:

```
<WebService(Namespace:="http://tempuri.org/webservices")>
```

**NEW TERM**   This line is called an *attribute definition*. If you are an experienced .NET code developer, you may already have used these kinds of attributes in your code. If you haven't used them, just understand that they supplement the code you write. In this case, we are using the WebService attribute to specify the namespace for our Web Service.

Because Web Services can be exposed to the rest of the world on the Internet, each one needs a unique namespace. This namespace is exactly the same kind of thing you would use in an XML file that you were going to share with another company, as we explained

13

on Day 8, "Using XML with Your Applications." If you are developing a Web Service for an organization, you should use your organization's public URL instead of tempuri.org.

Next, Line 6 (which is actually a continuation of Line 5) defines the `TimeUtilities` class. Because the class defines a Web Service, it must derive from the `WebService` class in the `System.Web.WebServices` namespace.

Our next order of business (Lines 9–15) is to define the method that we want our Web Service users to call. Notice that the `GetTime` method is preceded by the `<WebMethod>` attribute. All methods that should be available to Web Service users must have this attribute. `GetTime` simply returns a string with the current time on the server.

## Testing the Web Service

To test the Web Service, you need to point a Web browser to the Web Service as if it were a regular Web page. ASP.NET automatically generates some simple documentation for the Web Service and provides Web pages to invoke methods on the service. If you're using the same computer where the Web Service resides to test, point your browser to the following URL. If not, substitute the name of the computer for *localhost* in the following URL:

```
http://localhost/TimeService/TimeUtilities.asmx
```

You should see a page that resembles Figure 13.1. From the figure, you can see that ASP.NET has created a page with a list of the methods that the TimeUtilities Web Service exposes.

Click the GetTime link to see a page that has some template documentation for the `GetTime` method, as shown in Figure 13.2.

**FIGURE 13.1**

*ASP.NET output for the TimeUtilities.*

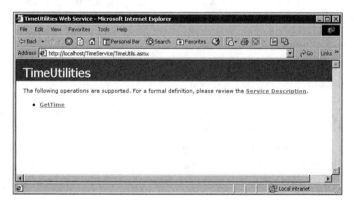

**FIGURE 13.2**

*ASP.NET boilerplate documentation for the* `GetTime` *method.*

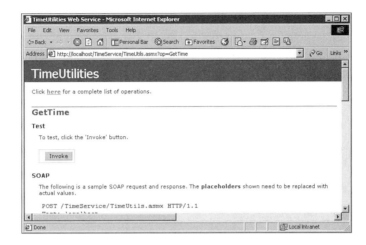

By clicking the Invoke button on this page, you see a response similar to the following code lines in your browser. The Web server (IIS) returns an XML document that contains the response from the Web Service.

```
<?xml version="1.0" encoding="utf-8" ?>
  <string xmlns="http://tempuri.org/webservices">
    The current time on the server is: 7/7/2001 3:55:41 PM
  </string>
```

## Describing the Web Service

Web Services need a way to tell client programs what methods they implement, the parameters each method takes, and the return values each method gives back. They do so through a WSDL file. WSDL, which stands for Web Services Description Language, provides Web Service clients with all the necessary details they need to connect to and use the Web Service.

WSDL files are XML files. To see what the WSDL file looks like for our TimeUtilities application, point your browser to the URL of the TimeUtilities.asmx file and append the string ?WSDL to the URL, as in the following line:

```
http://localhost/TimeService/TimeUtilities.asmx?WSDL
```

**13**

**Tip**

> You can also see the WSDL file for the TimeUtilities application by browsing to the main Web Service page and then clicking the Service Description link (refer to Figure 13.1).

The WSDL file returned from our sample Web Service looks like Listing 13.2. The WSDL is quite large, even for our simple Web Service. Luckily, you should never have to create WSDL files yourself; the Web Service will generate the files automatically using the plumbing built into ASP.NET.

**LISTING 13.2**   The WSDL File for the TimeUtilities Web Service

```
 1:   <?xml version="1.0" encoding="utf-8" ?>
 2:   <definitions
 3:        xmlns:s="http://www.w3.org/2001/XMLSchema"
 4:        xmlns:http="http://schemas.xmlsoap.org/wsdl/http/"
 5:        xmlns:mime="http://schemas.xmlsoap.org/wsdl/mime/"
 6:        xmlns:tm="http://microsoft.com/wsdl/mime/textMatching/"
 7:        xmlns:soap="http://schemas.xmlsoap.org/wsdl/soap/"
 8:        xmlns:soapenc="http://schemas.xmlsoap.org/soap/encoding/"
 9:        xmlns:s0="http://tempuri.org/webservices"
10:        targetNamespace="http://tempuri.org/webservices"
11:        xmlns="http://schemas.xmlsoap.org/wsdl/">
12:   <types>
13:    <s:schema attributeFormDefault="qualified"
14:              elementFormDefault="qualified"
15:              targetNamespace="http://tempuri.org/webservices">
16:     <s:element name="GetTime">
17:      <s:complexType />
18:     </s:element>
19:     <s:element name="GetTimeResponse">
20:      <s:complexType>
21:       <s:sequence>
22:        <s:element
23:              minOccurs="1"
24:              maxOccurs="1"
25:              name="GetTimeResult"
26:              nillable="true"
27:              type="s:string" />
28:       </s:sequence>
29:      </s:complexType>
30:     </s:element>
31:     <s:element name="string" nillable="true" type="s:string" />
32:    </s:schema>
33:   </types>
34:   <message name="GetTimeSoapIn">
35:    <part name="parameters" element="s0:GetTime" />
36:   </message>
37:   <message name="GetTimeSoapOut">
38:    <part name="parameters" element="s0:GetTimeResponse" />
39:   </message>
40:   <message name="GetTimeHttpGetIn" />
41:    <message name="GetTimeHttpGetOut">
42:     <part name="Body" element="s0:string" />
```

LISTING **13.2**   continued

```
43:     </message>
44:     <message name="GetTimeHttpPostIn" />
45:     <message name="GetTimeHttpPostOut">
46:      <part name="Body" element="s0:string" />
47:     </message>
48:     <portType name="TimeUtilitiesSoap">
49:      <operation name="GetTime">
50:       <input message="s0:GetTimeSoapIn" />
51:       <output message="s0:GetTimeSoapOut" />
52:      </operation>
53:     </portType>
54:     <portType name="TimeUtilitiesHttpGet">
55:      <operation name="GetTime">
56:       <input message="s0:GetTimeHttpGetIn" />
57:       <output message="s0:GetTimeHttpGetOut" />
58:      </operation>
59:     </portType>
60:     <portType name="TimeUtilitiesHttpPost">
61:      <operation name="GetTime">
62:       <input message="s0:GetTimeHttpPostIn" />
63:       <output message="s0:GetTimeHttpPostOut" />
64:      </operation>
65:     </portType>
66:     <binding name="TimeUtilitiesSoap" type="s0:TimeUtilitiesSoap">
67:      <soap:binding transport="http://schemas.xmlsoap.org/soap/http"
68:                    style="document" />
69:      <operation name="GetTime">
70:       <soap:operation soapAction="http://tempuri.org/webservices/GetTime"
71:                    style="document" />
72:       <input>
73:        <soap:body use="literal" />
74:       </input>
75:       <output>
76:        <soap:body use="literal" />
77:       </output>
78:      </operation>
79:     </binding>
80:     <binding name="TimeUtilitiesHttpGet" type="s0:TimeUtilitiesHttpGet">
81:      <http:binding verb="GET" />
82:      <operation name="GetTime">
83:       <http:operation location="/GetTime" />
84:       <input>
85:        <http:urlEncoded />
86:       </input>
87:       <output>
88:        <mime:mimeXml part="Body" />
89:       </output>
90:      </operation>
91:     </binding>
```

**13**

LISTING **13.2**   continued

```
 92:   <binding name="TimeUtilitiesHttpPost" type="s0:TimeUtilitiesHttpPost">
 93:    <http:binding verb="POST" />
 94:    <operation name="GetTime">
 95:     <http:operation location="/GetTime" />
 96:     <input>
 97:      <mime:content type="application/x-www-form-urlencoded" />
 98:     </input>
 99:     <output>
100:      <mime:mimeXml part="Body" />
101:     </output>
102:    </operation>
103:   </binding>
104:   <service name="TimeUtilities">
105:    <port name="TimeUtilitiesSoap" binding="s0:TimeUtilitiesSoap">
106:     <soap:address
107:              location="http://localhost/timeservice/timeutilities.asmx"
/>
108:    </port>
109:    <port name="TimeUtilitiesHttpGet" binding="s0:TimeUtilitiesHttpGet">
110:     <http:address
111:              location="http://localhost/timeservice/timeutilities.asmx" />
112:    </port>
113:    <port name="TimeUtilitiesHttpPost"
114:              binding="s0:TimeUtilitiesHttpPost">
115:     <http:address
116:              location="http://localhost/timeservice/timeutilities.asmx" />
117:    </port>
118:   </service>
119:  </definitions>
```

## Analyzing the WSDL File

ANALYSIS   To get a general sense of what the WSDL file describes, let's take a detailed look
at Listing 13.2. The top-level XML nodes for the TimeUtilities WSDL file are as
follows:

```
<definitions >
 <types>

 <message name="GetTimeSoapIn">
 <message name="GetTimeSoapOut">
 <message name="GetTimeHttpGetIn">
 <message name="GetTimeHttpGetOut">
 <message name="GetTimeHttpPostIn">
 <message name="GetTimeHttpPostOut">

 <portType name="TimeUtilitiesSoap">
```

```
<portType name="TimeUtilitiesHttpGet">
<portType name="TimeUtilitiesHttpPost">

<binding name="TimeUtilitiesSoap">
<binding name="TimeUtilitiesHttpGet">
<binding name="TimeUtilitiesHttpPost">

<service name="TimeUtilities">

</definitions>
```

You can see that the WSDL file contains several kinds of nodes: types, message, portType, binding, and service. The types node describes the names, parameters, and return values of each method in the Web Service. The message, portType, binding, and service definitions describe how a client should communicate with the Web Service.

Let's analyze each WSDL definition node in reverse order.

## The service Node

The service node defines the name of our Web Service—in this case, TimeUtilities—and then defines ports:

```
104:    <service name="TimeUtilities">
105:     <port name="TimeUtilitiesSoap" binding="s0:TimeUtilitiesSoap">
106:      <soap:address
107:          location="http://localhost/timeservice/timeutilities.asmx" />
108:     </port>
109:     <port name="TimeUtilitiesHttpGet" binding="s0:TimeUtilitiesHttpGet">
110:      <http:address
111:          location="http://localhost/timeservice/timeutilities.asmx" />
112:     </port>
113:     <port name="TimeUtilitiesHttpPost"
114:              binding="s0:TimeUtilitiesHttpPost">
115:      <http:address
116:          location="http://localhost/timeservice/timeutilities.asmx" />
117:     </port>
118:    </service>
```

Each port corresponds to a certain protocol that the Web Service will support. Our Web Service supports the SOAP, HTTP Post, and HTTP Get protocols.

**13**

**Note** Not every Web Service supports HTTP, because some complex parameters can't be passed in and out of Web Services using HTTP. We'll explain the rules surrounding when HTTP is supported later today. SOAP supports any kind of data type.

## The `portType` Node

Each port supports an "operation." Each operation corresponds to a method that the Web Service supports. You can see that the following SOAP `portType` supports the `GetTime` operation for our Web Service. Each operation consists of "messages": an input message for when the method is called and an output message for when the method returns a value.

```
48:    <portType name="TimeUtilitiesSoap">
49:     <operation name="GetTime">
50:      <input message="s0:GetTimeSoapIn" />
51:      <output message="s0:GetTimeSoapOut" />
52:     </operation>
53:    </portType>
```

## The `message` Node

The `message` definition for the `GetTimeSoapIn` method is as follows:

```
34:    <message name="GetTimeSoapIn">
35:     <part name="parameters" element="s0:GetTime" />
36:    </message>
```

The `message` definition describes how parameters will be passed into and out of the Web Service. The `GetTime` method doesn't receive any parameters, so the `message` definition is trivial.

## The `types` and `schema` Nodes

The `types` node describes each method, parameter, and return value for a Web Service. These Web Service elements are detailed in a `schema` node. A simplified version of the schema node for our Web Service follows:

```
<s:schema>
 <s:element name="GetTime">
  <s:complexType />
 </s:element>
 <s:element name="GetTimeResponse">
  <s:complexType>
   <s:sequence>
    <s:element name="GetTimeResult" type="s:string" />
   </s:sequence>
  </s:complexType>
 </s:element>
 <s:element name="string" nillable="true" type="s:string" />
</s:schema>
```

Here, the `schema` node describes the `GetTime` and `GetTimeResponse` messages that our Web Service deals with. Our Web Service returns a `GetTimeResponse` message after the `GetTime` method is invoked. The definition shows that the response message includes a string.

# Implementing the Web Service Client

Although being able to access a Web Service from a Web browser is nice, a more realistic use is to create custom client programs that access a Web Service remotely, such as Web pages and standalone applications. To demonstrate how to create such programs, we'll create two different clients for our TimeUtilities Web Service: a console application and a Web page.

> **Tip**
>
> You can create Web Service clients easily by using Visual Studio .NET; we'll explain how to create them a little later today. However, to show some of the "plumbing" behind Web Services, let's continue using a text editor to create our client programs.

**NEW TERM**  Before creating the client to our TimeUtilities application, we need to create a proxy class. A *proxy class* allows us to call the GetTime method without worrying about how to connect to the server and how to pass and return parameters to and from the method. In general, a *proxy* is an object that wraps up method calls and parameters, forwards them to a remote host, and returns the results to us. Proxies serve the role as a middleman on the client computer.

.NET comes with a special utility called WSDL.exe for creating Web Service proxies. As you might imagine from the utility's name, WSDL.exe takes a Web Service's WSDL description and creates a proxy. Follow these steps to create the proxy with WSDL.exe:

1. Open a Visual Studio .NET command prompt (from the Start menu, choose Visual Studio .NET, Visual Studio .NET Tools, and then Visual Studio .NET Command Prompt). This DOS command prompt contains all the paths for the .NET tools.

2. Create a new directory for the client projects, such as C:\src\timeclient.

3. Type the following command at the prompt (try to fit the entire command at the second prompt onto one line):

```
C:>cd src\timeclient
C:\src\timeclient> wsdl /l:vb /n:WebBook
   ➥/out:TimeProxy.vb
   ➥http://localhost/TimeService/TimeUtilities.asmx?WSDL
```

This command creates the TimeProxy.vb file, which you can use in your client applications:

- /l:vb tells the utility to create the proxy using Visual Basic.

- /n:WebBook specifies a namespace for the WSDL tools to use when it creates the proxy class. You can use any namespace name you want.

**13**

- /out:TimeProxy.vb specifies the name of the output file.
- The last parameter is a URL for getting a WSDL description of the Web Service. You can also specify a file containing WSDL. However, if you use an URL, as in this example, the utility will automatically browse to the Web address and use the WSDL file that it finds.

4. Compile the new proxy file:

```
C:\src\timeclient> vbc /t:library TimeProxy.vb
```

The proxy that the WSDL.exe utility creates should look like the file shown in Listing 13.3. Notice that several very long lines have been broken up for readability.

**LISTING 13.3**  An Automatically Generated Proxy Class for the TimeUtilities Client

```
 1: '_ _ _ _ _ _ _ _ _ _ _ _ _ _ _ _ _ _ _ _ _ _ _ _ _ _ _ _ _ _ _ _.
 2: ' <autogenerated>
 3: '     This code was generated by a tool.
 4: '     Runtime Version: 1.0.2914.16
 5: '
 6: '  Changes to this file may cause incorrect behavior and will be lost if
 7: '  the code is regenerated.
 8: ' </autogenerated>
 9: '_ _ _ _ _ _ _ _ _ _ _ _ _ _ _ _ _ _ _ _ _ _ _ _ _ _ _ _ _ _ _ _.
10:
11: Option Strict Off
12: Option Explicit On
13:
14: Imports System
15: Imports System.Diagnostics
16: Imports System.Web.Services
17: Imports System.Web.Services.Protocols
18: Imports System.Xml.Serialization
19:
20: '
21: 'This source code was auto-generated by wsdl, Version=1.0.2914.16.
22: '
23: Namespace WebBook
24:
25:     <System.Web.Services.WebServiceBindingAttribute _
26:     (Name:="TimeUtilitiesSoap", _
27:     [Namespace]:="http://tempuri.org/webservices")> _
28:     Public Class TimeUtilities
29:         Inherits System.Web.Services.Protocols.SoapHttpClientProtocol
30:
31:         <System.Diagnostics.DebuggerStepThroughAttribute()> _
32:         Public Sub New()
33:             MyBase.New
34:             Me.Url = "http://localhost/timeservice/timeutilities.asmx"
```

**LISTING 13.3**   continued

```
35:            End Sub
36:
37:            <System.Diagnostics.DebuggerStepThroughAttribute(), _
38:             System.Web.Services.Protocols.SoapDocumentMethodAttribute _
39:                ("http://tempuri.org/webservices/GetTime", _
40:                RequestNamespace:="http://tempuri.org/webservices", _
41:                ResponseNamespace:="http://tempuri.org/webservices", _
42:                Use:=System.Web.Services.Description.SoapBindingUse.Literal, _
43:                ParameterStyle:=System.Web.Services. _
44:                Protocols.SoapParameterStyle.Wrapped)> _
45:            Public Function GetTime() As String
46:                Dim results() As Object = Me.Invoke("GetTime", _
47:                    New Object(-1) {})
48:                Return CType(results(0),String)
49:            End Function
50:
51:            <System.Diagnostics.DebuggerStepThroughAttribute()> _
52:            Public Function BeginGetTime(ByVal callback As _
53:                    System.AsyncCallback, _
54:                ByVal asyncState As Object) As System.IAsyncResult
55:                Return Me.BeginInvoke("GetTime", New Object(-1) {}, _
56:                    callback, asyncState)
57:            End Function
58:
59:            <System.Diagnostics.DebuggerStepThroughAttribute()> _
60:            Public Function EndGetTime(ByVal asyncResult As _
61:                    System.IAsyncResult) As String
62:                Dim results() As Object = Me.EndInvoke(asyncResult)
63:                Return CType(results(0),String)
64:            End Function
65:        End Class
66: End Namespace
```

**ANALYSIS**   The proxy file contains a new definition for the TimeUtilities class, different from the one created earlier in Listing 13.1. This new definition is the version that all our client programs will use. Although this new class is defined differently than the original created for the Web Service, this new TimeUtilities class will work the same way for any client program that uses it. Rather than execute code directly, this new class will call the Web Service to execute each method.

Notice also the two new methods in the proxy class, BeginGetTime (Lines 51-54) and EndGetTime (Lines 57-60). These methods are created so that we can call the Web Service asynchronously. This means that we can call the Web Service in our client program and then do other work immediately. Then, when the Web Service returns a result, we can process the results at that time. This asynchronous method for calling remote Web Services might not be responsive because of a slow network connection. Day 16

**13**

will contain detailed samples that show how to use asynchronous calling methods and
Web Services.

Now that we've created our proxy class, we can create client programs that use our Web
Service. To begin, let's create a simple console application to call the Web Service. The
client is shown in Listing 13.4.

**LISTING 13.4**   CallService.vb: A Console Application That Calls the TimeUtilities Web
Service

```
Imports System
Imports WebBook

namespace WebBook
  public class CallService
    public static sub Main()
      Dim remoteService as new TimeUtilities()
      Console.WriteLine("Calling web service...")
      Console.WriteLine(remoteService.GetTime())
    End Sub
  End Class
End Namespace
```

If you save the CallService.vb client in the `TimeClient` project directory that you created, you can compile it by using this command:

`vbc CallService.vb /r:TimeProxy.dll`

This command creates a file named CallService.exe in the client directory, which you
can run now. For this command to work, you must have compiled the proxy class in
Listing 13.3 according to the instructions in step 4 of this section.

After running the CallService.exe program you created, you should see output like the
following:

 Calling web service...
The current time on the server is: 7/9/2001 12:19:08 PM

## Creating a Web Service Client

Now that you've seen how to create a Web Service proxy and client program manually,
let's use Visual Studio .NET to make a Web page that calls the TimeUtilities Web
Service. Visual Studio .NET automates the process by creating a proxy file using a wizard. For the example in this section, we'll create an ASP.NET page that calls the Web
Service.

To create the client application, follow these steps:

1. Create a new ASP.NET Web application by selecting New Project on Visual Studio's start page.

2. In the New Project dialog, select Visual Basic Projects in the Project Types list and then select ASP.NET Web Application from the Templates list. Name the Web application ASPClient and click OK (see Figure 13.3).

**FIGURE 13.3**

*The New Project dialog.*

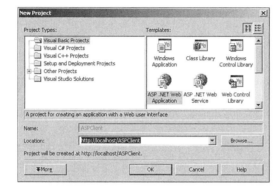

3. From the Project menu, choose Add Web Reference. You should see a dialog similar to Figure 13.4.

**FIGURE 13.4**

*The Add Web Reference dialog.*

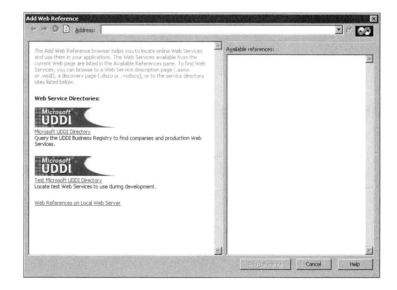

13

4. In the Address text box, enter
   **http://localhost/TimeService/TimeUtilities.asmx** and then click the Add
   Reference button to create a proxy file for the Web Service and add it to your
   project.

5. Change the Page_Load method in WebForm1.aspx to use the code in Listing 13.5.

6. Run the project.

**LISTING 13.5**   Page_Load Method for the Visual Studio Client ASP.NET Page

```
private sub Page_Load(sender as object, e as System.EventArgs)

    Dim remoteService as new localhost.TimeUtilities()
    Response.Write(remoteService.GetTime())

End Sub
```

If the remote Web Service resides on another machine, the localhost string in Listing
13.5 changes to the name of that machine. After running the project, you should see a
screen similar to Figure 13.5.

**FIGURE 13.5**

*The ASP.NET client for
the Web Service.*

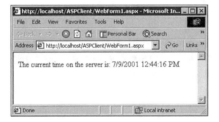

# Understanding How Web Services Work

Web Services communicate with clients using SOAP (Simple Object Access Protocol),
which is built on top of the HTTP and TCP Internet protocols. Figure 13.6 shows how
SOAP is used with these other two protocols between a Web Service and its client.

SOAP uses XML and defines how a function should be called on a remote machine. It
also specifies how parameters should be passed to and from a function on a remote
machine. For example, Listing 13.6 shows the SOAP message that a client sends to the
TimeUtilities Web Service.

**FIGURE 13.6**

*Internet protocols used by a Web Service and its clients.*

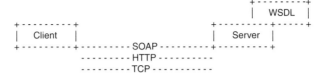

```
                                                      +---------+
                                                      |  WSDL   |
          +---------+                        +---------+-----+
          | Client  |                        | Server  |
          +---------+---------- SOAP --------+---------+
                   ---------- HTTP ----------
                   ---------- TCP -----------
```

**LISTING 13.6**   A SOAP Request to the TimeUtilities Web Service

```
1: <?xml version="1.0" encoding="utf-8"?>
2: <soap:Envelope xmlns:xsi="http://www.w3.org/2001/XMLSchema-instance"
3:                xmlns:xsd="http://www.w3.org/2001/XMLSchema"
4:                xmlns:soap="http://schemas.xmlsoap.org/soap/envelope/">
5:   <soap:Body>
6:     <GetTime xmlns="http://tempuri.org/webservices" />
7:   </soap:Body>
8: </soap:Envelope>
```

**ANALYSIS** From Listing 13.6, you can see that each SOAP request is an XML file that contains the name of a method to call and any parameters that the method might need. Because SOAP uses the HTTP protocol, the HTTP headers (Lines 1–5) in Listing 13.7 are placed before the SOAP message (Lines 2–8) in Listing 13.6. The HTTP request using SOAP for the TimeUtilities looks like Listing 13.7.

**LISTING 13.7**   An HTTP Request Containing a SOAP Method Call

```
 1: POST /timeservice/timeutilities.asmx HTTP/1.1
 2: Host: localhost
 3: Content-Type: text/xml; charset=utf-8
 4: Content-Length: 484
 5: SOAPAction: "http://tempuri.org/webservices/GetTime"
 6:
 7: <?xml version="1.0" encoding="utf-8"?>
 8: <soap:Envelope xmlns:xsi="http://www.w3.org/2001/XMLSchema-instance"
 9:                xmlns:xsd="http://www.w3.org/2001/XMLSchema"
10:                xmlns:soap="http://schemas.xmlsoap.org/soap/envelope/">
11:   <soap:Body>
12:     <GetTime xmlns="http://tempuri.org/webservices" />
13:   </soap:Body>
14: </soap:Envelope>
```

**13**

Because SOAP uses HTTP, you can create a program that responds to SOAP requests using a Web server. This is why Web Services promise to become a popular way to create distributed programs. Currently, a huge number of Web servers are already in place, and given the right plumbing utilities, each one can be made to accept SOAP calls and return SOAP responses.

Because Web Services use SOAP and can run using Web servers, all .NET Web Services use ASP.NET as a foundation. ASP.NET is designed so that it can handle SOAP requests and dispatch them to your custom Web Services. If you create a Web Service using an ASP.NET page with an .asmx extension, ASP.NET will recognize it as a Web Service and dispatch SOAP requests to your Web server.

**Note**

> As you might suspect, you can use SOAP without a Web server. By using .NET, you can also create server programs that use SOAP and communicate with client programs without the use of a Web server. This process, called *remoting* in .NET, is beyond the scope of this book. However, the documentation that comes with Visual Studio .NET contains detailed information and examples on how to set up servers using SOAP. Look under the Remoting keyword.

Finding out how to communicate with a remote Web Service is difficult unless there's a standard way to find out what methods the Web Service offers. As you saw earlier today, WSDL files supply this information. Any developer who needs to use a Web Service can look at the WSDL file and then build programs that call the remote Web Service. Of course, .NET automates this feature with the WSDL.exe tool and Visual Studio .NET.

### The Web Services Vision

If the programming community adopts Web Services, expect to see many companies supplementing their Web sites with Web Services. They could include airline reservation services, music and book pricing, shipping services, and a host of other services that Web sites provide now.

You may be in a position to supplement your own company's Web or intranet site with a Web Service. For instance, if your company's intranet provides phone book and contact directories, you might implement a Web Service that provides the same information. This would allow other developers in your company to create desktop applications or other Web pages that access this contact information.

If you are a more ambitious developer, you may be contemplating a Web Service that provides a service to the general public, such as music CDs. Whatever your goal, the .NET Framework provides all the tools you will need to create a Web Service of any size.

## Summary

Today's lesson explained how to create and use Web Services. Now that you know the basics of Web Services and how they work, you are well equipped to learn more advanced techniques to use with Web Services, such as sending and returning custom data structures and ADO.NET datasets.

Today you learned how to create Web Service proxies with the .NET Framework tools and automatically with Visual Studio .NET. You learned how a client program can use proxy class to call remote Web Services.

You also learned how Web Services communicate with client programs using the SOAP protocol. You saw examples of SOAP requests and learned why Web Services are used together with Web servers such as IIS.

# Q&A

**Q If I implement a Web Service using ASP.NET, will my service's clients be tied to the Microsoft platform?**

**A** No. You can use any platform and language combination that supports TCP/IP. This makes your choice of client implementation almost unlimited. Client operating systems can include Windows 3.11 through Windows XP, all flavors of UNIX and Linux, VAX, mobile device operating systems, and many others. Your choice of language to use for the client program could include Java, C, C++, Visual Basic, or any language that includes TCP/IP support.

**Q How much about the SOAP protocol do I need to know to create Web Services?**

**A** If you use .NET to create Web Services and their clients, you don't need to know much more than what you've seen in this chapter. ASP.NET and the .NET Framework provides all the SOAP protocol plumbing for you. This situation is similar to the HTTP protocol and Web site programming, in that most Web pages can be created without detailed knowledge of HTTP requests and responses. To learn more about the SOAP protocol, visit `http://www.w3c.org`.

**13**

# Workshop

The workshop provides quiz questions to help you solidify your understanding of the material covered today as well as exercises to give you experience using what you have learned. Try to understand the quiz and exercise before continuing to tomorrow's lesson. Answers are provided in Appendix A, "Answers to Quizzes and Exercises."

## Quiz

1. What file extension does ASP.NET use for Web Services?
2. Why do Web Services use WSDL files?

3. How do you retrieve the WSDL description for an ASP.NET Web Service?

4. Why should you use proxies for Web Service clients?

5. What files are created when you select Add Web Reference in Visual Studio?

6. Why do Web Services use ASP.NET?

7. Do all Web Services support HTTP Get and HTTP Post for calling functions?

8. List each standard in today's lesson that uses XML for its data format.

9. If a Web Service offers a method called HelloWorld, what two methods would a proxy program define for asynchronous calling?

10. What programming attribute do you use to make a method accessible to the public in a Web Service?

## Exercises

1. Create a new method in the TimeUtilities Web Service that returns the time of day in military and standard format. Have the method receive a bool parameter that specifies which format to use.

2. Create a Web Service using Visual Studio. What new files did Visual Studio create that we didn't in the TimeUtilities example?

3. Create a Web Service that calls another Web Service. How could a Web Service like this be useful?

# WEEK 2

# DAY 14

# Publishing Web Services

After you start to create your own Web Services, you will need a way to let the rest of the world know about them. Today's lesson will explain how clients discover Web Services and how to publish information about your Web Services.

The first section of today's lesson will explain exactly how the Add Web Reference dialog works in Visual Studio and will examine Web Service discovery files. These files can be used so that when Web Service consumers know the domain name of a Web server, they can easily find the complete specifications for all the services that the server provides.

Today's lesson will then introduce UDDI, an industry standard for listing Web Services with widespread support from many key leaders in the software industry. Even Microsoft and Sun, along with more than 80 major industry leaders, agree that UDDI should be the standard for Web Service discovery. You will learn about the structure and content of entries in the UDDI registry and see how to create entries for your own organization's Web Services.

Today's lesson covers the following topics:

- Dynamic and static Web Service discovery files and tips for how to choose between them

- UDDI, including an introduction and explanation of the UDDI registry
- Ways to add your own UDDI entries
- A sample UDDI entry

# How Do Web References Work?

After yesterday's lesson, you may be wondering exactly how the Add Web Reference dialog works in Visual Studio. To refresh your memory, you display this dialog box by choosing Add Web Reference from the Project menu. You can use this dialog box to locate Web Services published by other companies; just click the `Microsoft UDDI Directory` link (you'll find more details on UDDI directories later today). Or, you can use it to list Web Services available on your local computer by clicking the `Web References on Local Web Server` link. How is this list of locally available Web Services obtained?

**NEW TERM**   The secret lies in what are called *discovery files*, or *disco files*. Visual Studio discovery files end in the extension .vsdisco. After .NET is installed on a computer, Internet Information Services (IIS) is configured so that it will hand off all .vsdisco files to ASP.NET whenever any application browses to one of these files.

So, what do discovery files do? They provide URL references to Web Services Description Language (WSDL) files, or to other discovery files. Recall from yesterday's lesson that WSDL files provide detailed information about a Web Service's public methods. By looking at a WSDL file for your Web Service, any program (or programmer) can create a Web Service proxy to use your Web Service. Discovery files provide, in XML format, the URL that any program (or programmer) needs to find a WSDL file for your Web Service. Discovery files can also provide the URL of another discovery file.

Discovery files, like almost everything else associated with Web Services, have an XML format. Each discovery file contains an XML document with elements that contain references to your Web Service's WSDL file. Listing 14.1 shows an example of a discovery file.

**LISTING 14.1**   Example1.vsdisco: A Sample Discovery File

```
<?xml version="1.0" encoding="utf-8" ?>
<discovery xmlns="http://schemas.xmlsoap.org/disco/">
  <discoveryRef ref="http://localhost/WebBook/WebBook.vsdisco" />
  <discoveryRef ref="http://localhost/ComAspNet/ComAspNet.vsdisco" />
</discovery>
```

Three kinds of XML elements are ,used in discovery files: `discovery`, `discoveryRef`, and `contractRef`. Listing 14.1 shows the first two kinds. The `discovery` element is used as the root element in every static discovery file. The `discoveryRef` element gives a reference to another discovery file. Listing 14.1 contains references to two more discovery files, in the WebBook and ComAspNet virtual directories.

Listing 14.2 shows a discovery file that contains `contractRef` nodes.

**LISTING 14.2**    Example2.vsdisco: Referencing WSDL Contracts

```
<?xml version="1.0" encoding="utf-8" ?>
<discovery xmlns="http://schemas.xmlsoap.org/disco/">

  <contractRef ref="http://localhost/WebBook/AverageTiming.asmx?wsdl"
               docRef="http://localhost/WebBook/AverageTiming.asmx"
               xmlns="http://schemas.xmlsoap.org/disco/scl/" />

  <contractRef ref="http://localhost/WebBook/NorthwindService1.asmx?wsdl"
               docRef="http://localhost/WebBook/Timing.asmx"
               xmlns="http://schemas.xmlsoap.org/disco/scl/" />
</discovery>
```

The `contractRef` element references a WSDL file for a Web Service. It can also include a `docRef` attribute that points to a URL to find documentation about the Web Service. Because ASP.NET automatically generates documentation for a Web Service, the URLs for the Web Services themselves are given for the `docRef` attribute.

In general, each virtual directory that houses a Web Service also has a discovery file, which enables client programs to find the WSDL contract for the service. Also, the root virtual directory contains a discovery file with references to all the discovery files for each Web Service. Thus, by finding the discovery file in the root virtual directory, you can find all other disco files and the WSDL contracts for all available Web Services.

Web references in Visual Studio ,work by using discovery files. When you click the `Web References on Local Computer` link, Visual Studio opens the file default.vsdisco in the root Web directory of your computer. At this point, ASP.NET takes over, processes the discovery file, and hands back an XML file containing references to all the Web Services on your computer. Visual Studio then uses its own version of the WSDL.exe tool to create a Web Service proxy, using the WSDL contract that the discovery file points to.

## Dynamic Discovery Files

NEW TERM    The good news is, that you don't have to create and maintain discovery files yourself. Instead, you can use a second flavor of discovery files, called *dynamic* discovery files. The disco files covered in the preceding section are called *static* discovery files.

14

When a client program browses to a dynamic discovery file, the dynamic discovery file searches for WSDL contracts by itself and then returns an XML discovery document to the client. ASP.NET handles and creates the output for dynamic discovery files.

To make the discussion concrete, let's examine a dynamic discovery file. After a new .NET installation, a default.vsdisco file that uses dynamic discovery is put in the root of your Web server. Listing 14.3 shows what the default.vsdisco file looks like.

**LISTING 14.3**    Default.vsdisco: The Default Discovery Document in the Root of a Web Server

```
<?xml version="1.0" ?>
<dynamicDiscovery xmlns="urn:schemas-dynamicdiscovery:disco.2000-03-17">
<exclude path="_vti_cnf" />
<exclude path="_vti_pvt" />
<exclude path="_vti_log" />
<exclude path="_vti_script" />
<exclude path="_vti_txt" />
</dynamicDiscovery>
```

For dynamic discovery ,documents, ASP.NET searches through all the virtual directories on the Web server looking for more discovery (.vsdisco) files. It adds each discovery file that it finds to a list and outputs the results in a file that looks like a static discovery file. If you use your Web browser to look at the default.vsdisco file on your Web server root, you see something that looks like Listing 14.1.

Listing 14.3 contains XML elements labeled <exclude>. They instruct ASP.NET to avoid searching for more discovery files in the subdirectories named with the path attribute. By using the <exclude> element, you can hide directories from being discovered.

For dynamic discovery documents that reside in a virtual directory, ASP.NET searches for all Web Services in the directory (specifically for all files with an .asmx extension) and then outputs a static discovery file, such as Listing 14.1.

## Preventing Dynamic Discovery

You may not want people, browsing your Web server for all the services that it houses. You can easily disable dynamic discovery; to do so, just delete the .vsdisco file in the root virtual directory.

You can use these tips for the Web Service discovery issue:

- If you don't want the general public to find out what Web Services you have on your machine, remove the .vsdisco file from your Web server's root virtual directory.

- If you want to control which Web Services the general public can discover, replace the dynamic discovery files on your server with static discovery files, such as the code in Listing 14.1. Unfortunately, this option involves more work on your part because you have to maintain the discovery files yourself.

- To discover Web, Services on a remote computer, browse for the discovery files or use the Add Web References dialog in Visual Studio.

# What Is UDDI?

Today, finding a Web site that contains information that you need involves using a Web search engine. As you are no doubt well aware, finding Web sites this way isn't an easy task. Web search engines have become very sophisticated over the few short years that the Internet has been in popular use. Many Web search engines use a combination of sophisticated HTML parsing algorithms in combination with programs that automatically surf the Internet to gather the current information about Web sites. These search engines condense and index Web pages into large databases that you can browse using keywords or view by category. Unfortunately, Web search engines aren't perfect, and finding a Web site you need sometimes takes several search attempts. Even then, you still may never find the best Web site for the information you need.

Now that Web Services are appearing in greater numbers, the searching problem is even more difficult. Web Services rarely contain HTML pages that can be scanned for keywords. It doesn't take long to realize that Internet users need a new way to find information about organizations providing services on the Web.

UDDI (Universal Description, Discovery, and Integration) has been proposed as the solution to the problem of discovering a Web Service. UDDI is a global registry that contains information about organizations and the public Web Services that they provide. UDDI is similar to an online yellow pages for Web Services.

As of this book's writing, three companies host the UDDI registry. Ariba, IBM, and Microsoft all share the hosting responsibilities. Each company periodically synchronizes the contents of the UDDI registry on its servers with the other two. This means that no single company controls the UDDI registry.

The UDDI project is still in its early stages. All companies contributing to the current UDDI project (currently more than 80) will hand off the UDDI concept to a standards body sometime in 2002. The home Web site for all information about UDDI is `www.uddi.org`.

**14**

## Web Services and UDDI

**NEW TERM** UDDI uses the term *Web Service* in a broader way than today's lesson. A *UDDI Web Service* doesn't have to be a program that allows for remote method invocation using SOAP and XML. Instead, a UDDI Web Service can be as simple as a Web site that offers real estate listings as HTML pages. This sample real estate site is providing a service, after all.

The UDDI standard has three main goals:

- To let consumers quickly find Web Services that serve a specific purpose.
- To provide a place that describes how Web Service transactions should take place.
- To create a standard way for businesses that offer Web Services to communicate with potential customers.

UDDI has been designed so that standard Web search engines can use it to supplement their own searching algorithms. Rather than find ad hoc methods to index Web Services, Web search engines can use a standard API to browse the UDDI registry.

However, you don't need to be a company such as Yahoo! to use UDDI. You can list all your company's Web Services in the UDDI registry by using a simple Web-based registration process, as you will see later today. You can search and browse the UDDI registry online. By using .NET, you can easily create programs that search the UDDI registry.

Let's look for some Web Services using IBM's Web site (www-3.ibm.com/services/uddi/findbusiness). You can also use the Microsoft UDDI directory, which is available directly from the Add Web Reference dialog. Both sites contain nearly identical features. Figure 14.1 shows the search page at the IBM site.

As an example, let's search for some of the Web Services that Microsoft has to offer. Enter **Microsoft** in the Business Name box. After you do so, the company listing appears, along with a link labeled services. Following this link displays a listing containing a number of Web Services (with *Web Service* defined in the most general sense), including links to the company's home page, online shopping, and many others. One link includes an entry called Web Services for smart searching. Clicking this link brings up a list of two Web Service pages, both of which link to the mscomsearchservice.asmx service. This list is shown in Figure 14.2.

## Creating Your Own UDDI Entry

If you create a public Web Service, listing it in the UDDI registry is one way to generate interest. Even if you don't have a Web Service ready yet, your company may provide general Web Services that you can list right now. You can easily list your own organization in the UDDI registry as follows:

FIGURE 14.1

*Searching for a business using a UDDI Web search site.*

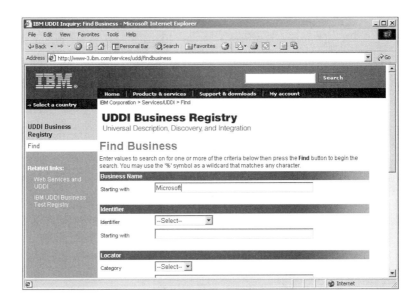

FIGURE 14.2

*A page containing links to public Web Services from a UDDI search site.*

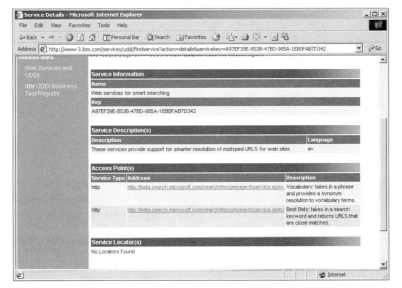

1. Point your Web browser to `http://www.uddi.org/register.html`.
2. Choose from the list of UDDI registry provider companies. All companies share the same UDDI information among themselves, so your choice depends only on which Web site you prefer.

**14**

3. Create an account when the UDDI registry provider asks you to do so. Note that any information you give won't be available to the public.

4. Complete the Web site's easy-to-follow steps for adding a listing. This section won't give detailed instructions on this point. When you create your UDDI entry, you have the option of adding a technical contact. This contact person's information will be available to the public.

## What's Inside a UDDI Entry?

UDDI entries can contain the following types of information:

- **A business name and description.** This information is required for every entry.

- **Technical contacts.** You can add any number of contacts for your organization.

- **Classifications for your organization's services.** UDDI uses a number of industry standard classification systems, such as the North American Industry Classification System and the Standard Industrial Classification. You should choose at least one classification for each service that your organization provides.

- **Classification bindings.** They are the actual references to your Web Services. They can include URLs to a Web site, URLs to a Web Service (in the specific sense), e-mail addresses, fax and phone numbers, or a reference of your own choosing.

- **A specification signature.** It describes the type of binding and can include entries such as http://WSDL-interface for a Web Service application. Other services, such as Web sites and e-mail addresses, don't have a specification signature.

- **Identifiers.** They identify your organization and can contain a D-U-N-S number.

**Note**

> Dun & Bradstreet identifies many organizations by using D-U-N-S® (Data Universal Numbering System) numbers. These numbers are used to verify the origin and status of a business. You can find out more about them at www.dnb.com.

- **Discovery URLs.** They contain URLs to Web pages giving more information about the services your organization provides.

- **Service types.** They contain descriptions of the services that your organization provides. Service types can contain classifications and identifiers (both discussed earlier in this list). Service types can also contain an overview document, which describes how the particular service type works, what kind of input it expects, and what kind of output it generates.

UDDI entries have a tree type format. To make the preceding list a little clearer, Figure 14.3 shows the structure of a UDDI entry.

FIGURE **14.3**

*The structure of a UDDI entry.*

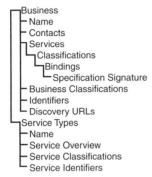

```
Business
  Name
  Contacts
  Services
    Classifications
      Bindings
        Specification Signature
  Business Classifications
  Identifiers
  Discovery URLs
Service Types
  Name
  Service Overview
  Service Classifications
  Service Identifiers
```

UDDI entries can contain quite a bit of information, and after a first glance at Figure 14.3, you might think it duplicates information. In particular, the Service Types node seems to duplicate the Services node in the Business node. The distinction is that the Service Types node contains specifications for Web Services. The Services node in the Business tree contains a reference to a specific Web Service. This specific Web Service is linked to a specification in the Service Types tree by using the Bindings node.

In particular, the Service Types entry contains a reference to the WSDL document for a Web Service that your organization provides. This WSDL reference is stored in the Service Overview node.

## tModels and UDDI Entries

NEW TERM   A *tModel* is a data structure (in XML, of course) that contains a reference to a WSDL file for a Web Service. When you create a Service Type (from Figure 14.3) using the UDDI provider's Web interface, you are creating a tModel for your Web Services. Other programs can find all your organization's tModels, use them to find the WSDL files for each of your Web Services, and then create proxy code to interact with your Web Service.

The idea of a tModel is more general than a specific WSDL file. One goal of the UDDI project is to build an industry standard set of tModels. This way, if your organization wants to provide a service to the public, you should implement a Web Service that corresponds to an industry standard tModel.

## UDDI Entry Example

Let's examine what a specific UDDI entry would look like for a fictitious company called Bill's Discount Software. The lead software engineer at Bill's, named Sue, would

**14**

like to create a UDDI entry for the company. She wants to create this entry because the Information Technology department has just created a new Web Service that allows client programs to receive and pay invoices. The Web Service, called SoftPay, is located at `https://www.billsdiscountsoftware.com/services/softpay.asmx`. The Web Service was designed to be used with a custom program called EZSoftwarePay. Bill's provides customers with the EZSoftwarePay client program for free, in hopes that the clients will use the program to pay their invoices quickly.

Sue first creates an account at one of the UDDI registry providers by following the links from `www.uddi.org/register.html`. This process takes a couple of days to complete because the UDDI provider needs to verify Sue's organization. After she receives an e-mail with a user ID and password, she logs into the provider site and begins to create an entry.

Sue has three main tasks:

- Create background information for her company in the UDDI entry.
- Optionally create a new Service Type if the Web Service her organization provides doesn't conform to an industry standard or if no industry standard service type is now defined for her organization's Web Service.
- Create a new Web Service definition for her organization and bind it to a Service Type.

Sue performs these steps to create background information for her company:

1. She adds the company name and description ("Bill's Discount Software" and "Provides software at a deep discount").
2. She adds two contacts for the company from the information technology department.
3. She adds the company's D-U-N-S number.
4. She adds a classification from the North American Industry Classification System (NAICS) for the business. She chooses Electronic Shopping and Mail-Order Houses from the Retail Trade group.

**Note**

UDDI uses several standard classification systems for businesses, called *taxonomies*. These contain categories for most kinds of businesses. The NAICS taxonomy is one of several different classification systems available with UDDI.

Sue knows that her company is an industry leader in providing new Web Services, so for her second task, she wants to establish a new Service Type definition for the SoftPay service. She does so because she wants other companies to implement the SoftPay Web Service, in hopes that software invoicing can be automated through the industry. Sue follows these steps:

1. She adds a new Service Type called SoftPay with a description of Automatic Software Invoicing.

2. She adds an URL to the online technical documentation for developers who want to create their own Web Service that conforms to the SoftPay standard. This technical documentation contains links to WSDL contracts, in addition to detailed descriptions for how SoftPay services should work. This document URL is added to the Overview Document entry.

3. She adds a classification for the SoftPay service standard, using the NAICS classification system.

Last, Sue adds a new Web Service definition for her company. This Web Service definition will contain the URL for the company's implementation of the SoftPay service.

1. She adds a new service type, called Electronic Invoicing.

2. She adds a binding to the service to the URL `http://www.billsdiscountsoftware.com/webservice/invoicing.asmx`.

3. She adds a specification type of SoftPay to the binding she just created.

4. She adds a classification for the service.

Figure 14.4 shows what the new Bill's Discount Software UDDI entry looks like.

---

One benefit of the UDDI specification and infrastructure is that you can create your own programs to access a UDDI registry. You could create your own search engine to traverse the UDDI registry, find Web Services, and then connect to and use those services. Creating a program like this is an advanced topic beyond the scope of this book. However, you can use the Microsoft UDDI SDK to create .NET programs that access any publicly available UDDI registry. The SDK comes with a sample project that contains a program to browse UDDI registries and copy the contents of a registry onto your own machine. The SDK allows you to program against the UDDI API, which is defined at `www.uddi.org`. You can download the latest SDK from `www.microsoft.com/downloads`.

**14**

**FIGURE 14.4**

*Sample UDDI entry.*

```
Business
├─ Name  Bill's Discount Software
├─ Description  Provides Software at a Deep Discount
├─ Contacts
│     Name  Sue
│     Phone  555-555-5555
│     eMail  sue@billsdiscountsoftware.com
├─ Services
│     Name  Softpay Invoicing
│     Description  Automatic payment for invoices
│     Classifications
│       Name  Invoice Payment Automation
│       Bindings
│         Access Point  http://www.billsdiscountsoftware/webservice/invoicing.asm
│       Specification Signature
│         Name  Softpay
│     Business Classifications
│       Name  Software Services
│     Identifiers
│     └─ D-U-N-S  123456
└─ Discovery URLs
      (provided by registry host)
Service Types
├─ Name  Softpay
├─ Service Overview
│     Overview Document  http://www.billsdiscountsoftware/doc/SoftPay.htm
├─ Service Classifications
│     Name  Software Services
└─ Service Identifiers
      D-U-N-S  123456
```

# Summary

Today's lesson began by explaining discovery (disco) files and how you can use them to allow clients to browse all the Web Services available on a particular server. You saw two versions of discovery files: static and dynamic. Static discovery files contain XML documents that contain references to Web Services or other discovery files. Dynamic discovery files are handled by ASP.NET, which processes the file and returns a static discovery file as output.

The second half of today's lesson introduced the UDDI project and showed you how to use UDDI to publish Web Services in a global registry. You saw examples illustrating the structure of UDDI entries and a sample entry for a fictitious company. UDDI entries can define specific Web Services that an organization supports and can also be used to create new specifications for Web Services so that other organizations can create Web Services that implement this standard. You saw a sample Web Service standard called SoftPay, used for invoicing.

The next two lessons will dive into the nuts and bolts of creating real-world Web Services. You will learn how to pass complex data structures to Web Services in tomorrow's lesson, and Day 16 will give details on advanced Web Service programming techniques.

# Q&A

**Q I want to publish my Web Service. Should I use disco files or UDDI?**

**A** Use both disco and UDDI. Disco files aren't listed to the Internet community at large, but are useful for Web Service users once they know exactly what computer houses the Web Service. UDDI is a public record that anyone can use to find your Web Service. UDDI provides a great deal of supplementary information about a Web Service, including details about the organization providing the Web Service, contact information, and references to documentation.

**Q Which UDDI provider should I use to publish my Web Service?**

**A** Choosing a UDDI provider is only a matter of personal preference. All UDDI providers share the same database of information. After you make a UDDI entry in one provider, the entry propagates to all other UDDI providers within a short amount of time.

**Q Is UDDI an industry standard now? If not, when will it become one?**

**A** UDDI is presently an initiative that hasn't yet been ratified by a computer standards body. However, the UDDI initiative is scheduled to be handed over to a standards body in 2002.

# Workshop

The Workshop provides quiz questions to help you solidify your understanding of the material covered today as well as exercises to give you experience using what you've learned. Try to understand the quiz and exercises before continuing to tomorrow's lesson. Answers are provided in Appendix A, "Answers to Quizzes and Exercises."

## Quiz

1. What's the difference between static and dynamic discovery files?
2. What is UDDI and what does it stand for?
3. How can you create a UDDI entry?
4. Name the two top-level nodes in a UDDI registry entry.
5. What's a tModel?

## Exercises

1. Create a static discovery file for use with the TimeService example from yesterday's lesson.

**14**

2. Browse the www.uddi.org site for the latest developer documentation for the UDDI project. What's the complete definition of a tModel?

3. Download the Microsoft UDDI SDK. You will need to have SQL Server or MDAC installed on your computer first. Try using the sample .NET project to browse the Microsoft UDDI registry.

# WEEK 2

# In Review

8

9

10

11

12

13

14

Congratulations! You've completed the second week of your lessons and are well on your way to becoming an expert .NET Web developer. The first week concentrated mainly on ASP.NET. This past week, you learned several new, exciting Web technologies and how they are used in .NET. You now have enough knowledge to create real-world Web applications within the .NET Framework.

Day 8 covered XML and a few of the classes in the .NET Framework that you can use to integrate XML into your Web development efforts. The next three lessons explained how to use ADO.NET and XML in your Web applications so that you can store and retrieve data in a scalable and high performance way.

Through the past two weeks of study, you've learned a great amount of practical knowledge that you can apply to your own Internet applications. Take some time to review your progress—you should be pleasantly surprised!

# WEEK 3

## At a Glance

After finishing the second week of lessons, you should be quite adept at building Internet applications with .NET. You now know how to create Web sites and Web Services with .NET and how to manage data in your applications using ADO.NET and XML. Congratulate yourself—you've mastered a large amount of practical knowledge.

Week 3 will complete your study of Internet programming with .NET. You will learn how to publish your Web Services in the UDDI registry, send and receive complex data structures to Web Services, and try out some advanced techniques such as asynchronous Web method invocation.

Days 18, 19, and 20 will explain how to configure, secure, and deploy your Web applications with .NET. These lessons will give you practical information for the final, critical stages of your .Net web projects.

The last lesson, Day 21, "Creating Your Application Architecture," will focus on design considerations for your Web application. This lesson will explain techniques for making your Internet application scalable, maintainable, and fast.

15

16

17

18

19

20

21

# WEEK 3

# DAY 15

# Accessing Complex Data with Web Services

Many Web Services that you write will contain methods that use custom data structures. For example, you may write a Web Service that stores an appointment schedule. Such a Web Service needs to have information about the name, start time, duration, and location of the appointment. A Web Service like this may need to receive complex data structures to be useful. Today's lesson will show how you can send and receive almost any kind of parameter to and from a Web Service.

After explaining how to define and use complex parameters, today's lesson will present a sample Web Service that uses the ADO.NET dataset object. This service will demonstrate some of the problems that can arise when more than one user tries to change the same data records at the same time. The example in today's lesson will offer one solution to the problem and give tips for solving the issue for your own projects.

Today you will learn about the following topics:

- How to define Web Service methods compatible with the HTTP protocol
- What data types can be used with the HTTP protocol
- What new types can be used with the SOAP protocol
- How to define custom data structures for use with a Web Service
- How to send and receive datasets to a Web Service
- How to deal with multiuser access to a Web Service
- How to use record-locking strategies in your own Web Services

# Passing Parameters and Web Services

You may be wondering about what kinds of data structures you can send to a Web Service and what kinds of results can be returned. This section will detail the different methods that you can use to pass parameters to Web Services and give several examples showing how to send complex parameters and receive them from Web methods.

## Revisiting the Protocols Used for Web Services

Day 13, "Introducing Web Services," gave only a small amount of detail concerning the Internet protocols that Web Services use to communicate. Understanding how to send and receive variables and objects to Web Services requires knowledge of a few key facts about Web Service protocols. This section will explain these protocols so that you are well equipped to learn about sending and receiving parameters in your own services.

.NET Web Services can use four different protocols without any extra work on your part: HTTP GET, HTTP POST, HTTPS, and SOAP. This section will explain each except for HTTPS, which will be explained on Day 19, "Securing Internet Applications." To begin the discussion, let's use the TimeUtil Web Service created on Day 13. It's not repeated here, but you can refer to Listing 13.1 if you want to review the source code.

Let's start by looking at a typical HTTP GET request and response, as shown in Listings 15.1 and 15.2.

**LISTING 15.1**   A Sample HTTP GET Request to a Web Service

```
GET /TimeService/TimeUtils.asmx/GetTime? HTTP/1.1
Host: localhost
```

So, what is an HTTP GET request? The request is just a stream of characters sent from a client program to a Web server, containing something like the text in Listing 15.1. Note that GET requests are limited to 1,024 characters.

> **Note**
>
> Try it yourself! Use Telnet to make an HTTP GET request by adding the following at the command-line prompt:
>
> ```
> telnet localhost 80
> ```
>
> Type the text in Listing 15.1 exactly and press Enter twice at the end. You can't see what you're typing, but you get the response shown in Listing 15.2.

**LISTING 15.2**   A Sample HTTP GET Response from a Web Service

```
 1: HTTP/1.1 200 OK
 2: Server: Microsoft-IIS/5.0
 3: Date: Fri, 01 Aug 2001 21:48:21 GMT
 4: Cache-Control: private, max-age=0
 5: Content-Type: text/xml; charset=utf-8
 6: Content-Length: 139
 7:
 8: <?xml version="1.0" encoding="utf-8"?>
 9: <string xmlns="http://tempuri.org/">The current time on
10: the server is: 8/1/2001 5:48:21 PM</string>
```

**ANALYSIS**   The GET response contains a standard header (Lines 1–6) and then the actual result from the Web Service call (Lines 8–10). HTTP POST requests are similar, with a slight change in the way parameters are passed in the request.

Now that you are well versed in the details of the GET request, you can understand one key limitation of using this protocol. By using HTTP, you can't send complicated parameters to the Web server. For a GET request, you can't do so because the request, including the parameter being passed in, has to fit on the first line of the request (first line of Listing 15.1). You might be able to convert a parameter into a string that would fit in the GET request. However, you could easily exceed the 1,024-character limit, and converting the parameter back and forth would be a messy operation.

In a nutshell, requests made to a Web server using the HTTP protocol are limited to the data types listed in Table 15.1.

**TABLE 15.1**  Parameters That Can Be Passed to a Web Service Using the HTTP Protocol

| Data Type | Description |
| --- | --- |
| Primitive Types | char, int, long, float, double, Boolean, Int16, Int32, Int64, Single, Double, Currency, and unsigned versions of all numerical types |
| Strings | String |
| Enumerations | For example, `enum myopinion {good, bad, indifferent}` |
| Arrays | Arrays of any of the preceding types |

As you saw in Listing 15.2, HTTP responses can contain any XML data, so there's no limitation on the parameters returned by using the HTTP protocol.

## Sending and Receiving Parameters with SOAP

You can send *any* parameter you create in Visual Basic to and from a Web Service using SOAP—well, almost any. If the parameters that you create contain unmanaged code (code written using Visual C++, pre-.NET Visual Basic, assembly language, COM parameters, or parameters that you craft using the "hexadecimal" option in a text editor), they probably won't work. Parameters have to be transformed into XML format to work with SOAP. Luckily, every .NET class you create and all the built-in .NET framework classes can be transformed into XML. Furthermore, you don't have to transform the parameters yourself; the .NET classes in the `System.Web.WebServices.Protocols` namespace takes care of this task automatically.

To see how a parameter is passed to a Web Service, look at the steps that happen when the client program invokes a Web Service method:

1. The client program calls a Web Service method using its Web Service proxy. Day 13 explained how to use Visual Studio .NET and the WSDL.exe tool to create Web Service proxies.
2. The proxy serializes each parameter into XML format.
3. The proxy creates a SOAP request using the XML version of the parameter.
4. The proxy opens a connection to the Web server hosting the Web Service.
5. The proxy transmits the SOAP request.

A reversed version of this process happens on the Web server so that the Web Service has a copy of the parameter that it can use.

## Parameter Passing in Practice

You are now aware of the theory behind parameter transmission and Web Services. Let's put the theory into practice with some practical examples. To begin, let's create a Web

Service that returns a complex parameter. The sample Web Service will extend the TimeUtils sample from Day 13 by adding a new method, GetTimeEx. This method returns a structure containing detailed information about the current time on the server.

First, create a definition for the parameter that the GetTimeEx method will return. Listing 15.3 shows the structure, TimeStruct.

**LISTING 15.3** A Definition for the `TimeStruct` Structure, Which Will Be Returned by a Web Service

```
public structure TimeStruct
  public Millisecond as Integer
  public Second as Integer
  public Minute as Integer
  public Hour as Integer

  public DayName as String
  public MonthName as String
  public YearName as String

  public CurrentTime as DateTime
  public  CurrentTimeUtc DateTime

End Structure
```

Listing 15.3 is a little contrived because the first seven member variables could easily be found using the CurrentTime variable. However, Listing 15.3 demonstrates one important point about passing parameters to and from Web Services: Any parameter that you want to pass to and from a Web Service must have a public class or struct definition. Also, any variable within the structure or class defining the parameter must be public.

Listing 15.4 shows the TimeUtilities2 Web Service, which is the same as the TimeUtilities service except with the new GetTimeEx method added.

 **Note**
Remember that to create and compile a Web Service outside Visual Studio, you must place the .asmx file in its own folder and create a virtual directory for that folder. Then, use your browser to navigate to the .asmx file to compile and test the service.

**LISTING 15.4** TimeService2.asmx: Adding the `GetTimeEx` Method

```
1: <%@ WebService Language="vb" Class="TimeUtilities2" %>
2: Imports System
```

**LISTING 15.4** continued

```
 3: Imports System.Web.Services
 4:
 5: public structure TimeStruct
 6:
 7:    public Millisecond as integer
 8:    public Second as integer
 9:    public Minute as integer
10:    public Hour as integer
11:
12:    public DayName as String
13:    public MonthName as String
14:    public YearName as String
15:
16:    public CurrentTime as DateTime
17:    public CurrentTimeUtc as DateTime
18:
19: end structure
20:
21: <WebService(Namespace:="http://tempuri.org/webservices")> _
22: public class TimeUtilities2
23:      Inherits WebService
24:
25:    <WebMethod> public Function GetTime() as string
26:
27:      Dim ret as string = "The current time on the server is: "
28:      return ret & DateTime.Now.ToString()
29:
30:    end function
31:
32:    <WebMethod> public function GetTimeEx() as  TimeStruct
33:
34:      Dim curTimeDT as DateTime = DateTime.Now
35:      Dim curTime as new TimeStruct()
36:
37:      curTime.CurrentTime    = curTimeDT
38:      curTime.CurrentTimeUtc = curTimeDT.ToUniversalTime()
39:      curTime.Millisecond    = curTimeDT.Millisecond
40:      curTime.Minute         = curTimeDT.Minute
41:      curTime.Hour           = curTimeDT.Hour
42:      curTime.DayName        = curTimeDT.DayOfWeek.ToString()
43:
44:      Dim monthAndDay as String = curTimeDT.ToString("m")
45:      Dim monthAndDaySplit() as String = monthAndDay.Split(" ")
46:      curTime.MonthName = monthAndDaySplit(0)
47:      curTime.YearName = curTimeDT.Month.ToString()
48:
49:      return curTime
50:
51:    end function
52: End Class
```

**ANALYSIS** Lines 5–19 define the `TimeStruct` structure from Listing 15.3.

The `GetTimeEx` method (Lines 32–51) creates a new `TimeStruct` object (Line 35) and returns the populated object (Line 49). Lines 44–46 contain a small trick to find the name of the current month. First, the `"m"` format string returns the month and date (Line 44). A sample string returned from this format string might be `"January 25"`. This string is split into two strings using the `Split` method (Line 45) so that the full month name can be found in the first element of the array that's returned (Line 46).

 **Note**

> Listing 15.4 doesn't take any special steps to return the structure because they aren't required; the code used here is similar to something you might write in any .NET application.

To complete the example, write a small client program to call the method. Listings 15.5 and 15.6 show a sample Web form and code behind files that call the Web Service. In a more realistic situation, the Web Service and Web page would be located on different server machines. If you have more than one computer at your disposal, try running the two listings separately.

**Note**

> Listing 15.5 requires a Web Service proxy to work. This listing will work "as is" with a proxy generated by Visual Studio. Yesterday's lesson explained how to create Web proxies. As a quick reminder, you can use the following steps to create the test project and the needed proxy:
>
> 1. Make sure the source Web Service has been compiled without errors, as described earlier in this chapter.
> 2. Start a new ASP.NET Web application and name it TimeClient2.
> 3. Choose Add Web Reference from the Project menu. Enter the URL for the source service's WSDL file in the Address field. For this example it will be something like this:
>    http://localhost/TimeService/TimeUtilities2.asmx?WSDL.
> 4. Click the Add Reference button to create the proxy.
> 5. Rename the project's .aspx page to DisplayTime.aspx.
> 6. Change the name of the project's Web form to DisplayTime.aspx, and paste the code from Listing 15.5 into the form, replacing code already in the file (but not the Web Form Designer–generated code). Paste the code from Listing 15.6 into DisplayTime.aspx.vb, again replacing existing code.
>
> When you run the project, it will access the new TimeUtilities2 Web Service and display the day, date, and time in your browser.

**LISTING 15.5**   DisplayTime.aspx: A Web Form That Uses Today's TimeUtils Web Service

```
<%@ Page language="vb" Codebehind="DisplayTime.aspx.vb"
        Inherits="TimeClient2.TimeService2.DisplayTime" %>
<html>
  <body>
    <h3>Current Time on the Server..</h3>
    <asp:Label id="Time" Runat="server"/>
  </body>
</html>
```

**LISTING 15.6**   DisplayTime.aspx.vb: The Code-Behind File for **Listing 15.5**

```
 1: Imports System.Web.UI
 2: Imports System.Web.UI.WebControls
 3: Imports TimeClient2.localhost
 4:
 5: Namespace TimeService2
 6:     Public Class DisplayTime
 7:         Inherits Page
 8:
 9:         Protected Time As Label
10:         Private Sub Page_Load(ByVal sender As Object, _
11:             ByVal e As System.EventArgs)
12:
13:             Dim ts As New TimeStruct()
14:             Dim timeServer As New TimeUtilities2()
15:             ts = timeServer.GetTimeEx()
16:             Time.Text = ts.DayName & " " & ts.MonthName & " " & _
17:                         ts.CurrentTime.Day.ToString() & " , " & _
18:                         ts.Hour.ToString() & ":" & _
19:                         ts.Minute.ToString()
20:         End Sub
21:     End Class
22: End Namespace
```

**ANALYSIS**   Listing 15.6 includes the namespace from the automatically generated proxy on Line 3. If you've used a different name to reference the Web server that contains the TimeUtilities2 Web Service, you may have to change Line 3.

Lines 13–14 use the Web Service proxy to create a new TimeStruct and a new instance of the TimeUtilities2 proxy class. The code in Listing 15.5 connects to the Web Service when the GetTimeEx method is called (Line 15). After Line 15 executes, the TimeStruct object will contain the values from the Web Service. Lines 16–19 set the Label control using the returned object.

As you can see from these listings, you don't have to write any special code to pass structures back from Web Services. The only tricky part of the process is generating the Web proxy class. You can rely on Visual Studio to create the proxy class simply by adding the Web reference.

## Sending Parameters by Reference and by Value

**NEW TERM**  Two other ways to pass parameters to a Web Service are known as *call by value* and *call by reference*. This section will explain what these terms mean and how they apply to Web Services.

Calling a method by value, or *byval* for short, means that when you pass a parameter into the method, the parameter will remain unchanged after the method is returned. Most programming languages make a copy of the parameter, pass this copied parameter into the method, and let the method change the parameter at will. When the method is done, the original parameter remains the same. The following code lines demonstrate the process:

```
sub MyMethod(intParam as integer)

  intParam = intParam * 1000

end sub
...
Dim I as integer = 1
MyMethod(i)
'i is still equal to 1 at this point
```

Calling a method by reference, or *byref* for short, means that the parameter passed into the method can be changed by the method, and the changes will "stick." For instance, when the method changes all of a parameter's variables, the parameter will keep the changes after the method is returned. Most programming languages implement this by passing in the original parameter to the method; no copies are made. Calling by reference is useful when you want a method to return multiple parameters. Simply pass in each parameter by reference, and use them as though they were return values from the method. This simple code shows the idea:

```
sub MyMethod(byref intParam as integer)

  intParam = intParam * 1000

end sub
...
Dim i as integer = 1
MyMethod(i)
'i is equal to 1000 at this point
```

Of course, the situation gets a little more complicated when Web Services are thrown into the mix. Passing a parameter to a Web Service by value involves making a copy of the parameter, persisting the parameter as XML, and passing the XML over the network to the Web Service.

Passing a parameter by reference to a Web Service uses the same method as the by value technique, with one extra step. After the method is finished, the same parameter is converted into XML by the Web Service and sent back to the client. The client program now has a modified parameter.

> **Caution**
>
> When you use the HTTP protocol (either GET or POST requests), all parameters must be passed by value, because HTTP doesn't support call by reference. In fact, the interface supplied by any ASP.NET Web service (the WSDL file) won't contain any by-reference method definitions. You must use SOAP to pass parameters by reference.

If you want to try passing a parameter by reference to a Web Service, add the following method to Listing 15.4:

```
<WebMethod>public sub GetTimeByRef(byref ts as TimeStruct)

  ts = GetTimeEx()

end sub
```

Next, change Line 15 of Listing 15.6 to the following:

```
timeServer.GetTimeByRef(ts)
```

The modified listings should produce the same result as before. If you need to write a method that modifies more than one parameter, simply make each parameter byref by adding the byref keyword.

# Accessing Data with Web Services

Because the SOAP protocol allows you to send any kind of parameter and receive any kind of return value, you can send and receive ADO.NET datasets. By using datasets in combination with Web Services, you can create Web Services that provide many kinds of data services. This section will describe a sample Web Service that manages a task list using dataset objects and XML files.

# The Shared Task Web Service

**15**

The sample Shared Task Web Service allows multiple users to add and change tasks in a central location. The service stores the tasks in an XML file and allows any number of users to add and update tasks in the list. Figure 15.1 shows an example of a client that uses the Shared Task Web Service.

FIGURE 15.1

*A Web form that uses the Shared Task Web Service.*

Any Internet application that allows more than one user to update data records has to deal with data concurrency issues. These issues consist of problems that can happen when two or more users update the same data record at the same time. You handle this problem by using a record-locking policy.

**NEW TERM** You can implement two kinds of record-locking policies to handle the simultaneous update problem: optimistic locking and pessimistic locking. *Optimistic locking* means that users can overwrite each other's changes. *Pessimistic locking* means that once a user obtains a lock on a data record, other users can't update that record until the first user releases the lock. Let's look at a scenario for each locking situation.

A typical pessimistic locking scenario might be the following:

1. User Joe reads a database record and sets a lock on the record.
2. User Sue reads the record but can't get a lock for it.
3. Sue tries to update the record but gets an error such as `The record is locked by Joe`.
4. Joe updates the record, saves changes, and releases the lock.
5. Sue can now update the record.

A typical optimistic locking scenario might be the following:

1. Joe reads a database record.
2. Sue reads the same record.

3. Sue updates the record.

4. Joe updates the record and overwrites Sue's changes.

From these scenarios, you might think that optimistic locking is a bad idea. Joe and Sue don't know that they overwrote each other's changes.

However, pessimistic locking can make a Web Service or Web application extremely slow because record locking takes up valuable database resources and can prevent other users from accessing other records. Most databases that use record locking must keep a permanent database connection open to the client program to preserve the lock. Database connections are a scarce resource. If a server has too many open database connections, it will perform extremely slowly. To compound the problem, if your Internet application uses XML to store data, you have to implement your own record-locking logic, which can be quite complex.

One solution to the pessimistic locking problem involves using record versioning. One way of implementing record versioning is to attach a timestamp to each record. The scenario works like this:

1. Joe reads a database record. The record contains a field with a timestamp of the last time the record was modified.

2. Sue reads the same record, along with the same timestamp.

3. Sue updates the record. The timestamp is changed to the current time because the record has been modified.

4. Joe tries to update the record. His record's timestamp doesn't match the timestamp of the current record. The server detects this difference and gives Joe the option of refreshing his record to get the latest changes or simply overwriting the current record.

In this solution, Joe knows that he is about to overwrite a record whose value has changed.

## Implementing Optimistic Locking

Let's implement the Shared Task Web Service so that it uses this record versioning solution to the optimistic locking program. Our first task is to design the look of the XML file that stores the shared tasks. Listing 15.7 shows an example.

**LISTING 15.7**   TaskStore.XML: A Sample XML File Containing Shared Tasks

```
<?xml version="1.0"?>
<sharedtasks xmlns="http://localhost/TaskServer/TaskStore.xsd">
  <task>
```

**LISTING 15.7** continued

```
      <name>Cross Reference Documentation</name>
      <due>2001-10-05T12:00:00</due>
      <owner>Joe</owner>
      <modified>2001-08-10T17:50:03</modified>
    </task>
    <task>
      <name>Print Documentation</name>
      <due>2001-12-05T12:00:00</due>
      <owner>Sue</owner>
      <modified>2001-08-08T08:45:04</modified>
    </task>
</sharedtasks>
```

Each task contains a name, due date, owner name, and modified field.

Next, create a schema for the XML file. As a first step, use Visual Studio to automatically generate the schema. Then you can modify the schema to make the name field a primary key and to establish the appropriate data types for each field. The name and owner fields should be strings, and the due and modified fields should be of type dateTime. If you are following along with the lesson, you can make these changes in the Design view of the XML Schema editor in Visual Studio. Day 11's lesson gave details on how to use the editor. The final XML Schema should look like Listing 15.8.

**LISTING 15.8** TaskStore.XSD: A Schema Definition for the Shared Tasks XML File

```
 1: <xsd:schema id="sharedtasks_id"
 2:            targetNamespace="http://localhost/TaskServer/TaskStore.xsd"
 3:            xmlns="http://localhost/TaskServer/TaskStore.xsd"
 4:            xmlns:xsd="http://www.w3.org/2001/XMLSchema"
 5:            xmlns:msdata="urn:schemas-microsoft-com:xml-msdata"
 6:            attributeFormDefault="qualified"
 7:            elementFormDefault="qualified">
 8:   <xsd:element name="sharedtasks"
 9:              msdata:IsDataSet="true"
10:              msdata:EnforceConstraints="true">
11:     <xsd:complexType>
12:       <xsd:choice maxOccurs="unbounded">
13:         <xsd:element name="task">
14:           <xsd:complexType>
15:             <xsd:sequence>
16:               <xsd:element name="name"
17:                            type="xsd:string"
18:                            minOccurs="0"
19:                            msdata:Ordinal="0"
20:                            msdata:AllowDBNull="false" />
21:               <xsd:element name="due"
```

**LISTING 15.8**   continued

```
22:                                          type="xsd:dateTime"
23:                                          minOccurs="0"
24:                                          msdata:Ordinal="1" />
25:                          <xsd:element name="owner"
26:                                          type="xsd:string"
27:                                          minOccurs="0"
28:                                          msdata:Ordinal="2" />
29:                          <xsd:element name="modified"
30:                                          type="xsd:dateTime"
31:                                          minOccurs="0"
32:                                          msdata:Ordinal="3" />
33:                       </xsd:sequence>
34:                    </xsd:complexType>
35:                 </xsd:element>
36:              </xsd:choice>
37:           </xsd:complexType>
38:           <xsd:unique name="task_con"
39:                    msdata:PrimaryKey="true">
40:             <xsd:selector xpath=".//task" />
41:             <xsd:field xpath="name" />
42:           </xsd:unique>
43:        </xsd:element>
44: </xsd:schema>
```

**ANALYSIS**   Lines 38–42 define a primary key for the XML file using the `unique` element. The name field is defined as the primary key field using the `selector` (Line 40) and `field` (Line 41) elements. Line 10 uses the `EnforceConstraints` attribute to make sure that ADO.NET uses the primary key when it reads the XML file. This way, ADO.NET will throw an exception if duplicated records with the same `name` field are added to the file.

Next, create a Web Service that allows users to add and modify tasks:

1. Create a new project using the Blank Web Project template. Name the project TaskServer.

2. Add a config.web file by choosing Add New Item from the Project menu.

3. Copy the TaskStore.xml file into the project directory. Add the file to the solution by choosing Add Existing Item from the Project menu.

4. Add the TaskStore.xsd file into the project.

5. Create a new typed dataset using the TaskStore.xsd file. To do so, select the TaskStore.xsd file from the Solution Explorer window and open it. Then select the Generate DataSet option from the Schema menu.

6. Add a new Web Service file by using the Project menu's Add Web Service option. Call the Web Service TaskServer.asmx.

Import the System.Data namespace at the start of the .asmx file. Create a method called GetTasks to return all tasks in the TaskStore.xml file to the user. Listing 15.9 shows what the method should look like.

**LISTING 15.9** Returning a Dataset Containing All Shared Tasks

```
1: <WebMethod> _
2: public function GetTasks() as sharedtasks
3:
4:    Dim ds as new sharedtasks()
5:    ds.ReadXml(Server.MapPath("TaskStore.xml"))
6:    return ds
7:
8: end function
```

**ANALYSIS** Line 2 declares that the GetTasks method should return an object of type sharedtasks. The sharedtasks class is defined in the typed dataset file that was just created in step 5. Lines 4–5 create a new typed dataset and read the content from the TaskStore.xml file. Line 6 returns the new typed dataset.

Now create a method that will add a new task. The method, called AddTask, should accept the sharedtasks typed dataset, which will contain one new task. The method should check to make sure that the new record doesn't have a duplicate name field. Listing 15.10 shows an example of the AddTask method.

**LISTING 15.10** Adding a New Shared Task

```
 1: <WebMethod()> _
 2:    Public Function AddTask(ByVal dsNewTask As sharedtasks, _
 3:        ByRef ErrorMsg As String) As Boolean
 4:
 5:        Dim bSuccess As Boolean = True
 6:        Dim newRow As sharedtasks.taskRow = dsNewTask.task(0)
 7:        Dim ds As sharedtasks = GetTasks()
 8:
 9:        Try
10:            ds.task.ImportRow(newRow)
11:            ds.WriteXml(Server.MapPath("TaskStore.xml"))
12:        Catch ex As ConstraintException
13:            bSuccess = False
14:            ErrorMsg = "A task with the name " & _
15:                newRow.name & " already exists."
16:        Catch ex As Exception
```

**LISTING 15.10**    continued

```
17:              bSuccess = False
18:              ErrorMsg = "Error: " & ex.Message
19:          End Try
20:          Return bSuccess
21:
22:      End Function
```

**ANALYSIS**  Line 6 creates a reference to the row containing the data for the new task called
newRow by selecting the row at index 0 from the task table. Line 7 gets the current
task list by calling the GetTasks method and assigns it the typed dataset called ds.

Lines 10–11 try to add the new row to the dataset by calling the ImportRow method (Line
10). ImportRow will throw a ConstraintException object if the new record contains a
duplicate name field. Line 11 will write the new version of the shared task list back to
disk if the ImportRow call was successful.

Lines 12–14 deal with a ConstraintException, if it occurs. Lines 14–15 create an error
message that client programs can display to the user.

Next, add a method to the TaskService that will modify a row in the shared tasks file.
This method needs to check the "modified" field of the record and match it against the
"modified" field in the current record. If the two match, the client's original data was
valid. If the two modification times are different, the client's data is out of sync with the
data on the server. In this case, the method should return an error message. Listing 15.11
shows an example of the ModifyTask method.

**LISTING 15.11**    Modifying a Task, and Checking to See Whether Another Client Has
Modified the Record

```
 1: <WebMethod()> _
 2: Public Function ModifyTask(ByRef dsTask As sharedtasks, _
 3:     ByRef ErrorMsg As String) As Boolean
 4:
 5:     Dim bSuccess As Boolean = True
 6:     Dim modifiedRow As sharedtasks.taskRow = dsTask.task(0)
 7:     Dim ds As sharedtasks = GetTasks()
 8:     Dim taskTable As sharedtasks.taskDataTable = ds.task
 9:     Dim matchingRows() As DataRow = _
10:         taskTable.Select("name = '" & modifiedRow.name & "'")
11:
12:     If matchingRows.Length = 1 Then
13:         Dim rowToModify As sharedtasks.taskRow = _
14:             CType(matchingRows(0), sharedtasks.taskRow)
15:
```

LISTING **15.11** continued

```
16:          If rowToModify.modified = modifiedRow.modified Then
17:              modifiedRow.modified = DateTime.Now
18:              ds.Merge(dsTask)
19:              ds.WriteXml(Server.MapPath("TaskStore.xml"))
20:          Else
21:              bSuccess = False
22:              ErrorMsg = "This task has been changed by another user.  " & _
23:                         "Please refresh your view of the data."
24:          End If
25:      Else
26:          bSuccess = False
27:          ErrorMsg = "No task named " & dsTask.task(0).name + " found."
28:      End If
29:
30:      Return bSuccess
31:
32: End Function
```

**ANALYSIS** Line 6 creates a reference to the modified row that the client sent, called modifiedRow. Line 7 gets the current set of shared tasks by calling the GetTasks method.

Lines 9–10 return an array of DataRow objects in the shared task database that have the same name as the modified row that the client sent. Presumably, this array of matching rows contains only one value.

Lines 13–14 create a reference to the target row to be modified in the shared task database by retrieving the first object from the array of matching rows created previously.

Line 18 contains the key check to compare the modification timestamps between the client's record and the server's record. If they are identical, the client's data is up-to-date, and the changes should be accepted. Line 19 updates the server's version of the data and persist the data to disk.

Lines 21–23 create an error message if the client's data is out of sync with the server's version of the data.

As a final step, compile the new service.

## Implementing a Client Web Form

This section will give an example of a Web form client that accesses the shared task service. You can use this Web form project to create multiple clients to the service and simulate the data concurrency problems that can occur. To create the client project, follow these steps:

1. Add a new project to the current solution using the Blank Web Project template (choose Add Project from the File menu). Name the project `TaskClient`.

2. Add a config.web file by using the Project menu's Add New Item option.

3. Add a new Web reference from the TaskService by using the Add Web Reference option on the Project menu.

4. Rename the proxy class created by Visual Studio to `TaskServerProxy`. To do so, right-click the localhost Web reference in the Solution Explorer window and select Rename.

5. Add a new Web form by using the Add Web Form option on the Project menu. Call the Web form TaskUI.aspx.

Next, create a user interface for the Web form. The form should contain a DataGrid to display the shared tasks and three buttons to add records, modify records, and refresh the grid. Also, add text boxes so that users can specify the name, due date, and owner of each new or modified record. Listing 15.12 shows what the Web form code will look like.

**LISTING 15.12**   TaskUI.aspx: A Web Form Client for the Task Service

```
1: <%@ Page Language="vb" AutoEventWireup="false"
2:     Codebehind="TaskUI.aspx.vb" Inherits="TaskClient.TaskClient.TaskUI"%>
3: <!DOCTYPE HTML PUBLIC "-//W3C//DTD HTML 4.0 Transitional//EN">
4: <html>
5:   <body>
6:     <font face="arial">
7:     <form runat="server" ID="Form1">
8:       <h3>Shared Tasks</h3>
9:       <asp:DataGrid ID="taskGrid" Runat="server"
10:                     HeaderStyle-Font-Bold="True"/>
11:       <hr>
12:       Task Name: <asp:TextBox Runat="server" ID="Name"/><br>
13:       Due (dd/mm/yy): <asp:TextBox Runat="server" ID="Due"/><br>
14:       Owner: <asp:TextBox Runat="server" ID="Owner"/><br>
15:       <br>
16:       <asp:Button Runat="server" OnClick="AddTask"
17:                   Text="Add Task" ID="Button1" />
18:       <asp:Button Runat="server" OnClick="ModifyTask"
19:                   Text="Modify Task" ID="Button2"/>
20:       <asp:Button Runat="server" OnClick="OnRefresh"
21:                   Text="Refresh View" ID="Button3"/>
22:       <br>
```

**LISTING 15.12**   continued

```
23:        <asp:Label Runat="server" ID="ErrMessage" ForeColor="Red"/>
24:        </form>
25:      </font>
26:    </body>
27:  </html>
```

**ANALYSIS**   Lines 9–10 define a data grid for the tasks, called `taskGrid`. Lines 12–14 define new text box controls that allow users to specify the task name, due date, and owner. Lines 16–21 define button controls to add tasks, modify tasks, and refresh data. Using the data grid for task editing could enrich this interface, but this example keeps things simple.

Next, set up the infrastructure for the client Web form. The client should keep its version of the task list in session state and contain methods to load the grid from the Web Service on the first page hit. Listing 15.13 shows the infrastructure for the Web form.

**LISTING 15.13**   TaskUI.aspx.vb: The Infrastructure Code for the Web Form Client

```
 1: Imports System
 2: Imports System.Data
 3: Imports System.Web.UI
 4: Imports System.Web.UI.WebControls
 5: Imports TaskClient.TaskServerProxy
 6:
 7: Namespace TaskClient
 8:
 9: Public Class TaskUI
10:     Inherits System.Web.UI.Page
11:
12:     Protected taskGrid As DataGrid
13:     Protected ErrMessage As Label
14:     Protected Name As TextBox
15:     Protected Owner As TextBox
16:     Protected Due As TextBox
17:
18:     Private Sub Refresh()
19:
20:         Dim ts As New TaskServer()
21:         Dim ds As sharedtasks = ts.GetTasks()
22:         ds.EnforceConstraints = False
23:         Bind(ds)
24:
25:     End Sub
26:
27:     Private Sub Bind(ByVal ds As sharedtasks)
28:
```

**LISTING 15.13**  continued

```
29:              Session("Data") = ds
30:              taskGrid.DataSource = ds.task
31:              taskGrid.DataBind()
32:
33:      End Sub
34:
35:      Protected Sub Page_Load(ByVal Sender As Object, _
36:              ByVal e As EventArgs)
37:
38:          If Not IsPostBack Then
39:              Refresh()
40:          Else
41:              Dim ds As sharedtasks = CType(Session("Data"), sharedtasks)
42:              Bind(ds)
43:          End If
44:      End Sub
45:
46:      Protected Sub OnRefresh(ByVal Sender As Object, _
47:              ByVal e As EventArgs)
48:
49:          Refresh()
50:
51:      End Sub
52:
53: End Class
54: End Namespace
```

**ANALYSIS**  The Refresh method (Lines 18–25) is responsible for fetching the latest version of the task list from the Web Service. The Bind method (Lines 27–33) binds the taskGrid Web control to a dataset and stashes the dataset in session state.

The Page_Load method (Lines 35–44) will either refresh or rebind the data grid, depending on whether this is the first time the page has been rendered or if this request is from a control postback.

The OnRefresh method (Lines 46–51) reloads the data grid by calling the Refresh method. The Refresh button, defined in the Web form user interface, calls this method.

The final two steps involve creating event handlers for the Add and Modify buttons. First, create the AddTask event handler, which should use the contents of the text boxes in the user interface to construct a new dataset. It should pass this dataset to the Web Service by calling the Web Service's AddTask method. Listing 15.14 shows an example of the client's AddTask method.

**LISTING 15.14** Adding a New Task by Calling the Remote Web Service

```
 1: Protected Sub AddTask(ByVal Sender As Object, ByVal e As EventArgs)
 2:
 3:     Dim ds As sharedtasks = CType(Session("Data"), sharedtasks)
 4:     ds.AcceptChanges()
 5:
 6:     Dim dt As sharedtasks.taskDataTable = ds.task
 7:     dt.AddtaskRow(Name.Text, DateTime.Parse(Due.Text), _
 8:                  Owner.Text, DateTime.Now)
 9:     Dim delta As sharedtasks = _
10:         CType(ds.GetChanges(DataRowState.Added), sharedtasks)
11:
12:     Dim ts As New TaskServer()
13:     Dim ErrorMsg As String
14:     Dim bOk As Boolean = ts.AddTask(delta, ErrorMsg)
15:
16:     If bOk Then
17:         ds.AcceptChanges()
18:         ErrMessage.Text = ""
19:     Else
20:         ds.RejectChanges()
21:         ErrMessage.Text = ErrorMsg
22:     End If
23:     Bind(ds)
24:
25: End Sub
```

**ANALYSIS** Lines 3–4 get the contents of the client's version of the task list from session state and call the AcceptChanges method to prepare the dataset for the new changes that are about to occur.

Lines 6–8 add a new row to the dataset, using the contents of the text boxes in the Web form. Lines 9–10 create a new dataset object, called delta amd containing just this changed row, by calling the GetChanges method.

Lines 12–14 invoke the AddTask method from the Shared Task Web Service, passing the delta dataset.

If the Web Service successfully adds the task, the AcceptChanges method is called (Line 17) so that the client's version of the dataset reflects this new record. If the task can't be added, Line 20 calls RejectChanges, which prevents the new record from being added to the dataset's client copy.

The last method that needs to be added to the code behind file should handle record modifications. This event handler, ModifyTask, should modify the due date and owner fields only. The Web Service will take care of modifying the timestamp associated with the record. If the client's original copy of the record is synchronized with the server's record, the server will update the record's timestamp to reflect the change. If another user has changed the record, the server won't update the timestamp but will return an error message instead. Listing 15.15 shows an example of the `ModifyTask` event handler.

**LISTING 15.15**   Modifying a Task by Calling the Remote Web Service

```
 1: Protected Sub ModifyTask(ByVal Sender As Object, ByVal e As EventArgs)
 2:
 3:     Dim ds As sharedtasks = CType(Session("Data"), sharedtasks)
 4:     ds.AcceptChanges()
 5:
 6:     Dim matchingRows() As DataRow = _
 7:         ds.task.Select("name = '" + Name.Text + "'")
 8:     If matchingRows.Length = 0 Then
 9:         ErrMessage.Text = "No task with this name exists"
10:         Return
11:     End If
12:
13:     Dim modifiedRow As sharedtasks.taskRow = _
14:         CType(matchingRows(0), sharedtasks.taskRow)
15:
16:     'don't change modified time - server will do this on success
17:     'add stuff for get changes.
18:     modifiedRow.due = DateTime.Parse(Due.Text)
19:     modifiedRow.owner = Owner.Text
20:
21:     Dim delta As sharedtasks = _
22:        CType(ds.GetChanges(DataRowState.Modified), sharedtasks)
23:     Dim ErrorMsg As String
24:     Dim ts As New TaskServer()
25:     Dim bOk As Boolean = ts.ModifyTask(delta, ErrorMsg)
26:
27:     If bOk Then
28:         modifiedRow.modified = delta.task(0).modified
29:         ds.AcceptChanges()
30:         ErrMessage.Text = ""
31:     Else
32:         ds.RejectChanges()
33:         ErrMessage.Text = ErrorMsg
34:     End If
35:     Bind(ds)
36:
37: End Sub
```

**ANALYSIS**   Lines 6–11 contain code to find the row in the local dataset to modify by matching what the user entered into the name text box with records in the local dataset.

Lines 18–19 modify the fields in the row to match what the user entered in the Due and Owner text boxes.

Lines 21–22 create a new dataset, called `delta`, that contains the modified records. Lines 24–25 send the `delta` dataset to the Web Service by calling the service's `ModifyTask` method.

If the modification proceeds without any errors, the timestamp for the modified record is updated (Line 28), and Line 29 calls the `AcceptChanges` method. If the server returns an error, the `RejectChanges` method is called on Line 32.

## Trying Out the Client

To simulate two different users making changes to the same record, start two Web browsers. In the first Web browser, use the URL `http://localhost/TaskClient/TaskUI.aspx`. In the second browser, use the URL `http://127.0.0.1/TaskClient/TaskUI.aspx`. Using these different URLs has the effect of creating two different ASP.NET sessions, so you can simulate two different users.

Try adding and modifying records using the two different clients. Figure 15.2 shows an example in which one user tries to modify a record changed by another user.

FIGURE 15.2

*Two shared task clients that modify the same record.*

# Summary

Today's lesson showed how to create Web Services that use and return custom data structures and complex parameters. The first section detailed each kind of data type that you can use with HTTP and SOAP. You saw how HTTP restricts many of your options for a Web Service and how you can use SOAP to transmit almost any kind of data.

The second half of today's lesson gave an advanced example of a Web Service that handles conflicting data modification requests from multiple clients. You learned the difference between optimistic and pessimistic locking and saw one strategy for overcoming some of the limitations of the optimistic locking scheme. The example used a record versioning strategy, which added a timestamp to each record. You can use the techniques presented in this sample in your own Web Service applications. These record-locking techniques aren't unique to Web Services and can be applied in many kinds of applications.

## Q&A

**Q  Because the HTTP protocol is limited to call by reference, what practical effect does this have for my Web Service clients?**

**A**  Web Service clients that use HTTP instead of SOAP won't be able to use any Web Service methods that use call by reference parameters. ASP.NET generates the WSDL interface file automatically, and it won't generate method definitions for methods that use reference parameters for the HTTP protocol. All methods will contain definitions for the SOAP protocol.

**Q  I'm not sure if I should use an optimistic or pessimistic locking scheme for my Web Service. What are the critical issues?**

**A**  Optimistic locking works well when a large number of client programs don't modify the same records frequently. This situation can be described as the "low contention" scenario, because client programs don't contend to modify the same records to often. However, if multiple client programs update the same records frequently, optimistic locking doesn't work very well. Use pessimistic locking for this "high contention" scenario, when many users want to modify the same data record.

## Workshop

The Workshop provides quiz questions to help you solidify your understanding of the material covered today as well as exercises to give you experience using what you've learned. Try to understand the quiz and exercises before continuing to tomorrow's lesson. Answers are provided in Appendix A, "Answers to Quizzes and Exercises."

### Quiz

1. Can the HTTP protocol support methods that use the ADO.NET dataset as a parameter? Why or why not?

2. What is an "out" parameter?

3. What is a "byref" parameter?

4. What is optimistic locking?

5. Why is optimistic locking used in Web applications and services?

6. What method can you use to check the validity of a record modification request when using optimistic locking?

## Exercises

1. The Task Server contains a major defect that will show up if used by many clients simultaneously. The problem is that the Update method might change the contents of the source XML file while the AddTask method is being called. Use the .NET Monitor class to synchronize access to the XML file in the Web Service.

2. Change the Task Server to use a SQL Server database or a database server of your choice. How much of the code needs to be changed?

# DAY **16**

# Putting It All Together with Web Services

By reading the last three days' lessons, you've gained a good knowledge base to use when creating your own Web Services. Today's lesson will build on the last three and will teach you some more advanced techniques that you can use in your own Web Services.

Today's lesson will begin by explaining how to *manage state* in your Web Services. This issue arises when you need to store information about particular Web Service clients between the calls that they make to your service. You will learn how to use the built-in Application and Session objects within your Web Services. As you will see, managing state can get complicated depending on the capabilities of the client accessing your service. This lesson will give solutions to many of these complex issues.

Today's lesson will continue by introducing a new technique called *asynchronous calling*. Web Service clients can use this method to call Web Service methods that may take a long time to complete. Clients can create a request to execute a Web method, perform other work, and then be signaled when the method is complete. You will see two examples that use this technique, including a Web form–based client.

After today's lesson, you should be well equipped to create your own Web Service applications. The remainder of this book will focus on deployment and configuration issues in Web applications and Web Services.

Today you will learn how to

- Use ASP.NET session state and application state in your Web Services
- Work around problems associated with ASP.NET session cookies
- Use asynchronous calling techniques for Web Service clients
- Create Web application client programs that use asynchronous calling

# Managing State in Web Services

The following sections will explain how to use ASP.NET session and application state with Web Services. There's no quicker way to start a debate among .NET developers than to ask the question, "How do I manage per-user data in my Web Service using sessions?" Opinions vary on the use of session state in Web Services. Some regard the combination of session state and Web Services to be a terrible approach because some Web Services—maybe even your own—are designed so that thousands of users can call the service's methods at the same time. A Web Service that makes airline reservations might fit this description. If a Web Service like this uses session state, thousands of Session objects will be created at the same time. The creation of all these Session objects could quickly consume all of a Web server's resources. Web Services like these probably need to manage per-user data differently. Day 21, "Creating Your Application Architecture," will detail Web application and Web Service architectural issues. Until then, let's postpone the debate on ASP.NET sessions and Web Services. For now, we will show you how to use session state without making any pronouncements regarding whether you should use it.

## Using Session State

In the lessons covering Web applications, you saw examples that use the Session object to store data for Web forms. For a quick review, remember that you can store data associated with each specific user of your Web site in the Session object with statements such as the following:

```
Session("User Name") = "Joe Smith"
```

and

```
Dim userName As String = CStr(Session("User Name"))
```

The `Application` object can be used similarly. The lesson for Day 3, "Using Web Forms," contained an example that used the `Application` object to store objects for a Web application.

You can also use the `Session` and `Application` objects when developing ASP.NET Web Services. By using the `Session` object, you can keep track of information about clients that access your Web Service. Listing 16.1 shows a sample Web Service that keeps track of the amount of time spent on the server in a method called `DoWork`.

**16**

**LISTING 16.1**   Timing.asmx: Keeping Track of the Time Spent in the *DoWork* Method

```
 1: <%@ WebService Language="vb" Class="Timing" %>
 2: Imports System
 3: Imports System.Threading
 4: Imports System.Web
 5: Imports System.Web.Services
 6:
 7: <WebService(Namespace:="WebBook")> _
 8:  public class Timing
 9:      Inherits System.Web.Services.WebService
10:
11:    private sub AddTime(starttime as DateTime, endtime as DateTime)
12:
13:      Dim oTime as Object = Session("TotalTime")
14:      dim ts as TimeSpan
15:      if oTime is nothing then
16:        ts = new TimeSpan(0, 0, 0, 0, 0)
17:      else
18:        ts = ctype(oTime, TimeSpan)
19:      end if
20:      ts = ts.Add(endtime.subtract(starttime))
21:      Session("TotalTime") = ts
22:
23:    end sub
24:
25:    <WebMethod(EnableSession:=true)> _
26:    public sub DoSomeWork()
27:
28:      Dim startTime as DateTime = System.DateTime.Now
29:      '  do some work
30:      Thread.Sleep(1000)
31:
32:      dim endTime as DateTime = System.DateTime.Now
33:      AddTime(startTime, endTime)
34:
35:    end sub
36:
37:    <WebMethod(EnableSession:=true)> _
38:    public  function GetTimeSpent() as String
```

**LISTING 16.1**    continued

```
39:
40:          if not Session("TotalTime") is nothing then
41:              return CType(Session("TotalTime"),System.TimeSpan).ToString()
42:          else
43:              return new System.TimeSpan().ToString()
44:          end if
45:      end function
46:  end class
```

**ANALYSIS**  The AddTime utility method (Lines 11–23) adds time to a total stored in the Session object. The method takes two DateTime objects representing the start and end times of a method call and calculates the difference between them by using the TimeSpan object, and then adds the difference in time to the total time and stores the updated value in Session (Lines 20-21). Lines 13–19 contain logic to deal with the possibility that the total time isn't already stored in Session.

The DoSomeWork method (Lines 26–35) calls the Thread.Sleep method (Line 30) rather than perform any real work. It takes a snapshot of the current time on the server at the beginning and end of the method (Lines 28 and 32) and uses the AddTime method to update the current user's time count.

The GetTimeSpent method (Lines 38–45) returns a string containing the latest total time figure for the DoSomeWork method. Of course, this Web Service doesn't accurately reflect the amount of CPU time that the server spent executing the code. It reports only the amount of elapsed time that the DoSomeWork method took to execute.

Using the Timing Web Service works normally if it's accessed from a Web form client. We won't show a Web form client here. You could use the following few lines of code to exercise the Web Service within your own Web form:

```
Dim timingServ as new Timing()
timingServ.DoSomeWork()
timingServ.DoSomeWork()
timingServ.DoSomeWork()
Response.Write(timingServ.GetTimeSpent())
```

The result from this code might look like the following line:

```
00:00:03.0043200
```

This output shows that the Web server spent just over 3 seconds to execute the three DoSomeWork calls, as expected.

Let's test the Timing service by using a console application for a client. Listing 16.2 shows just such an application. In Visual Studio, be sure to add a reference to the Web Service using the techniques you learned previously.

**LISTING 16.2** CallTiming.vb: Calling the Timing Web Service, with Unexpected Results

```vb
Imports System
Imports System.Net
Imports CallTiming.localhost

Module Module1

    Public Sub Main()

        Dim timingServ As New Timing()
        timingServ.DoSomeWork()
        timingServ.DoSomeWork()
        timingServ.DoSomeWork()
        Console.WriteLine("Time spent using web service: " & _
            timingServ.GetTimeSpent())
        Console.ReadLine()
    End Sub

End Module
```

The output from Listing 16.2 looks like Figure 16.1.

**FIGURE 16.1**

*Calling a Web Service using a console application.*

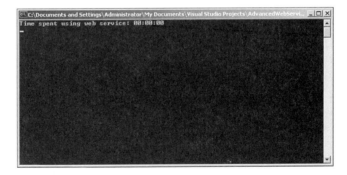

Clearly, there is a problem here; the application should report a time of about 3 seconds, but it reports zero.

To understand the problem, let's revisit how sessions work. ASP.NET normally uses browser cookies to keep track of sessions. When a new Web browser accesses a Web site or Web Service, ASP.NET generates a new empty Session object and new cookie for this browser. The cookie contains an ID number for the newly generated session. On each subsequent page hit from a browser, ASP.NET uses the ID number in the cookie to look up the user's session data, which is normally stored in memory in the Web server. ASP.NET takes the ID, looks up the session in memory, and then places that session into the Session object so that the Web Service (or Web form) can use it.

The problem with the Timing Web Service is that not all client programs support cookies. In fact, most clients, such as a Windows Forms application or console application, don't support cookies.

The solution to the problem involves a little trickery in two steps. First, stop ASP.NET from using cookies by changing one line of code in the web.config file.

> **Note**  Day 3, "Using Web Forms," gave some introductory information on the web.config file, and Day 18, "Configuring Internet Applications," will explain all the options you can set in the file. As a quick review, you use the web.config file to change compilation settings, session state settings, debugging settings, and many more options. The web.config file should reside in the same directory as your Web Service.

You can use a web.config file such as the one in Listing 16.3 to stop ASP.NET from using cookies. This file would go in the Web Service's folder.

**LISTING 16.3**   A web.config File That Turns Off Cookies for Session Management

```
1: <configuration>
2:   <system.web>
3:     <compilation defaultLanguage="vb" debug="true"/>
4:     <sessionState cookieless="true" />
5:   </system.web>
6: </configuration>
```

**ANALYSIS**  Line 3 makes sure that debugging is enabled, and Line 4 turns off cookies.

**NEW TERM**  Now that cookies are disabled, ASP.NET will use a technique called *URL munging* to keep track of sessions. URL munging works by taking the ID for a session that's normally stored in a cookie and appending it to the URL for the Web Service or Web form. This means that on the first method call to the Web Service, the client will be redirected to a new "munged" URL, such as the following:

```
http://localhost/WebBook/(ylotjcyo4hhe00nkqwmr1r55)/Timing.asmx
```

Unfortunately, this new URL will cause an exception in the console application client when it invokes the Web proxy. The standard Web proxy doesn't work when the Web Service redirects it to a new URL.

At this point, the second part of the solution is necessary. You have to make a small modification to the client program so that it will go to the new URL after the first call to the

Web Service. Listing 16.4 shows one way to implement the solution. In this solution, the error message that was returned when the Web Service redirects the client contains the proper URL. By extracting that URL, the program can work as it's supposed to.

**LISTING 16.4**   CallTiming2.vb: Handling Redirection to a Munged URL

```
 1: Imports System
 2: Imports System.Net
 3: Imports CallTiming2.localhost
 4:
 5: Module Module1
 6:
 7: Public Sub Main()
 8:
 9:    Dim timingServ As New Timing()
10:
11:     'Make an attempt to call a method.  This will result in
12:     'an exception, because the web server redirects us to a
13:     ' "munged" url
14:     Try
15:         timingServ.DoSomeWork()
16:     Catch ex As WebException
17:         ' Handle the exception.  The message of the exception
18:         ' will contain a reference to the new URL
19:         Dim err As String = ex.Message
20:
21:         ' Create a search string to find the new URL
22:         Dim search As String = "Object moved to <a href='"
23:
24:         Dim newUrlPos As Integer = err.IndexOf(search)
25:
26:         If newUrlPos > 0 Then
27:             ' We found the magic string, so redirect ourselves
28:             Dim rightString As String = err.Substring(newUrlPos)
29:
30:             ' Split the string using the ' character. The second element
31:             ' will contain the new URL - the first and third elements
32:             ' contain the rest of the error message
33:             Dim segmentedString() As String = rightString.Split("'")
34:             Dim newUrl As String = segmentedString(1)
35:
36:             ' Redirect ourselves by changing the URL in the
37:             ' web server proxy
38:             timingServ.Url = "http:\\localhost" & newUrl
39:         Else
40:             ' this must be a different error
41:             Throw ex
42:         End If
43:     End Try
```

LISTING **16.4** continued

```
44:
45:     timingServ.DoSomeWork()
46:     timingServ.DoSomeWork()
47:     timingServ.DoSomeWork()
48:     Dim timeSpent As String = timingServ.GetTimeSpent()
49:     Console.WriteLine("Time spent using web service: " & timeSpent)
50:     Console.ReadLine()
51:
52: End Sub
53:
54: End Module
```

**ANALYSIS** The new code to redirect the Web proxy to the munged URL is contained in the try...catch block in Lines 14–43. The catch block in Lines 16–43 searches for a "magic" string in the exception's error message (Line 24). If the search string is found, the code parses the new URL (Lines 28–34) and then replaces the URL for the Web Service proxy (Line 38). Now, the console client displays the correct time from the Web Service.

## Using Application State

ASP.NET application state doesn't have the complications that surround session state for Web Services because application state is independent of specific users. Application state doesn't need to be tracked using cookies. Not needing to use cookies simplifies your Web Service and Web Service client code significantly.

For instance, you could modify Listing 16.4 slightly to record statistics about a Web Service. Rather than record information user by user about the call time for the DoSomeWork method, the Web Service could record times for every user. You then could modify the GetTimeSpent method to return the average time spent in the DoSomeWork method for all the service's clients.

Listing 16.5 shows a sample Web Service that records average call times for a method.

LISTING **16.5** AverageTiming.asmx: A Web Service That Records Average Call Time for a Method

```
1: <%@ WebService Language="vb" Class="AverageTiming" %>
2: Imports System
3: Imports System.Threading
4: Imports System.Web
5: Imports System.Web.Services
6:
7: <WebService(Namespace:="WebBook")> _
```

Listing 16.5    continued

```
 8:   public class AverageTiming
 9:       Inherits WebService
10:
11:     private sub AddTime(starttime as DateTime, endtime as DateTime)
12:
13:       Dim calls as integer
14:       Dim oTime as object = Application("TotalTime")
15:       dim ts as TimeSpan
16:       if oTime is nothing then
17:         ts = new TimeSpan(0, 0, 0, 0, 0)
18:       else
19:         ts = Ctype(oTime, TimeSpan)
20:         calls = Cint(Application("Calls"))
21:       end if
22:       ts = ts.Add(endtime.subtract(starttime))
23:       Application("TotalTime") = ts
24:       Application("Calls") = calls + 1
25:     end sub
26:
27:     <WebMethod> _
28:     public sub DoSomeWork()
29:
30:       dim startTime as DateTime = System.DateTime.Now
31:       '  do some work
32:       Thread.Sleep(1000)
33:
34:       dim endTime as DateTime = System.DateTime.Now
35:       AddTime(startTime, endTime)
36:
37:     end sub
38:
39:     <WebMethod> _
40:     public function GetAverageTimeSpent() as String
41:
42:       Dim ts as TimeSpan = CType(Application("TotalTime"), TimeSpan)
43:       dim numCalls as integer = CInt(Application("Calls"))
44:       Dim avgTime as double = (ts.Seconds * 1000 + _
45:           ts.Milliseconds)/numCalls
46:       return avgTime.ToString()
47:
48:     end function
49:
50:   end class
```

**16**

**ANALYSIS**   The AddTime method (Lines 11–25) has been changed to use the Application object. Also, the AddTime method records the total number of calls and stores this figure in the Application object (Lines 20 and 24). The AddTime method also records the total amount of time spent inside the calling method (Lines 22–23).

The DoSomeWork method (Lines 28–37) is unchanged from Listing 16.4. The GetAverageTimeSpent method (Lines 40–48) finds the average call time so far in milliseconds and returns the value.

# Dealing with Slow Services

Web Service methods may take a long time to complete, especially if the method performs a complicated operation or must access other slow components. For instance, an airline reservation Web Service may have to wait on a legacy reservation system that takes a few seconds to complete. In this case, the client program may be blocked waiting for the Web Service method to complete. This blocking behavior could make the client program appear to be frozen to users, and they might get impatient and stop the client program. The solution to this problem is to call Web Service methods asynchronously.

 Calling a Web Service method *asynchronously* means that each method call is broken into two steps:

1.  The client program generates a request to the Web Service. This request contains all the necessary parameters for the Web Service method. The client sends the request to the Web Service and, rather than wait for a response, performs other tasks, such as displaying a progress bar. When the client makes the request, it also gives the Web Service a reference to a callback method.

2.  When the Web Service is finished, it returns the data and the Web Service proxy invokes the callback method. The callback method can examine the results from the Web Service and process the results. For the airline reservation example, the client program can inform users about the status of their reservation requests.

If the Web Service doesn't return a result in time, the client can abort the connection and take steps to tell users that the method failed.

.NET has built-in support for asynchronous calling, and Web Services and Web Service proxies use the .NET classes. If you are experienced with asynchronous calling techniques in .NET, the following explanation for Web Services won't be any different from what you are used to already. If you've never implemented a program that uses asynchronous calling, don't worry; the rest of this section will give you step-by-step instructions.

The following steps outline how to create a program to call Web Service methods asynchronously. The following sections will explain each step in detail.

1.  Create a callback method.

2.  In the callback, make a call to the EndXXX proxy method, where XXX is the name of the Web method. This method will return the results from the Web Service method.

3. In the method that calls the Web Service, create an `AsyncCallback` object that wraps the actual callback method.

4. Invoke the Web Service method by using the `BeginXXX` proxy method, where *XXX* is the name of the Web method.

5. Write code to do other work or wait for the method to complete. You can abort the call at any time.

Let's see how to carry out each one of these steps. To simplify the task of learning about asynchronous calling, we'll use a console application as a client in this first example. However, you can apply the same techniques to any kind of client application. At the end of this section, you'll create a Web form that uses asynchronous calling.

Of course, we need a Web Service that contains a slow method to see how this process works. Listing 16.6 shows just such an example.

**LISTING 16.6**   SlowService.asmx: A Slow Web Service

```
 1: <%@ WebService Language="vb" Class="SlowService" %>
 2: Imports System
 3: Imports System.Threading
 4: Imports System.Web
 5: Imports System.Web.Services
 6:
 7:   <WebService(Namespace:="WebBook")> _
 8:   public class SlowService
 9:      Inherits WebService
10:
11:    <WebMethod> _
12:    public Function SlowMethod(waitSec as integer) as string
13:
14:      Thread.Sleep(waitSec * 1000)
15:      return "The answer is...43."
16:
17:    end function
18:
19:  end class
```

**ANALYSIS**   The `SlowMethod` (Lines 12–17) uses one parameter, `waitSec`, to determine how many seconds it should wait. This parameter allows you to set exactly how slow the method will be in a client program, which is useful for experimentation. The `SlowMethod` returns an arbitrary string.

## Creating a Callback Method

Creating a callback method is the first step to take for the "asynchronous" client. The code in Listing 16.7 shows a sample callback method.

**LISTING 16.7**  A Sample Callback Method

```
 1: public sub MyCallBack(ar as IAsyncResult)
 2:
 3:   try
 4:     Dim result as String = slowServ.EndSlowMethod(ar)
 5:     Console.WriteLine("Callback:Web Service returned: " & result)
 6:   catch ex as Exception
 7:     Console.WriteLine("Callback:The call was aborted!")
 8:   end try
 9:
10: end sub
```

**ANALYSIS**   All callback methods must follow the pattern on Line 1. That is, the callback method can't return a value, and the method must take one parameter of type IAsyncResult. The IAsyncResult object contains the result of the call to the Web method.

Line 4 contains the code to process the result object and extract the return value from the Web method. Notice that Line 4 uses the EndSlowMethod call from the Web proxy. Every Web proxy generated by Visual Studio (or WSDL.exe) contains a method like this. For each Web Service method, such as *ExcellentMethod*, there will be an End*ExcellentMethod* and Begin*ExcellentMethod* in the Web proxy by default.

The callback method uses a try...catch block (Lines 3–8) in case the asynchronous call is aborted. The next section will explain how to abort asynchronous calls. When a method is aborted, the callback is invoked immediately, and the EndSlowMethod call throws an exception.

## Calling the Web Method Asynchronously

Now that the callback is written, you need to create code to call the Web method asynchronously. As you might have guessed, you must use the BeginSlowMethod (or Begin*AppropriateMethod*) call to do so. Before doing so, you must take some preparatory steps:

1. Create a new AsyncCallback method that contains a reference to the callback you created in the preceding section. For this example, you use the following code line:

   ```
   Dim callbackRef as new AsyncCallback(AddressOf MyCallBack)
   ```

2. Call the Web method using a line like the following:

   ```
   Dim ar as IAsyncResult
   ar = slowServ.BeginSlowMethod(5, callbackRef, nothing)
   ```

16

**ANALYSIS** To understand the preceding code, let's examine it from right to left. The `BeginSlowMethod` call takes three parameters:

- The value 5 corresponds to the first parameter that the original `SlowMethod` receives, so this Web method will take at least 5 seconds to complete.
- `callbackRef` is the `AsyncCallback` object created in the preceding section.
- The third parameter is used for extra information. This parameter should always be `nothing` for the current version of .NET.

The asynchronous call returns an `IAsyncResult` object, which you can use to get information about the asynchronous call's status. Listing 16.8 uses the asynchronous result object to wait on the method.

**LISTING 16.8** Partial Code Sample to Wait for an Asynchronous Call by Polling the Result Object

```
 1: Console.WriteLine("Waiting on the web service...")
 2: Dim totalWaitTime as integer = 6000  'wait 6 seconds
 3: ' Dim totalWaitTime as integer = 1000 'Uncomment this line to be impatient
 4:
 5: 'replace this with code to do some real work
 6: ar.AsyncWaitHandle.WaitOne(totalWaitTime, false)
 7:
 8: if ar.IsCompleted then
 9:   Console.WriteLine("The call completed!")
10: else
11:   Console.WriteLine("The call did not complete in time.  Aborting...")
12:   slowServ.Abort()
13: end if
```

**ANALYSIS**

**NEW TERM** Line 2 sets the `totalWaitTime` variable to the total amount of time to wait in milliseconds. Line 6 calls the `WaitOne` method, which waits for the `IAsyncResult` object (the object named `ar`) to become set to a completed state. This is known as waiting for the object to be *signaled*. The `WaitOne` method will return as soon as the asynchronous call is complete or when the timeout period expires, whichever comes first.

Lines 8–13 test whether the method is completed in time by using the `IsCompleted` property. If the method isn't completed in time, the code calls the `Abort` method (Line 12) to stop the asynchronous call immediately.

## Completing the Asynchronous Client

Listing 16.9 contains the complete code for the console application client. This console application is called `SlowServiceClient`. As always, be sure to add a reference to the Web Service to the project.

**LISTING 16.9**   Calling a Web Service Asynchronously

```
 1: Imports System
 2: Imports System.Threading
 3: Imports SlowServiceClient.localhost
 4:
 5: Module Module1
 6:
 7:     Public Sub Main()
 8:
 9:         Dim obj As New WebServiceCaller()
10:         obj.CallSlow()
11:         Thread.Sleep(50)
12:
13:     End Sub
14:
15:     Public Class WebServiceCaller
16:
17:         Dim slowServ As SlowService
18:
19:         Public Sub MyCallBack(ByVal ar As IAsyncResult)
20:
21:             Try
22:                 Dim result As String = slowServ.EndSlowMethod(ar)
23:                 Console.WriteLine("Callback:Web Service returned: " & _
24:                     result)
25:             Catch ex As Exception
26:                 Console.WriteLine("Callback:The call was aborted!")
27:             End Try
28:
29:         End Sub
30:
31:         Public Sub CallSlow()
32:
33:             slowServ = New SlowService()
34:             Dim cb As New AsyncCallback(AddressOf MyCallBack)
35:
36:             Dim ar As IAsyncResult = slowServ.BeginSlowMethod _
37:                 (5, cb, Nothing)
38:
39:             Console.WriteLine("Waiting on the web service...")
40:             Dim totalWaitTime As Integer = 6000  'wait 6 seconds
41:             'totalWaitTime = 1000 'Uncomment this line to be impatient
42:
```

**LISTING 16.9** continued

```
43:                ar.AsyncWaitHandle.WaitOne(totalWaitTime, False)
44:
45:            If ar.IsCompleted Then
46:                Console.WriteLine("The call completed!")
47:            Else
48:                Console.WriteLine("The call did not complete in time." & _
49:                    " Aborting...")
50:                slowServ.Abort()
51:            End If
52:        End Sub
53:    End Class
54:
55: End Module
```

16

After running this sample, you should see output similar to Figure 16.2. If you uncomment Line 41, recompile, and then rerun the client, you should see output similar to Figure 16.3.

**FIGURE 16.2**

*Calling a Web Service using an asynchronous client console application.*

**FIGURE 16.3**

*An aborted asynchronous call to a Web Service.*

**ANALYSIS** The preceding discussion already detailed most of the code in Listing 16.9. However, one line is worth noting. Line 11 contains a `Sleep` call after Line 10's

CallSlow method. This line is optional and was inserted into this sample so that you can see the result from the callback when the asynchronous call is aborted. Without the delay, the program would exit before the callback had a chance to complete. Removing the delay won't break the example; the program will still complete gracefully.

Listing 16.9 is fine for demonstration purposes, but a console application probably isn't your first choice for a Web Service client. Let's use the concepts in Listing 16.9 to create a Web form client for the SlowService Web Service in Listing 16.6. This client will model a request for an airline reservation, using SlowService as the back-end "reservation system."

The client will work using the following steps:

1. The Web form will display the message Making Reservation..., similar to Figure 16.4.

**FIGURE 16.4**

*A Web Form that calls a Web Service asynchronously.*

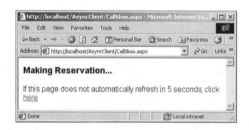

2. In the Page_Load event, the Web form will generate an asynchronous call to the SlowService Web Service.

3. The Web form will contain HTML code so that the browser will automatically refresh after 5 seconds.

4. The Page_Load event will contain code to detect whether it has been called twice. If so, it will check for a result. If the asynchronous call is completed, the results will be shown. If not, the Web form will display a Still waiting... message.

Listing 16.10 shows a Web form to call the SlowService Web Service, and Listing 16.11 shows the code-behind file that calls a Web Service asynchronously using the four preceding steps.

**LISTING 16.10** CallSlow.aspx: A Prototype Reservation Page that Calls a Web Service Asynchronously

```
1: <%@ Page Language="vb" Codebehind="CallSlow.aspx.vb"
2:    Inherits="CallSLow.CallSlowService"%>
3: <!DOCTYPE HTML PUBLIC "-//W3C//DTD HTML 4.0 Transitional//EN">
4: <HTML>
```

**LISTING 16.10** continued

```
 5: <HEAD>
 6: <meta http-equiv='refresh' content='5' id='metatag' runat='server'/>
 7: </HEAD>
 8: <body>
 9: <h3><asp:Label ID="Message" runat="server"></asp:Label></h3>
10: <div id="refreshMessage" runat="server">
11: If this page does not automatically refresh in 5 seconds, click
12: <a href="CallSlow.aspx">here</a>
13: </div>
14: </body>
15: </HTML>
```

**ANALYSIS** Lines 5–6 contain a `<meta>` tag that tells the browser to refresh the current page after 5 seconds. This `<meta>` tag is defined as a server control so that it can be disabled by the code behind file after the reservation is completed successfully. Lines 10–13 contain a `<div>` tag that's used exactly the same way as the `<meta>` tag. The `<div>` tag will be hidden by the code behind file after the reservation is completed.

**LISTING 16.11** CallSlow.aspx.vb: The Code-Behind File for Listing 16.10

```
 1: Imports System
 2: Imports System.Web.UI
 3: Imports System.Web.UI.WebControls
 4: Imports System.Web.UI.HtmlControls
 5: Imports System.Web.Services.Protocols
 6: Imports CallSLow.localhost
 7:
 8: Public Class CallSlowService
 9:     Inherits System.Web.UI.Page
10:
11:     Dim slowServ As SlowService
12:     Protected Message As Label
13:     Protected refreshMessage As HtmlGenericControl
14:     Protected metaTag As HtmlGenericControl
15:
16:     Public Sub MyCallBack(ByVal ar As IAsyncResult)
17:         Dim result As String
18:         Session("Result") = slowServ.EndSlowMethod(ar)
19:         Session("Done") = True
20:     End Sub
21:
22:     Protected Sub CallIt()
23:         Message.Text = "Making Reservation..."
24:         slowServ = New SlowService()
25:         Dim cb As New AsyncCallback(AddressOf MyCallBack)
26:         slowServ.BeginSlowMethod(4, cb, Nothing)
```

16

LISTING **16.11**   continued

```
27:            Session("CalledMethod") = True
28:        End Sub
29:
30:        Private Sub Page_Load(ByVal sender As Object, _
31:                ByVal e As System.EventArgs)
32:
33:            Message.Text = "Starting"
34:            If Session("CalledMethod") Is Nothing Then
35:                CallIt()
36:            ElseIf Session("Done") Is Nothing Then
37:                Message.Text = "Still waiting...."
38:            Else
39:                Message.Text = "Your reservation has been made."
40:                metaTag.Visible = False
41:            End If
42:
43:        End Sub
44: End Class
```

**ANALYSIS**   Lines 16–20 contain the custom callback method for the Web form. This callback
varies from the console application example because it stores the asynchronous
result object into session state. Although the program doesn't use this value, a real program might. The callback also sets a "done" flag in session state.

Lines 22–28 contain the CallIt method. This method varies only slightly from the console application example because it stores a flag indicating that the Web method has been
called.

Lines 30–43 contain the Page_Load method. This method contains some complexity
because it can be called under a number of different circumstances. First, the method
checks to see whether the Web Service has been called (Line 34). If not, it invokes the
CallIt method to call the service. If Page_Load is called after the Web Service is
called—for example, if the user clicks the refresh button—the code then checks whether
the Web Service has returned (Line 36). If not, a "still waiting" message is displayed. If
so, a "reservation made" message is displayed and the page's automatic refreshing is
turned off.

Figure 16.5 shows the result of a successful call by the asynchronous client.

16

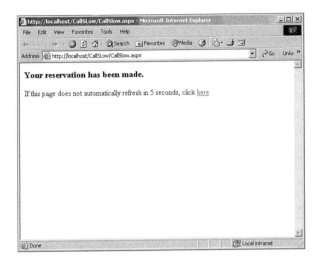

**FIGURE 16.5**

*Asynchronous Web
Form client results
after a Web method
call has completed.*

# Summary

Today's lesson showed how to use session state in a Web Service by giving an example that tracked the amount of time a Web Service spent in a method call for a user. Clients that don't support cookies, such as Windows forms programs and console applications, can have trouble dealing with Web Services that use session state. You saw some techniques for dealing with the issue in the first part of today's lesson.

You learned how to make asynchronous calls to Web Services in the second part of the lesson. This advanced technique can be especially helpful for Web Services that don't return results immediately. You saw how to create client programs that use asynchronous calls from a Web form and from a console application.

Today's lesson is the last one that deals explicitly with Web Services. Future lessons, such as Day 18, "Configuring Internet Applications," will show you how to configure Web Services, and Day 19, "Securing Internet Applications," will include sample programs that allow you to create secure services.

# Q&A

**Q I plan on using a commercial Web Service for one of my projects and I don't have any control over the way this service is implemented. Can I still use asynchronous calling techniques, like the ones described in this lesson?**

**A** Yes. Creating an asynchronous Web Service client doesn't depend on the remote Web Service that you are using. Visual Studio .NET and the .NET Framework allow you to create asynchronous clients for any kind of Web Service. The key methods in the Web Service proxy class, such as BeginSomeMethod and EndSomeMethod, are generated for you automatically.

**Q I plan on creating a standalone Windows Forms application that will call a Web Service asynchronously. Which technique in this lesson should I use?**

**A** Windows Forms applications are similar to the console application from Listing 16.9, in that they don't support client-side cookies. You can use the techniques from Listing 16.9 in Windows Forms applications to call a Web Service asynchronously. You would need to move the code in the console application's Main method into the Form event handler that calls the Web Service.

# Workshop

The Workshop provides quiz questions to help you solidify your understanding of the material covered today as well as exercises to give you experience using what you have learned. Try to understand the quiz and exercise before continuing to tomorrow's lesson. Answers are provided in Appendix A, "Answers to Quizzes and Exercises."

## Quiz

1. What attribute must be used to enable session state for a public Web method?
2. Why does using session state in a Web Service cause complications for some client programs?
3. Does a special attribute enable application state for Web Services?
4. What technique is used to deal with Web Services that take a long time to return a result from a method call?
5. Do you have to take any special actions to enable asynchronous calling for a Web Service?
6. What interface do objects returned from asynchronous method calls support?
7. Do Web forms support asynchronous method calls to Web Services?

## Exercises

1. Modify SlowService to return error messages at random.
2. Modify one of the asynchronous clients to handle the randomly generated error messages from the new SlowService created in Exercise 1.

# WEEK 3

# DAY 17

# Using Legacy Code with .NET

Now that you've seen how to create Web applications and Web Services with .NET, we hope you will want to use it in your own applications. However, you or your organization may have a large base of existing code that can't be thrown away just because yet another new development technology is available. Fortunately, you don't have to scrap all your existing code to start using .NET. In fact, .NET components, Web forms, and Web Services can coexist with existing applications written using previous versions of Visual Studio or other development technologies. Some programmers debate whether trying to port legacy code to .NET is worth the trouble, suggesting that rewriting an application from scratch is a better approach. That's not a decision we can make for you, but after you decide to do so, this chapter will get you started.

Today's lesson will begin by explaining how to use ASP.NET and ASP simultaneously. The lesson won't give explicit instructions for porting individual lines of code; it assumes that you already know enough about Visual Basic to begin this task yourself. Instead, the first part of today's lesson will give examples for sharing session objects between ASP and ASP.NET.

The second part of today's lesson will detail how to use legacy code in .NET applications, specifically in Web forms and Web Services. Using the techniques in the second part of today's lesson will allow you to leverage your existing code base when you start developing Web applications with .NET.

Today's last section will give step-by-step instructions for using .NET code from your legacy applications. The section will show how to create .NET components that can be called from any existing legacy application, including ASP.

Today's lesson will show you how to

- Make ASP and ASP.NET coexist without problems
- Transfer ASP sessions into ASP.NET sessions automatically
- Use legacy code from Web forms and Web Services
- Create .NET components that can be used in legacy applications
- Make sure that your .NET component can be called from scripting languages such as VBScript

 **Caution**  Today's lesson requires that you have a good understanding of COM. If you don't, please consult *Essential COM* by Don Box (Addison-Wesley, ISBN 0-201-63446-5), which gives detailed information on what COM is all about.

# Using ASP and ASP.NET Together

Happily, ASP and ASP.NET pages will run alongside each other in the same directory without any problems. This capability allows you to migrate your ASP pages in steps, rather than have to convert your entire site all at once.

## The Session Problem

One complication arises when you use old and new versions of ASP together. ASP.NET and ASP pages won't share the `Session` or `Application` object. This limitation can cause some headaches if both sets of pages need to share state information. However, you can transfer information stored in ASP sessions into ASP.NET sessions by using XML files. To share session information, create a function in your ASP code to persist the contents of the `Session` object to an XML file. Then read the XML file from ASP.NET, placing all the data into ASP.NET session state.

Listing 17.1 shows a sample ASP page that adds a few sample objects, including an array, to session state. The example then calls the `PersistSession` function, which writes out the contents of the particular session to an XML file in a special directory, C:\private\sessions. This directory will be accessible only to ASP and ASP.NET; users can't see what it contains. The PersistSession method will create a unique filename for the XML file, using the native session ID and current time. The page then contains a link to an ASP.NET page that will read the XML file and load the contents into ASP.NET session state (as in Listing 17.2).

**LISTING 17.1**    TransferSession.asp: Persisting the Contents of Its Session to an XML File

```
 1: <%@ LANGUAGE="VBSCRIPT" %>
 2:
 3: <%
 4:     'Create some sample objects and put them in session
 5:     Dim myArray(2)
 6:     myArray(0)="firstvalue"
 7:     myArray(1)="secondvalue"
 8:     myArray(2)="thirdvalue"
 9:     Session("myArray")=myArray
10:
11:     Session("stringval")="1234567890ABCDEFG"
12:
13:     set objConn=server.createobject("adodb.connection")
14:     set Session("conobject")=objConn
15:
16:     dim g_key
17:     g_key = PersistSession
18: %>
19: <html>
20: <body>
21: Array, string, and object added to session..
22: <br>
23: Click <a href="ReadSession.aspx?seskey=<%=g_key%>">here</a>
24: to go to the ASP.NET page
25: </body>
26: </html>
27: <%
28: function PersistSession
29:     dim fso, xmlfile, key, sessitem
30:     key = GetSessionKey
31:     Set fso = CreateObject("Scripting.FileSystemObject")
32:     Set xmlfile = fso.CreateTextFile("C:\private\sessions\" & key & _
33:                     ".xml", true)
34:     xmlfile.WriteLine "<?xml version=""1.0"" ?>"
35:     xmlfile.WriteLine "<session>"
36:     For Each sessitem in Session.Contents
37:       xmlfile.WriteLine FormatSessionValue(sessitem)
38:     Next
39:     xmlfile.WriteLine "</session>"
```

17

**LISTING 17.1**    continued

```
40:    xmlfile.Close
41:    PersistSession = key
42: end function
43:
44: function GetSessionKey
45:    dim curTime
46:    curTime = split(FormatDateTime(now, 3), " ")
47:    dim newTime
48:    newTime = Replace(curTime(0), ":", "-")
49:
50:    GetSessionKey = Session.SessionID & "-" & newTime
51: end function
52:
53: function FormatSessionValue(sessitem)
54:     dim name
55:     name = sessitem
56:     dim value
57:     value ="<" & name & ">"
58:     If IsObject(Session.Contents(name)) Then
59:       value = value & "Error:Objects cannot be persisted"
60:     Else
61:        If IsArray(Session.Contents(name)) Then
62:          Dim idx
63:          idx = 0
64:          For each objArray in Session.Contents(sessitem)
65:              value = value & "<item>"
66:              value = value & Session.Contents(sessitem)(idx)
67:              value = value & "</item>"
68:              idx = idx + 1
69:          Next
70:        Else
71:              value = value & Session.Contents(sessitem)
72:        End If
73:     End If
74:     value = value + "</" & name & ">"
75:    FormatSessionValue = value
76: end function
77: %>
```

**ANALYSIS**   Lines 3–14 create some sample objects, including an array, string, and ADO connection object, and place them in session state. Line 17 calls the PersistSession function (Lines 28–42), which returns a unique key name for this session. The key name will look something like 894131997-11-09-07, which is a concatenation of the native session ID and current time. Line 23 contains a link to the ASP.NET page that will read the session information. Line 17 uses the key (g_key) that the PersistSession function returned.

Lines 27–75 contain the utility methods that persist session state. They might be put in an .inc file for reuse. These methods are explained in the following paragraphs.

The `PersistSession` function (Lines 28–42) creates a new file in the C:\private\sessions directory, using the key name from the `GetSessionKey` call on Line 30. Lines 34–35 write out the XML header and begin tag for the file. Lines 36–38 loop through the session object, calling `FormatSessionValue` to format each object as an XML element.

The `GetSessionKey` function (Lines 44–51) returns the magic session key string. It uses string manipulation functions to append the current time to the native session identifier and return the result.

`FormatSessionValue` (Lines 53–76) formats a session value for the XML file. Notice Lines 58 and 59, which test whether the value is of type `Object`. The function can't persist object type values because they could contain COM objects, which would be difficult to serialize as XML and import into an ASP.NET session. Your applications shouldn't store COM objects in ASP session state anyway, so this shouldn't be a problem.

**Note**

> The preceding paragraph assumes that your ASP program doesn't store COM objects in session state. Storing COM objects this way is a bad idea because COM objects that use single-threaded apartments (STA) will bring your Web server to a crawl if they are stored in ASP or ASP.NET session state. All COM objects created using Visual Basic 6.0 and earlier use single-threaded apartments.

A typical XML file created by Listing 17.1 looks like this:

```
<?xml version="1.0" ?>
<session>
 <myArray>
  <item>firstvalue</item>
  <item>secondvalue</item>
  <item>thirdvalue</item>
 </myArray>
 <stringval>1234567890ABCDEFG</stringval>
 <comobject>Error:Objects cannot be persisted</comobject>
</session>
```

The next task is to create a utility method to read this XML file and a Web form to put the method to use. Listing 17.2 shows a sample Web form that uses the `XmlDocument` class to read the session file. This example doesn't use any HTML; it simply calls the `Response.Write` method to output raw text to the client browser.

**LISTING 17.2**    ReadSession.aspx: Reading an XML File Containing Session Data

```
 1: <%@ Import Namespace="System.Xml" %>
 2: <script language="vb" runat="server">
 3: public sub XmlToSession(sessionKey as String)
 4:
 5:   Dim reader as XmlTextReader
 6:   try
 7:     reader = new XmlTextReader("c:\private\sessions\" & _
 8:                   sessionKey & ".xml")
 9:     Dim sessionDoc as new XmlDocument()
10:     sessionDoc.Load(reader)
11:
12:     Dim sessionNode as XmlNode = sessionDoc.LastChild
13:     Dim childNode As XmlElement
14:     for each childNode in sessionNode
15:
16:       Dim name as String = childNode.Name
17:       Dim val as String
18:       if childNode.ChildNodes.Count = 1 then
19:         val = childNode.InnerText
20:         Session.Add(name, val)
21:       else
22:         Dim vals(childNode.ChildNodes.Count) as String
23:         Dim idx as Integer = 0
24:         Dim child2Node As XmlNode
25:         for each child2Node in childNode.ChildNodes
26:           vals(idx) = child2Node.InnerText
27:           idx += 1
28:         next
29:         Session.Add(name, vals)
30:       End If
31:     Next
32:     reader.Close()
33:   catch ex as Exception
34:     reader.Close()
35:   End Try
36: End Sub
37:
38: private sub WriteSessionContents()
39:
40:   Dim oname as string
41:   for each oname in Session.Keys
42:     if Session(oname).GetType() Is GetType(String()) then
43:       Response.Write(oname & ":<br>")
44:       Dim vals() As String = CType(Session(oname), String())
45:       Dim i as integer
46:       for i = 0 to UBound(vals)
47:         Response.Write(vals(i) & "<br>")
48:       Next
49:     else
```

**LISTING 17.2** continued

```
50:       Response.Write(oname + ": " & _
51:                       Session(oname).ToString() & "<br>")
52:     End If
53:   Next
54: End Sub
55:
56: private sub Page_Load(sender as object, e as System.EventArgs)
57:
58:   Dim sessionKey as string = Request.Params("seskey")
59:   XmlToSession(sessionKey)
60:   WriteSessionContents()
61:
62: End Sub
63: </script>
```

**17**

**ANALYSIS**  Lines 3–36 contain the XmlToSession method, which reads the XML generated by Listing 17.1 and places the contents into ASP.NET session state. The method receives the session key value, which it uses to find the XML file (Lines 7–8). Lines 9–10 create a new XmlDocument and load it from the file. Lines 14–31 contain a loop that processes XmlElement objects contained in the XmlDocument.

Line 18 tests to see if the current node has more than one child node. If it does, the node contains an array of values, so special action is taken to process the subelements (Lines 22–29).

The WriteSessionContent method (Lines 38–54) demonstrates that the whole process actually worked by printing the contents of the current session. The Page_Load method (Lines 56–62) queries the Params collection to find the key to the XML file (Line 58), and then reads the session from disk and writes the result to the browser.

You can make several enhancements to this code. For instance, you could add utility methods to shuffle ASP.NET session state to ASP sessions to each listing. Code to persist the Application object could also be added. This task is left as an exercise at the end of today's lesson.

## Migrating ASP

Besides changing your existing ASP code into ASP.NET Web forms, the thorniest issue you will have to deal with concerns COM objects. You may not want to rewrite all your existing COM objects immediately, and you don't have to. The next few sections will detail how to use COM objects in .NET applications, including Web forms and Web Services.

# Using COM Components

The simplest way that .NET code will interact with "legacy" code is through COM and COM+ objects. If you have a large set of COM or COM+ objects already, you don't need to throw away your existing code; you can use it without too much trouble in your new .NET code. If your existing code is in the form of standard executable files (.exe files) without a COM interface, you will have to "wrap" the code inside a COM object.

**Note**

You can choose from at least two other methods for interacting with legacy code:

- Use the .NET managed C++ compiler. (Using managed C++ is beyond the scope of this book.)
- If your code is contained in a standard dynamic link library (DLL), you can invoke the code by using the DllImport code attribute.

Adding COM objects to your .NET Web forms and Web Services is a simple operation. Follow these steps inside a Visual Studio project:

1. From the Project menu, choose Add Reference.
2. In the Add Reference dialog, click the COM tab. All registered COM components on your computer that contain a type library will appear in the list.
3. Double-click an entry. If you want to follow along with the next few examples in today's lesson, select the Microsoft ActiveX Data Objects 2.0 entry to add a reference to ADO.old to your project.
4. Click OK. You will be greeted by a dialog similar to the one shown in Figure 17.1.

**FIGURE 17.1**

*Creating a wrapper for a legacy COM object.*

5. The dialog is essentially asking, "Should Visual Studio create a wrapper for the COM object?" Answer by clicking Yes. A new reference for the COM object, called ADODB in this case, will appear in the Solution Explorer under the References node.

**NEW TERM**
Figure 17.1 shows a dialog asking whether you would like to create a *primary interop assembly* in step 4. This term refers to a new assembly that sits between a .NET application and a COM component, as Figure 17.2 shows. This intermediate

assembly is called a *Runtime Callable Wrapper (RCW)*, a proxy that allows .NET code to call COM components.

**FIGURE 17.2**

*The Runtime Callable Wrapper and a .NET application.*

Your application doesn't call the component directly; instead, it calls this intermediate assembly. The proxy deals with all the messy details of calling the COM component, including converting .NET objects into data structures that the component can use and converting returned data back into .NET objects.

Let's create a Web form that uses ADO.old through the proxy created in the preceding steps. Listings 17.3 and 17.4 show a Web form that returns all the shippers in the Access Northwind database. (Of course, you can easily modify the code to use the Northwind database supplied by SQL Server using the methods from Day 9.) Listing 17.4 mixes ADO.NET and ADO.old, creating a standard ADO.NET `DataSet` object but using ADO.old rather than a .NET data adapter to populate the dataset.

**LISTING 17.3**   Displaying the Shippers in the Northwind Database

```
<%@ Page language="vb" Codebehind="LegacyShippers.aspx.vb"
    Inherits="aspold.LegacyShippers" %>
<html>
  <body >
    <form runat="server">
    <h3>Northwind's Shippers</h3>
    <asp:DataGrid ID="shippersGrid" Runat="server"/>
    </form>
  </body>
</html>
```

**LISTING 17.4**   LegacyShippers.aspx.vb: Using ADO to List the Shippers in the Northwind Database

```
1: Imports System
2: Imports System.Data
3: Imports System.Web.UI
4: Imports System.Web.UI.WebControls
5: Imports System.Xml
6: Imports ADODB
7:
8: Namespace aspold
```

**LISTING 17.4**   continued

```
 9:
10:    Public Class LegacyShippers
11:      Inherits System.Web.UI.Page
12:
13:      Protected shippersGrid As DataGrid
14:
15:      Private Sub Page_Load(ByVal Sender As Object, ByVal e As EventArgs)
16:
17:        Dim ds As New DataSet()
18:        Dim dt As New DataTable("Shippers")
19:        ds.Tables.Add(dt)
20:        dt.Columns.Add("ShipperID", GetType(Int16))
21:        dt.Columns.Add("CompanyName", GetType(String))
22:        dt.Columns.Add("Phone", GetType(String))
23:
24:        Dim con As New ADODB.Connection()
25:        Dim connectionString As String = "Provider=Microsoft.Jet. " & _
26:            " OLEDB.4.0;Data Source=C:\Program Files\Microsoft Office\" & _
27:            "Office\Samples\Northwind.mdb;" & _
28:            "User ID=;Password=;"
29:        Dim cmd As New ADODB.Command()
30:        con.Open(connectionString, "", "", 0)
31:        cmd.ActiveConnection = con
32:        cmd.CommandText = "SELECT ShipperID, CompanyName, " & _
33:            "Phone FROM Shippers"
34:        Dim oRowsAffected As New Object()
35:        Dim Params As New Object()
36:        Dim rs As ADODB.Recordset = cmd.Execute(oRowsAffected, Params, 0)
37:        rs.MoveFirst()
38:        While Not rs.EOF
39:          Dim vals(3) As Object
40:          vals(0) = rs.Fields("ShipperID").Value.ToString()
41:          vals(1) = rs.Fields("CompanyName").Value.ToString()
42:          vals(2) = rs.Fields("Phone").Value.ToString()
43:          dt.Rows.Add(vals)
44:          rs.MoveNext()
45:        End While
46:
47:        rs.Close()
48:        con.Close()
49:
50:        ' Important!
51:        con.Dispose()
52:
53:        shippersGrid.DataSource = ds ' ds
54:        shippersGrid.DataBind()
55:      End Sub
56:    End Class
57: End Namespace
```

**ANALYSIS**   Listing 17.4 uses standard ADO.old techniques to read the contents of a dataset's table.

> **Note**   This analysis assumes that you've used ADO.old before. If you haven't, don't worry about the meaning of specific calls in the listing. The important point to notice is that the calls to ADO here are exactly the same types of calls made to a regular .NET object.

The most important piece of information to take away from Listing 17.4 is the call on line 51 to the `Dispose` method. Every COM proxy will contain a `Dispose` method. This method isn't part of the original COM component. *You must call the `Dispose` method on every COM proxy* after you're finished with the object. If you don't call `Dispose`, the COM object will stay in memory permanently, even after the method returns and the original proxy object goes out of scope. This could also cause other .NET components that have a reference to the COM object proxy to stick in memory.

The rule about calling `Dispose` is a good one to remember, even for .NET objects. For any object in .NET that contains a `Dispose` method, you must *always* call `Dispose` after you are done with the object.

This rule about calling `Dispose` makes your life as a programmer painful, especially after you become used to .NET's automatic garbage collection features. This single rule will probably be the cause of countless memory leaks and developer hours spent for many years to come. A full explanation of the reasons you must call `Dispose` involves knowing specific details about COM reference counting and .NET garbage collection. If you're interested in the specifics, search for "garbage collection" and "reference counting" in the Visual Studio MSDN documentation.

> **Note**   You can use a type library importer tool called Tlbimp.exe to create Runtime Callable Wrappers (COM proxies). The following line shows how you use the tool, assuming that you have a COM component called MyComObject.dll:
>
> ```
> tlbimp /out:MyComObjectRCW.dll /namespace:MyComProxy
> MyComObject.dll
> ```
>
> You can specify the output filename and namespace using the /out and /namespace parameters. You also can use a number of special parameters with the Tlbimp tool to customize how the wrapper should be generated.

17

# Using .NET Components in Legacy Applications

With all the great new features that .NET offers you as a developer, you might want to migrate your existing application by porting existing components into Visual Basic .NET. This section will show you how to use .NET components inside your existing applications.

You can interact with .NET components by treating them as though they are COM components. Your .NET component needs a proxy called a COM Callable Wrapper (CCW). This wrapper, created on demand by the .NET runtime environment, calls code in your .NET assemblies. To your existing code, the .NET assembly appears as though it is a standard COM object.

Although your existing code won't have any problem using your .NET components, you will have to go through some trouble to expose the component to legacy code. Follow these steps:

1. Create a public interface in your .NET project to be used as the COM interface in the COM Callable Wrapper.
2. Define each method that you want to expose in the interface.
3. Create a class to implement the interface. Add custom .NET code to make the class do something.
4. Create public and private keys to sign your .NET assembly, using the sn.exe tool.
5. Add attributes to your code so that your assembly will use the public and private keys in its signature.
6. Compile the project, thereby creating a signed assembly.
7. Add the assembly to the Global Assembly Cache (GAC) using the gacutil.exe tool.
8. Register the assembly in the Windows Registry by using the regasm.exe tool.

At first, this process seems daunting. However, it's not difficult to execute in practice. Before going into the details of each step, the next section will explain the Global Assembly Cache and application signing.

## The Global Assembly Cache

COM and COM+ components need to be registered, which is the process of adding numerous keys to the Windows Registry. COM+ components also store references in the COM+ catalog, which is similar in structure to the Windows Registry.

If you've been developing COM and COM+ components for any amount of time, you are painfully aware of the problems associated with inconsistent Registry settings and your component. Depending on exactly how inconsistent the Registry becomes, your COM component may not be accessible to any client applications.

The bad news is that .NET adds a third "catalog" to the mix, called the Global Assembly Cache. The GAC contains references to .NET components, just like the Windows Registry does for COM and COM+ components. The good news is that the GAC isn't corrupted easily and is easy to inspect and repair.

The GAC contains references to .NET assemblies that need to be used as COM objects or distributed to the general public. The GAC is used for .NET component versioning, just like the Windows Registry is used for COM component versioning. The GAC allows you to control which version of a .NET component your own code should use.

To view what's in the GAC, browse to the directory C:\winnt\assembly. (Use a different path if Windows is installed somewhere else besides C:\winnt.) You should see something like Figure 17.3.

**17**

**FIGURE 17.3**

*The Global Assembly Cache.*

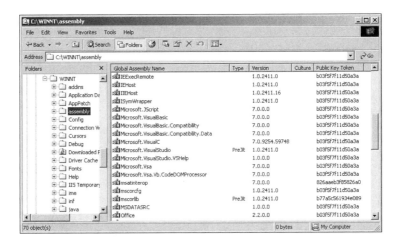

The GAC uses public and private keys to identify each .NET assembly.

**Note**

Public and private key pairs are used in many places. By using a public/private key pair, you can encrypt information using the private key. You can give the encrypted information and public key to anyone you want to read the encrypted information. That person can decrypt the information using the public key. The public key will decode only information that has been encoded using the private key. This way, whoever has your public key knows the information came from you, not an imposter.

If you want to add your own assembly to the GAC, you have to "sign" the assembly with a public and private key pair. Signing involves generating an identification string, encrypting the identification string, and including the encrypted identification string along with the assembly. .NET does all this work for you automatically when compiling an assembly; all you need is a file containing your public and private keys.

You can easily generate a public and private key pair to sign an assembly. Type the following command at the Visual Studio command prompt:

```
sn -k MyKeyPairFile.snk
```

The sn.exe tool generates a new public and private key pair this way.

When you have an assembly that's signed with the key pair (the next section will explain how to sign assemblies), you can add the assembly to the GAC by using the following command:

```
gacutil /i MyAssembly.dll
```

To remove the assembly, type the following:

```
Gacutil /u MyAssembly
```

Omit the filename extension when removing the assembly.

## Exposing a .NET Class

Let's write a .NET class that we can call from ASP. Listing 17.5 shows an example. If you're following along with the examples, make sure that you create a public/private key pair file. If you're using Visual Studio, create a new Class Library project called MyInteropExample.

**LISTING 17.5**   HelloUtility.vb: A Component That You Can Use as a COM Component

```
 1: Imports System
 2: Imports System.Reflection
 3: Imports System.Runtime.InteropServices
 4:
 5: 'Change the path below to the location of your public/private
 6: 'key file generated with the sn.exe tool
 7:
 8: <assembly:AssemblyKeyFileAttribute("mykey.snk")>
 9:
10: namespace MyInteropExample
11:
12:    public interface HelloInterface
13:
14:       Function GetUsefulResult() as string
```

**LISTING 17.5**   continued

```
15:
16:    End Interface
17:
18:    <ClassInterface(ClassInterfaceType.None)> _
19:    public class HelloImplementation
20:        Implements HelloInterface
21:
22:      Public Function GetUsefulResult() as string _
23:          implements HelloInterface.GetUsefulResult
24:
25:        return "Here is something useful..."
26:
27:      End Function
28:    End Class
29: End Namespace
```

**ANALYSIS**   Listing 17.5 uses two new attributes. The first, on Line 8, instructs the compiler to sign this assembly with the specified public/private key pair file. The second, on Line 18, is necessary only because we are going to use this program from ASP. Notice that lines 18 and 19 are actually one line, split for readability. The `ClassInterface` attribute modifies how the COM Callable Wrapper is generated. Using the `ClassInterfaceType.None` setting ensures that clients using late binding, such as VBScript and other scripting languages, can use this component.

Lines 12–16 declare the public interface that legacy applications will see when using this class. Lines 18–27 define an implementation for the public interface. Clients will use this implementation class when invoking the object.

To prepare Listing 17.5 for use by ASP and other legacy applications, follow these steps:

1. Compile the listing (you can find the source code at `www.samspublishing.com`). The code won't compile without the public/private key pair file referenced on Line 7. Create the key pair using the sn.exe tool, as the preceding section explained. You could use a command like the following:

   `sn -k mykey.snk`

2. Register the assembly in the Windows Registry by running the following command from the Visual Studio command prompt:

   `regasm HelloUtility.dll /tlb:HelloUtility.tlb`

   The regasm.exe tool registers a .NET assembly as though it were a COM component. The `/tlb` option makes the utility generate a type library in addition to registering the component. The Registry will contain a reference to the .NET runtime, instead of directly to your assembly. The .NET runtime will create the proxy object for the assembly.

3. Add the HelloUtility.dll assembly to the GAC by using the following line:

```
gacutil /i HelloUtility.dll
```

This line allows .NET to find your assembly so that it can create the proxy object for the legacy application.

4. Every time you change and recompile your program, repeat steps 2 and 3.

Now that we've prepared the .NET class, let's write an ASP page to use it. Listing 17.6 shows an ASP page that calls the HelloUtility component.

**LISTING 17.6**  CallNet.asp: A Legacy Program That Calls a .NET Component

```
<%
  set obj = createobject("MyInteropExample.HelloImplementation")
  Response.Write obj.GetUsefulResult
  set obj = nothing
%>
```

Listing 17.6 is a standard snippet of ASP code that invokes a COM object. Now that you've gone through the necessary steps to expose the .NET component, you can see that writing client code is simple.

# Summary

Today's lesson explained many of the issues surrounding the use of legacy code in your .NET applications. The first section showed an example that moved data from ASP sessions into ASP.NET sessions. You can use an example like this in your own applications if you need to share session state.

The second section in today's lesson gave an example using a legacy COM object in a Web form. You saw how to create Runtime Callable Wrappers using Visual Studio for any COM object and how to use the wrapper in .NET code. The section also explained the importance of the Dispose method.

The last section in today's lesson explained how to create .NET assemblies that you can use in legacy applications. Using .NET this way can make the transition to this new technology a more practical endeavor. You saw how the Global Assembly Cache enables any legacy application to use a .NET assembly.

# Q&A

**Q Where can I find out more information about COM+, and using COM+ in .NET applications?**

**A** The System.EnterpriseServices namespace contains all the .NET support for COM+. Dan Fox's book *Building Distributed Applications with Visual Basic .NET* (Sams Publishing, ISBN 0-672-32130-0) provides an in-depth look at COM+ and .NET.

**Q What are the advantages to porting my COM objects to .NET, if I can simply use them as is in Web forms and Web Services?**

**A** There are several advantages to "pure" .NET code:

- .NET offers many new features that legacy COM objects may not have taken advantage of.

- Deployment becomes a much simpler task if all project code is written using managed .NET code. Day 20 will explore this issue in detail.

- Many COM components, especially those written in Visual Basic 6.0 and earlier, use COM single-threaded apartments (STA). Using these components in Web forms and Web Services can limit an application's performance.

- Any COM objects used by a .NET application must go through the runtime callable wrapper (RCW), which slows performance.

# Workshop

The Workshop provides quiz questions to help you solidify your understanding of the material covered today as well as exercises to give you experience using what you've learned. Try to understand the quiz and exercise, before continuing to tomorrow's lesson. Answers are provided in Appendix A, "Answers to Quizzes and Exercises."

## Quiz

1. Can ASP.NET be used with ASP? Are there any problems when using the two technologies together?

2. What's the name of the proxy used to call COM objects in .NET applications.

3. How can you generate a Runtime Callable Wrapper for a COM object?

4. What is the Dispose method, and why is it used?

5. What is the Global Assembly Cache?

6. Why must public assemblies by signed?

7. What cryptographic technology do assemblies use for signing?

8. What utility can you use to generate your own public and private keys?

9. What tool registers assemblies so that legacy applications can use them?

## Exercises

1. Create a COM object by using Visual Studio 6.0 and use the object from a Web form.

2. Add a method to the HelloUtility.vb sample that returns an XmlDocument object. Explore how this object can be used from legacy code.

# WEEK 3

# DAY 18

# Configuring Internet Applications

Today's lesson covers the many different configuration options available to you when creating ASP.NET applications or Web Services. By modifying the built-in configuration files that ASP.NET provides, you can customize many different aspects of your Web application. You will probably configure your Web application in at least two different ways, depending on whether the application is in development or is about to be deployed into a production environment. ASP.NET allows you to change your application's behavior easily by using simple XML files that you can copy into your application directories.

ASP.NET uses a special file, web.config, to store configuration options in XML format. You already saw a glimpse of web.config on Day 3, "Using Web Forms," when we described some simple options that you can use with your Web application. Today we will cover in detail the different options available to you with the web.config file.

Today you will learn how to configure the following areas of your Internet application:

- Tracing and debugging to simplify development
- Compilation options for your ASP.NET pages and services
- Error handling for ASP.NET pages, to give your site a professional look
- Session state, including how to store sessions in a separate process
- ASP.NET process configuration, including how to fine-tune ASP.NET
- Custom configuration sections that you can use in your own code

# XML and the Web.Config File

ASP.NET uses the web.config file to control specific options for Web applications and Web Services. This file contains all the settings the applications use. Each ASP.NET Web application on a Web server can contain different configuration options because each application can contain its own unique web.config file. In fact, every directory within an ASP.NET Web application or Web Service can contain a web.config file, which allows you to apply different configuration options within a single application.

The web.config file is structured in an XML format. The root node of the web.config file is called configuration. Beneath this node are several different child nodes that control different aspects of ASP.NET and your application. The following shows a sample web.config file:

```
<configuration>
  <system.web>
    <compilation defaultLanguage="vb" />
  </system.web>
</configuration>
```

**Tip**

web.config files use XML, which is case sensitive. This means that each element, attribute, and value in the web.config file is case sensitive.

Storing configuration data using XML format offers several advantages when you are developing ASP.NET applications and services:

- The configuration files are easy to read and modify.
- Most importantly, web.config files are easy to manage if your Web site is being hosted by a third party. You can simply FTP a new configuration file to the remote site whenever you need to make a configuration change. Whenever ASP.NET

detects a new or modified web.config file, it automatically restarts the corresponding Web application or service. This saves you from having to restart IIS or reboot the remote Web server.

> **Tip**   Whenever you change an application's web.config file, ASP.NET restarts that application. This means that all ASP.NET sessions for the application will be deleted. We will explore two methods for preserving session state between restarts later today.

Many configuration file settings can be changed within each subdirectory of a Web application or service; to do so, you use a modified web.config file within the subdirectory. For instance, you might disable session state within one or more subdirectories of your application. Each web.config file in a subdirectory overrides the settings in the one above. You don't have to duplicate each configuration file to make this work; you need to include changes only in the new web.config file in the child directory. All settings not explicitly set in the subdirectory default to whatever is set in the parent directory's web.config file.

You might be wondering where the default settings for the web.config file in the root Web application directory come from. The default configurations come from a file called machine.config, which is stored in the system directory where the .NET Framework is installed. (Usually, the location is something like C:\winnt\Microsoft.net\\*Version*\machine.config.)

# Examining Configuration Files

As the example in the preceding section showed, the root node of each web.config file is called `configuration`. Within the `configuration` node, most modifications that you will make fall under the `system.web` child node. You can add custom configuration nodes; they are put outside the `system.web` node. We'll explore custom configuration later today.

**NEW TERM**   Within the `system.web` node, ASP.NET uses configuration *sections*. Sections are XML elements that contain configuration information for a particular area of ASP.NET, such as compilation or globalization options. Listing 18.1 shows a sample web.config file with these sections.

**18**

**LISTING 18.1**   web.config: Top-Level XML Nodes

```
<configuration>
  <system.web>
    <compilation>
      <!-- XML elements that define how compilation should work -->
    </compilation>
    <globalization>
      <!-- XML elements that define how globalization should work -->
    </globalization>
    <!-- More sections -->
  </system.web>
</configuration>
```

Each section can contain child XML elements and attributes that further specify how a particular part of ASP.NET should work for an application.

Table 18.1 shows the web.config sections that we'll cover today. Several other sections in the web.config file are used for security settings and advanced configuration. We'll cover many of the security sections, such as the authentication, authorization, and identity sections, in tomorrow's lesson. The remaining sections, such as `httpHandlers` and `httpModules`, can be used to configure advanced page handling code; they are beyond the scope of this book.

**TABLE 18.1**   web.config Sections Covered in Today's Lesson

| Section | Description |
|---------|-------------|
| appSettings | Defines custom configuration information for your application. You create the entries in this section that your application reads. |
| compilation | Controls how the application is compiled, including debugging options. |
| customErrors | Defines pages to which the user should be redirected when specific errors occur. |
| pages | Customizes the behavior of ASP.NET for specific Web pages. You can configure session and compilations settings here. |
| processModel | Controls the ASP.NET process itself. Allows you to control when ASP.NET should restart itself. |
| sessionState | Controls where and how ASP.NET sessions are tracked. Allows you to store sessions on another computer or in a SQL Server database. |
| trace | Allows you to enable tracing for ASP.NET pages. |

# Adding Tracing and Debugging

Adding tracing and debugging to your Web application and service is very helpful during the development process. As you are no doubt aware at this point, ASP.NET Web pages show debugging information inside the page. You also can use Visual Studio.NET to step through methods in your code behind files or Web Service files. By using the web.config file, you can turn on tracing and debugging applicationwide or in the application's subfolders.

To debug an individual page, you can set the Debug attribute of the Page directive, as the following line shows:

```
<%@ Page Debug="True" %>
```

Adding this directive to the top of every page can be cumbersome, especially if your application contains many pages. A better idea is to use the web.config file to configure debugging. You do so in the compilation section. The following sample configuration file turns on debugging for the entire application. This flag sets the compilation mode for both ASP.NET pages and Web Services.

```
<configuration>
  <system.web>
    <compilation debug="true" />
  </system.web>
</configuration>
```

>
> **Tip**
>
> If you try to start an ASP.NET application from Visual Studio .NET in debug mode by choosing Start from the Debug menu and the debug flag isn't set within the web.config file, you get an error message similar to Figure 18.1. This error message tells you to set the debug attribute of the compilation section as in the preceding example.

**FIGURE 18.1**

*Visual Studio .NET error message when debugging hasn't been set correctly in the web.config file.*

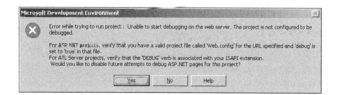

The compilation section controls many other important aspects determining how the ASP.NET pages and Web Services are compiled. For example, it controls common namespaces and assemblies to be included and the default language that each file is written in. We'll explore these options in the next section.

## Adding Tracing to ASP.NET Pages

The trace section of the web.config file adds ASP.NET built-in tracing features to your pages. After you enable tracing, ASP.NET prints a number of statistics for a page, including performance measures, cookie information, and HTTP headers. Figure 18.2 shows a sample page that uses the ASP.NET tracing features.

**FIGURE 18.2**

*A sample ASP.NET page rendered using the built-in ASP.NET tracing features.*

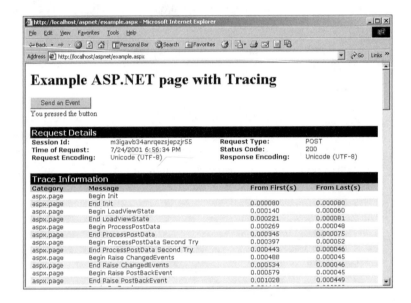

You can add tracing to a single page by using the Trace flag within the Page directive, as the following line shows:

```
<%@ Page Trace="True" %>
```

By using the web.config file, you can set up tracing applicationwide. Also, using the web.config file gives you finer grained control over tracing. For instance, you can set ASP.NET to show tracing only on the local computer; remote requests won't see and trace output by using the pageOutput attribute. As an example, the following web.config file configures tracing:

```
<configuration>
  <system.web>
    <trace enabled="true" localOnly="true"/>
  </system.web>
</configuration>
```

Table 18.2 shows the entire list of tracing options available to you in the web.config file. Set each option as attributes within the trace node.

**TABLE 18.2**  Tracing Options for ASP.NET Pages

| Option | Description |
| --- | --- |
| enabled | Set to `true` to enable tracing, `false` to disable tracing. |
| requestLimit | Set this option to the maximum number of trace output listings to store on the Web server. Defaults to 10. |
| localOnly | Set to `true` to make tracing appear on local browsers only. |
| traceMode | Can be set to `SortByTime` or `SortByCategory`. You can create custom categories for tracing output. |
| pageOutput | Set to `false` if you don't want tracing output sent to the default tracing page. |

The `pageOutput` attribute (the last entry of Table 18.2) allows you to direct all tracing output to a special page, called trace.axd. If `pageOutput` is set to `false`, all tracing messages are appended to the trace.axd page. This page resides in the same directory containing the web.config file. Normally, this page contains tracing output for the last 10 page requests. You can change this number by setting the `requestLimit` attribute of the `trace` section to a different value.

# Customizing Project Compilation

In addition to debugging settings, the `compilation` section of the web.config file contains entries for other features, including the default language to use when compiling pages and adding default references and assemblies.

Many code examples in this book set the `Language` option to Visual Basic inside the `Page` directive, such as in the following code line:

```
<%@ Page Language="vb" %>
```

Writing this directive is tedious when you're creating many pages. You can set the default language for all ASP.NET files, code behind files, and global files by using the `defaultLanguage` option in the `<compilation>` tag, as the following code demonstrates:

```
<configuration>
  <system.web>
    <compilation defaultLanguage="vb" />
  </system.web>
</configuration>
```

## Adding References

In large applications, many pages may include the same .NET Framework namespace, such as `System.Collections`. You can use the web.config file to automatically include such a namespace in every application file by using the `<namespaces>` tag inside the `<compilation>` tag, as the following shows:

```
<configuration>
  <system.web>
    <compilation>
      <namespaces>
        <namespace add="System.Collections" />
      </namespaces>
    </compilation>
  </system.web>
</configuration>
```

Adding references this way saves you from repeatedly adding Imports statements to your source files.

## Adding Assemblies

When creating a Web application, you may have written a utility class, such as an error logging class, that you compiled into an assembly. Often you may want to give every other class in the project access to this assembly by default. You can configure this access with the web.config file by using the `<assemblies>` tag, as the following shows:

```
<configuration>
  <system.web>
    <compilation>
      <assemblies>
        <assembly add="Logger" />
      </assembly>
    </compilation>
  </system.web>
</configuration>
```

Notice that the assembly name here is *not* a filename. In this example, the actual file for the Logger assembly is called Logger.dll and is stored in the bin subdirectory of the ASP.NET application.

> In most cases, any assembly that you use in your ASP.NET application must reside in the bin subdirectory. The only exception is shared assemblies, which can be placed anywhere. Day 17, "Using Legacy Code with .NET," covered shared assemblies.

# Adding Error Handling to ASP.NET Pages

To give your Web site a professional finish, you might want to write custom code to handle ASP.NET errors. When you create a custom error handling page, any unhandled exceptions or compilation errors are displayed using the custom error page. For production Web sites, adding this type of page allows you to put a nicer finish on an undesirable situation. Rather than show your users an ugly message such as Unhandled exception in MyApplication.MyMethod, you can direct them to an error page informing them that the system has experienced a temporary error and will soon be fixed. You can also use your custom error handling page to log all errors internally.

To set up your custom error handling page or pages, use the customErrors section of the web.config file. Listing 18.2 shows a sample web.config file, and Listing 18.3 shows a sample page that could be used to handle errors.

LISTING 18.2   Configuring Your Application to Use a Custom Error Page

```
1: <configuration>
2:   <system.web>
3:     <customErrors defaultRedirect="/globalerror.aspx" mode="RemoteOnly">
4:     </customErrors>
5:   </system.web>
6: </configuration>
```

**ANALYSIS**   Listing 18.2 uses the mode and defaultRedirect attributes (Line 3). The defaultRedirect flag species an URL where all errors should be redirected. The mode flag sends all requests that aren't from the local Web server to the custom error page. If you want to redirect all errors, even from a Web server's local browser to the custom error page, you can remove this flag.

**18**

LISTING 18.3   globalerror.aspx: Some Basic Error Handling Code

```
 1: <%@ Page language="vb" %>
 2: <%@ Import Namespace="System.Diagnostics" %>
 3: <html>
 4:   <body>
 5:     <h2>
 6:       We're sorry, there was an internal error in the application
 7:     </h2>
 8:     The problem has been recorded, and the system administrators have
 9:     been notified. Please try again later.
10:   </body>
11: </html>
12: <script runat="server">
13: sub Page_Load(sender as object, e as System.EventArgs)
14:
15:   dim el as new EventLog()
16:   el.Source = "Application"
17:   el.WriteEntry("Unexpected error at " & DateTime.Now & _
```

**LISTING 18.3** continued

```
18:                          " from " & Request.QueryString("aspxerrorpath"))
19:
20: end sub
21: </script>
```

 **ANALYSIS** Listing 18.3 logs the time and page that was at fault to the event log inside the Page_Load method (Lines 13–20). So far, no lessons have used the EventLog class (Line 15). You can use the EventLog class to log errors to the Windows event log. In this example, we log errors to the Application log, one of the built-in Windows event logs. The only error information passed to the error page is the aspxerrorpath variable (Line 18), which contains the path to the offending page.

> **Tip**
>
> Use custom error logging for production Web sites. For development, using the built-in ASP.NET error logging pages is often useful because they show the offending code lines.

Setting up error handling in using the customErrors section will influence only the way that ASP.NET page errors and your custom code errors are handled. These errors are different from HTTP errors, such as the 404 not found error shown in Figure 18.3. You must configure Internet Information Server (IIS) to change the way these errors are handled.

**FIGURE 18.3**

*Error page generated by Internet Information Server when a page isn't found.*

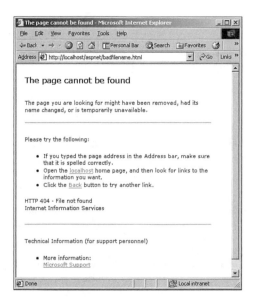

You can configure HTTP errors generated by IIS by following these steps:

1. Open the Internet Information Server Manager.

2. Select the virtual directory containing your application.

3. Right-click and select Properties.

4. On the properties dialog that appears, select the Custom Errors tab, as in Figure 18.4.

**FIGURE 18.4**

*The Custom Errors tab within the Internet Information Server Manager.*

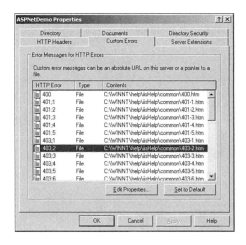

5. Double-click any error listed. You can select a new HTML file to display for each one.

# Configuring Session State

On Day 3 we explored the ASP.NET Session object, which is used for storing per-user state data for Web pages. Today's lesson will detail the many different session options available to you. They include the ability to disable cookies, change the default session timeout, and store session state on another computer or in a database.

## Changing Session Timeout

ASP.NET sessions expire after 20 minutes of user inactivity. You may want to change this timeout value if your site experiences a lot of short-lived traffic. To change this value, use a web.config file similar to the following:

```
<configuration>
  <system.web>
    <sessionState timeout="5" />
  </system.web>
</configuration>
```

You can also disable sessions altogether by using a web.config file similar to the following:

```
<configuration>
  <system.web>
    <sessionState mode="Off" />
  </system.web>
</configuration>
```

Of course, you can customize session preferences at the directory level. For instance, your Web site may have a subdirectory that contains searching features. You may want to disable session state for the search feature; in this case, just copy the preceding file into this subdirectory.

## Disabling Cookies

Sessions and the data they contain are stored on the Web server by default. Normally, ASP.NET creates a cookie on the client machine to contain a randomly generated reference key. Every time the user hits an ASP.NET page, this reference key is used to look up session information on the Web server. Because the reference key is a very large randomly generated value, the odds of a malicious user being able to create a session with a fake key are very low.

If you are making a Web site that can't rely on cookies, you can still use sessions. To do so, you must use "cookieless" sessions, which work by storing the reference key for the user's session in the URL for each page. This process is called *URL munging*, as you learned on Day 16, "Putting It All Together with Web Services." Figure 18.5 shows a sample page with a typical munged URL used with cookieless sessions.

**FIGURE 18.5**

*An ASP.NET page with a munged URL that uses cookieless sessions.*

The URL for the page in Figure 18.5 contains a random string; this is the session key. Users don't have to type in the session key every time they use the Web page. Instead, they enter the normal URL into their browser, and ASP.NET automatically redirects them to the munged URL for the page.

To configure cookieless sessions, use a web.config file similar to the following:

```
<configuration>
  <system.web>
```

```
      <sessionState cookieless="true" />
    </system.web>
</configuration>
```

## Storing Sessions in the State Server

 **Caution**     This section and the next ("Storing Sessions in a SQL Server Database") will work only if you are using the Windows NT/2000/XP operating systems in your development. These sections do not apply to Windows 98 or ME.

Whenever you change the web.config file, ASP.NET restarts your Web application or Web Service. This restart includes deleting all active sessions. However, you can preserve session state through application restart by storing sessions in the ASP.NET State Server. The State Server is a Windows service application that keeps track of all session data independently of the ASP.NET process.

To use the ASP.NET State Server, you must start the Windows service called ASP.NET State, using the Computer Management utility. After you start it, use a web.config file similar to Listing 18.4 to use the State Server.

**LISTING 18.4**   Configuring ASP.NET to Use the State Server

```
1: <configuration>
2:   <system.web>
3:     <sessionState mode="StateServer"
4:                   stateConnectionString="tcpip=127.0.0.1:42424" />
5:   </system.web>
6: </configuration>
```

**ANALYSIS**    Listing 18.4 sets the mode flag to StateServer (Line 3) to force ASP.NET to use the State Server for the current application. You must also specify a connection string for the State Server; in this case, we use a connection string for the local computer (Line 4).

The connection string allows you to specify an IP address and TCP/IP port for the State Server. By changing the IP address to the name or number of a different computer, you can use a remote computer to store ASP.NET sessions. To make this work, you must start the ASP.NET State service on the remote computer.

**NEW TERM**    Although it's beyond the scope of this book, storing ASP.NET sessions in a remote computer is a useful technique for implementing a Web farm. A *Web farm* is a set of two or more computers, each running a Web server. Normally, all computers

18

in the farm contain identical content. This makes a Web site more reliable; if one server experiences a hardware problem or software bug, other computers in the farm can take over and service requests. The Web site also can service more requests this way because each Web request can be distributed among all the servers in the farm. To properly implement a Web farm, you need a way to share Internet requests among multiple machines; this is called *load balancing*. Windows 2000 Advanced Server contains built-in load-balancing software. Configuring a Web farm is an advanced topic. See *Deploying and Managing Microsoft .NET Web Farms* by Barry Bloom (Sams Publishing, ISBN 0-672-32057-6) for an excellent explanation of the topic.

## Storing Sessions in a SQL Server Database

Another advanced option available with ASP.NET is the ability to store sessions in a SQL Server 7.0/2000 database. Storing user sessions in a database makes a Web site even more reliable than using a remote State Server because sessions can then survive computer power failures and reboots.

To store sessions in a SQL Server database, you must follow these steps:

1. Find the installation script called InstallSqlState.sql. It should be located in the directory where the .NET Framework is installed. A typical path would be c:\winnt\Microsoft.Net\Framework\\*Version*.

2. Using the SQL Query Analyzer tool, run the InstallSqlState.sql script.

3. Configure your web.config file similar to Listing 18.5.

**LISTING 18.5**    Using SQL Server to Store User Sessions

```
1: <configuration>
2:   <system.web>
3:    <sessionState mode="SQLServer"
4:                  sqlConnectionString="data source=localhost;uid=sa;pwd=;" />
6:   </system.web>
7: </configuration>
```

**ANALYSIS**    To use SQL Server for user sessions, you must set the mode (Line 3) and sqlConnectionString (Lines 4–5). You can change the sqlConnectionString to suit your own database configuration, including setting the data source property to the name of a remote SQL server. You certainly won't want to use a blank password, as this example does.

# Configuring the ASP.NET Process

**NEW TERM** ASP.NET contains a new feature called *process recycling*, which means that ASP.NET will restart itself when certain conditions are met. You can think of process recycling as extra insurance against program bugs. Although you may never write software that runs in an infinite loop or gobbles up all free memory, other developers may do so. By configuring ASP.NET process recycling, you can force ASP.NET to start with a clean slate if one of the undesirable situations just mentioned occurs.

ASP.NET can be triggered when any or all of the following events take place:

- A user-specified amount of time has passed.
- The Web site has been inactive for a certain amount of time.
- A specified number of hits has taken place.
- ASP.NET's memory consumption has passed a certain threshold.
- The number of unserviced page hits has grown past a limit.

To force ASP.NET to restart every 24 hours, use a web.config file similar to the following:

```
<configuration>
  <system.web>
    <processModel enable="true" timeout="1440" />
  </system.web>
</configuration>
```

In addition to the `timeout` flag, the `<processModel>` section contains several related attributes, as listed in Table 18.3.

**TABLE 18.3**  Frequently Used Process Recycling Attributes

| Attribute | Description |
| --- | --- |
| timeout | Indicates the number of minutes between restarts |
| idleTimeout | Forces ASP.NET to restart after this many minutes of inactivity |
| requestLimit | Forces ASP.NET to shut down after this many requests |
| requestQueueLimit | Forces ASP.NET to shut down after this number of unserviced paged requests |
| memoryLimit | Forces ASP.NET to shut down after this percentage of system memory is consumed by the ASP.NET process |
| enable | Set to `true` to enable process recycling |

18

Tomorrow's lesson on security will explain how to change the Windows account that ASP.NET runs as.

# Configuring ASP.NET Pages

The last ASP.NET configuration section that we'll discuss today concerns page-specific configuration using the pages section handler. This section handler allows you to disable user sessions and ViewState for each directory within your application.

Recall from Day 4, "Working with Web Controls," that each ASP.NET Web control saves its state into a hidden field on each page, called ViewState. Although this feature makes programming with Web controls easy, it can make ASP.NET pages perform more slowly because all the state information for each control is transmitted from the client browser to the Web server on every page request or postback.

You can disable ViewState on a per-control basis by setting the EnableViewState property to false within a control. For instance, the following lines show an ASP.NET DataGrid control with ViewState disabled:

```
<asp:DataGrid runat="server"
              EnableViewState="false"
              DataSource="MyDataView" />
```

Rather than mark each control's EnableViewState property to false, you can use a web.config file similar to the following:

```
<configuration>
  <system.web>
    <pages enableViewState="false"
          enableSessionState="false" />
  </system.web>
</configuration>
```

This file also disables sessions for the pages within its directory.

# Adding Custom Configuration Sections

In addition to specific ASP.NET configuration, you can create your own configuration entries within the web.config file. By moving all configuration data for your Web application or Web Service into the web.config file, you can create a centralized location for all configuration data. Centralizing your configuration data this way will make this information easy to manage. Storing custom configuration data in the web.config file also makes deploying your Web application onto another server a much easier task: Simply copy all web.config files, along with any page and user control files.

You can add your own configuration data using the `appSettings` node inside the web.config file. Listing 18.6 shows an example that contains login credentials for a database.

**LISTING 18.6** Adding Custom Configuration Settings to the web.config File

```
<configuration>
  <appSettings>
    <add key="DatabaseLoginID" value="ASPUser"/>
    <add key="DatabaseLoginPassword" value="secret"/>
  </appSettings>
</configuration>
```

To read custom configuration settings, use the `ConfigurationSettings` class, which is contained in the `System.Configuration` namespace. Listing 18.7 shows an ASP.NET page that will read the configuration file in Listing 18.6.

**LISTING 18.7** ReadSettings.aspx: Reading Custom Configuration Settings from the web.config File

```
 1: <%@ Page Language = "vb" %>
 2: <%@ Import NameSpace = "System.Configuration" %>
 3:
 4: <script runat="server">
 5: sub Page_Load(Sender as Object, e as EventArgs)
 6:
 7:   dim DatabaseID as String = _
 8:       ConfigurationSettings.AppSettings("DatabaseLoginID")
 9:   dim DatabasePwd as string = _
10:       ConfigurationSettings.AppSettings("DatabaseLoginPassword")
11:
12:   LoginLabel.Text = DatabaseID
13:   PasWdLabel.Text = DatabasePwd
14:
15: end sub
16: </script>
17:
18: <html>
19: <body>
20:
21: <h3>Reading configuration settings</h3>
22: Read the following values from web.config: <br><br>
23: Login ID = <asp:Label runat="server" id="LoginLabel"/> <br>
24: Login Password = <asp:Label runat="server" id="PasWdLabel" />
25:
26: </body>
27: </html>
```

**18**

**ANALYSIS** Listing 18.7 includes the System.Configuration namespace (Line 2) using the Import directive. The code then uses the AppSettings collection from the ConfigurationSettings class to access the values stored inside the web.config file (Lines 7–10). After reading the values, the listing stores them in Label controls (Lines 12 and 13).

> **Tip**
>
> Storing configuration information in the AppSettings section of an XML configuration file is a general method that you can implement in all .NET programs. If your application is named SuperApp.exe, you can create a custom configuration file called SuperApp.config and read the contents using the same method in Listing 18.7.

> **Note**
>
> You can store private configuration data inside any web.config file. ASP.NET will block any requests to read the web.config file directly from a Web browser.

# Summary

Today's lesson surveyed many of the important configuration options available under ASP.NET for Web pages and Web Services. Today you learned about the XML format of the web.config file and how you can use it to change the behavior of an ASP.NET application. Different web.config files can be stored inside each directory in an Internet application, allowing you a great deal of flexibility in your application configuration. Each web.config file in a subdirectory supplements the configuration file in parent directories, with the machine.config file holding all default configuration information.

Today you also explored debugging and tracing settings, compilation settings, and custom error handling pages. You also saw how to configure user sessions in ASP.NET, using cookieless sessions and the ASP.NET State Server. The ASP.NET process can be configured to recycle itself after certain conditions have been met, allowing you to compensate for bugs that creep into an application from time to time. Last, you saw how to add your own configuration settings into the web.config file.

We covered quite a bit of information today. Please test yourself using the following Q&A and Workshop sections. After doing so, you should be comfortable configuring your own ASP.NET application.

# Q&A

**Q** **Can malicious users read my configuration files and find out confidential information about my Web site?**

**A** No. ASP.NET blocks all HTTP requests for the web.config file. However, if you choose to store your custom configuration information in different files, you must be certain that others can't see these files. Using the web.config file is the recommended way to store configuration information.

**Q** **I want to make sure the user session information is persisted, even when I restart my Web server. How can I do that?**

**A** You can accomplish this goal easily by using the ASP.NET State Server. See the section "Configuring Session State" for complete details.

**Q** **The web.config file is fine, but I prefer placing application settings into the Windows Registry. Why shouldn't I place them there?**

**A** You can certainly read and write any information that you want into the Windows Registry. However, storing information in the web.config file makes deployment from development computers to production servers an easier task.

**Q** **I keep having problems making configuration settings in my own web.config files. For instance, I see errors like `Unrecognized Configuration Section` and `Unrecognized Attribute` when I try to view my pages. What's going on here?**

**A** Remember that the web.config file is case sensitive. Errors like these usually occur when a section doesn't have the proper capitalization or is spelled incorrectly.

18

# Workshop

The Workshop provides quiz questions to help you solidify your understanding of the material covered and exercises to provide you with experience in using what you've learned. The answers to the quiz questions and exercises are provided in Appendix A, "Answers to Quizzes and Exercises."

## Quiz

1. How do you turn debugging on for an entire Web application or Web Service?

2. What's an easy way to find performance figures of ASP.NET Web pages?

3. What's the easiest way to include a .NET Framework namespace in every source file in a Web application or Web Service?

4. How can you direct all ASP.NET compilation errors to a custom page so that Web site users aren't exposed to the details of your application?

5. How can you use ASP.NET sessions without using cookies?

6. How do you override settings for a web.config file in a subdirectory of a Web application?

7. What sections do you use to create your own custom configuration settings in the web.config file?

8. How can you configure ASP.NET to restart if its CPU utilization climbs above 80%?

## Exercises

1. Create a web.config file that uses cookieless sessions with an expiration time of 5 minutes. Also, make the web.config file set the default compilation language to Visual Basic.

2. Create a Web application that contains two subdirectories, one of which doesn't use sessions or Web control ViewState.

# DAY 19

# Securing Internet Applications

Security is one of the most important aspects of any Web application or Web Service. Your application must be secure from the attacks of malicious users. Unfortunately, enforcing security in an Internet application is a difficult undertaking; security is a complex topic. When tackling security issues, you often delve into areas outside your normal software development skills. Also, Internet standards are open to the public. This means that virtually anyone can try to compromise your application.

Today's lesson will focus on the fundamental aspects of security in .NET Internet applications. At the day's end, you will have a grasp of the most important security issues surrounding your Internet applications. This lesson is divided into three main sections:

- You will learn some fundamental concepts of network security.
- We will explain the actions that you can take to enforce security in an ASP.NET application.
- We will explain code access security in the .NET Framework and how it applies to your own Internet applications.

More specifically, today you will learn about the following:

- Fundamental security concepts
- Network security, including dealing with denial of service attacks
- How to encrypt all network traffic to and from your Web application
- .NET authentication and authorization schemes
- How impersonation works
- Code access security

Today's lesson is a little longer than many of the others, because security is such an important topic. After you master today's concepts, you should be well on your way to creating secure Web applications and Web Services. Today's lesson also provides you with enough information so that you understand more advanced security information provided in Microsoft's online documentation and the Visual Studio documentation.

Caution | Almost all security techniques explained today require you to run your Web application or service using Windows NT 4.0/2000/XP or higher. Securing an Internet application using Windows 98/ME is extremely difficult. We recommend that you deploy any of your Internet applications for public use by using the recommended operating systems.

# Understanding Network Security Issues

Any discussion of Web application and Web Service security wouldn't be complete without mentioning common network security issues that occur when you use the Internet. Network security is a very broad topic, and although this section certainly isn't an exhaustive treatment of the subject, it should give you an understanding of some of the fundamental issues involved with Web applications. Network security concerns how malicious users can use the Internet or an intranet to gain access to services that reside on server computers. Internet servers can offer a wide range of services, including Web pages, .NET Web Services, FTP, Telnet, and many more.

Internet servers, and the services they offer, use Transmission Control Protocol/Internet Protocol (TCP/IP) to communicate with client computers. In fact, all Internet-based applications of any kind use TCP/IP to communicate with other computers. TCP/IP is a standard that specifies how messages should be formatted and sent over the different network hardware that makes up the infrastructure of today's Internet.

**NEW TERM** TCP/IP uses *ports* to communicate messages between computers. Ports, in this context, aren't hardware ports; instead, they are mechanisms in networking software that act like a physical port. Each port is numbered between 1 and 65,534. For instance, Web browsers try to open port 80 on Web servers to fetch HTML pages. Web browsers open a second port on the local computer (usually above port 2000) to receive HTML back from Web servers. Other types of communications have their own ports assigned to them, by convention. The process of opening ports for communication between two computers is called creating a *socket*, an abstraction for communicating information between two computers using TCP/IP. After a socket is established, programs can send and receive information by writing and reading to the socket, just as they might do with a local file.

**NEW TERM** TCP/IP ports between 1 and 1024 are sometimes referred to as *well-known ports* because many network services use these ports, and most people agree to use the same port for each service. For instance, FTP services use ports 20 and 21, and Telnet uses port 23.

## Denial of Service Attacks

**NEW TERM** In the past few years, commercial Web sites have suffered a number of *denial of service attacks*. A typical denial of service attack involves connecting one or many rogue client applications to a well-known port, such as port 80 for a Web server. Then, each rogue program sends so much data that the service either crashes or slows down to a crawl. More sophisticated denial of service attacks involve sending bad data, or data that's known to crash a particular Internet service. Your own .NET Web applications and Web Services can be vulnerable to a denial of service attack if a client can send specific bad data that causes your program to crash.

There aren't any sure-fire ways of stopping the first kind of denial of service attack, other than seeking legal action against people who are trying to overload Internet service applications. Most Internet services, such as Internet Information Services (IIS, Microsoft's Web server), have patches that you can install to prevent them from crashing when they receive bad data. Of course, IIS isn't the only Internet service that's vulnerable to denial of service attacks. Virtually any server on any platform—whether it's Linux, UNIX, or VAX—can be attacked this way.

**NEW TERM** The most common way to protect servers that run Internet services is to use a *firewall*. A firewall is either a special hardware device or software program that blocks TCP/IP ports. If a port is blocked, it's invisible to the outside world, making an attack by a malicious user very difficult. As much as your local network administrator would like to, you can't block all ports with a firewall. If you did, you couldn't run Web servers or other Internet services.

19

As a developer, you are probably not responsible for configuring your company's firewall or network architecture. Given this fact, it's your job to secure your Internet application by using an authentication and authorization scheme. The remainder of this lesson will explore security in .NET Internet applications from this standpoint.

# Using HTTPS for Encryption

Before we delve into security fundamentals as they apply to .NET Internet applications, let's explore the area of encryption. Everyone who has used a Web site that requires credit card or other sensitive information, has sent and received Web pages using Secure Hypertext Transfer Protocol (HTTPS).

When you use HTTPS, all data sent from a Web server to a Web browser and back is encrypted using the Secure Sockets Layer (SSL), making eavesdropping nearly impossible. Complete details for the SSL protocol are numerous and complex, as with most security-related topics. However, the process is simple from a high level:

1. The client Web browser and remote Web server's goal is to generate a *session key* that can be used to encrypt communication between them. The session key is a randomly generated string of bytes, long enough so that an outside party can't guess it. When the key is used, all data can be scrambled so that eavesdroppers can't read the data. Of course, both client and server have to be able to trust the session key; if a malicious user intercepts the data between them and creates a fake session key, that person could access sensitive information.

2. To create the session key, the client browser sends a message to the Web server requesting its certificate. The Web server's certificate contains a public key that can be used to encrypt communication. Anyone (including the client browser) can encrypt data with the server's public key. However, only the server can decrypt the data by using its own private key.

> **Note**
>
> Many popular encryption schemes rely on the concept of public and private keys. *Public keys*, made available to anyone, are used to encrypt sensitive information being sent to you. *Private keys*, which only you have, are required to decrypt the coded message.

3. When the client computer has the server certificate, it generates a set of random temporary keys. The client encrypts these keys using the Web server's public key. Only the server can decrypt these temporary keys because only it has the matching private key.

4. The client and server exchange a set of messages using the client's temporary keys and server's public keys until they agree on a random session key that can be used for all future communication.

Of course, this explanation leaves out quite a few details of the process. For a complete treatment, read the SSL Specification at
`http://home.netscape.com/eng/ssl3/draft302.txt`.

## Using Certificates

To use HTTPS, you need to get an SSL certificate for your Web server. Certificate authorities, such as VeriSign or Thawte, issue certificates to business and other organizations. If you don't already have an SSL, you can buy one from a certificate authority. This process necessarily involves your national postal authority to send documentation about your organization, so don't expect to get an SSL certificate immediately.

You can also download temporary SSL certificates for testing purposes only. Most certificate authorities are willing to issue test certificates.

## Configuring a Test Certificate

This section outlines the steps for creating a certificate request and installing the certificate on IIS 5.0. If you're using a different Web server, such as Personal Information Server, you may not be able to use HTTPS. Check the documentation of your Web server to be sure.

One important fact to remember about SSL certificates is that they are bound to a particular machine name, URL, or IP address. This means that a certificate bound to `www.mydomain.com` won't work if the user enters `test.mydomain.com` or even `mydomain.com`.

To generate the certificate request, use the Internet Information Services tool and follow these steps:

1. Open Internet Information Services via the Windows Control Panel (double-click Administrative Tools to find the IIS icon).
2. Select the Default Web Site node in the tree.
3. Right-click the Default Web Site node and select Properties to open the Default Web Site properties dialog box.
4. On the Directory Security page, click the Server Certificate button. The Server Certificate Wizard will appear (see Figure 19.1).

**19**

**FIGURE 19.1**

*The Server Certificate Wizard generates certificate requests and installs new certificates.*

5. Follow the steps in the wizard. Be sure to set the Bit Length field to 1028 in the Name and Security Settings step. Also, carefully enter an URL or IP address associated with the certificate in the Your Site's Common Name step. In the final step, Certificate Request File Name, be sure to put your certificate request in a place that you can find easily in the future.

After the request is generated, you can send the certificate request text file to a certificate authority, usually by copying and pasting the file into a Web site. The certificate authority may issue you a test certificate immediately or e-mail you a file with the test certificate enclosed.

The file will look similar to Listing 19.1.

**LISTING 19.1** A Sample Certificate File Issued from a Certificate Authority

```
-----BEGIN CERTIFICATE-----
VZIIwcNAQElcmlTaWduDQYJKoZIhvLCBJbm/WwzfKwEBQAwgakxFjAUMxRze21aoyT
...
-----END CERTIFICATE-----
```

After you receive a certificate file, you can install the certificate by using the same Server Certificate Wizard that you used to generate the request. You have the option of Processing a Pending Request in the wizard. Simply direct the wizard to the name of the text file containing your certificate.

## Trying Out the Certificate

You can try out the certificate by browsing to an existing page on your Web server using HTTPS, similar to `https://myserver.mypage.com`. If you experience a problem, Microsoft's tech support site contains a number of articles to help. You can reach the site at `http://www.microsoft.com/support`.

# Understanding Security Terms

Configuring HTTPS for your Web server is just the first step in securing your Internet application. To completely secure your site, you must create an authentication and authorization scheme.

 The following terms are essential for understanding and implementing security in your own Web site or Web Service:

- *Authentication* is the process of verifying a user's identity. Simply put, this means checking that the user is who he says he is. The most common way to implement authentication is to give each user a username and password combination that only he knows. You can create your own custom authentication scheme, or you can rely on the built-in support that Windows provides for you. We'll explore each method in the following section.

- *Authorization* is the process of granting permission to an authenticated user. A typical permission that you might grant includes the ability to access a certain part of your application, such as allowing a manager to browse employee records. At a lower level, you might authorize a specific user to make modifications to a table in a database or read certain files. You can manage authorization in .NET in several ways, which will be detailed in the "Understanding Authorization and Impersonation" section later today.

- *Impersonation* is a process in which one program assumes the identity of an authenticated user and then acts on her behalf. Typically, IIS or ASP.NET impersonates a specific user and then accesses a database or the local file system. Impersonation techniques will be illustrated later today in the "Understanding Authorization and Impersonation" section.

- *Security policy* is a set of rules that define how authentication and authorization work. .NET contains tools for managing a computer's security policy. We'll touch on this subject briefly at the end of today's lesson.

Now that the theoretical definitions used in today's lessons are out of the way, let's begin learning how to apply security to Internet programs.

# Understanding Authentication

You can use one of four possible authentication schemes in your .NET Web application. These authentication schemes include Windows, Forms, Passport, and custom authentication. Let's explore each in turn.

**19**

## Windows Authentication

Windows authentication involves creating a new Windows account for each user whom you want to be able to access your Web site or Web Service. Windows authentication doesn't work with Windows 98 or ME; you must use one of the Windows NT–based Windows operating systems, such as Windows NT 4.0, 2000, or XP. After a Windows user is created, you use IIS to verify each user. By using Windows authentication, you are relying on IIS to perform authentication for you.

Within the Windows authentication scheme, IIS uses three distinct flavors of authentication: basic, digest, and integrated. Digest and integrated authentication requires that all users run Internet Explorer. Because this requirement limits the availability of your Web site or service, we won't explore these two options here further. However, you can find detailed information on integrated and digest authentication at http://msdn.microsoft.com.

Basic authentication works on both IE and Netscape, from older to newer versions. Basic authentication works by sending usernames and passwords directly over the Internet without encryption. Sending information this way may seem like a poor choice for security, but you can combine Basic authentication with HTTPS for a highly secure authentication process.

Let's look at how to configure Basic authentication with Windows 2000, IIS, and ASP.NET:

1. Locate a virtual directory that corresponds to an ASP.NET application. If you've been following along with the examples in this book, you will have at least one or two. If not, create a new Web project with Visual Studio .NET.

2. Open the Internet Information Services Manager from the Windows Control Panel (again, double-click Administrative Tools to find the IIS icon).

3. Within the IIS Manager, open the virtual directory that corresponds to your Web application.

4. Right-click the virtual directory and select Properties.

5. In the properties dialog box, select the Directory Security tab at the top (see Figure 19.2).

6. Click the Edit button at the top in the Anonymous Access and Authentication Control section. The Authentication Methods dialog box will appear.

7. Clear the Anonymous Authentication check box to force users browsing to the Web application to authenticate themselves.

8. Select the Basic Authentication check box. A warning dialog box will appear; click Yes to turn on Basic authentication.

9. Clear the Integrated Windows Authentication and Digest Authentication for Windows Domain Servers check boxes, if they are checked. Your dialog box should look like Figure 19.3. Click OK.

10. Click OK in the properties dialog box.

**19**

Try browsing to your Web application. You should be greeted by a dialog box asking you to enter your username and password.

Implementing Basic authentication in combination with HTTPS is a secure option for your Internet application. Because HTTPS requests are encrypted, any usernames and passwords exchanged between browsers and Web servers are safe.

In the "Understanding Authorization and Impersonation" section later today, you will see how to execute your own ASP.NET code as the particular user that logged in using Basic authentication. That section will also show a Web Service and Web client that use Basic authentication.

# Forms Authentication

Forms authentication is similar to Basic authentication, except that the usernames and passwords you use are independent of actual Windows accounts. Forms authentication allows you to configure user accounts and passwords yourself, either by hand or in code. Forms authentication can be used only with ASP.NET Web applications; you can't use Forms authentication with ASP.NET Web Services.

Forms authentication works by storing usernames and passwords into a web.config file. If ASP.NET detects that a user has browsed to any page in your Web application without logging on first, it automatically redirects the user to a login page that you create. With Forms authentication, similar to Basic authentication, you must use HTTPS for your login page; otherwise, usernames and passwords are sent without encryption or "in the clear."

Let's see how to configure Forms authentication by using ASP.NET.

## Step 1: Establishing User Accounts in web.config

You first need to establish one or more user accounts within the web.config file. To do so, use a web.config file similar to Listing 19.2.

**LISTING 19.2**   A web.config File Containing Two Sample Users, Jane and Joe

```
 1: <configuration>
 2:   <system.web>
 3:     <authentication mode="Forms">
 4:       <forms name="MyFormsAuthentication" loginUrl="login.aspx">
 5:         <credentials passwordFormat="Clear">
 6:           <user name="Jane" password="Janespassword" />
 7:           <user name="Joe" password="joespassword" />
 8:         </credentials>
 9:       </forms>
10:     </authentication>
11:     <authorization>
12:       <deny users="?" />
13:     </authorization>
14:   </system.web>
15: </configuration>
```

**ANALYSIS**   Listing 19.2 sets the authentication method for the current virtual directory to Forms using the <authentication> tag and mode attribute in Line 3. Next, the file sets the name of the login page, using the loginUrl attribute in Line 4.

Each sample user is added in the <credentials> element (Lines 5–8). For this example, passwords are stored "in the clear." Passwords can also be stored in encrypted format. In addition, usernames and passwords can be stored in another file or in a database, as described later in this section.

To ensure that all users authenticate themselves, the `<authorization>` section (Lines 11–13) is set to deny access to anonymous users. Notice that the file uses a question mark (Line 12) to single out anonymous users. This forces anonymous users to authenticate by using the login.aspx page.

## Step 2: Creating a Login Page

To implement Forms authentication, you next need to create a login page, such as the login.aspx page declared in Line 4 of Listing 19.2. When creating the login page, you must use the `FormsAuthentication` class to check usernames and passwords.

Listing 19.3 shows a simple login page that you can use with the web.config file from Listing 19.2.

**LISTING 19.3**   Login.aspx: Using the *FormsAuthentication* Class to Authenticate Users

```
 1: <%@ Page language="vb" %>
 2: <html>
 3: <body>
 4: <form runat="server">
 5: Please log in.<br>
 6: Username: <asp:TextBox id="UserName" runat="server"/> <br>
 7: Password: <asp:TextBox id="Password" runat="server"/> <br>
 8: <asp:Button Text="Log in" OnClick="Authenticate" runat="server"/> <br>
 9: <hr>
10: <asp:Label id="Status" runat="server" />
11: </form>
12: </body>
13: </html>
14: <script runat="server">
15: sub Authenticate(Sender as Object, e as EventArgs)
16:
17:   dim UserID as String = UserName.Text
18:   dim PassWd as String = Password.Text
19:   if FormsAuthentication.Authenticate(UserID, PassWd) then
20:     'The user logged in ok
21:     FormsAuthentication.RedirectFromLoginPage(UserID, false)
22:   else
23:     Status.Text = "Unknown username and password combination."
24:   end if
25: end sub
26: </script>
```

**ANALYSIS**   Lines 1–13 contain HTML and ASP.NET code for a simple login screen. The Authenticate button on Line 8 calls the Authenticate method on Line 15 when the user logs in.

19

The `Authenticate` method calls the `FormsAuthentication.Authenticate` method (Line 19) to check the username and password against the entries stored inside the web.config file from Listing 19.2. This method returns `true` if the username and password match an entry in the file.

If the username and password are correct, the Login.aspx file in Listing 19.3 calls the `FormsAuthentication.RedirectFromLoginPage` method (Line 22) to return the user to the original page she hits. If the user started from the login page directly, she is directed to a page named Default.aspx. You must supply this page also.

Try using Listings 19.2 and 19.3 inside one of your own virtual directories. As you can see, implementing Forms authentication is quite simple. Just as you do with Basic authentication, you must use HTTPS to ensure that usernames and passwords can't be intercepted.

The `FormsAuthentication` class contains various other useful methods, as shown in Table 19.1.

**TABLE 19.1**  Commonly Used `FormsAuthentication` Methods

| Method | Purpose |
| --- | --- |
| `Authenticate` | Verifies the supplied username and password against the configuration file |
| `GetRedirectURL` | Gets the URL of the original page that the user hits before being redirected to the login page |
| `HashPasswordForStoringInConfigFile` | Encrypts a password and stores it in the configuration file |
| `RedirectFromLoginPage` | Redirects a user after successfully logging in |
| `SignOut` | Ends a user's session |

If you want to use an XML file or a database table to store usernames and passwords, you must implement the `Authenticate` method with your own custom code and remove the `<credentials>` section from the web.config file because you are keeping track of usernames and passwords yourself.

## Passport Authentication

Passport authentication involves using Microsoft's Passport site to verify users. Microsoft has created an authentication infrastructure that allows anyone with an e-mail account to create his own Passport account. After a user creates a Passport account, she can use her "passport" at any Web site that accepts them, much as real passports are used.

**NEW TERM** Microsoft has termed the combination of passport accounts and Web Services as the *.NET My Services* initiative (previously called *Hailstorm*). This initiative uses Web Services, Passport accounts, and the existing Internet infrastructure so that users can access useful services from anywhere. For instance, a business might create a personal appointments application that allows users to store information about upcoming meetings in a centralized location. One part of the appointment application may involve a Web Service to store and retrieve appointment information. Users could then use mobile devices and their desktop computer to access the appointment service. User authentication would be taken care of by the Microsoft Passport service, which provides an infrastructure that Web sites and Web Services can use to verify a user's credentials. .Net My Services contains a broad vision for integrating Web Services with the rest of the Internet infrastructure. You can read more about the initiative at `www.microsoft.com/net/netmy-services.asp`.

Passport authentication has many desirable properties. Users can (although they aren't required to) enter personal information and preferences, which you can use to gather statistics on your Web site. Implementing passport authentication requires the Passport SDK, and is beyond the scope of this book. However, you can download the Passport SDK at `www.passport.com`. Passport authentication takes away much of the drudgery surrounding the implementation of authentication schemes. Because Microsoft is pledging full support for the service, you can count on Passport having high reliability and availability. Furthermore, using Passport relieves you of the burden of creating and managing authentication services for your Web application or service.

## Custom Authentication

19

Now that you've seen the built-in options for authentication in .NET Web applications, you have a good idea for how authentication should work. If none of the existing schemes fit your needs, consider implementing your own custom authentication schemes. Here are three ideas for implementing your own authentication schemes:

- You may want to store usernames and passwords in a database. Of course, you must make sure that the database itself is secure. Often, ensuring security involves storing the database on a separate computer that's behind a restrictive firewall.

- Windows employs user groups, which allows permissions to be assigned to a group rather than to an individual user. You may want to implement your own scheme for allowing users to be part of groups.

- You may want to leverage the existing security features in Windows, such as file permissions, in your own site. Windows contains a rich security infrastructure; don't reinvent the wheel if you can help it.

# Understanding Authorization and Impersonation

**NEW TERM** — *Authorization* involves restricting or granting rights to users. *Impersonation* occurs when a program, or process, acts with the security credentials of a legal user. Impersonation is a perfectly valid programming technique, often used to simplify security-related code in an application. The most common case of impersonation in ASP.NET Web applications and Web Services involves setting the ASP.NET process to run as a Windows user.

To make the concept more concrete, imagine the following situation. You've configured two special Windows accounts for your Web application, called WebGuest and WebAdmin. Further suppose that you are using Basic authentication in your Web application so that all users must log on as one of these two accounts. Suppose also that your Web application contains a top-level virtual directory called MyApp and a subdirectory called ChangeSite. The top-level directory contains general ASP.NET pages that anyone can browse, and the ChangeSite directory contains ASP.NET pages that configure the main site.

**NEW TERM** — You can set file read *permissions* inside this application's directory so that WebGuests can read all files in the top directory, and WebAdmins can read files in all directories. A file permission allows or disallows particular users from creating, reading, writing, or modifying a particular file.

By using impersonation, ASP.NET can act as the WebGuest account or WebAdmin account, depending on who is visiting the site. When a guest user tries to access the ChangeSite directory (through ASP.NET), Windows will deny access. When an admin user browses to the ChangeSite directory, there will be no access problems.

**NEW TERM** — Using a scenario like this involves ASP.NET impersonation and *file authorization* because you've set read permission on files. Of course, file authorization and impersonation work only using Windows authentication. If you decide to use Forms or Passport authentication, you must use a different method for securing your site. Today's lesson will explain just such an example later in the "Using URL Authorization" section.

## Configuring ASP.NET Impersonation

By default, ASP.NET doesn't impersonate users, even if they have logged on using Basic authentication. Instead, it runs with the identity of the special "anonymous user" account. This account has a name similar to IIS_*COMPUTERNAME*; in my case, it's IIS_SYME2. The anonymous user account is created by IIS during installation and usually has quite limited security rights.

To make ASP.NET impersonate users for a certain application, use a web.config file similar to Listing 19.4.

**LISTING 19.4** Configuring ASP.NET to Impersonate Windows Users

```
<configuration>
  <system.web>
    <identity impersonate="true" />
  </system.web>
</configuration>
```

You can also make ASP.NET impersonate a specific Windows user at all times no matter who has been authenticated by using a file similar to Listing 19.5.

**LISTING 19.5** Configuring ASP.NET to Impersonate a Specific Windows User

```
<configuration>
  <system.web>
    <identity impersonate="true" userName="WebUser" password="secret" />
  </system.web>
</configuration>
```

## Trying Out Impersonation

You might try out ASP.NET impersonation in combination with Windows authentication yourself. To do so, follow these steps:

1. Create a project directory, such as C:\src\security, and a subdirectory called ChangeSite that you will use for special security settings.

2. Create a virtual directory pointing to the project directory created in step 1, such as SecurityApp.

3. Follow the steps in the "Windows Authentication" section earlier today to enable Basic authentication for the SecurityApp virtual directory.

4. Create two special accounts, WebGuest and WebAdmin, on your local computer. In the Windows Control Panel, double-click the Users and Passwords icon. Follow the steps in the Add New User Wizard, making sure that each new account is a Restricted User.

5. Place a new web.config file similar to Listing 19.4 into the project directory.

Now that the application is configured, add two ASP.NET pages to the project, such as those in Listings 19.6 and 19.7. Place the file named Top.aspx in the top-level directory and Special.aspx in the subdirectory.

**19**

**LISTING 19.6**   Top.aspx: A File That All Windows Accounts Can See

```
<%@ page language="vb" %>
<html>
  <body>
    <a href="ChangeSite/Special.aspx">Click here to administer the site</a>
    <br>
    <h2>Here is some text that all users can read</h2>
    Text....
  </body>
</html>
```

**LISTING 19.7**   Special.aspx: Locked Using File Permissions So That Only the WebAdmin Account Can Access It

```
<%@ Page Language="vb" %>
<html>
<body>
  Placeholder for many interesting administrative options...
</body>
</html>
```

Using the Windows Explorer, you can set the permissions to deny the WebGuest account access to the Special.aspx file. To do so, follow these steps:

1. Browse to the ChangeSite project subdirectory that you created in step 1 of the preceding steps. Right-click the Special.aspx file and select Properties.

2. On the Security tab, click the Add button on the upper right. Choose the WebGuest account and click Add.

3. Select all check boxes under the Deny column. Your properties dialog box should now look like Figure 19.4.

4. Repeat step 2, except this time add the WebAdmin account. Leave the default permissions intact and click OK.

Try logging in to the site both as WebAdmin and WebGuest. When using the WebGuest account, you should see an error page denying access after you click the Administer link on the Top.aspx page, similar to Figure 19.5.

As you might imagine, you can apply security this way to other operating system objects and programs, including databases. SQL Server integrates with the Windows security system so that you can configure database tables and stored procedures the same way you would for files. Unfortunately, Access isn't integrated with the Windows security system.

**FIGURE 19.4**

*Disabling access to a file.*

**FIGURE 19.5**

*An access denied error from ASP.NET.*

**19**

# Setting Up URL Authorization

ASP.NET contains two systems for authorizing users: File authorization and URL authorization. File authorization was explained in the preceding section. Remember that File authorization can be used only with Windows authentication.

**NEW TERM** The second authorization system, *URL authorization*, allows you to grant or deny access to URLs in your Web application or Web Service by using the web.config file. URL authorization is used in combination with Forms authentication.

To learn about URL authorization, let's use the Forms authentication examples in today's lessons: Listings 19.2 and 19.3. You already saw a brief glimpse of URL authorization in the web.config file of Listing 19.2. In this example, we used the `<authorization>` section to force all users to log in if they hadn't already. Let's extend the web.config file from Listing 19.2 by allowing only Jane to use the Web application. Listing 19.8 shows the new web.config file.

---

**LISTING 19.8** An Extended web.config File to Allow Access to Only One User

```
 1: <configuration>
 2:   <system.web>
 3:     <authentication mode="Forms">
 4:       <forms name="MyFormsAuthentication" loginUrl="login.aspx">
 5:         <credentials passwordFormat="Clear">
 6:           <user name="Jane" password="janespassword" />
 7:           <user name="Joe" password="joespassword" />
 8:         </credentials>
 9:       </forms>
10:     </authentication>
11:     <authorization>
12:       <allow users="Jane" />
13:       <deny users="*" />
14:     </authorization>
15:   </system.web>
16: </configuration>
```

---

 The file in Listing 19.8 configures Forms authentication (Line 3) and the default login page location (Line 4). The file also adds Jane and Joe as possible users (Lines 5–8).

The file explicitly allows Jane to access the site (Line 12) and denies access to everyone else (Line 13). Notice that the code uses an asterisk character to deny all users.

> **Tip**
>
> By copying web.config files into each subdirectory of your application, you can modify the authorization behavior for the different components of your application.

# Setting Up Authentication for Web Services

All four authentication methods described today work for ASP.NET Web Services. This section will describe Windows and Forms authentication but won't cover Passport authentication.

## Windows Authentication and Web Services

To learn about Windows authentication in combination with Web Services, let's create a simple Web Service that returns a success message when the client calls a test method. Listing 19.9 shows such a simple Web Service. You should install and compile this service for use with later projects in today's lesson.

LISTING **19.9**    StubbedService.asmx: Testing Authentication

```
<%@ WebService Class="Stub.Test" Language="vb" %>
Imports System
Imports System.Web.Services

namespace Stub

  <WebService(Namespace:="http://temuri.org/test")> _
  public class Test
    Inherits WebService

    <WebMethod> _
    public Function TestMethod() as string

      return "Test successful"

    end function
  end class
End Namespace
```

You can create this service by using Visual Studio .NET or by hand using the techniques from previous lessons. If you create the service manually, be sure to place StubbedService.asmx in its own project directory and create a virtual directory that points to it. For the examples that follow, this directory will be called SecurityApp.

The last step you must take is to enable Basic authentication for the virtual directory that contains Listing 19.9. Use the steps in the "Windows Authentication" section earlier today.

## Creating a Secure Client

You can easily create a client that will log on to the Web Service using Basic authentication. At a minimum, you need to add only three lines of code to any client you created previously. Listing 19.10 shows a sample console application client that logs on to the Web Service.

```
1: Imports System
2: Imports System.IO
3: Imports System.Net
4: Imports SecureClient.localhost
5:
6: Module Module1
7:
```

LISTING **19.10**   continued

```
 8: Public Sub Main()
 9:
10:     Try
11:         Dim webServiceClient As New Test()
12:         Dim cred As New NetworkCredential("webGuest", "web*secret!", _
13:             "SYME2")
14:         webServiceClient.Credentials = cred
15:         Dim s As String = webServiceClient.TestMethod()
16:         Console.WriteLine(s)
17:     Catch e As WebException
18:         Console.WriteLine("Could not access the web service.")
19:         Console.WriteLine(e.Message)
20:     End Try
21:     Console.ReadLine()
22:
23: End Sub
24:
25: End Module
```

**ANALYSIS**   Listing 19.10 creates a new instance of a Web Service proxy object (Line 11).
Then the program creates a new NetworkCredential object, using a Windows
username, password, and domain (Lines 12–14). Of course, these settings will change for
your own Windows accounts. On Line 14, the NetworkCredential object is assigned to
the Credentials property of the Web Service proxy.

The file in Listing 19.10 also contains an exception handler (Lines 17–20) that will display any error message associated with accessing the Web Service.

## Using Forms Authentication and Web Services

Using Forms authentication and Web Services will work, but the implementation for
doing so is more than a little convoluted. Forms authentication presupposes a Web
browser as a client, so it stores and transmits authentication information using cookies.
Any program can connect to a Web Service, such as a console application, and not all of
them support cookies. Further compounding the problem, Forms authentication redirects
each user to the standard login ASP.NET page.

The solution to this dilemma is a little roundabout. To solve the problem, you must make
the Web Service accept any incoming anonymous connections, authenticate users manually, and then re-authenticate the user on every method call. Furthermore, you must make
your Web Service open the cookie that the FormsAuthentication class creates and transmit its contents as an authentication "ticket." To summarize, this means the following for
the Web Service:

- A web.config file will allow all anonymous users access to the site without authentication.
- A *Login* method will return the contents of an authentication cookie as a ticket.
- Every other Web method in the Web Service must accept the ticket and re-authenticate the user.

The following are required from the Web Service client:

- The client must call the *Login* method and get an authentication ticket.
- The client must pass the ticket to every method it calls in the Web Service.

Listing 19.11 shows a web.config file that allows all anonymous users, and Listing 19.12 shows a sample Web Service that uses Forms authentication.

**LISTING 19.11**  A web.config File That Allows Anonymous Access to a Web Service

```
<configuration>
  <system.web>
    <authentication mode="Forms">
      <forms name="MyFormsAuthentication" >
        <credentials passwordFormat="Clear">
          <user name="Jane" password="Janespassword" />
        </credentials>
      </forms>
    </authentication>
    <authorization>
      <allow users="?" />
    </authorization>
  </system.web>
</configuration>
```

**19**

**LISTING 19.12**  FormsService.asmx: Allowing Users Forms Authentication

```
 1: <%@ WebService Class="Stub.Test2" Language="vb" %>
 2: Imports System
 3: Imports System.Web
 4: Imports System.Web.Services
 5: Imports System.Web.Security
 6:
 7: namespace Stub
 8:
 9:   <WebService(Namespace:="http:\\temuri.org/test")> _
10:   public class Test2
11:      Inherits WebService
12:
13:     <WebMethod> _
14:     public function Login(UserName as String, Password as String)
```

LISTING **19.12**   continued

```
15:               as String
16:           if FormsAuthentication.Authenticate(UserName, Password) then
17:             dim cookie as HttpCookie = _
18:                 FormsAuthentication.GetAuthCookie(UserName, false)
19:             return cookie.Value
20:           else
21:              return ""
22:           end if
23:
24:       end function
25:
26:       ' Authenticate a user using a Ticket string.
27:       private function Authenticate(Ticket as string) as boolean
28:
29:          dim formticket as FormsAuthenticationTicket
30:          try
31:            formticket = FormsAuthentication.Decrypt(Ticket)
32:          catch e as Exception
33:            return false
34:          end try
35:
36:          if not formticket is nothing then
37:              if not formticket.Expired then
38:                ' other checks here, formticket.Name is the user name
39:                 return true
40:              end if
41:          end if
42:          return false
43:
44:       end function
45:
46:       <WebMethod> _
47:       public function TestMethod(strTicket as String) as String
48:
49:          ' We must authenticate the user inside of every WebMethod
50:          if Authenticate(strTicket) then
51:            return "You executed the method successfully!"
52:          else
53:            return "Not authenticated - please call the Login method."
54:          end if
55:
56:       end function
57:    end class
58: end namespace
```

**ANALYSIS**   Listing 19.12 is one of the most advanced programs in this book. To begin with, the Login method (Lines 14–24) authenticates the user in the standard way, using the Authenticate method (Line 16). Then the method creates a ticket string. It does so by first getting a cookie that contains the ticket string by calling GetAuthCookie (Line 17). It then returns the string using the Value property of the ticket.

The Authenticate method (Lines 27–44) uses the Decrypt method to create an authentication ticket from a ticket string. Then it checks to make sure that the ticket is not null (Line 36) and not expired (Line 37).

The sample method TestMethod (Lines 47–56) calls the Authenticate method (Line 50) to verify every call.

Writing the client for this Web Service is a little more simple. Listing 19.13 shows an example.

**LISTING 19.13** A FormServiceClient.vb: A Console Application Client for the FormsService Web Service

```
 1: Imports System
 2: Imports System.IO
 3: Imports System.Net
 4: Imports FormServiceClient.localhost
 5:
 6: Module Module1
 7:
 8:     Public Sub Main()
 9:
10:         Try
11:             Dim webServiceClient As New Test2()
12:             'Log in and get a ticket
13:             Dim Ticket As String = webServiceClient.Login("Jane", _
14:                 "janespassword")
15:             'Call a web method.  Must use the ticket on every call
16:             Dim Result As String = webServiceClient.TestMethod(Ticket)
17:             Console.WriteLine(Result)
18:         Catch e As WebException
19:             Console.WriteLine("Could not access the web service.")
20:             Console.WriteLine(e.Message)
21:         End Try
22:         Console.ReadLine()
23:
24:     End Sub
25:
26: End Module
```

**ANALYSIS** Listing 19.13 creates a new proxy for the Web Service (Line 11). Then it calls the Login method (Lines 13–14) and gets a ticket string. It then calls TestMethod (Line 16), using the ticket obtained from the Login method.

19

Although the Forms authentication process for Web Services is much uglier than Windows authentication, it's easier to implement than your own custom scheme. Use your own good judgment when selecting an authentication method for your Web Service.

# Summary

Today's lesson covered many of the techniques that you will use to secure your Web application. Early in the lesson, you familiarized yourself with the basic issues of network security, including some techniques used to interfere with Web servers. Next, you learned how to generate a certificate request so that you can encrypt communication using HTTPS and SSL. The rest of the lesson was devoted to authentication, authorization, and impersonation using ASP.NET.

Today you also learned how to authenticate users of your Web site or service using Windows authentication. You saw how to use Forms authentication in a Web site. Today's lesson should have given you enough ideas to help you start designing your own authentication mechanism if you choose to do so.

Today's lesson also covered impersonation, especially as it applies to Windows authentication and ASP.NET. You saw how you can use impersonation in combination with the built-in security features of the Windows operating system to build a secure Web site.

We hope that this lesson will inspire you to read more about security issues. You should have a good foundation for understanding any new security document that you might find.

# Workshop

**Q Hackers keep breaking into my Web site. What can I do about it?**

**A** After reading the section on network security in today's lesson, you should have a starting point for defending against hackers. Explore putting a firewall in place on your network and apply all the latest security patches to your Web server.

**Q No matter how hard I try, I can't seem to get HTTPS and my trial certificate to work with my Web server. What can I do?**

**A** Setting up HTTPS and SSL is tricky, even though IIS provides you with a wizard. Here are some tips:

- Use the Certificates MMC snap-in to manage the certificates for your local machine.

- Use the Windows NT Event Log viewer to check for any error messages that IIS writes.

- Use the Microsoft Knowledge Base at *www.microsoft.com/support* for articles discussing common problems and solutions to them.

**Q I want to use Passport authentication in my own site. Where can I find information about it?**

**A** A number of sites online provide information about setting up Passport authentication, including *www.passport.com* and *msdn.Microsoft.com*. You must download the Passport SDK to use Passport authentication.

# Quiz

1. What is a firewall?
2. What does SSL stand for, and why is it used?
3. What's one difference between Windows authentication and Forms authentication?
4. What is Basic authentication, and why would you use it?
5. Why is it crucial to use HTTPS in combination with Basic authentication?
6. What is impersonation, and why is it used?
7. What's the `NetworkCredential` class used for?
8. What is URL authorization, and can it be used with Windows authentication?
9. *True or False:* When using ASP.NET impersonation, you can't force ASP.NET to assume the role of a specific user.
10. What class is used to validate users when using Forms authentication?

# Exercises

1. Create a web.config file that uses Forms authentication. Add three users: Guest, Member, and Admin. Force all users to authenticate themselves to a page called MyAuth.aspx by denying access to anonymous users.
2. Create your own XML file that's used to store usernames and passwords. Use it in combination with Forms authentication in a test site.

19

# WEEK 3

# DAY 20

# Deploying Internet Applications

Deployment issues are frequently overlooked until the end of a project. The biggest reason for overlooking these issues is that deployment doesn't directly involve writing code. However, thinking ahead about how to correctly deploy your Internet application can save you from some of the late nights that inevitably occur at the end of a project. By investing a little bit of energy into deployment issues, you should be able to transfer your application from your development computers onto a production machine without trouble.

One of the most common methods for creating a production environment for an Internet application is to use a third-party Web hosting company. Before .NET, moving an Internet application to a hosted setting was a frustrating process, including pleas to the hosting company's support personnel to restart the Web server or reboot the server computer. As today's lesson will show, such phone calls are no longer necessary when you're deploying your .NET applications. In fact, you may never have to deal with an unfriendly support technician from a Web hosting company again.

By using .NET, you have a number of choices for application deployment ranging from simple file-copy operations to custom installation programs. You don't have to purchase third-party installation tools even when your Internet application requires complex installation tasks. Visual Studio contains facilities that allow you to create relatively complex installation programs by using *setup projects*. This feature comes as a welcome change from previous versions of the product. Today's lesson will show you how to use these features with a hands-on example.

Today's lesson will explain the following topics:

- When you can use XCOPY and FTP deployment and how to do so
- How to use Visual Studio in simple deployment scenarios
- What kinds of application components require more complex installation programs
- How to employ installation program concepts
- How to use Visual Studio to create custom installation programs

# Deploying Web Applications with XCOPY and FTP

If your Internet application is written entirely using Visual Basic and ASP.NET, and doesn't use any legacy COM, COM+ objects, or a database, deployment and installation are trivial. Because the application is written using managed code, you have to perform only three tasks to set up the server computer:

1. Create the folder structure for your application on the target server.
2. Create a virtual directory on the target system for your application.
3. Copy all necessary files.

You can accomplish steps 1 and 3 by using the XCOPY command from the command line or by using an FTP client program. Step 2, creating a virtual directory, involves some manual work, but you need to do it only once.

You will likely deploy your Internet application to a server computer to which you have direct access, or you will use a third-party Web host. In the first case, creating a virtual directory is easy, as we explained on Day 2, "Introducing ASP.NET." In the second case, almost all hosting companies provide an administration interface (usually a specific set of pages that you have access to) that you can use to easily create virtual directories. Usually, these administration sites also allow you to transfer files.

**Note**

For applications that use ASP.NET, remember that all assemblies must be put in the bin directory. This directory must be located immediately off the root virtual directory.

## XCOPY Tips

If your target server is located on your own local area network, the directory that contains your Internet application should be accessible through a Windows file share. If you don't know how to set up file sharing, or your local administrator prohibits it, you must resort to using an FTP client program.

You can copy an entire project, including all its subdirectories, in one fell swoop by using the XCOPY command as follows:

```
xcopy c:\src\myproject\*.* x:\project /e /y
```

In this example, all the files, including those in the subdirectories, are copied from the myproject directory to the project directory on the x drive, which is a sample drive used for file sharing. The /e option copies files within subdirectories and the /y command overwrites files without prompting you for permission.

The XCOPY command contains many other command-line switches that you can use to copy files modified after a certain date (/d), showing what files would be copied instead of copying them (/l), and creating only directories and not files(/t). Type **xcopy /?** for a full list of options.

**Note**

The example in this section uses the X drive, a so-called *mapped drive*. This means that a directory on the target server has been mapped to a drive (the X drive) on the local development computer. Mapped drives are available only on a local area network. To create a mapped drive, choose Map Network Drive from the Tools menu in the Windows Explorer.

**20**

## Database Installation

If your Internet application uses a database, you will have to take more steps than simply copying files. Most database applications require configuration using their own interface. One exception is Microsoft Access; you can simply copy your source database, usually ending in an .mdb extension, to the target server.

If a third-party company is hosting your application, make sure that you talk with the technical support staff about how to configure and upload data for your database. Many hosting companies that use SQL Server allow you administrative rights to a database so that you can configure the database yourself. If you have the SQL Server client utilities installed on your local computer, you can easily connect to the host database by using the SQL Server Enterprise Manager.

One problem that occurs frequently is configuring the SQL Server client tools to use TCP/IP to communicate with the server. Run the program cliconfg.exe, which is located in your Windows system directory, to make sure that TCP/IP is the default network protocol.

Investigate your Web hosting company's policies and the quality of its technical support before investing in a long-term contract. You can choose from many hosting companies. Of course, your hosting company must support .NET.

# Copying Projects with Visual Studio

A second method for deploying an Internet application is to use Visual Studio's built-in Copy Project feature. Visual Studio copies your project to a destination server by using Windows file sharing or FrontPage extensions. You can selectively copy only necessary files, all files in your project solution, or every file in your project directory.

For this process to work, the server computer must have the latest FrontPage Server extensions installed or have file sharing enabled. If you are in charge of the remote Web server, you can install FrontPage Server Extensions by using the Internet Services Manager. Right-click the Default Web Site node, select the All Tasks option, and then select the Install Server Extensions subitem. A wizard will help you complete the process.

Follow these steps to copy projects using Visual Studio:

1.  Select Copy Project from the Project menu. The Copy Project dialog box will appear (see Figure 20.1).

2.  Choose either FrontPage or a file share as your Web Access Method. The file share method works only for servers that are part of your local network. Many Web hosting companies configure FrontPage Server Extensions, which allows you to use FrontPage to access the site.

*Copying an Internet application using Visual Studio and FrontPage extensions.*

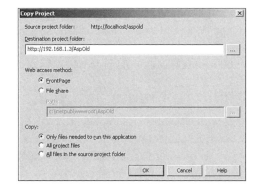

3. Select the file type you want to copy. Normally, you should use the first option, Only Files Needed to Run This Application, so that your source code isn't deployed.

4. Click OK. Visual Studio will try to create a new virtual directory for your project on the Web server if it doesn't exist.

5. At this point, you may be prompted to log in to the server, as Figure 20.2 shows. Enter the account name of a user with author permissions (this name should be provided by your Web hosting provider). If you installed FrontPage extensions yourself, you already created an authors group when following the installation wizard.

**FIGURE 20.2**

*Logging in to a remote server using FrontPage extensions.*

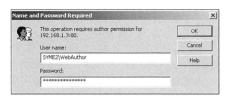

The directory structure, virtual directories, and necessary files are then created and copied onto the destination server.

# Creating Powerful Setup Programs

Your Internet project may not consist of only "pure" .NET code. For instance, your project may rely on COM and COM+ objects, legacy code, and other code not directly related to .NET. In this case, copying your project using the methods described previously in this lesson won't work.

20

Fortunately, Visual Studio .NET contains features that allow you to create your own setup programs that can contain any files. By using Visual Studio .NET, you can create setup programs that install legacy COM objects, create Registry entries, and add Start menu items. The remainder of this lesson will explain how to do so.

## Using Visual Studio to Create Setup Programs

Visual Studio .NET comes with a number of template projects that you can use to create setup programs for your Internet applications. After you create a setup program, deploying your project is as simple as running the new setup program on the server. By using Visual Studio, you can even bundle the .NET Framework with your programs so that you can install your application on a server that doesn't currently have .NET installed.

You can create four kinds of setup projects using Visual Studio, as listed in Table 20.1.

**TABLE 20.1**   Visual Studio Setup Projects

| Project | Description |
| --- | --- |
| Web Setup Project | Creates a setup program specifically for Internet applications. |
| Setup Project | Creates a setup program for any kind of .NET application. |
| Cab Project | Creates a Windows Cabinet File, a compressed binary file containing application items, for use by Web browsers to install programs. |
| Merge Module Project | Creates Windows merge modules, which can be included in other setup programs. Also used for common application components that are shared among multiple applications. |

Today's lesson will focus on the first kind of setup application, so-called Web Setup Projects. You will use the code from Day 17, "Using Legacy Code with .NET," because these samples consist of legacy COM objects, ASP pages, and .NET components. Using this code will exercise many of the features available in Web setup projects.

Both the Web Setup Project and Setup Project options create installation programs that rely on the Windows Installer. These program names end in the .msi extension. Many applications rely on the Windows Installer, including all programs that Microsoft releases, so it's a safe bet that your setup program will function properly on a target computer.

The Windows Installer has a number of nice features, including the capability to roll back a partially complete setup, clean up an installed program, and be aware of COM object and DLL versions. This last feature ensures that your installation program won't break other applications by installing an old version of a shared library. Because the setup programs created by Visual Studio use the Windows Installer, your custom setup programs get all these features with no additional work on your part.

To follow along with today's lesson, create a new Web Setup Project as follows:

1. Select the New Project option on the Visual Studio Start Page or from the File menu.

2. In the New Project dialog box, click the Setup and Deployment Projects node on the left. Your dialog should look like the one shown in Figure 20.3.

**FIGURE 20.3**

*Creating a new Web Setup Project using Visual Studio.*

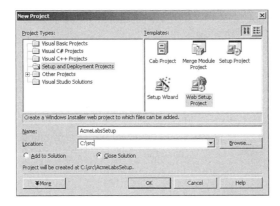

3. Select the Web Setup Project template on the right.

4. Name the project and click OK. You will now see a project that looks similar to Figure 20.4.

**FIGURE 20.4**

*A blank Web Setup Project in Visual Studio.*

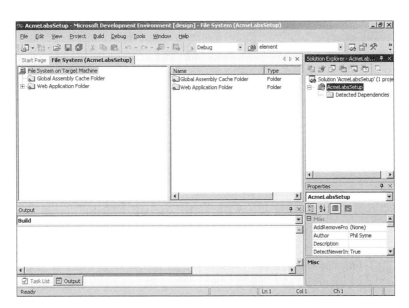

**20**

## Navigating a Web Setup Project

NEW TERM Each piece of the setup project is organized into *views*, which are windows that contain information and settings about a specific aspect of the new setup program. You can select each view by right-clicking the project node in the Project Explorer and then selecting View. Table 20.2 lists the views available in Visual Studio.

**TABLE 20.2**   Views of a Web Setup Project

| View | Description |
| --- | --- |
| File System | Shows the files and assemblies that make up your application. They includes .NET assemblies and files ending in .aspx, .asmx, .asax, .ascx, .disco, and .config. You also add any COM and COM+ components, ASP, and any other files needed for your application. |
| Registry | Shows additional Registry entries that your application requires. Visual Studio takes care of COM object registration entries for you and doesn't display them in this view. |
| File Types | Shows custom file types. If you need to create custom file types so that the user can double-click the file and be directed to a program, add the types here. |
| User Interface | Shows each screen that the setup program will display. You can add custom screens here, such as splash screens, license agreements, and read-me screens. |
| Custom Actions | Shows any custom scripts or executables that the setup program should run. You can add actions for the Install, Commit, Rollback, and Uninstall modes of the setup program. |
| Launch Conditions | Shows rules that you've added before the installation can launch, such as checks for a certain version of Windows and Internet Information Services. |

Web Setup Projects offer you a huge number of features, as you can see from the views in Table 20.2. It's likely that you will have to configure only the File Types and Registry portions of the setup project. After all, you are deploying your Web project to a server, not the general public.

## Configuring Files in Your Setup Project

The first step to take when configuring a Web Setup Project is to create the directory structure for the target application. To do so, select the File System view and then select the Web Application Folder at the left. Right-click and select Add, and then add all the necessary subdirectories.

Step two involves adding all the files necessary to make your Internet application function. They include all the file types in the first entry of Table 20.2. Add all .NET assemblies, Web forms, user controls, Web Services, discovery files, and web.config files first by selecting Add from the Project menu. You can add more than one file at the same time if each file is located in the same directory.

As you add files, Visual Studio computes all dependent files that you need for your project and adds these files automatically. By default, Visual Studio makes your application dependent on a file named dotnetfxredist_x86_enu.msm. This dependency is shown in the Solution Explorer window. This particular file is a merge module that contains the entire .NET Framework installation. You should remove this merge module if your target computer already has .NET installed, because the file is quite large.

Next, add all items other than COM and COM+ objects, including ASP.old pages, Access database files, XML files, and help files.

Finally, add COM and COM+ objects. You must take some special actions to make sure that the setup program registers the objects. To do so, select one of the COM or COM+ objects. In the properties window, locate the `Register` attribute and change it to the value `vsdraCOM`. Change the `SharedLegacyFile` attribute to read `true`. Finally, each object must be added to the Global Assembly Cache Folder at the left. Add each object again to this folder to ensure that the objects are placed in the GAC.

If you are following along by using Visual Studio, you need to add the following items into the File System view from Day 17:

- **Assemblies.** The main assembly for Day 17, such as aspold.dll. Also, the HelloUtility.dll assembly, used by the ASP.old pages.
- **.NET files.** They include ReadSession.aspx and LegacyShippers.aspx.
- **ASP.old files.** WriteSession.asp and CallHello.asp.

When you add these files, the dependent assembly called Interop.ADODB_2_0.dll is added automatically. It is the wrapper assembly used to call ADO.old functions.

Next, you need to add the HelloUtility assembly to the Global Assembly Cache Folder. Also, change the properties for the assembly so that it will be registered as a COM component by using the steps outlined earlier in this section.

## Generating and Testing the Setup Program

To generate a new setup application, build the setup project using the Build menu's Build option. As with other Visual Studio projects, the setup project is compiled with debugging information by default. This is fine for testing purposes; after the setup program is working properly, it can be recompiled in Release mode.

**20**

To test the setup program properly, you need a second computer that doesn't have the examples from Day 17 installed. It's critical to use a "clean" computer to test the installation program, especially when legacy components are included in the installation program. A clean test computer guarantees that the Registry entries your installation program creates are correct.

When you start the setup program, you should be greeted by a window similar to Figure 20.5. The setup program comes with installation, repair, and uninstall features by default. Try deleting a few files on the server, repairing the installation, and then uninstalling the application.

**FIGURE 20.5**

*A setup program created using Visual Studio.*

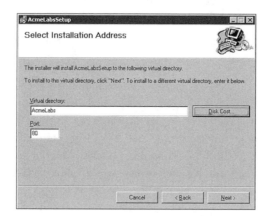

## Setting Up Advanced Projects

Some of the more advanced tasks you can perform with a setup program include setting custom Registry keys and values, creating rules for how the setup program can be launched, adding licensing and read-me screens, and using custom scripts. Let's explore how to implement these features using Visual Studio.

### Adding Registry Keys

Custom settings for Web applications should be stored in the web.config file. However, your application may contain legacy components that use the Registry to load configuration information. If so, your setup program must be able to create and set Registry keys and values.

Configuring your setup program to create custom Registry keys and values isn't difficult. To do so, switch to the Registry view inside the Web Setup Project. You will see the four root Registry keys: HKEY_CLASSES_ROOT, HKEY_CURRENT_USER, HKEY_LOCAL_MACHINE, and HKEY_USERS. You generally use the Local Machine and Current User keys for your Internet application's custom settings. For settings that should be available to all users on the destination computer, use the Local Machine key. Settings customized for each user, or that each user can set to her own preference, should be put in the Current User key.

Adding your application keys to the Registry view is quite similar to using the Windows RegEdit tool. If you've used RegEdit before, the Registry view interface will be easy to learn. The general process uses the following steps:

1. Add Keys to the nodes on the left by clicking each node and selecting the Add option.
2. Continue adding keys until the Registry structure for your application is complete.
3. Add Values inside each key. Values can be of type String, DWORD (an unsigned integer), and Binary.

Any keys that you add to the Registry view are copied onto the target machine during installation. Conversely, if your Internet application is uninstalled, the values and keys are removed.

## Adding Launch Conditions

**NEW TERM** Each setup project created with Visual Studio can specify *launch conditions,* which are rules that the setup program will test before running and can be created in the Launch Conditions view. By running these rules, you can, for example, make sure that the current user running the installation program has administrative rights, ensure that the proper version of IIS is installed on the target server, and make sure that the current Windows operating system on the server is compatible with your application.

The format for the rules that you use in the Launch Conditions view is somewhat complex. These rules are in a format that the Windows Installer can understand; the Windows Installer is in charge of running the rules and deciding whether your setup program can run.

A default rule added to all Web Setup Programs is called IIS Condition. This rule looks like the following:

```
IISVERSION >= "#4"
```

This rule checks to see that IIS version 4 or higher is installed on the target computer. Rules like this involve three parts: a property (IISVERSION in this case), an operator (>=), and a value (#4). You can create your own properties such as IISVERSION by creating new search conditions, which will be explained shortly. The Windows Installer also contains a number of built-in keywords that you can use. Table 20.3 shows some keywords you might commonly use in a setup program.

**20**

**Table 20.3**  Commonly Used Windows Installer Keywords

| Keyword | Description |
| --- | --- |
| ADMINUSER | Nonzero if the current user has administrative rights. |
| WINDOWS9X | Version number of Windows, if a non-NT version is installed. This includes Windows 95, 98, and ME. |
| WINDOWSNT | Version number of Windows if an NT version is installed. This includes Windows NT, 2000, XP, and all Server/DataServer versions. |
| SERVICEPACKLEVEL | The service pack version number. |
| WINDOWSBUILD | The Windows build number. |

In the previous example, IISVERSION was used to check the current version of IIS on the target machine. Visual Studio created the IISVERSION property by adding a new Registry key search. This Registry search has a property name of IISVERSION and a RegKey property pointing to the location in the Registry where IIS stores its current version.

You can create your own properties that search for specific files, Registry entries, and Windows Installer merge modules. You can specify each custom property by adding an element to the Search Target Machine node in the left pane of the Registry view. The IISVERSION property demonstrated Registry searches. As another example, file searches can be made by name, date, size, or any combination of these properties.

## Customizing the User Interface

The windows displayed by Visual Studio setup programs can be customized to display other windows besides the normal Click Next to Install screen. You can add custom windows to the setup program by using the User Interface view. When you do so, you see a diagram of the windows that appear in the installation program. If you want to add more steps to the installation program, choose from the list in Table 20.4.

**TABLE 20.4**  Custom Steps That You Can Add to a Setup Program

| Step | Description |
| --- | --- |
| Splash | A splash screen that can contain a message and an image file |
| Register User | A screen that gathers registration information, such as a product key |
| License Agreement | A screen full of legal jargon that has a low likelihood of ever being read |
| Customer Information | A screen that gathers information about the user, such as contact information |
| RadioButton Screens | Various flavors of screens that allow users to choose installation options |
| Read Me | A screen containing miscellaneous information |

# Summary

Today's lesson explored several different methods for Internet application deployment under .NET. The first section explained how to deploy Internet applications to a hosted site using simple tools such as FTP or XCOPY.

The second section explained how to use Visual Studio for simple XCOPY-style deployment by using the Copy Project option. You saw two different methods, one that used FrontPage extensions and the second that used a network file share.

In the last section, you saw how to use Visual Studio to create powerful custom installation programs. These setup programs can be used if your application contains legacy code or a .NET object that needs to be registered in the Global Assembly Cache. You saw how to add custom rules and user interface elements to your setup programs. Using Visual Studio this way gives you a great amount of flexibility when you need to deploy your application to another computer.

# Q&A

**Q I'm not sure about which Internet service provider (ISP) to use to host my .NET application. What are some things I should look for?**

**A** First, make sure that the ISP supports .NET programs. Ask the ISP how many other .NET sites it has running right now. Next, investigate how the ISP handles databases, especially if your Web application uses SQL Server. Next, find out about their turnaround time for technical problems. Last, call their technical support line, and talk with their support staff. You should be able to gauge their support staff's competence with a short conversation.

**Q I've heard that third-party applications are available to create installation programs. Should I use these or rely on Visual Studio .NET?**

**A** You can use a number of third-party tools to create complex installation programs. One critical factor in the decision is whether your setup programs needs to conditionally install certain parts of a program. For instance, many applications allow users to choose typical, minimal, or custom installation options. If this is the case with your application, you may want to investigate third-party tools.

**Q How important is using a "clean" computer to test my setup program?**

**A** The answer depends on how complex your installation program is. The best practice is to always use a separate computer that has never run your setup program before for testing. You can choose to bend the rules if you are confident that your application can be uninstalled cleanly. In this case, always uninstall your application before running a new setup program.

20

# Workshop

The Workshop provides quiz questions to help you solidify your understanding of the material covered today as well as exercises to give you experience using what you've learned. Try to understand the quiz and exercise before continuing to the next lesson. Answers are provided in Appendix A, "Answers to Quizzes and Exercises."

## Quiz

1. What three steps are needed to deploy a "pure" .NET Internet application?
2. What two methods are available for deployment in Visual Studio .NET?
3. What factors influence the choice of deployment method for a .NET Internet application?
4. What different views are offered in a Web Setup Project?
5. Name two custom screens that you can add to your Web Setup Project.
6. What's the name of objects used in custom launch condition clauses?
7. What kinds of launch condition properties can you create?

## Exercises

1. Create a custom setup program that copies documents containing help information to the target computer.
2. Create a custom setup program that registers some .NET assemblies for use by legacy code, such as an ASP page. Investigate what Registry entries are added to the target machine. What happens when the application is uninstalled?

# DAY **21**

# Creating Your Application Architecture

You've learned quite a bit about Internet programming with .NET and Visual Basic during the past three weeks. By reading each of the past 20 lessons, you should have a broad foundation of knowledge that you can use to create new Internet applications or to extend existing ones.

Before you embark on your own project, take some time to read today's short lesson, which details programming rules, designs, and techniques that should lead to a solid architecture for your Internet application. As the saying goes, rules are meant to be broken, so please adapt this lesson's suggestions to the unique constraints of your project.

This lesson doesn't contain much in the way of code examples. Rather, it contains opinions shared by most of the development community that you might apply to your own projects. Because the lesson contains more advice than programming examples, take the opinions here and use them where needed.

Today's lesson will cover:

- Six important aspects of a Web application, and what they mean
- Applications tiers, including logical and physical tiers
- Performance considerations
- Scalability considerations, including scaling up and scaling out
- Standard high-level application architecture models for Web applications and Web Services
- Tips for improving scalability, reliability, and performance for your application

# Applications with Great "PARSSeM"

The PARSSeM acronym is a convenient way to pack the following words together:

- **Performance.** How quickly does your application respond to requests?
- **Availability.** What percentage of the day does your application work, on average?
- **Reliability.** How often does your application crash?
- **Scalability.** If you need to service more user requests, can you simply throw more hardware into the mix or does your code have to change to accommodate the hardware?
- **Security.** Is your application's private data safe?
- **Maintainability.** How easy is it for other developers (or you, for that matter) to extend your application?

Systems with great PARSSeM make everyone happy. Unfortunately, making an Internet application that has all these qualities at the same time is difficult. For example, code that implements security almost always makes the entire application perform more slowly; authenticating and authorizing users takes time. Similarly, making your application maintainable often means that you sacrifice some performance because the code is designed for easy consumption by both computers and people.

You can create an application with all these qualities, however, by creating and designing good software architecture from the beginning of the project. It also helps to have a stockpile of money so that you can buy fast computers and network equipment. This book can't help with the financial angle, but the rest of today's lesson will describe industry standard architectural techniques for your application.

# Looking at Logical and Physical Architecture

**NEW TERM** You can view your application's structure from the software or hardware perspective. Your application's software structure is often referred to as the *logical architecture*, and how your application is distributed across different computers is called the *physical architecture*.

Both software and hardware architecture contain tiers. Here, a *tier* means a set of components responsible for the same function. Software tiers are called *logical* tiers, and hardware tiers are called *physical* tiers. For instance, a logical data tier might include a database and some utility code to allow the rest of the application to use the database easily. A physical data tier might include five computers, each containing the same database program, connected to a set of disks to store the data.

Logical and physical tiers don't have to correspond to each other exactly. For instance, your application might have three logical tiers for the user interface, business rules, and data. The same application could be run on one computer, so it would have a trivial physical tier. Conversely, an application could be one huge pile of monolithic code (one logical tier) that uses two computers, one for the application and one for the database (two physical tiers). In many cases, distributing an application with one single logical tier onto several physical tiers is impossible.

What's the big deal about tiers? Breaking your application into several logical tiers makes solving scalability, security, and maintainability issues easier for several reasons. Let's consider maintainability as an example. If your application has several logical tiers, changes and additional features usually affect only one tier. For instance, you might want to change your database from Access to SQL Server or Oracle. Rather than rip apart code in every single file that makes database calls, you have to change only the logical data access tier, which might involve only a few files.

Physical tiers are important for almost all PARSSeM qualities of an application. For instance, you might have different computers for the data tier of your application. By doing so, you can put a firewall (explained on Day 19, "Securing Internet Applications") in front of the database servers, isolating them from the rest of the network that the application uses. This way, you can limit all data to specific TCP/IP ports that only your application uses so that malicious users have a tough time reaching any important data. You can also optimize each physical tier for the job it's supposed to do. Does the application have problems with lengthy SQL queries? No problem at all—just plow a few thousand dollars into a massive data server, and the problem disappears almost by magic.

The rest of today's lesson will focus on logical tiers because, as a developer, you have the most control over this aspect of your application.

**21**

## What Makes a Logical Tier?

A logical tier contains code that works for a common set of functionality, and has a boundary defined by one or more interfaces. Each interface contains a general set of functions that perform related tasks. For instance, a logical data tier has methods for retrieving, adding, deleting, and modifying data. It doesn't have methods that draw graphics onscreen. For a human resources application, it also doesn't have methods that check to see if an employee's salary is too high for his job classification. These kinds of checks are specific to the business problem that the application solves and should be put somewhere else. A good data tier manages the number of open database connections, for example, and handles database transactions.

## Two-Tiered Applications

In the good old days, cutting-edge applications used two logical tiers: the database code and everything else. We recommend that you avoid this approach because your code won't be very maintainable.

## Three-Tiered Applications

Software architects never met a logical tier they didn't like, so when three-tiered applications came along, they inspired admiration from all quarters. Three-tiered applications have user interface, business logic, and data tiers. The goal for this kind of architecture is to isolate all code that creates windows or renders HTML pages into the user interface tier. This means that code to check whether the user entered a ZIP code from a company's home state and then added sales tax to the bill goes into the business logic tier. Of course, these decisions are always more complicated in the real world. The great thing about software—at least early in a project—is that you can shuffle functionality between tiers until you get it right.

## *N*-Tiered Applications

**NEW TERM**  People would have kept going by designing four-, five-, and six-tiered applications until someone put a stop to the process and invented the term *n-tier*. This term came about because software architects were trying to reconcile the three-tiered logic model with Internet applications. One key issue is that many Internet applications have a user interface tier that renders HTML and JavaScript for browsers. This might provide for workflow and a resulting small amount of logic for each page. In this case, the code at this level contains essentially two tiers: one to render HTML and JavaScript, and another to provide a user interface "facade," providing workflow and page navigation logic.

With the advent of Web Services, the three-tiered model gets thrown out the window. You can have a complicated *n*-tiered Web Service combined with a complicated *n*-tiered client application that uses the service. You can also have different kinds of clients, such as cell phones and PDAs, or complex client applications. As you can imagine, trying to partition an application like this gets difficult unless you have an "*n*-tiered" perspective.

# Performance and Scalability

Performance and scalability don't always go together hand in hand. To see why, let's explore scalability in a little more depth.

NEW TERM     *Scalability* essentially means that you can use your wallet to allow your application to service more requests rather than rewrite your code. Put another way, scalability means that you can add hardware to your physical tiers without having to rewrite application code.

You can employ two methods to increase the scale of your application: scaling up and scaling out. *Scaling up* means that you replace a computer running your application with a bigger, better computer. This computer might have a faster processor, more memory, bigger and faster disks, or whatever other piece of new technology has recently arrived. Scaling up is easy, reliable, and involves no work on your part. Scaling up is guaranteed to increase performance, and is every developer's first choice.

Sometimes you just don't have the budget to scale up, or you don't have time to wait for the current speed of server computers to double. In this case, your second option is to *scale out*. This means that rather than replace computers, you add computers to each physical tier. Scaling out involves much more software complexity because the application needs to be able to run on more than one computer at the same time. Scaling out may even slow an application because of extra code to distribute user requests to more than one computer.

Previous lessons mentioned that you can make your Web application or Web Service stateless by not using ASP.NET session objects. *Stateless* essentially means that any specific per-user data, such as a user's Social Security number and credit card number, is stored in a database or XML file (both referred to as *the database* in this discussion), instead of in session state. Every time your code wants to do something for users, such as debiting their credit card $1000, it needs to retrieve user information from the database, make changes, and save the changes back to the database. This means that the per-user state for the application is loaded and modified on every user request. The alternative is to retrieve user information once and then store it in memory, such as the ASP.NET session. Storing the information in session avoids having to reload user information on

21

every request. This approach is certainly faster because no database access is involved. Stateless applications don't store user information in the user interface or business logic tiers between browser requests or Web Service method requests.

You make an Internet application stateless so that you can easily scale out the user interface and business logic tiers. As a side effect, making the application stateless increases the reliability and availability of the application. If you have 10 Web server computers serving up your popular (stateless) airline reservation Web service and 3 computers burst into flames, your Web Service clients are inconvenienced only temporarily, or not at all. At the worst, a particular Web Service call will fail, but no data will be corrupted, and the call can be retried.

Building a scaled-out application is tough and usually involves specialized hardware to route Web Service and browser requests randomly to each Web server. The hardware must also be aware of the status of each Web server, in case the computer melts. This hardware is called a *network load balancer* (NLB) and is sold by various companies. Windows 2000 Advanced Server and its various versions contain support for load balancing; you just add a second network card to each server computer. Figure 21.1 shows such a configuration.

**FIGURE 21.1**

*Physical application configuration using network load balancing.*

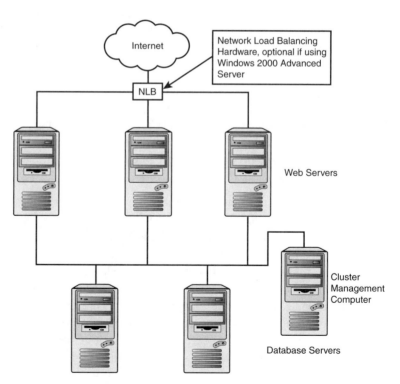

Unfortunately, scaling out a database and the data tier for increased reliability and avail-ability is a difficult task. This process usually involves using duplicate database servers that store exact copies of the same data and can also involve splitting up database files among different computers. This advanced topic is beyond the scope of today's lesson. Check with your database vendor for specific instructions. Luckily, the database is usual-ly the last piece of your application that you have to worry about because all popular commercial databases are far more reliable than any custom code you or I might write—not because database programmers are more intelligent than other humans, but because they've been solving the same problem for the past 30 years.

So far, this section has focused purely on scalability issues. However, an application's performance has a profound effect on scalability. Scalability is all about handling more and more user requests in a given amount of time. An application that performs well and uses fewer system resources will naturally scale. This means that it makes sense to invest resources in creating application components that are thrifty with their use of system memory, database connections, and disk I/O. Such thrifty components will scale well as a matter of course.

Another important point to remember is that dividing an application into multiple physi-cal tiers will, in most cases, decrease performance. This is because function calls among multiple computers (from one tier to another) contains much overhead. Each call must be packaged and sent over a network, unpackaged, and processed, with the reverse process for each result value. In terms of machine cycles, this overhead is enormous, even with a very fast network connecting the two computers.

# DNA for .NET

Microsoft has made its own recommendations on the PARSSeM issue by inventing the Distributed interNet Architecture model (DNA). The model has evolved from its first ver-sion, before Web Services and .NET, to the current Web Service-aware, .NET-aware model. This section will explain the model, shown in Figure 21.2.

**FIGURE 21.2**

*Microsoft DNA and .NET.*

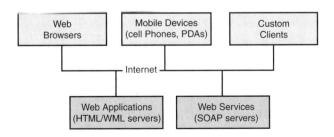

21

Figure 21.2 shows client applications at the top and server applications at the bottom, all connected using the Internet. Let's drill down into the architecture of each component in the diagram.

Web browsers and mobile devices have a simple architecture; they usually run some kind of program that parses HTML or WML and displays it on the client device. Custom clients can vary from simple browser-like applications to complex applications, such as an application that calculates the stress of gravity on a new building. Custom client applications can be divided into multiple logical and physical tiers, just like any other.

After the past 20 days, you are quite familiar with Web applications and Web Services in .NET. Let's examine the logical architecture for a Web Service, shown in Figure 21.3.

**FIGURE 21.3**

*Sample logical architecture for a .NET Web Service.*

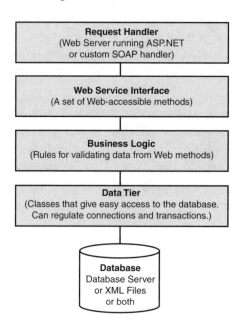

Looking at Figure 21.3 from the top down, the request handler is a program that can receive requests in SOAP format and send SOAP responses, usually over TCP/IP so that the Web Service will work with the Internet. Of course, ASP.NET and your Web server perform this task for you, as you saw this past week. You don't have to worry about this layer.

The Web Service interface contains a set of methods that clients can call. You saw how to create Web-accessible methods in the past few lessons: You simply add the WebMethod attribute to a function.

The business logic layer contains code that validates data according to the specific needs of the particular business that the application is concerned with. For example, an airline reservation business layer would contain code to calculate an exorbitant fine for a last-minute reservation change.

The data tier in .NET is usually a thin wrapper around the built-in ADO.NET `DataSet` and `DataTable` classes, which you saw in Week 2. A typed dataset (discussed on Day 11, "Using ADO.NET and XML Together") is a typical example.

The database for a .NET Web Service is usually SQL Server, Oracle, or even Access. Depending on the needs of the application, it could simply consist of XML files. In this case, the Windows file system would play the role of the database server.

A logical architecture for a Web application looks similar to Figure 21.3. The main difference is in the top two layers, as shown in Figure 21.4.

**FIGURE 21.4**

*Sample logical architecture for a .NET Web application.*

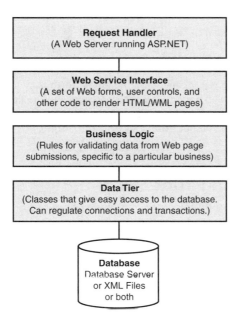

Because the two architectures are so similar, you might consider combining a Web Service and Web application. Combining them is certainly a great way to offer broad access to your application.

**21**

# PARSSeM and .NET

We are sorry to report that writing all your code using .NET won't cure all PARSSeM-related issues. Making a PARSSeM Web site or Web Service still takes careful design, good architecture, and great code.

> **Tip**
>
> Anyone who tells you that technology X (where X can be any of but not limited to .NET, Java, C++, Windows, Unix, mainframes, and supercomputers) will cure all performance, availability, scalability, security, and maintainability problems is trying to sell you a certain product and most likely doesn't have your best interests at heart.

With that said and the preceding tip in mind, we can say that .NET can help you make better applications when used correctly. Next, we offer some ideas to help you in your quest to make an exceptional application.

> **Caution**
>
> This caution is just common sense but is worth scanning once. Use your experience and good judgment when applying the tips in the rest of today's lesson. Don't take this book's advice or anyone else's advice about software architecture without careful analysis and testing.

## Tips for Designing Your System

You may find these tips useful for the design phase of your project:

- Prototype your system. This means you must write test code for any part of your application that uses a new technology or a technology that you don't have detailed knowledge about.

- Read everything you can about design, architecture, and the technology you're using.

## Tips for Scaling Out Your Service

To scale out the user interface and business logic tiers of your application, you can use the following tips:

- Avoid using ASP.NET session state. Instead, pass parameters to retrieve necessary user information from a database.

- If you must use ASP.NET session state, store the sessions on a different computer so that multiple computers can access the "session server." Day 18, "Configuring Internet Applications," explained how to store them. You can also store ASP.NET sessions in a SQL Server database.

- Decide between the preceding two tips; see the prototyping tips in the previous section to make an intelligent choice.

- Put down your object-oriented programming references briefly. Don't create massive class libraries with objects that contain every bit of information about each particular user and fill up the classes on every service or page request. Instead, create classes that are tuned for each scenario that your application will handle. This way, each class can load only the pertinent information for each service request. For example, in your airline reservation system, you don't need to load a passenger's flight history, contact information, and credit history when making a reservation request.

- Pick up your object-oriented programming references and find the classic techniques for handling batch-oriented tasks.

- Design for scalability but don't scale out more than the load on the current servers necessitates because doing so will cause a performance hit.

## Tips for Improving Performance

You can use the following programming techniques to improve Web site and Web Service performance:

- Make your Web Service calls and Web page requests *chunky*. A chunky call contains a lot of data. Rather than use individual Web Service methods that return one property each, return a custom data structure or XML file that contains all properties. This point is important because Internet requests are slow.

- Minimize dynamic ASP.NET Web controls if possible. Programming for Web controls is easy, but they involve a processing time penalty on the server. Static ASP.NET Web controls can be cached, which greatly improves their performance.

- If you use Web controls, disable their view state if possible. This way, the view state data in the hidden control in each Web page isn't transmitted to the server.

- Cache data. For Web pages, ASP.NET contains built-in facilities for caching user controls, as Day 6, "Working with User Controls," showed. For Web Services, you have to design your own caching mechanisms.

- Profile your application to find the slow areas and then make the slow parts faster. You can buy profiling programs that measure .NET application performance from third-party vendors. For ASP.NET Web pages, you can set the Trace flag to true, as explained on Day 18.

21

## Tips for Improving Reliability

NEW TERM One key reliability concept that hardware engineers have been aware of for a long time is called *redundancy*. This means that for any piece of hardware that can fail, use two or more of them. The space shuttle contains five separate computer systems that all do the same thing, just in case. This concept easily applies to your application's physical tiers.

To apply redundancy to software, you can do the following:

- Back up your data. Now you have two copies of your data. If possible, create full backups of your data, not just differential or "delta" backups that contain only data changes. Life is too short to spend restoring data.

- Write code to check each module in your application. Now you have code to check your code.

- Have a friend check your code. Now two people are writing the same code.

- Have someone else review your design.

- Have someone else test your code. You can't check your own application to see whether it functions properly.

# Summary

Today's lesson explored some of the general issues that you will confront when you create a larger scale Internet application. You saw a list of some of the important factors that make an Internet application successful, including performance, availability, reliability, scalability, security, and maintainability.

Today's lesson described logical and physical application tiers. You saw recommended ways for partitioning your Web application or Web Service so that it can fulfill high-level architectural requirements such as performance and scalability.

Today's lesson concluded with tips that you can apply to your own Internet applications. These ideas will be useful for your own projects. Creating a large-scale Internet application is a difficult task. With the lessons you've learned from this book, you should be well equipped for your own projects. Good luck!

# Q&A

**Q I'm coming from a Java/Sun background, and I don't understand all this fuss about physical tiers. Java applications that I've written don't use multiple physical tiers, because Sun's servers are powerful enough to get the job done**

**alone. Programming with .NET and multiple physical tiers sounds unnecessarily complex. Why use all these tiers?**

A The issue of scaling out, using multiple physical tiers, and stateless approaches, are a source of hot debate. All large-scale implementations of Web applications use some form of redundancy. In some applications, one application server may contain redundant hardware; in other applications, redundant servers are used to accomplish the same result, and some implementations use a mix of the two techniques. Your approach will be probably be based on cost and your own (and your team members') particular skill sets. Almost any configuration of hardware and physical tiers can be made to work.

# Workshop

The Workshop provides quiz questions to help you solidify your understanding of the material covered today as well as exercises to give you experience using what you've learned. Try to understand the quiz and exercise before continuing to the next lesson. Answers are provided in Appendix A, "Answers to Quizzes and Exercises."

## Quiz

1. What is a logical application tier?
2. What is an *n*-tier design?
3. Why is it important to prototype a software design?
4. What is a stateless Internet application?
5. What does *scale out* mean?
6. Why make a stateless design?

## Exercises

1. Search the msdn.microsoft.com site for articles dealing with software architecture issues. How do they extend today's lesson?
2. Search the java.sun.com site for articles about software architecture in the Java environment. How do these articles differ from those in the first exercise?

21

# WEEK 3

# In Review

You're finished! Take a moment to congratulate yourself on a job well done. You've learned a great deal of information in the past three weeks. It was a lot of material to cover, but that was simply a reflection of all the powerful tools that .NET brings to Internet development. During this final week, you learned about some of the most important parts of Web development, including design, configuration, security, and deployment.

The first part of this week extended your knowledge of Web Services, including how to find other companies' Web Service offerings and how to publish your own Web Services by using the UDDI directory. Day 17 provided tips and techniques for moving your existing code to the .NET Framework. Days 18, 19, and 20 showed you the ins and outs of configuration, security, and deployment in .NET. Last, on Day 21, you learned how to design your Web applications for scalability, reliability, and performance.

Be sure to check this book's Web site at www.samspublishing.com for more complex project samples and project ideas.

Now that you've completed these lessons, you are ready to take on almost any kind of Web project. Perhaps you need to write a Web application as part of your job, or maybe you just want to add some pizzazz to your personal Web site. Whatever the programming task, .NET can handle it—and now, so can you!

15

16

17

18

19

20

21

# APPENDIX A

# Answers to Quizzes and Exercises

## Day 1, "Introducing Web Programming with .NET"

### Quiz Answers

1. The common language runtime (CLR) is a set of class libraries and services that .NET provides for all .NET programs. The CLR provides memory management services (garbage collection), program type checking, and support for multiple applications running in one Windows process.

2. An assembly is a dynamic link library (.dll) or executable file (.exe) that contains Microsoft intermediate language (IL), machine code (native code), and type information (metadata).

3. A namespace is a grouping of .NET classes with a specific name. .NET contains many stock namespaces, which group all the base classes that you can use in your applications. Some examples include `System` , `System.Web`, and `System.Net`.

4. Internet Information Services (IIS) is a Web server used to run Internet applications.

5. Program code that you write makes a Web page dynamic. Dynamic pages respond to user input and perform useful services.

6. A Web Service is a program that offers functions that other programs can call over the Internet.

7. A Web Service uses custom code to provide functions to client programs located somewhere on the Internet. A Web server listens for Internet requests, such as HTTP or SOAP requests, and responds with files. Most Web Services use a Web server to "feed" them with requests from clients and to "push" data back to client programs.

## Exercise Answers

1. Depending on how IIS was installed on your computer, the online help files may or may not have been installed. If the help files were installed, they should appear in the virtual directory labeled IISHelp.

2. Of course, you can create a directory by using the Windows File explorer. Make sure that you create the directory in a place that you can locate easily. For instance, you might use c:\src\lesson2 as a project directory.

   To create a virtual directory pointing to the source directory, use ISM, and select New Virtual Directory from the right-click menu. The beginning of Day 2 gives detailed instructions.

3. To add HTML files, you need a text editor at the minimum. You can also use Visual Studio to add HTML files by choosing Add New Item from the Project menu.

# Day 2, "Introducing ASP.NET"

## Quiz Answers

1. No, you don't have to implement the `Page_Load` event. You should implement this method when you must perform some kind of work before the page is rendered.

2. There are two different ways to use code-behind:

   - Add the `src` attribute into the page's `Page` directive, which should contain the name of the file containing the code behind.

- Compile the code-behind file into an assembly, and put the assembly in the bin subdirectory for your Web project.

In both cases, you should also use the `inherits` attribute within the `Page` directive.

3. The simplest possible way to write an HTML string is to use the `Response.Write` method.

4. The `HttpResponse` class reads the content of the form. You access this class using the `Response` object, where you can use the `Form` or `Parameters` collection to find each form entry.

5. The `Form` collection contains input from an HTML form. The `QueryString` collection contains information from a HTTP `GET` request, such as from the link

   `<a:href="thispage.aspx?Parameter1=Value1">Click Me</a>`

6. `MapPath` retrieves the full path of a physical directory, given the name of a virtual directory. Always use `MapPath` wherever possible; this way, you can change the physical location of your Web project without having to change your code.

7. Use the `HttpBrowserCapablities` class to determine the browser type. In particular, use the `Request.Broswer.Type` property to find the type of the remote Web browser.

8. Use the `Response.Redirect` method to direct users to different pages. Remember that you must call this method before any HTML is rendered for a page.

9. Use the `Parameters` collection because it contains the contents of both the `Form` and `QueryString` collections. This would allow your code to examine one combined collection for any user response or parameters that were passed to the page.

10. There's no one correct answer for this question. You might use the TextBox, DropDownList, and Button Web controls in a survey form, although your own form may vary.

## Exercise Answers

1. There are several ways to implement this exercise. At a minimum, you need to change the lines that write out the results of the login attempt into lines that call `Response.Redirect`. Listing 2.2 with these changes is repeated here as Listing A.1.

**LISTING A.1**  LoginControl.aspx: Using Web Controls Instead of HTML Controls

```
<%@ Page language="VB" %>
<script runat="server">
sub LoginClicked(Sender as Object, e as EventArgs)
```

A

**LISTING A.1** continued

```
' If the page has posted back results, then check them
if IsPostBack then
  ' Grab the username and password fields
  dim strUserName as string = Request("username")
  dim strPassword as string = Request("password")

  ' Write out a success/failure message
  if (strUserName = "Joe Smith") and (strPassword = "secret") then
    Response.Write("<h2>Logon successful " & strUserName & "</h2>")
  else
    Response.Write("<h2>Your username/passwordwere not found.</h2>")
  end if
 end if
end sub
</script>

<html>
<body>
<h2>Welcome to the Sample Login Page</h2>
<form runat="server">
<table>
  <tr>
   <td>UserName:</td>
   <td><asp:textbox id="username" runat="server"/></td>
  </tr>
  <tr>
   <td>Password</td>
   <td><asp:textbox id="password" textmode="password" runat="server"/></td>
  </tr>
  <tr>
    <td></td>
    <td>
      <asp:button text="Login" onClick="LoginClicked" runat="server"/>
    </td>
  </tr>
</table>
</form>
</body>
</html>
```

2. Use the `Request.Browser.Type` object to find out the browser now in use. A sample program that filters for Internet Explorer version 5, and redirects the user, is shown here:

```
<%@ Page language="VB" %>
<script runat="server">
sub Page_Load(Sender as Object, e as EventArgs)
  if ucase(Request.Browser.Type) = "IE5" then
    Response.Redirect("ie/beginpage.aspx")
```

```
      else
        Response.Redirect("nonms/beginpage.aspx")
      end if
    end sub
</script>
```

# Day 3, "Using Web Forms"

## Quiz Answers

1. A *postback* is the name for the page request that an ASP.NET page sends to itself when a Web control is activated, such as when users click a button. Most Web forms use the HTML form control, which allows users to submit data using HTTP Post requests.

2. You can handle state in ASP.NET Web applications by using cookies, query strings, hidden fields, and the Session and Application objects.

3. Cookies are stored on each user's computer, through their Web browser. Cookies can contain string data.

4. Store an object in application state when the data it contains isn't specific to an individual user.

5. You can change the timeout for a Session object by setting its Timeout property or by using the web.config file.

6. The HttpSession class supports the Load and Unload events.

7. The global.asax file handles Session and Application events.

8. Use the <object> tag to declare an object in the global.asax file.

9. Use the web.config file to configure Web applications.

10. The .NET collection classes use the Synchronized method to return thread-safe versions of themselves.

## Exercise Answers

1. Visual Studio will create an AssemblyInfo.vb file, which contains version information about the assembly for the Web project. Visual Studio will also create a discovery file with a .disco extension, which will be explored in Week 3. Visual Studio also creates web.config and global.asax files, as well as a default web form, as discussed in today's lesson.

2. To ensure that the method is thread-safe, use the thread-safe collection (m_colSync).

3. There's no single answer for this exercise; you can implement this in various ways.

A

# Day 4, "Working with Web Controls"

## Quiz Answers

1. Each ASP.NET page that processes events must contain a form tag, as follows:

   ```
   <form runat="server">
   ```

   Without the form tag, ASP.NET Web controls can't create postback events, which are generated by submitting forms.

2. The LinkButton generates the `Click` event when users click the link.

3. Set the `AutoPostBack` property to true to force the control to send a form request when users change a selection.

4. To suppress a control generation, set the `Visible` property to false. The control won't be rendered. You might take this action in the `Page_Load` event after some conditional logic.

5. The CompareValidator control compares the contents of two controls.

6. To suppress the error message, set the `DisplayError` property to false. You might do this if you've created custom error handling code with error messages that shouldn't be displayed with the control.

7. Cascading Style Sheets (CSS) are used to set the look and feel of a Web page or Web site.

8. The `CSSClass` property binds a Web control to an element of a Cascading Style Sheet.

9. You must always call the `ApplyStyle` method to apply a `Style` object to a control.

10. As with all Web controls, use the `Width` property to set the display width of a TextControl.

## Exercise Answers

1. Listing A.2 shows a modified version of Listing 4.1 with an Update button.

**LISTING A.2**   Updated Code to Handle Common Events in Some Web Controls

```
<html>
  <body>
  <script runat="server" language="VB">
  sub MyUpdate(Sender as Object, e as EventArgs)
    'Call event handlers manually
    MyCheckSelChange()
    MyDropSelected()
  end sub
```

**LISTING A.2** continued

```
sub ButtonPress(Sender as Object, e as EventArgs)
  lblOutput.Text = "You pressed the button<br>"
end sub
sub MyDropSelected()
  lblOutput.Text = ExDrop.SelectedItem.ToString() & _
    " is selected in the drop down box<br>"
end sub
sub MyCheckSelChange()
  dim i as integer
  lblOutput.Text = ""
  for  i=0 to ExCheck.Items.Count - 1
    if(ExCheck.Items(i).Selected) then
      lblOutput.Text += "Check box " + i.ToString() & _
                        " is checked<br>"
    else
      lblOutput.Text += "Check box " + i.ToString() & _
                        " is not checked<br>"
    end if
  next
end sub
</script>
<form runat="server">
<asp:Button id="ExButton" text="Press Me" OnClick="ButtonPress"
        runat="server"/>
<br>
<asp:DropDownList id="ExDrop" runat="server" />
  <asp:ListItem>Item 1</asp:ListItem>
  <asp:ListItem>Item 2</asp:ListItem>
  <asp:ListItem>Item 3</asp:ListItem>
</asp:DropDownList>
<br>
<asp:CheckBoxList id="ExCheck" runat="server" />
  <asp:ListItem>Check 1</asp:ListItem>
  <asp:ListItem>Check 2</asp:ListItem>
  <asp:ListItem>Check 3</asp:ListItem>
</asp:CheckBoxList>
<hr>
<asp:Label id="lblOutput" runat="server" />
<asp:Button id="Update" text="Update" OnClick="MyUpdate"
        runat="server"/>

</form>
</body>
</html>
```

A

2. Listing A.3 shows code for a sample page containing a bound HashTable object.

**LISTING A.3**   Using a Bound `HashTable` Object on a Page

```
<%@ Page Language="VB" %>

<script runat="server">
dim Hash as new Hashtable()

sub Page_Load(Sender as Object, e as EventArgs)

    Hash.Add("Sunday",     "Ending my weekend.")
    Hash.Add("Monday",     "Start my workweek.")
    Hash.Add("Tuesday",    "Still working.")
    Hash.Add("Wednesday",  "Playing golf.")
    Hash.Add("Thursday",   "Working until Friday.")
    Hash.Add("Friday",     "Getting ready for the weekend.")
    Hash.Add("Saturday",   "Mowing the lawn.")

  if not IsPostBack then
    MyDropList.DataSource = Hash.Keys
    MyDropList.DataBind()
  end if
end sub

sub MyListSelected(Sender as Object, e as EventArgs)
  dim Entry as string = MyDropList.SelectedItem.ToString()
  Status.Text = CStr(Hash(Entry))
end sub

</script>
<html>
<body>
<h3>Please select one of the days of the week to see what I am doing</h3>
<form runat="server">
<asp:DropDownList runat="server"
                  id="MyDropList"
                  autopostback="true"
                  OnSelectedIndexChanged="MyListSelected"/>
<br>
This is what I'm doing today:
<asp:Label runat="server" id="Status"/>
</form>
</body>
</html>
```

3. An example style sheet might look like the following:

```
body
{
  background: blue
}
H1
{
```

```
    height: 10px
  }

  A
  {
    border-right: 1px solid;
    border-top: 1px solid;
    border-left: 1px solid;
    border-bottom: 1px solid;
  }
```

# Day 5, "Using Advanced ASP.NET Web Controls"

## Quiz Answers

1. The `LiteralControl` class adds HTML tags to the Panel control.

2. A template is a set of HTML or ASP.NET code displayed in a list or grid format by the Repeater, DataGrid, or DataList control.

3. The `DataBinder.Eval` method binds data items to ASP.NET Web controls.

4. The `ItemTemplate` and `AlternatingItemTemplate` change the style of even- and odd-numbered rows.

5. Yes, by using the `TemplateColumn` definition.

6. By using the `EditCommandColumn`. See Listing 5.6 for an example.

7. The viewstate for a large grid, such as the one in the Listing 5.6, contains a large amount of data. Listing 5.6 doesn't need to use view state, because the contents of the grid are kept in session state. This makes the page display more quickly, and minimizes the amount of network traffic between client and server, because the grid's view state doesn't need to be transmitted.

## Exercise Answer

Both exercises for today's lesson are open-ended, so no definitive answers are available.

**A**

# Day 6, "Working with User Controls"

## Quiz Answers

1. User controls are the main mechanism for code reuse.

2. User controls allow you to encapsulate code so that your Web application's code is organized around discrete modules. You can use any .NET language in user controls, which allows greater development flexibility for your Web application. You can cache user controls for higher performance.

3. Yes. User controls support custom properties. To use them, declare public methods within the user control to allow access to a property.

4. Yes. User controls support events, just as Web forms do. You can declare any kind of event handler for Web controls within a user control, just as you would for a Web form.

5. No. You should use the <form> tag only in a Web form. Contained user controls rely on the <form> tag of their parent Web form.

6. Fragment caching is the process of caching individual user controls.

7. The Duration parameter specifies the lifetime of a cached Web form or user control. It specifies the number of seconds that the object should be held in memory.

8. The OutputCache directive enables caching.

9. The VaryByParam parameter stores multiple versions of a cached Web form or user control.

## Exercise Answers

1. Add the following code to Listing 6.3 after the Width property declaration:

```
public property Height() as unit
  get
    return ZipCode.Height
  end get
  set
    ZipCode.Height = value
  end set
end property
```

2. ASP.NET allows you to cache objects by using the Cache collection on the Page object. To add an object to the cache, just call the Insert or Add method, along with a key of your choice. For instance, the following line would insert an object containing stock quotations into the cache:

```
Cache.Insert("StockQuotes", objStockData)
```

You can use the sample program in Listing A.4 to experiment with the Cache collection.

**LISTING A.4**   A Sample Program for Experimenting with Caching

```vb
<%@ Page Language="vb" %>
<html>
<body>
<script runat="server">
public class CacheItem
  public readonly property Message() as String
   get
     return "I exist"
   end get
  end property
end class

sub Add_Click(Sender as object, e as EventArgs)

  Dim dSeconds as double = 0.0
  try
    dSeconds = Double.Parse(Seconds.Text)
  catch ex as Exception
    'ignore parsing exceptions
  end try
  if dSeconds = 0 then dSeconds = 100000

  dim depend as CacheDependency
  if File.Text.Length > 0 then
    depend = new CacheDependency(Server.MapPath(File.Text))
  end if

  if Type.SelectedItem.Text = "Absolute" then
    Cache.Insert("MyItem", new CacheItem(), depend, _
        DateTime.Now.AddSeconds(dSeconds), TimeSpan.Zero)
  else
    Cache.Insert("MyItem", new CacheItem(), depend, _
        DateTime.MaxValue, TimeSpan.FromSeconds(dSeconds))
  end if
 end sub

sub Remove_Click(Sender as object, e as EventArgs)

  Cache.Remove("MyItem")

end sub
</script>

<%
  dim item as CacheItem = Cache.Get("MyItem")
  if item is nothing then
    Response.Write("<b>Item does not exist in cache.</b>")
  else
```

A

**LISTING A.4**    continued

```
     Response.Write("<b>Found item!</b> Its meassage is: " & item.Message)
   end if
%>

<form runat="server">
Expire item in
<asp:TextBox id="Seconds" runat="server"/>
seconds. (Enter 0 for no limit)<br>

Expiration Type:
<asp:DropDownList id="Type" runat="server">
 <asp:ListItem>Absolute</asp:ListItem>
 <asp:ListItem>Sliding Window</asp:ListItem>
</asp:DropDownList>

<br>
<asp:Button id="Add" runat="server"
           Text="Add Object to Cache" OnClick="Add_Click" /><br>
<asp:Button id="Remove" runat="server"
           Text="Remove Object from Cache" OnClick="Remove_Click" /><br>
<asp:Button id="Check" runat="server"
           Text="Check on Item" /><br>

Make item depend on the following file in the application root:
<asp:TextBox id="File" runat="server"/>

</form>
</body>
</html>
```

# Day 7, "Writing Internet Applications for Mobile Devices"

## Quiz Answers

1. Some examples include the UP simulator from Openwave, the Microsoft Mobile Explorer Emulator, and the Desktop Pocket PC emulator.

2. WML, or Wireless Markup Language.

3. The `Paginate` property controls automatic pagination. Set the property to `true` to turn on pagination.

4. The List, SelectionList, and ObjectList controls display list data.

5. The `Request.Browser` and device filters are used to render specialized content.

6. No, many devices don't support CSS. You can use the StyleSheet Web control styles.

7. ASP.NET mobile stores view state in the `session` object.

8. You can use the `HiddenVariables` collection.

## Exercise Answers

1. To create a mobile page that allows for numerical passwords, use the Textbox control. Set the `Numeric` and `Password` properties to true.

2. A device filter that will test for the presence of a cell phone might look like the following:

```
1: <configuration>
2:   <system.web>
3:     <deviceFilters>
4:       <filter name="IsCell"
5:               compare="PreferredRenderingType"
6:               argument="wml11" />
7:     </deviceFilters>
8:   </system.web>
9: </configuration>
```

Line 5 checks for the default rendering type of the device. Cell phones use WML version 1.1, and so the `argument` parameter on Line 6 checks for the string `"wml11"`.

# Day 8, "Using XML with Your Applications"

## Quiz Answers

1. A well-formed XML document can only have one top-level element, because the elements in an XML document must have a "tree" structure.

2. A leaf element in an XML document contains no child nodes by definition.

3. XML is used in ADO.NET, for SOAP messages to Web Services, in all of the XML base classes, configuration data, serialization, and in XML schemas.

4. XML namespaces are used to create a context for the elements in an XML file. You might want to use them if your XML data is sent to another organization.

5. An element node can contain other elements, while a text node contains data.

6. Three resulting formats could be XML, XSL, or a custom text format.

7. XSL templates specify how an XML document should be transformed using an XSL style sheet.

A

8. XPath is used to create matching expressions, so that XSL templates can be applied to specific XML elements.

9. It would be better to use the XMLDocument class when you need to access an XML file in a non-sequential way. Since the XMLDocument class stores the entire source XML file in memory, you can traverse the document in any order you like.

10. You can use the XML Web control to apply an XSL style sheet to an XML file.

## Exercise Answers

1. This exercise is open-ended; you can perform it in several different ways.

2. A simple way to construct such a program would be to take Listing 8.6 and comment out the if check in the CountData method. The new method would look like the following:

```
Function CountData(Node as XmlNode) As Integer

    Dim Count As Integer = 1
    Dim ChildNode As XmlNode

    for each ChildNode in Node.ChildNodes

      Count = Count + CountData(ChildNode)
    Next
    return Count
End Function
```

3. This exercise is open-ended; you can perform it in several different ways.

# Day 9, "Introducing ADO.NET"

## Quiz Answers

1. ADO.NET contains the SQL data provider and the OLE DB data provider. Use the SqlDataProvider for SQL Server because it's optimized specifically for this database. Use the OLE DB provider for other databases.

2. Use the SqlConnection and OleDbConnection classes to connect to a database using ADO.NET.

3. Use the SqlDataReader and OldDbDataReader classes to read data in a forward direction only.

4. The SqlCommand and OleDbCommand classes are used to execute SQL commands using ADO.NET.

5. The ExecuteNonQuery method executes SQL commands that don't return a result set.

6. The `ExecuteScalar` method executes SQL commands that return single values.

7. The preferred method is to use the `SqlParameter` and `OleDbParameter` objects, as detailed in the section "Using Parameters with the `Command` Object."

8. Objects of type `SqlError` and `OleDbError` are thrown by the ADO.NET classes.

9. You can use the `IDataReader`, `IDbCommand`, and `IDataAdapter` classes to abstract the data provider.

## Exercise Answers

1. Listing A.5 shows the new code for Listing 9.1.

**LISTING A.5**   Using the SQL Data Provider to Read Records from a Table

```
<%@ Control Language="vb" %>
<%@ Import Namespace="System.Data" %>
<%@ Import Namespace="System.Data.SqlClient" %>
<script runat="server">

private _TableName as  String

public property TableName() as  String
  get
    return _TableName
  end get
  set (byval v as string)
    _TableName = v
  end set
end property

</script>
<%
  'Create a connection to the local NorthWind database
  Dim con as new SqlConnection("data source=localhost;uid=sa;" & _
                  "pwd=;database=Northwind")
  con.Open()

  'Create a simple command that will select every record from a table
  SqlCommand cmd = new SqlCommand("Select * from " & _TableName, con)

  'Create a data reader which will read each record from the select
  'command in a forward-only, read-only mode
  Dim rdr as SqlDataReader = cmd.ExecuteReader()

  'Loop for every record
  while rdr.Read()

    'Loop through every column - 0 to FieldCount
```

A

**LISTING A.5** continued

```
       dim fldNum as integer
       for fldNum = 0 to rdr.FieldCount - 1

         Dim strFieldItem as String

         'If the value in the column is not null, retrieve it as
         'a String value
         if not rdr.IsDBNull(fldNum) then
           strFieldItem = rdr.GetString(fldNum)
         end if

         'Write out the value
         Response.Write(strFieldItem)
         if fldNum < rdr.FieldCount - 1 then
           Response.Write(", ")
         else
           Response.Write("<br>")
         end if
       Next
     End While
     'Close the data reader and the connection - no need to close
     'the command object
     rdr.Close()
     con.Close()
  %>
```

2. Listing A.6 shows code using the abstract interfaces.

**LISTING A.6** Using the ADO.NET Abstract Data Provider Interfaces to Read Records from a Table

```
<%@ Control Language="vb" %>
<%@ Import Namespace="System.Data" %>
<%@ Import Namespace="System.Data.OleDb" %>
<script runat="server">

private _TableName as String

public property TableName() as  String
  get
    return _TableName
  end get
  set (byval v as string)
    _TableName = v
  end set
end property

</script>
```

**LISTING A.6** continued

```
<%
  'Create a connection to the local NorthWind database
  Dim con as new OleDbConnection("Provider=Microsoft.Jet.OLEDB.4.0;" & _
        "Data Source=C:\Program Files\Microsoft Office\" & _
        "Office\Samples\Northwind.mdb;" & _
        "User ID=;Password=;")
  con.Open()

  'Create a simple command that will select every record from a table
  Dim cmd as IDbCommand = con.CreateCommand()
  cmd.CommandText = "Select * from " & _TableName

  'Create a data reader which will read each record from the select
  'command in a forward-only, read-only mode
  Dim rdr as IDataReader = cmd.ExecuteReader()

  'Loop for every record
  while rdr.Read() {

    'Loop through every column - 0 to FieldCount
    Dim fldNum as integer
    for fldNum = 0 to rdr.FieldCount - 1

      Dim  strFieldItem as String

      'If the value in the column is not null, retrieve it as
      'a String value
      if not rdr.IsDBNull(fldNum) then
        strFieldItem = rdr.GetString(fldNum)
      end if

      'Write out the value
      Response.Write(strFieldItem)
      if fldNum < rdr.FieldCount - 1 then
        Response.Write(", ")
      else
        Response.Write("<br>")
      end if
    next
  End While
  'Close the data reader and the connection - no need to close
  'the command object
  rdr.Close()
  con.Close()
%>
```

A

# Day 10, "Working with Datasets"

## Quiz Answers

1. The `Fill` method populates a dataset with records.

2. Use two `Connection` objects and two `Adapter` objects. Open a connection to both databases, and then fill the same `DataSet` with the two `Adapters`.

3. You can use a `Command` object with a SQL statement such as the following:

    `UPDATE Products set Price = Price * 1.10`

4. Use the `AcceptChanges` method after the underlying database is updated with the changes in the current `DataSet`. If no errors occur, call `AcceptChanges` so that each row in each table of the `DataSet` is set to the `Unmodified` state.

5. You can create event handlers for each error by using the techniques from the section "Handling `DataAdapter` Errors." You can also add `try...catch` blocks around the code that uses the `DataAdapter` to catch errors.

6. Primary keys are fields that specify a unique value for every row in a database table. A foreign key field contains the value of a primary key from a parent table. The two are different because foreign key fields don't make individual rows unique in a table; instead, they refer to parent records.

7. Use primary and foreign keys to create a parent-child relationship between tables. The parent table must have a primary key, and the child table must have a foreign key that refers to the parent table's primary key.

8. The `ForeignKeyConstraint` class ensures consistency between records in a `DataSet`.

9. An expression column is derived from columns in a database table. You might use one to create a virtual column that contains a modified version of an original column.

10. The `DataAdapter` class uses `RowStates` to extract modified, added, or deleted records.

## Exercise Answers

1. Listing A.7 shows the modified code.

**LISTING A.7**  Displaying Data with ADO.NET and the DataSet Web Control

```
<%@ Page Language="vb" %>
<%@ Import Namespace="System.Data" %>
<%@ Import Namespace="System.Data.OleDb" %>
```

**LISTING A.7**   continued

```
<script runat="server">
sub Page_Load(Sender as Object, e as EventArgs)

  Dim con as _
     new OleDbConnection("Provider=Microsoft.Jet.OLEDB.4.0;" & _
        "Data Source=C:\Program Files\Microsoft Office\" & _
        "Office\Samples\Northwind.mdb;" & _
        "User ID=;Password=;")
  Dim adpt as new OleDbDataAdapter("SELECT * FROM Orders", con)

  Dim ds as new DataSet()

  adpt.Fill(ds, "Orders")
  MyGrid.DataSource = ds
  MyGrid.DataBind()
end sub
</script>
<html>
<body>
<font face="Arial">
<asp:DataGrid id="MyGrid" runat="server" />
</body>
</html>
```

2. The solution in Listing A.8 uses a derived column, using the formula
`UnitPrice + .05`.

**LISTING A.8**   Using Derived Columns in ADO.NET DataTables

```
<%@ Page Language="vb" %>
<%@ Import Namespace="System.Data" %>
<%@ Import Namespace="System.Data.OleDb" %>
<script runat="server">
sub Page_Load(Sender as Object, e as EventArgs)

  Dim con as _
     new OleDbConnection("Provider=Microsoft.Jet.OLEDB.4.0;" & _
        "Data Source=C:\Program Files\Microsoft Office\" & _
        "Office\Samples\Northwind.mdb;" & _
        "User ID=;Password=;")
  OleDbDataAdapter adpt = _
    new OleDbDataAdapter("SELECT * FROM Products", con)

  Dim ds as new DataSet()

  adpt.Fill(ds, "Products")
  ds.Tables(0).Columns.Add("PricePlus", _
```

A

**LISTING A.8**  continued

```
        Type.GetType("System.Single"), _
        "UnitPrice + 0.05")

    MyGrid.DataSource = ds
    MyGrid.DataBind()

end sub
</script>
<html>
<body>
<font face="Arial">
<asp:DataGrid id="MyGrid" runat="server"
              AutoGenerateColumns="false">
  <Columns>
    <asp:BoundColumn DataField="ProductName"/>
    <asp:BoundColumn DataField="PricePlus" />
  </Columns>
</asp:DataGrid>
</body>
</html>
```

# Day 11, "Using ADO.NET and XML Together"

## Quiz Answers

1. Use the ReadXml method from the DataSet class.

2. Inference.

3. Yes, you can apply constraint objects to an ADO.NET dataset even when the source data comes from an XML file. Constraint objects were explained on Day 10.

4. XML Schema is an XML-based technology that allows you to specify the structure and format of a target XML file.

5. Use the xmlns namespace keyword to specify the URI of the XSD file. For instance, if the XSD file is available on the Web at www.mycomany.com/name-spaces/xsd/employees.xsd, you would use the following line:

   ```
   xmlsn = "http:// www.mycompany.com/namespaces/xsd/employees.xsd"
   ```

6. Use either Visual Studio or the XSD.exe tool.

## Exercise Answers

1. Only the DataGrid definition needs to be changed to solve this exercise. The new definition is as follows:

```
<asp:DataGrid HeaderStyle-Font-Bold="True"
              Font-Name="Arial"
              Font-Size="10pt"
              ID="MyDataGrid" Runat="server">
  <Columns>
    <asp:BoundColumn HeaderText="Name"
                     DataField="name"/>
    <asp:BoundColumn HeaderText="Operating System"
                     DataField="os"/>
    <asp:BoundColumn HeaderText="Speed"
                     DataField="speed"/>
    <asp:BoundColumn HeaderText="Memory"
                     DataField="memory"/>
  </Columns>
</asp:DataGrid>
```

2. A new XML file with the applications element added to each computer element is as follows:

```
<?xml version="1.0" encoding="utf-8" ?>
<computers>
  <computer nic="true" modem="false" server="false">
    <name>Alice 1</name>
    <os>Windows 2000</os>
    <speed>800</speed>
    <memory>256</memory>
    <applications>
      <application>IIS</application>
      <application>Visual Studio</application>
      <application>Notepad</application>
    </applications>
  </computer>
  <computer nic="false" modem="true" server="false">
    <name>Bob</name>
    <os>Windows ME</os>
    <speed>500</speed>
    <memory>128</memory>
    <applications>
      <application>Word</application>
      <application>Excel</application>
      <application>PowerPoint</application>
    </applications>
  </computer>
</computers>
```

The structure of the XSD file generated from this XML file contains a nested table for the list of applications. The XSD also contains foreign key constrains for the elements of the new applications nested table.

A

# Day 12, "Putting It All Together with ASP.NET"

## Quiz Answers

1. Either `ICollection`, `IListCollection`, or `IEnumerable`.

2. The `DataTextField` property specifies source data.

3. The `DefaultView` returns a stock `DataView` object.

4. Use the string `"Like *Inc*"`.

5. You must set the `ApplyDefaultSort` property to `true`.

6. For read-only data grids, view state is an excellent choice because you don't have to manage the data in the grid in session or write extra code.

7. View state is transferred over the Internet on every page hit. This brings a penalty that's especially large for users with a dial-up connection.

8. If your site experiences a large number of concurrent users, your Web server may not be capable of handling a large number of sessions.

9. ASP.NET sessions can be stored on another server or in the database. Guessing at the performance figures for a particular site is difficult and should be backed up by test results.

10. Use the `HyperLinkColumn` to implement this style of page.

## Exercise Answers

1. To filter the data set in Listing 12.6 by the current year, you can change the SELECT statement, or set the Filter property of the default DataView, as the "Filtering Data" section showed. One possible SELECT statement might be

```
"SELECT * FROM Orders WHERE EmployeeID = " + empId + " AND
            OrderDate >= #1/1/1998#"
```

2. To get you started on a solution, an XML file containing the new nodes might look like the following:

```xml
<?xml version="1.0" encoding="utf-8"?>
<music xmlns="http://tempuri.org/Music.xsd">
  <cd>
     <name>Mozart Symphony Number 40</name>
     <location>Bill's Music</location>
     <location>Classic Records Inc</location>
  <cd>
  <cd>
    <name>Anthem of the Sun</name>
```

```
      <location>Sue's Music</location>
      <location>Record Warehouse</location>
   </cd>
</music>
```

The complete details for implementing a master-detail record view for this XML file aren't included. However, you can use the same techniques shown in today's lesson. Create an XSD schema for this new XML file, and then copy the code from Listings 12.6 and 12.7, using the XML file as a data source instead of the Northwind database.

# Day 13, "Introducing Web Services"

## Quiz Answers

1. ASP.NET uses the .aspx extension for Web Service files.

2. Web Services use WSDL files so that client programs know exactly how to communicate with them. Because of WSDL, automated tools such as Visual Studio and the WSDL.exe program can generate proxy files simply by examining the WSDL file.

3. To retrieve the WSDL description, append the string "?WSDL" to the URL for the .asmx page associated with the Web Service, and place this URL in your favorite browser. ASP.NET generates the WSDL file for the Web Service automatically and sends the XML file back as a response to the HTTP request from the browser.

4. Proxies are essential for any client that consumes (uses) a Web Service. The proxy handles details such as packaging parameters into SOAP requests, contacting the remote Web Service, and unpacking the SOAP response into objects that clients can use.

5. Visual Studio creates a number of files, including the service proxy (*webservivename*.vb), a static WSDL file for the service (*webservivename*.wsdl), and a discovery file (*webservivename*.disco). Tomorrow's lesson explains discovery files.

6. Web Services use ASP.NET because ASP.NET provides supporting infrastructure and plumbing for the service. Specifically, ASP.NET automatically generates WSDL files for any client of the Web Service, provides code that translates SOAP requests into method requests, and provides code that packages method responses in to SOAP responses for Web Service clients.

7. Not all Web Services provide support for all public Web methods, because the HTTP protocol doesn't support some of the more complex parameters that Web Services can use. Tomorrow's lesson provides an in-depth discussion of the issue.

A

8. From this chapter, WSDL files, SOAP requests and responses, and HTTP Web Service calls all use XML.

9. The proxy program defines the methods `BeginHelloWorld` and `EndHelloWorld` for asynchronous calling. Day 16's lesson gives a detailed discussion for implementing asynchronous calling.

10. Use the `[WebMethod]` attribute to make a method publicly accessible to Web Service clients.

## Exercise Answers

1. One possible implementation for the method follows:

```
<WebMethod> public FUnctionGetTimeMil(useMilitary as boolean) as String

    Dim currentTime as DateTime = DateTime.Now
    Dim formattedTime as string
    if useMilitary then
      formattedTime = currentTime.ToString("HH:mm:ss")
    else
      formattedTime = currentTime.ToString("hh:mm:ss tt")
    end if
    return "The current time on the server is: " & formattedTime

End Function
```

2. Visual Studio creates the following additional files when using the Web Service template:

   - A stock .asmx file to start a Web Service implementation, with a small `HelloWorld` method

   - A Global.asax file, as explained on Day 3

   - A dynamic discovery file named *projectname*.vsdisco. Dynamic discovery files are explained in tomorrow's lesson.

   - A stock web.config file, explained in detail on Day 18

   - A file named AssemblyInfo.vb, which allows for application signing and versioning. Day 17's lesson will explain application signing.

3. This exercise is open ended, and code for a Web Service that calls another isn't provided. A scenario like this one could be useful if a custom client Web Service called a commercially available Web Service for utility methods.

# Day 14, "Publishing Web Services"

## Quiz Answers

1. Static discovery files contain XML with URL links. Dynamic discovery files generate static discovery content through ASP.NET.

2. UDDI (Universal Description, Discovery, and Integration) is a joint project among the leading companies in the software industry to provide a directory for public Web Services.

3. You can use one of the public UDDI registry sites. www.uddi.org/register contains links to Web sites that you can use.

4. The Business and Service Types nodes are at the top of the hierarchy.

5. A tModel is a definition of a Web Service type, in XML.

## Exercise Answers

1. The following shows an example static discovery file for the TimeUtils example from Day 13:

```
<?xml version="1.0" encoding="utf-8" ?>
<discovery xmlns="http://schemas.xmlsoap.org/disco/">

  <contractRef ref="http://localhost/WebBook/TimeService.asmx?wsdl"
               docRef="http://localhost/WebBook/TimeService.asmx"
               xmlns="http://schemas.xmlsoap.org/disco/scl/" />
</discovery>
```

2. This exercise is open ended. The complete definition for a tModel is contained in the UDDI Technical White Paper at http://www.uddi.org/whitepapers.html.

3. This exercise also is open ended. To use the sample .NET project in the UDDI SDK, you have to sign up for a Microsoft Passport account.

# Day 15, "Accessing Complex Data with Web Services"

## Quiz Answers

1. No. The HTTP protocol is limited because input data needs to be supplied in the form of simple strings.

2. An out parameter is returned only by a method and can be used as a substitute for a return value.

A

3.  A byref parameter is used to both send and retrieve data from a method.

4.  Optimistic locking locks data records only when they are being read; the lock is extremely short lived.

5.  Optimistic locking requires very few server resources because each lock has to be maintained only for a very short amount of time.

6.  You can version each record, using timestamps or numerical version IDs. When you're updating a record, check to make sure that the version from the client matches the current version in the data store.

## Exercise Answers

1.  To use a Monitor object for the sample, add a new private Monitor object,which you might call _monitor, to the `TaskServer` class. In the `TaskServer` constructor, add code to set the _monitor variable to a new `Monitor` object.

    Add a call to the Monitor Enter method in the first line of the `AddTask` method, as in the following code line:

    ```
    _monitor.Enter()
    ```

    Add a corresponding Monitor Exit call at the end of the `AddTask` method. Perform the same modifications to the `ModifyTask` method.

2.  To make the sample use a database, all code associated with reading and writing the TaskStore.xml file needs to be changed to use a new database table. To accomplish this, first create a new table in the database of your choice. Make sure that the table contains a field corresponding to each data node in the TaskStore.xml file. Next, replace the code that reads the XML file with ADO.NET code that reads from the database table. Then replace code that modifies the XML file with ADO.NET code that updates the database table. You can use the `OleDbDataAdapter` or `SqlDataAdapter` class to move data from the `DataSet` objects in the original sample into database tables.

# Day 16, "Putting It All Together with Web Services"

## Quiz Answers

1.  `<WebMethod(EnableSession:=true)>`

2.  The Web Service will use cookies to index the user's session, and not all client programs support cookies.

3.  No attributes are needed. The `Application` object is always available.

4. Asynchronous method calls.

5. No. Automatically generated proxies come with asynchronous methods by default.

6. `IAsyncResult`

7. Yes. See the "Dealing with Slow Services" section in today's lesson for an example.

## Exercise Answers

1. The enhanced `SlowMethod` is shown as follows:

```
<WebMethod> _
public function SlowMethod(waitSec as integer) as string

   dim rand as new Random(CInt(DateTime.Now.Millisecond))
   if rand.NextDouble() > 0.5 then
      dim e as new Exception("Random Error")
    throw e
   end if
   Thread.Sleep(waitSec * 1000)
   return "The answer is...43."

end function
```

This code throws an `Exception` object with its `Message` property set to the string `"Random Error"`.

2. When the `SlowService` returns an error, it will be detected in the exception handler for the `EndSlowMethod` call in each asynchronous client example. To distinguish the exception from other kinds of exceptions that can occur in asynchronous calls, check the exception's `Message` property.

# Day 17, "Using Legacy Code with .NET"

## Quiz Answers

1. Both technologies can be used together; however, ASP and ASP.NET use incompatible session objects.

2. The Runtime Callable Wrapper (RCW).

3. Choose Add References from Visual Studio's Project menu.

4. `Dispose` decrements the reference count on a COM object. If it's not called, the COM object can remain in memory indefinitely.

5. The GAC is a global registry for .NET assemblies. It's used for versioning and exposing assemblies to legacy applications.

A

6. Public assemblies must have a unique identity, usually from the organization that created the assembly. Signing is used for this purpose.

7. Assemblies use public/private key encryption for signing.

8. You can use the sn.exe utility.

9. Use the regasm.exe tool to register assemblies.

## Exercise Answers

1. One of the easiest ways to create a COM object using Visual Studio 6.0 is to use Visual Basic. Create a new project and select ActiveX DLL. Then add new public functions or subroutines to the main VB module file. Compile the file, and you should be able to use the object in a .NET Web form, using the methods described in today's lesson.

2. Add the following line to the public interface of the HelloUtility.vb file:

```
Dim ReturnDocument() As XmlDocument
```

Next, add the following function to the HelloImplementation class:

```
Public Function HelloInterface.ReturnDocument() as XmlDocument
Dim doc as new XmlDocument()
    return doc
End Function
```

You can also add code to the method to populate the XML document, although it's not necessary.

By using ASP pages, you can retrieve the XmlDocument with a code snippet like the following, which could be added to Listing 17.6:

```
Dim objDoc
    ObjDoc = obj.ReturnDocument
```

You can manipulate the document by using the public methods in the XmlDocument class.

# Day 18, "Configuring Internet Applications"

## Quiz Answers

1. Use the debug node in the compilation section, as demonstrated in the "Adding Tracing and Debugging" section of this lesson.

2. Use the tracing section of the web.config file. In particular, you may want to set the pageOutput flag to false so that you can view all trace output in the trace.axd file.

3. Use the `references` node in the `compilation` section of the web.config file, as explained in the "Customizing Project Compilation" section of today's lesson.

4. Use the `customErrors` section of the web.config file.

5. Set the `cookieless` attribute to `true` inside the `sessionState` section.

6. Create a new web.config file with the changed settings and place this file in the subdirectory.

7. Use the `appSettings` section of the web.config file for custom configuration settings.

8. Use the `memoryLimit` attribute of the `processModel` section.

## Exercise Answers

1. A sample web.config file that uses cookieless sessions with a timeout of 5 minutes and Visual Basic as the default compilation language follows:

```
<configuration>
  <system.web>
    <compilation defaultLanguage="vb" />
    <sessionState cookieless="true" timeout="5" />
  </system.web></configuration>
```

2. After creating a Web application with two subdirectories, you need only one new web.config file to disable sessions and `ViewState`. A sample web.config file that does so is shown here:

```
<configuration>
  <system.web>
    <pages enableViewState="false"
           enableSessionState="false" />
  </system.web>
</configuration>
```

# Day 19, "Securing Internet Applications"

## Quiz Answers

1. A firewall is a program or hardware component that blocks TCP/IP ports.

2. SSL stands for Secure Sockets Layer and is used to encrypt communication over TCP/IP. HTTPS is built on top of SSL.

3. Windows authentication uses actual Windows users. Forms authentication users are independent of the operating system.

4. Basic authentication is a form of Windows authentication in which information is sent "in the clear" without encryption. Almost every browser supports Basic authentication.

5. Basic authentication doesn't encrypt usernames or passwords. HTTPS encrypts all data. Without using HTTPS, an outsider could easily gain access to Windows accounts on your network.

6. Impersonation is the process of one application assuming the identity of a known user. It's used to save writing custom security logic in your own code.

7. This class is used to create credentials for Web Service clients. By using this class, clients can use a Web Service protected by Windows authentication.

8. URL authorization is the process of allowing or denying access to users using the web.config file. URL authorization is used in combination with Forms authentication, not Windows authentication.

9. False. You can force ASP.NET to run as a specific user by using the `username` and `password` attributes of the `identity` element in the web.config file. See Listing 19.5 for an example.

10. The `FormsAuthentication` class is used to validate, redirect, and log users out. See Table 19.1 for the common methods in this class and Visual Studio documentation for complete details.

## Exercise Answers

1. The following web.config file configures Forms authentication and the three users:

```
<configuration>
  <system.web>
    <authentication mode="Forms">
      <forms name="MyFormsAuthentication" loginUrl="MyAuth.aspx">
        <credentials passwordFormat="Clear">
          <user name="Guest" password="pass1" />
          <user name="Member" password="pass2" />
          <user name="Admin" password="pass3" />
        </credentials>
      </forms>
    </authentication>
    <authorization>
      <deny users="?" />
    </authorization>
  </system.web>
</configuration>
```

2. You can solve this open-ended exercise in a number of ways. There's no single answer.

# Day 20, "Deploying Internet Applications"

## Quiz Answers

1. Create a folder structure, create a virtual directory, and then copy all program files.

2. The Copy Project option and custom setup programs.

3. If the application uses legacy code, you must take special steps. Also, if you need to run custom database scripts and commands, this will make XCOPY deployment impossible.

4. The File System, Registry, User Interface, Custom Launch Conditions, and Custom Actions views.

5. Any two of Splash, Register User, License Agreement, Customer Information, or Radio Button screens.

6. They are called properties.

7. File, Registry, or Merge Module properties.

## Exercise Answers

1. This exercise is open ended. However, to create a setup program that installs help information, follow these steps:

    1. Create some sample help files.

    2. Create a Web setup program.

    3. Add the help files to the setup program via the File System view.

2. This exercise is open ended. However, you can use the methods from the section "Configuring Files In Your Setup Program" in today's lesson to add .NET assemblies for use by legacy code. After running the completed setup program, investigate Registry entries by using the RegEdit.exe program. Browse to the HKEY_CLASSES_ROOT Registry hive, and look for the names of the .NET assemblies and classes in the Registry.

# Day 21, "Creating Your Application Architecture"

## Quiz Answers

1. A logical application tier is a grouping of software modules that are all related to one general area of an application, such as the user interface.

**A**

2. An *n*-tier design uses multiple logical tiers in an application. The application may consist of different client and server components, each of which is partitioned into logical tiers.

3. Prototyping exposes issues that you didn't think of when a design is applied to your own particular software and hardware environment.

4. A stateless Internet application doesn't store data about its users in memory between browser requests or Web Service method requests.

5. Scaling out means adding extra computers to help satisfy requests from users in an Internet application.

6. A stateless design will allow you to scale out a portion of your application more easily.

## Exercise Answers

Answers to both exercises are open ended, so no definitive answers are available.

# Index

# Hey, you've got enough worries.

## Don't let IT training be one of them.

Get on the fast track to IT training at InformIT,
your total Information Technology training network.

 | **www.informit.com** | **SAMS**

■ Hundreds of timely articles on dozens of topics ■ Discounts on IT books from all our publishing partners, including Sams Publishing ■ Free, unabridged books from the InformIT Free Library ■ "Expert Q&A"—our live, online chat with IT experts ■ Faster, easier certification and training from our Web- or classroom-based training programs ■ Current IT news ■ Software downloads ■ Career-enhancing resources